T0315007

THE EVOLUTION OF MONEY

David Orrell and
Roman Chlupatý

COLUMBIA UNIVERSITY PRESS ♦ NEW YORK

Columbia University Press
Publishers Since 1893
New York   Chichester, West Sussex
cup.columbia.edu

Library of Congress Cataloging-in-Publication Data
Names: Orrell, David, author. | Chlupatý, Roman, author.
Title: The evolution of money / David Orrell and Roman Chlupatý.
Description: New York : Columbia University Press, [2016] |
Includes bibliographical references and index.
Identifiers: LCCN 2015050683 | ISBN 9780231173728 (cloth) Subjects:
LCSH: Money—History.
Classification: LCC HG231 .O77 2016 | DDC 332.4/9—dc23
LC record available at http://lccn.loc.gov/2015050683

COVER DESIGN: Noah Arlow

CONTENTS

ACKNOWLEDGMENTS

Many people contributed to this book. We would like to thank Myles Thompson and Robert Lecker for their advice and encouragement, and Stephen Wesley, Irene Pavitt, and Ben Kolstad for their expert editorial and copy-editorial advice. Credit also goes to all those who have shared their time and expertise on various subject matters related to *The Evolution of Money*, especially Parag Khanna, Tomáš Sedláček, Marek Palatinus, and Rob Carnell and James Knightley of ING's London office.

Roman would like to thank his dear friend and mentor Roger Tooze for providing him with invaluable advice and serving as a critical voice during the writing of this book. He would also like to extend his deepest and sincerest gratitude to his lovely wife, Klara, and his lively daughter, Dominika, for their help, support, and patience (not only) during the time spent writing this book. David would like to thank his wife, Beatriz (better than money), and his daughters, Isabel and Emma, who also evolved as this book was written.

Finally, the authors would like to thank each other for an enjoyable and mutually inspiring collaboration.

David would like to dedicate this book to Emma, and Roman would like to dedicate it to Sebastian.

THE EVOLUTION OF MONEY

Introduction

This book is about the nature and future of money—that mercurial substance that dominates so much of our lives, remains strangely elusive and misunderstood, can drive us forward or dash us against the rocks, and whose evolution may play a deciding role in the future success and prosperity of our species.

Money is one of mankind's earliest inventions. Its history appears to be as old as that of writing, and the two are closely connected—some of the oldest written artifacts in existence are 5,000-year-old clay tablets from Mesopotamia that were used to record grain deposits. Both money and writing are a way of using symbols to describe the world. Both are used as a means of communication, and thus are fundamentally social and central to the relationship between individuals and the state. Money, in many respects, is as closely tied to our way of thinking as words.

Like language, money is based on social conventions, the most important being agreement on what constitutes a standard of currency. In the same way that words for the same thing differ between languages, so the choice of money is flexible, everything from cowrie shells in ancient China to cigarettes in postwar Germany having served as lucre. The first metal coins appeared around 600 B.C.E. when the small but trade-friendly kingdom of

Lydia (in present-day Turkey) introduced tokens made from a naturally occurring alloy of gold and silver. Today, money has transcended a physical relationship with precious metals, or for that matter anything else. The concept of currency has become increasingly abstract, to the point where actual coins and notes form only a small portion of the money in existence. Like words in the cloud, money exists as an abstract set of symbols that can be created or destroyed with the press of a keyboard button or the touch of a screen. Cybercurrencies are revolutionizing the financial industry in the same way that e-books are revolutionizing the publishing industry.

This virtual, ethereal form of money underpins modern capitalism, and its pursuit determines much of the structure of our lives. Jobs are often seen largely as a means to obtain it. Our houses are seen not just as homes but as stores of wealth—where wealth is defined as something that can be converted, at least in principle, to money. An important measure of success for people is the numbers they make or the net worth they accumulate over their lives; for a country, its gross domestic product as measured in its national currency. Displays of wealth provide a form of validation within the community, and the pursuit of riches lends shape and meaning to our lives. Money, for many people, is not just a necessity of modern life; it is something closer to a religion (indeed, without such faith, the system would collapse). As the British Museum observes, money has become "the main motivating factor behind western culture . . . the prime focus of political debate and personal endeavor, both despite and because of its increasing elusiveness and power. This kind of attitude has been aptly termed 'fetishistic,' in the sense that it attributes a quasi-supernatural quality to the object of its adulatory devotion, in this case money."[1]

Money is also a source of worry. According to Gallup, "Half of Americans have substantial financial anxiety."[2] A survey by Britain's *Observer* newspaper portrayed a nation "anxious about numbers. We are, collectively, twice as worried about money as we are about family or health."[3] And yet, despite its obvious importance in our lives, we often tend to downplay money, saying it is nothing special in itself, no more than a glorified system for exchange and accounting. And despite the long history of our relationship with it, we don't seem to know it very well. Its properties are something of a blank page.

For example, the credit crunch in 2007 that kicked off the ensuing financial crisis was one of a long series of such events caused in large part by the dynamics of money and our inability to understand them. Like those other events, it came as a complete surprise to nearly everyone, including major financial institutions such as the International Monetary Fund (IMF) and the Organisation for Economic Co-operation and Development (OECD). We appear to be as helpless in the face of financial storms as our ancestors were to more natural cataclysms such as storms or volcanoes. Wealth that is built up over decades can seem to vanish into the ether, as if it had no substance.

A commonly held currency is seen as a unifying force, which bonds people together, like a shared national anthem. In Europe, the euro was intended to bring disparate member states together and eliminate the risks of the deadly conflicts that characterized much of its history. While that goal has been reached, the common currency has in some respects had the opposite effect, enhancing the differences between north and south, between Greeks and Germans. Indeed, money often seems to have a way of pulling people apart even within a single country: a defining feature of modern capitalism is extreme wealth inequality and the resulting threat of social conflict.

Our ignorance about money is not relieved by the field of economics, which—contrary to what one might expect—is surprisingly mute on the subject. Mainstream "neoclassical" economic theory, which has long shaped our attitude toward the economy, is based on the peculiar notion that money is just an inert medium of exchange, a passive facilitator of transactions that are based on rational decisions to optimize utility. As a result, most of the models used by economists and policy makers do not take money explicitly into account, treating it only as a metric rather than a thing in itself. But as marketers and advertisers know, financial decisions are often governed less by reason or calculation than by emotion—and money is about the most emotionally volatile substance imaginable. We will go to war for it, marry for it, sacrifice for it, obsess over it, go crazy for it—and never have enough of it!

Money is widely associated with happiness and well-being, which is one reason we desire it. However, the relationship between wealth and happiness is complicated and often paradoxical. For example, experiments show that we are often happier if we give money away than spend it on ourselves.[4] At the same time, the quest for wealth has the undesirable side effect of environmental destruction—affecting not just our happiness but the health of the planet.

Money is like oxygen: a substance that surrounds us, is usually invisible, but is vital for our survival. It is also potentially explosive. But we often seem about as advanced in our understanding of it as a clumsy nineteenth-century scientist tinkering with the confounding and dangerous properties of phlogiston (believed at the time to be the source of fire). This book investigates the properties of this mysterious substance that so affects our lives—and points the way to a future in which money may play a very different role.

The book is essentially divided into two main parts. The first part (chapters 1–5) traces the development of money from ancient times to the present day, explores its fundamental properties, and shows how modern alternative currencies are just the latest step in a long historical process. The evolution of money has involved a number of transitions. The first version of money (we'll call it Money 1.0) appeared as part of an elaborate credit system in ancient Mesopotamia. The first actual coins (Money 2.0) were minted in Lydia, and the idea soon spread (or appeared concurrently) around the world. In the Middle Ages, a shortage of precious metals, combined with the lack of a strong central government, meant that—like the bitcoins of today—Money 3.0 was more an accounting system than something you could weigh in your pocket.

The discovery of the New World by Spain—and the plunder of vast quantities of precious metal—marked the beginning of Money 4.0. Mercantilist governments attempted to accumulate the maximum amount of treasure, and value could be explicitly calculated in terms of a weight of gold. This led to the creation of a gold standard for currencies, enforced by the British Empire and the Bank of England. The collapse of the Bretton Woods agreement in 1971 marked the official end of the gold standard and the early stages of a major bifurcation toward what we call Money 5.0.

The second part of the book (chapters 6–10) focuses on the current state of currencies and on new ideas for directing the torrent of money and the accumulation of wealth. If money has alternated between virtual and metal-backed forms, then it is now certainly in a virtual regime, where most money is created at the whim of private banks, simply by entering a number into a computer account. When the Bank of England released a paper admitting this fact in 2014, it created ripples of shock in the media, even though the practice is not new.[5] The British pound and the U.S. dollar have more in common with alternative cybercurrencies than appearances suggest. We reveal the power relationships that hold the financial system aloft, show how its flaws and instabilities make alternatives particularly attractive, and explore the developments in both technology and economics that are changing the story and opening the door to new currency systems.

In recent years—especially since the crisis—there has been an explosion of interest in forms of money that do not just extend the idea of money but radically rewrite it. These range from local time-share schemes, in which people exchange hours spent performing services, to globally traded digital currencies like Bitcoin that exploit technologies such as peer-to-peer computer networks. Their development has been enhanced by the ubiquity of mobile computing devices, which in some countries are taking the place of wallets. New platforms such as the aptly named Ethereum extend the computer architecture to an ecosystem of cybercurrencies and other forms of transactions and services, thus moving entire business models into the ether.

Because money so strongly affects our society, and even our own personalities, the development of this new, fifth-generation money will have profound effects not just on business models for the financial sector but also on the way that we behave and interact. In fact, many of the new currencies, or alternatives to currencies, are explicitly designed to produce socially positive outcomes. These moneys should help provide an answer to some of the issues faced by an increasingly globalized and decentralized world.

Money has always told us much about human society. Today the shape and structure of finance, money, and wealth is being questioned like never before. *The Evolution of Money* will act as a guide to the inherent properties and contradictions of our current system and will make predictions about how it is likely to evolve. In ten years' time, what will be accepted as currency? How will we buy things? What kind of money will our purses, wallets, or mobile devices hold? And how will we measure our place in the economy?

The authors are a Canadian mathematician and author (Orrell) and a Czech-Canadian financial journalist (Chlupatý). We met in England and collaborated on a couple of shorter books, including a three-way discussion (*The Twilight of Economic Man*) with the Czech economist and philosopher Tomáš Sedláček. One of the topics we discussed then was how money and economic growth have been fetishized by society. Money is considered to be hard and absolute and drives out other values such as aesthetics or ethics that are considered soft and somehow secondary.

In this book, we argue that money can transcend its role of reducing everything to number and can become, like language, a more open and affirmative means of communication. For the world economy to be sustainable, capitalism needs to readjust. A first step is to rethink the function and purpose of money and the meaning of wealth. As they say, money talks—and soon it will be in a different voice.

1

Origins

In economics, money has traditionally been defined to be anything that is generally accepted as a medium of exchange. Money also acts as a store of value and as a unit of account. But where did it come from in the first place? Since Aristotle, economists have said that coin money emerged as a replacement for barter. This chapter tracks the development of money from credit systems in ancient Mesopotamia, to early coins in ancient Greece and Rome. As we'll see, its genesis was somewhat more interesting than is usually presented in standard economics—and so will be its future.

Money has been one of mankind's most successful inventions (it is no coincidence that to "coin" means to "invent"). Indeed, it is one of the things that best expresses our humanity. Other animals don't exchange labor for tokens or carry wallets or set up elaborate banking systems. Money has aided and encouraged the human delight in trade and has shaped our social and economic development. It also has a shadow side—money may not be the root of all evil, but it can certainly play a supporting role. The quest for money drives enterprise and innovation, but also leads to social ills varying from lack of free time to environmental destruction. It may be a sign of human-ity, but sometimes it is also a cause of behavior that we would call inhuman.

Money today is perhaps more powerful and pervasive than at any time in history, but—ushered into existence seemingly from nothing at the com-mand of banks—also seems little more than a kind of accounting trick. It is fitting that the creator of double-entry bookkeeping, Luca Pacioli, was a magician. What is its secret? Why does specie, as coinage used to be known, continue to have such a hold over the human species?

One of the most fundamental characteristics of money is that it acts as an easily transportable store of value. The fruits of our labor can be held in a crystallized form—instead of exchanging work directly for goods, we exchange it for cash, which can then be spent at our convenience. Money therefore holds value the same way a battery holds energy, and makes it movable both in time and space (unlike some other stores of value, such as land). A paycheck in one's pocket can be spent whenever and wherever one wants—providing, of course, that someone is willing to accept it. To be of use, money must be not just portable but also easily exchangeable.

In the United States during the Great Depression, a popular form of money, especially in remote logging or mining camps, was company scrip. A portion of wages was paid in scrip that could be redeemed only at the camp's store, rather like a modern gift certificate. Since the store was owned by the company, this increased the company's control over its workers and made it easy to mark up prices. Scrip could be exchanged for cash, but only at a discount, which reflected its limited range of use.

A similar arrangement known as the "truck system" was used during the Industrial Revolution in Britain (the word "truck" in this context is from the French *troquer*, which means "to trade or swap"). Again, a monetary drought during this period meant that factory workers were often paid with vouchers that were exchangeable in local stores, which were again often owned or controlled by the factory owner. However, such arrangements were eventually outlawed by a sequence of laws known as the Truck Acts. In the United States, President Franklin Delano Roosevelt banned scrips in 1933, as he struggled to get the faltering monetary system under control.

An important advantage of cash compared with such schemes, then, is its range—it is accepted not just by one employer-controlled retail outlet but also by the store down the road and a whole range of institutions. Money therefore stimulates trade, at least over the region in which it is accepted, by making transactions convenient. And it rep-resents a kind of freedom, since a person with money in his or her pocket is someone with the freedom to choose. As Fyodor Dostoyevsky put it: "Money is coined liberty." Or at least liberty to select from among an available selection of suppliers.

Money therefore acts as a store of value (though this does raise the question, what is value?) and a medium of exchange. Finally, its units—dollar, shekel, and other currencies—act as units of account. To compare the economic value of different items, we just need to compare their market prices. And unlike most physical objects, money can be easily divided into fractional amounts, which is useful—we don't need to say that a chicken egg is worth one-tenth of a chicken. As discussed later, the spread of the use of money—and the need for accounting techniques—helped to inspire the development of mathematics in ancient Greece. Today, financial wizards with degrees in particle physics are employed to keep track of money's incessant, turbulent flow around the globe.

Indeed, the adoption of money was part of a generalized shift toward the dominance of calculation in our lives. The main difference between monetary transactions and other social transactions such as gift exchange is that the former involve an exact amount—you can put a number on them. They therefore emphasize the left-brain functions of logic and quantification. As we'll see, money has a tendency to colonize and take over everything it comes into contact with, because like mathematics it is based on reducing the world to a common, self-contained system of thought. Like pure numbers, money has shed any physical attributes—luster, texture, weight—and now exists only on the higher plane of abstraction and mathematics.

This cold rationality and exactness introduces a note of finality to transactions, because once an exchange is complete, there is nothing left over—the numbers on either side of the ledger cancel out to zero. Money builds commercial relationships, but it can terminate them in a flash. By acting as a kind of prosthetic for trust, it also removes some of our need for creating and maintaining real trust with human beings. We trust in money more than we trust in one another. Our bond is with the bank.

The multiple properties of money, which can both complement and contradict one another, mean that it often arouses conflicting and paradoxical responses. For example, we want money to be attractive as a good store of value—but if it is too attractive relative to other options, it will be hoarded rather than allowed to circulate. We want money to be available in adequate quantities—but not so easily available that it causes inflation (for a period, tobacco served as legal tender in the state of Virginia, and when tobacco production surged to over twice its normal level in 1639, it was ordered that half the crop be destroyed). People without money want to borrow it, but bankers want to loan only to those who already have it. We think money will make us happy, but studies have shown that happiness levels of lottery winners are remarkably unchanged by their wins.[1] Money is "how our culture defines value," according to author Tim Kreider, but increasingly we expect to get our culture (or "content") from artists and authors for free, in what amounts to a modern version of a gift economy.[2] Attempts to reduce financial risk often have the effect of increasing it. Economic policies have surprising and counterintuitive effects. And so on.

As discussed later, mainstream economists have traditionally side-stepped some of these issues by focusing on money's role as what economist F. A. Harper called a "lubricant in exchange" so that money has no special or interesting powers of its own.[3] We defer our own definition until chapter 2, but as a start, an obvious question is where money came from in the first place. Just as philosophers have long speculated on the origins of the universe, so economists and others have wondered about the origins of money. It didn't just fall from the sky, so who invented it? As with other creation stories, the proposed answers are interesting not just for what they say about reality but for what they say about their authors; and for insights into not just the past but also the future.

Creation Myth

One of the first philosophers to write about the invention of money was Aristotle, who deduced that it must have replaced a barter system in response to increasingly complicated trade. As he wrote in *Politics*, the "more complex form of exchange [money] grew, as might have been inferred, out of the simpler [barter]. . . . For the various necessaries of life are not easily carried about, and hence men agreed to employ in their dealings with each other something which was intrinsically useful and easily applicable to the purposes of life, for example, iron, silver, and the like. Of this the value was at first measured simply by size and weight, but in process of time they put a stamp upon it, to save the trouble of weighing and to mark the value."[4]

Aristotle's argument that money replaced barter in this way appears to have been based more on speculation than detailed evidence or anthropological footwork on his part, but his opinions influenced much further thinking on the subject. In a book whose title translates to *A Guide to the Merits of Commerce and to Recognition of Both Fine and Defective Merchandise and the Swindles of Those Who Deal Dishonestly*, the Damascus merchant and writer Abu Ja'far al-Dimashqi noted the difficulties inherent in barter:

> [T]he time of need of a person does not often coincide with the time of need of another person, as in the case of a carpenter who may be in need of an ironsmith but could not find one (at that particular time). It may also happen that there is no equivalence between the respective quantities of what each need[s] from the other, and there is no way of knowing the value of each item of each kind of goods, and of knowing the rate of exchange between one item and another item of a part of the merchandise among all the parts of the rest of the merchandise, nor the relative value of each of the different crafts.[5]

As a result, "The ancients searched for something by which to price all things" and settled on coins of gold and silver, which were preferred "due to their being readily suited for casting, forging, combining, separating and shaping into any form required."

The story was picked up by the schoolmen who repeated Aristotle's teaching to a medieval audience in the first universities, and later by economists such as Adam Smith. In *The Wealth of Nations*, he agreed with Aristotle that money—and indeed the entire market economy—must have emerged naturally from barter. A "prudent man" would build up a stockpile of some commodity that "few people would be likely to refuse in exchange for the produce of their industry."[6] Again, the ideal material was gold or silver; originally these were used in the form of "rude bars" that constantly needed to be weighed and measured, but eventually the government would have stepped in to issue standardized coins. Mints, according to Smith, had exactly the same role in this process as "stamp-masters of woollen and linen cloth." He fleshed out the picture with the addition of vignettes of hunters and shepherds, with "bows and arrows" being exchanged "for cattle or for venison," which appear to be drawn from what was known at the time about peoples such as the Native Americans of North America.

Double Coincidence

In the late nineteenth century, neoclassical economists such as William Stanley Jevons attempted to reinvent economics as a mathematical discipline; part of that project was framing the emergence of money as a kind of logical necessity. "The earliest form of exchange," he wrote in his book *Money and the Mechanism of Exchange*, "must have consisted in giving what was not wanted directly for that which was wanted. This simple traffic we call barter or truck."[7] Echoing Al-Dimashqi, Jevons noted that barter relies on what he called a double coincidence of wants, since each person has to want what the other has: "A hunter having returned from a successful chase has plenty of game, and may want arms and ammunition to renew the chase. But those who have arms may happen to be well supplied with game, so that no direct exchange is possible."

The first money, according to Jevons, took the form of commodities: "In the traffic of the Hudson's Bay Company with the North American Indians, furs, in spite of their differences of quality and size, long formed the medium of exchange." Indeed, companies even used a unit of account called the Made Beaver to keep track. "In the next higher stage of civilization," Jevons went on, "the pastoral state, sheep and cattle naturally form the most valuable and negotiable kind of property. They are easily transferable, convey themselves about, and can be kept for many years, so that they readily perform some of the functions of money. . . . In countries where slaves form one of the most common and valuable possessions, it is quite natural that they should serve as the medium of exchange like cattle."

But of course you can't put furs, cattle, or slaves in your pocket; so again the best material, and the inevitable end result of this process, is coins made of precious metal:

> [I]n order that money may perform some of its functions efficiently, especially those of a medium of exchange and a store of value, to be carried about, it is important that it should be made of a substance valued highly in all parts of the world, and, if possible, almost equally esteemed by all peoples. There is reason to think that gold and silver have been admired and valued by all tribes which have been lucky enough to procure them. The beautiful lustre of these metals must have drawn attention and excited admiration as much in the earliest as in the present times.

The metals are also malleable enough to be formed easily into coins; a job Jevons thought should be left to "executive government and its scientific advisers" (though in his *Social Statics*, Herbert Spencer argued that private firms would do a better job).

Money's emergence from barter was therefore a natural, spontaneous process. In his article "On the Origins of Money," the Austrian economist Carl Menger attempted to demonstrate this through a kind of thought experiment; arguing that "we can only come fully to understand the origin of money by learning to view the establishment of the social procedure, with which we are dealing, as the spontaneous outcome, the unpremeditated resultant, of particular, individual efforts of the members of a society." As people traded among themselves, it turned out that some goods were more reliably marketable than others. People therefore stockpiled this substance (e.g., gold) and began to use it as a form of money. Money was therefore created not by the state but by the markets. As Menger wrote,

> Money has not been generated by law. In its origin it is a social, and not a state institution. Sanction by the authority of the state is a notion alien to it. On the other hand, however, by state recognition and state regulation, this social institution of money has been perfected and adjusted to the manifold and varying needs of an evolving commerce . . . the establishment and maintenance of coined pieces so as to win public confidence and, as far as possible, to forestall risk concerning their genuineness, weight, and fineness, and above all the ensuring their circulation in general, have been everywhere recognised as important functions of state administration.[8]

In his book *An Outline of Money*, Geoffrey Crowther (then editor of the *Economist* magazine) described money as the "radical invention . . . of some lazy genius who found himself oppressed by the task of calculating how many bushels of corn should exchange for one tiger-skin, if three bushels of corn were equal to five bananas, twenty bananas to one goat and twenty goats to one tiger-skin. And it undoubtedly was an invention; it needed the conscious reasoning power of Man to make the step from simple barter to money-accounting."[9] Paul Samuelson, in the ninth edition of his textbook *Economics*, which is the best-selling economics textbook of all time, brought the story up-to-date: "If we were to construct history along hypothetical, logical lines, we should naturally follow the age of barter by the age of commodity money. . . . The age of commodity money gives way to the age of paper money. . . . Finally, along with the age of paper money, there is the age of bank money, or bank checking deposits."[10]

As economist John Smithin noted in a collection of essays called *What Is Money?*, the idea that money spontaneously took over from barter as the solution to a practical problem, with the role of government limited to putting its stamp of approval on the whole thing, "has persisted to the present day" and is still featured in "almost every textbook."[11] Consider, for example, the explanation of the origins of money from the thirteenth edition of a modern best-selling Canadian textbook, *Economics*, by Christopher Ragan and Richard Lipsey:

> If there were no money, goods would have to be exchanged by barter. . . . The major difficulty with barter is that each transaction requires a double coincidence of wants. . . . The use of money as a medium of exchange solves this problem. . . . All sorts of commodities have been used as money at one time or another, but gold and silver proved to have great advantages. . . . Before the invention of coins, it was necessary to carry the metals in bulk. . . . The invention of coinage eliminated the need to weigh the metal at each transaction, but it created an important role for an authority, usually a king or queen, who made the coins and affixed his or her seal, guaranteeing the amount of precious metal that the coin contained. This was clearly a great convenience.[12]

We therefore see an eerie continuity between Aristotle, the first economists, and modern textbooks (as discussed later, this is not the only sense that economic theory remains Aristotelian). As the Banco Central do Brasil puts it: "At the beginning, there was no money. People engaged in barter."[13] Two things are worthy of note. The first is that, while Aristotle is still, of course, widely revered as one of the founders of Western philosophy, most scientific fields have been updated since his day (we don't still think the stars are made of ether and go round the earth). It therefore seems a very odd coincidence (a double coincidence?) that the mainstream theory about the emergence of money as recited to economics students has not changed much from the few sentences that he wrote about it more than 2,000 years ago.

The second point is that the story that has been thus embalmed over the ages is completely wrong. A noticeable feature of all these accounts is the lack of dates, references, or supporting details. As the British economist Alfred Mitchell-Innes observed in his article "What Is Money?": "So universal is the belief in these theories among economists that they have grown to be considered almost as axioms which hardly require proof, and nothing is more noticeable in economic works than the scant historical evidence on which they rest, and the absence of critical examination of their worth." He goes on: "Modern research in the domain of commercial history and numismatics, and especially recent discoveries in Babylonia, have brought to light a mass of evidence which was not available to the earlier economists, and in the light of which it may be positively stated that none of these theories rest on a solid basis of historical proof—that in fact they are false."[14]

With respect to "modern research" we should point out that Mitchell-Innes, whose work experience included a stint as financial adviser to the king of Siam, wrote his article in 1913. He argued that money is a proxy for government debt, which gains its value because it is needed to pay taxes (a school of thought known as chartalism). His work received a positive review from John Maynard Keynes, but then dropped out of sight, though it has recently made a comeback among "neochartalists" such as L. Randall Wray, who called Mitchell-Innes's contributions "the best pair of articles on the nature of money written in the twentieth century."[15]

Money did not emerge from barter. We know this because economies based purely on barter don't appear to ever have existed (box 1.1). According to anthropologist Caroline Humphrey, "No example of a barter economy, pure and simple, has ever been described, let alone the emergence from it of money."[16] Far from having sprung into the world as the pristine, elegant solution to a problem of logic, the history of money turns out to be a little richer, messier, and more complex.

Money 1.0

As Mitchell-Innes pointed out a hundred years ago, our knowledge of the ancient civilizations that were presumably the birthplace of money has improved somewhat since the time of Aristotle, Smith, or Jevons. The best-documented ancient money system is that of the Sumerians in Mesopotamia, a society of relentless record-keepers whose clay-tablet cuneiforms—when they were decoded by Victorian scholars in the mid-nineteenth century—turned out to be mostly about commercial transactions.

The Sumerians were responsible for a number of innovations that we still find useful today, including arithmetic, beer, the twenty-four-hour day, wheeled vehicles, and urban conglomerations. City-states such as

---

Box 1.1

Some Things That Have Been Used as a Means of Making Payment

- Bars made of precious metals (e.g., ancient Mesopotamia, central banks)
- Salt (vital commodity for preserving and flavoring food used as currency in North Africa, China, and the Mediterranean; salary is from Latin *sal* for salt)
- Cattle (e.g., ancient India and Africa; the word "pecuniary" is from the Latin *pecus* [cattle], while "capital" is from the Latin *capita* [head], and the Indian currency rupee is from *rupa* [head of cattle])
- Slaves (e.g., ancient Rome, Greece, parts of modern India)
- Cacao beans, cotton capes (ancient Mexico)
- Cowrie shells (e.g., ancient China, Maldives)
- Beads (used in African slave trade)
- Feathers (Santa Cruz archipelago, Solomon Islands)
- Dog teeth (Papua New Guinea)
- Whale teeth (Fiji)
- Very large, hard-to-move stone discs (Pacific islands of Yap)
- Knives or tools (parts of Africa)
- Iron rings and bracelets (parts of Africa)
- Brass rods (Tiv people of West Africa)
- Woodpecker scalps (Karok people of the Californian interior)
- Human skulls (Sumatra)
- Casino chips (some cities in nineteenth-century Siam [Thailand])
- Strings of wampum beads (American colonies)
- Tobacco, or receipts for warehoused tobacco (American colonies)
- Cigarettes (POW camps, postwar Germany, modern prisons—these are inflation-proof because if the value drops too far they get smoked)
- Carbon credits
- Binary information (e.g., bitcoins)

We would not describe all these as forms of money, since many are used as social currencies, which are rather different from the money used in markets.

Ur, whose location in modern-day Iraq is marked by the remains of its famous ziggurat, were home to tens of thousands of urban dwellers and were surrounded by farms that supplied them with agricultural produce. The system was controlled by temple bureaucrats, whose job of regulating this humming economy led to yet another invention—accountancy.

Transactions were recorded first using clay tokens, and then—more efficiently—by inscribing with a reed on clay tablets. Measurements of quantities such as weight of produce were made using a system of units based, like the Sumerian number system, on multiples of 60. A shekel weighed about 8.3 grams; 60 shekels made up a mina (about half a kilogram); and 60 minas were a talent (about 30 kilograms). Around 3000 B.C.E., the temple accountants began to use a shekel of silver as a unit of currency. The price of everything else, including commodities, labor, or legal penalties, was set by the state in terms of these shekels.

For example, the Laws of Eshnunna, named after a city near what is now Baghdad, specified that 1 shekel in silver was equivalent to 12 silas of oil, 15 silas of lard, 300 silas of potash, 600 silas of salt, 600 silas of barley, and so on, with a sila being about a liter in volume. A shekel of silver would buy 180 shekels-weight of copper or 360 shekels-weight of wool. A month's labor was 1 shekel of silver, while renting a wagon for a day together with oxen and driver would set you back one-third of a shekel.[17] If a man bit and severed the nose of a man, the fine was 60 shekels (1 mina). An eye was 60, a finger was 40, a tooth or an ear was 30, and a slap in the face was 10 shekels.[18] This last was weirdly the same as compensation for the loss of a slave. Of course, while the state could control legal penalties, attempts at price fixing would have been harder to enforce and maintain.[19]

The Sumerian economy was dominated by the day-to-day running of temples and palaces, and everything from wages to rents to taxes was being calculated and paid for in terms of shekels. In this sense silver did conform to our standard picture of money; however, because the economy was centrally planned and controlled (one imagines a version of North Korea without the nukes), the main use of the shekel was as an accounting device for bureaucrats, with transactions recorded as marks in a ledger. The actual metal did not circulate widely but was kept in carefully guarded vaults. If someone had to pay the palace, they weren't expected to show up with lumps of silver—they were more likely to use barley, wool, or some other commodity, with the value reckoned in shekels. Outside the palace, most market dealings were done on the basis of credit, so for example, one's beer consumption could be paid at harvest by delivery of the corresponding quantity of barley.[20]

In a way, this use of silver as an accounting device is reminiscent of the world's international gold reserves, of which a large fraction—some 7,055 tons—is kept underneath Manhattan in a very large basement vault belonging to the U.S. Federal Reserve. The owners are governments, central banks, and other official organizations from around the world. (A similar arrangement exists at the Bank of England, whose vaults contain a further 4,950 tons. Both are an inheritance from the days of the gold standard, which was controlled by first Great Britain and later the United States.)[21] When one entity decides to sell a portion of its gold to another, a bank employee just goes down and wheels the gold bars along to the correct room—but the metal rarely actually leaves the vault.[22] Everyone just needs to know it's there. Which it probably is.[23]

Back in Mesopotamia, larger debts were recorded on the cuneiforms, which were put inside clay envelopes and marked with the seal of the borrower. The creditor would keep the envelope and break it open when the debt was repaid. In cases in which the tablet promised to repay the bearer, rather than a specific individual, it was also possible to sell the tablet—and therefore the debt—to another person.[24] Such debt therefore became a tradable currency in itself—to use an expression from economics, it had been monetized. The principle was the same as that of paper money, which promises to "pay the bearer on demand."

The Sumerian system did not therefore rely on either barter or the widespread circulation of coins. Instead it would be better described as being based on a complex network of debts, specified in a scrip-like virtual currency—the shekel—that had the backing of the main employer and central administrator—the state. (Scrip is the same as money when there is only one company in town.) Cuneiforms were one way of expressing this debt in a tradable form that we would recognize as a kind of physical money object, but it would be more accurate to say that the real currency was the virtual silver that flitted invisibly through the economy, like fish at the bottom of a lake, just as money today is mostly electronic.

The interest charged on loans was known as *máš*, which was the word for "baby calf." For commercial loans this was set at one-sixtieth per month, which was an easy number to compute since the number system was based on sixty.[25] Interest payments on state loans went to the temple, from which they flowed back into the community, but private loans were made as well. For example, if a farmer had a bad harvest, debts could accumulate to the point where they became unpayable, to the point of forcing him into slavery. The concept of money may still have been in its infancy, but the numbers were real enough. To avoid social unrest, the Sumerian rulers occasionally canceled all debts, a practice that later came to be known as the Jubilee.[26]

Much less is known about how finance worked in the other early urban civilizations of Egypt or China; but again it seems clear that money first emerged as an accounting device. In ancient Egypt value was expressed in terms of *deben*, which originally referred to a measure of grain. Wheat was deposited in centralized, state-owned warehouses that functioned as banks and facilitated payments of debts and taxes.[27] Gold was sacred to the sun god Ra and did not serve as currency, unless perhaps with the gods: the primary use of the metal was to be buried with the dead.[28] Pre-imperial China was relatively less bureaucratic or centralized, and there appears to have been a patchwork of local arrangements. A common form of money was cowries— highly durable shells that have found use as a currency in many parts of the world—but a variety of credit instruments, such as knotted strings or notched pieces of bamboo, were also used. The first metallic coins to appear in China were imitations in bronze and copper of cowrie shells, and the Chinese character for money is said to be based on the shape of a cowrie shell.

Many of the examples used by Smith and later by Jevons were based on then-current ideas about tribal societies such as the Native Americans of North America. But when anthropologists actually investigated those cultures, they found that while barter certainly took place, it was a somewhat specialized form of transaction, usually involving parties who were borderline hostile and had little trust of each other. (Barter is also common in places where people are used to using money but are short of cash, such as jails.) More important were gift economies, in which transactions are framed as gifts; communal arrangements where goods are distributed by councils; and "social currencies" used to signify status, arrange marriages, compensate for damages, and so on. More on this later.

New inventions often result from a collision between existing technologies and cultural practices. The success of Johannes Gutenberg's printing press in the fifteenth century was due less to the novelty of its mechanism— the technology of mass-produced stamping had existed for some time— than its ability to fill a cultural need: the desire for uniformity in the enormous market for Catholic texts. The personal computer arose from the union of West Coast, hippie-ish, electronic hobbyists and tinkerers—who came up with the radical ideas—with the (mostly) East Coast, mainstream computer industry—which provided the applications and organization. Similarly, the invention of the next form of money can be seen as the offspring of a social technology—numeracy and accounting—with the ultimate "killer app": war.

Money 2.0

The first coins are believed to have been made in the seventh century B.C.E., not in Mesopotamia, but in the nearby kingdom of Lydia. They were discovered during the British Museum excavations of the Temple of Artemis at Ephesus (one of the seven wonders of the ancient world, whose construction was paid for by the Lydian king Croesus) in 1904/1905. The coins were oval (later circular, perhaps to deter tampering) pieces of a gold-silver alloy called electrum—or "white gold" by Herodotus—with a simple stamp on one side, showing, for example, the head of a lion, that certified the coin. They were made by placing a blank round of metal on top of a die and hammering it down with a punch. According to myth, King Midas—he who was cursed to turn whatever he touched, including his own daughter, into gold—was instructed by Dionysius to bathe in the river Pactolus to rid himself of the power. The gold flowed into the river bank, which was said to be the source of the naturally occurring electrum. Actual coins had a lower gold content and were probably from a man-made version of the alloy.

The denominations ranged from 1 stater (a translation of "shekel"), which weighed about 14 grams, down through various fractions to as small as a ninety-sixth of a stater. These were valuable coins: like a Sumerian shekel, 1 stater is believed to have been worth about a month's salary, and even a ninety-sixth stater coin could have fed a worker for a few days.[29] The commonest coins, which were one-third of a stater, would fetch about ten sheep, and so were not designed for everyday smaller transactions.

Lydian merchants dealt in a variety of commodities such as grains, oil, beer, as well as in goods such as ceramics and cosmetics, and they also had the first known brothels and gambling houses. It is not known how much coins were used for external trade, but it is clear that the *idea* of coinage quickly spread, first to the Greek cities of coastal Asia Minor, and from there to the mainland and surrounding islands.[30] By 600 B.C.E., most self-respecting Greek city-states were churning out their own coins as a sign of their independence, which can also be translated as power, as we shall see in chapter 6. The need to exchange between these coins, as well as make deposits and loans, meant that basic money-changing and banking services grew alongside their use.

As Jevons and colleagues pointed out, these new coins combined the advantages of commodity money with those of tokens. Coins were valuable in themselves because they were made of precious metals, but unlike commodities such as grain, they were easily transportable and didn't degrade with time. The stamp was also a reassurance that the coins would be accepted as currency within a certain region. Coins therefore always traded there for a value that was more than the cost of their content, since if this were not the case they would have been melted down. There was a constant tension between these two aspects of coin money, with the worth of a coin tending toward its stamp value within a city and toward its (lower) metal value when traded to foreigners.

While coins were certainly convenient for certain types of trade, the main motivation for the spread of coin money appears to have had less to do with the needs of the market—which historian Michael Crawford calls an "accidental consequence of the coinage"—than with those of the military.[31] The Greeks were enthusiastic warriors—their first great piece of literature, the *Iliad*, is mostly about warfare—and coinage was introduced at a time when the largest expense of Greek rulers was the mobilization of huge armies. Coins served as a device for payment but also as a tool to both motivate the troops and control the general public.

Long before gold and silver were being used as money, they were being used as jewelry and hoarded as treasure; and one of the positive spin-offs from military campaigns was that they usually involved plunder. What easier way to pay soldiers, and share the profits, than by giving each a small portion of the loot?[32] The coins, which were too valuable to be useful for small-scale transactions such as buying a loaf of bread, would have been perfect for a soldier's bonus. Also, soldiers and mercenaries needed money that could be transported easily and used in other countries. We were reminded of this in 2011 when the International Monetary Fund estimated that the former Libyan dictator Muammar Gaddafi had stockpiled about 165 tons of gold. As a gold analyst told the BBC, "Obviously for Gaddafi to have this anonymous highly liquid asset potentially is quite useful. . . . If you look back, gold is the ultimate means of payment, the ultimate form of exchange in crisis."[33]

At the same time, though, states wanted to encourage wider use of the coins, to solve logistical problems such as how to pay their own debts, to levy taxes on subject cities (Athens was exempt), and to supply the army and navy with supplies. Coins were ideal for use in this type of transaction, because they had a well-defined value that was enforced, guaranteed, and, of course, accepted by the state. Mints were located in temples, which were the traditional storehouses for captured wealth. The coins were distributed to soldiers and their suppliers, but also to the public at large through payments for service or the occasional handout. This ensured the development of markets that would accept the money. Because taxes and fees were paid by coin, people had to get their hands on money. This made them dependent on the state and motivated them to help provision the troops. Coinage was therefore spread around the area through war, conquest, and the distribution of the proceeds.

When in 359 B.C.E. the oracle at Delphi told Philip of Macedon that "with silver spears you may conquer the world," the ruler took over the silver mines of nearby kingdoms and used the proceeds as bribes against his opponents. The spread of coinage was accelerated by Philip's son, and Aristotle's student, Alexander the Great. During his conquest of the Persian Empire, salaries for his army of more than 100,000 soldiers amounted to about half a ton of silver per day. The silver was obtained largely from Persian mines, with the labor supplied by war captives, and was formed into Alexander's own coins. These had an image of the supreme god Zeus on the back and Hercules on the front (the image of a man who became a god after performing twelve superhuman tasks must have appealed to Alexander). Alexander would go on to invade the Babylonian Empire in Mesopotamia. He wiped out the existing credit system and insisted that taxes be paid in his own coins.

Rather than emerging naturally from barter, as mainstream economists like to imagine, the money system was imposed at the sharp end of a sword. However, even if its main function was for paying the army and collecting taxes, it certainly had a revolutionary effect on the structure of society. Money created its own markets and institutions, such as currency changers and banks, as well as its own demand. It promoted new kinds of social ties and connections by making it easier for people from different social circles or regions to carry out transactions. Its use turned computation into an essential skill and changed the way people thought and interacted. And it was a wonderful way of coordinating and controlling activity, because suddenly the rules were clear: everyone was on the same page.

The introduction of money was followed in Greece by a cultural blossoming in art, philosophy, literature, architecture, astronomy, mathematics, and democracy; and its spread around the world, both through imitation and independent reinvention, coincided with the start of what German philosopher Karl Jaspers called the Axial Age, in which "the spiritual foundations of humanity were laid simultaneously and independently in China, India, Persia, Judea, and Greece. And these are the foundations upon which humanity still subsists today."[34] It was as if a part of the human mind that had long laid dormant had suddenly been liberated by the arrival of cash (box 1.2).

Box 1.2

The Tetradrachm

The production of metallic money relied on extracting large quantities of gold and silver, and conquered armies were put to work as slaves in massive mines. The most popular coin in ancient Greece was the silver tetradrachm, which was equivalent to 4 drachmae (a drachma, from the Greek word for "grasp" or "seize," was a unit of weight, referring to a handful of grain). The coin sported an image of the goddess Athena on one side and an owl (the symbol of the wise Athenian people) on the other. The silver for the coin was extracted from mines such as the ones in Laurium, whose pits, which were up to 400 feet deep, are estimated to have employed (or rather, not employed) some 20,000 slaves.

Each coin contained around 15 to 20 grams of silver, depending on the mint, and would have paid about two weeks of unskilled labor.* Versions were in wide circulation from 510 to 25 B.C.E., when the mines ran out. The "thirty pieces of silver" paid to Judas for betraying Jesus are believed to have been Tyrian tetradrachms.

Greek silver tetradrachm of Athens (Attica), 520–510 B.C.E. Obverse shows the helmeted head of Athena; reverse side shows an owl with olive-sprig and moon crescent. (From H. A. Cahn, "Dating the Early Coinages of Athens," *Kleine Schriften zur Münzkunde und Archäologie* [1975]: 94, fig. 5a, http://commons. wikimedia.org/wiki/File%3AGreek_Silver_Tetradrachm_of_Athens_[Attica].jpg)

*Glyn Davies, *A History of Money: From Ancient Times to the Present Day*, 3rd ed. (Cardiff: University of Wales Press, 2002), 76.

Personal Property

At the time of Alexander's death at the age of thirty-two in 323 B.C.E., the area he had conquered included the Middle East, Persia, and Egypt, as well as parts of Afghanistan, Central Asia, and India. He founded some twenty cities in his own name; one of them, Alexandria in Egypt, became the major repository of Greek knowledge, including the teachings of his tutor Aristotle. It wasn't just coins that spread around the world, but a theory of money—which is one reason economics textbooks still include reworded versions of Aristotle. After Alexander's death, his empire was divided between his family and his generals. His coins continued to be minted for another 250 years, but were eventually replaced by those belonging to another, even larger empire, that of the Romans.

The Roman monetary system ran on similar principles to those of the Greeks, only on a more industrial scale. The army conquered foreign lands; slaves were put to work in mines extracting precious metals; millions of shiny Roman coins were stamped out by hand every year and distributed to the army as payment (as usual, this was the government's largest expense); and conquered populations were subjected to taxes, payable in those same coins, which ensured their circulation.[35] In Rome, coins were first minted in the temple of Juno Moneta—named for the goddess who was the protectress of funds—which is the origin of the word "money." Mints were later also set up in the provinces. In the second century B.C.E., the Senate gave generals the right to mint coins to pay their troops, so mobile mints sometimes accompanied the army.[36] Like Olympic medals, coins were available in gold, silver, and bronze (named for the metallurgists of Brindisi in southern Italy). One side would typically be adorned by the visage of the reigning emperor, while the other would feature a propagandist image, such as that of Romulus and Remus, the legendary founders of Rome.

Coins were, of course, less useful for very large transactions, such as the purchase of property. In a letter, the politician Cicero wrote that he bought a house for 3.5 million sesterces, which equated to about 3.8 tons of silver—rather a lot to deliver by hand then as now (for comparison, that amount of silver would cost about $2.2 million today). Instead, it seems that such transactions were based on credit: as Cicero elsewhere notes, "*nomina facit, negotium conficit*" (provides the bonds, completes the purchase).[37] The bonds (*nomina*) corresponded to entries in account books that could also be transferred from one person to another in a kind of proto–bond market. As he tells his financial adviser Atticus: "If I were to sell my claim on Faberius, I don't doubt my being able to settle for the grounds of Silius even by a ready money payment."

Cicero's follower Pliny the Younger asked a friend for advice on buying a piece of land: "It is three million sesterces, though at one time the price was five, but owing to the lack of capital of the tenants and the general badness of the times the rents have fallen off and the price has therefore dropped also. Perhaps you will ask whether I can raise these three millions without difficulty. Well, nearly all my capital is invested in land, but I have some money out at interest and I can borrow without any trouble."[38] Caesar apparently owed some 100 million sesterces in 61 B.C.E., though he soon earned it back through the military conquest of Gaul.[39]

In his *Ars Amatoria*, the poet Ovid showed that the temptation to also buy smaller items on credit is not a strictly modern phenomenon. When a young man wishes to please a lover who "has her purchase in her eye":

> If you complain you have no ready coin,
> No matter, 'tis but writing of a line;
> A little bill, not to be paid at sight:
> (Now curse the time when thou wert taught to write.)

The center for financial dealing was the Forum. Moneylenders, who took deposits, arranged loans, and changed money, tended to congregate around a vaulted passageway known as the Exchange; the names of debtors who defaulted on their loans were inscribed on a column called the Columna Maenia. The Romans therefore had access to a range of financial services, including a primitive credit-rating system. Cicero wrote that "this whole subject of acquiring money, investing money . . . is more profitably discussed by certain worthy gentlemen at the Exchange than could be done by any philosophers of any school."[40] The sprawling size of the Roman Empire also meant that it was frequently necessary to transfer funds from one region to another. This was accomplished through private companies known as *publicani*, which were responsible for tax collection in the provinces. To send money from Rome to some outpost in Spain or North Africa, you could deposit some silver or a *nomina* in the Rome branch, and some of the taxes would be made available for pickup at the other end.

Hundreds of millions of coins were struck, at a pace not matched until modern times; in the mid-second century C.E. imperial spending has been estimated at 225 million denarii per year, with about 75 percent going to supply the military.[41] The system was so successful that it actually outlasted the empire itself, at least in a virtual form. As discussed in chapter 3, people were still figuring debts and accounts in terms of Roman money centuries after the coins themselves were history.

The fall of the Roman Empire has been blamed on many factors, but the economy was certainly one of them. In the third century, the lack of new foreign conquests meant the supply of precious metals decreased. Since Rome produced very little itself, money was continuously draining away to foreign lands. The process accelerated as Romans consumed increasing quantities of exotic goods from India and China. As Cicero wrote, money is "the sinews of war," and these were stretched to breaking point as the army ballooned in size to 650,000 in the fourth century, even as the size of the empire itself was shrinking.[42] Coins were therefore debased, which contributed to severe inflation as more of them were issued to pay the state's expenses. During a spell of just one year (274–275 C.E.), prices multiplied by a factor of 100.[43] Like a pyramid scheme, the empire relied on ever more conquests to sustain itself; and when it ran out of new sources of funds, it collapsed.

The course of this inflation can be traced in the silver content of the denarius, the most common Roman coin, which was the equivalent of the Greek drachma. Its name came from the Latin for "containing ten" because it equaled ten smaller coins known as *asses*. The name lives on as the word for money in a number of languages, including Italian (*denaro*), Spanish (*dinero*), and Portuguese (*dinheiro*), and as the dinar currency in several (mostly Islamic) countries. When the small coin, with a diameter of about 2 centimeters, was first minted around 211 B.C.E., it contained about 4.5 grams of nearly pure (95–98 percent) silver and would pay a day's wages for a soldier or an unskilled laborer.[44] However, it became common for emperors to recall coins, reissue with a lower silver content, and keep the extra metal as profit. The silver content slowly reduced to about 50 percent by the middle of the third century C.E. and then plummeted to about 2 percent. In its final stages, around 280 C.E., the coin had a copper core and a silver surface that tended to rub off with use.[45] Like the empire itself, appearances were being maintained, but the core had transmuted into something less stable or enduring. When Constantine introduced the solidus coin (from which "soldier," since they liked to be paid with them) in 312 C.E., its 4.5 grams of solid gold was worth 275,000 denarii, and what counted was the weight of the metal, as opposed to the emperor's stamp.[46] The solidity of the bezant, as it was later known, is attested to by the fact that it remained in production for some seven centuries.

Law of the Land

While Rome's was the first empire to fully exploit the power of money and incorporate it into its structure and organization, the Romans never quite mastered the dynamics of money. The chaotic end of the Roman Empire—with emperors struggling to raise funds through taxation, confiscation, devaluation of the currency, or even the looting of their own temples under Constantine—still serves as a cautionary tale for any government that doesn't mind its budget (emperors didn't even have budgets until very late in the history of the empire).[47] The greatest contribution of the Romans to economic thought was not so much new theories of money—on which they tended to toe the Aristotelian line—but their legal system. Just as the straight lines of Roman roads still mark many countries in Europe, so the straight lines set by their legal codes continue to inform our understanding of things like property rights.

The Romans had enormous respect for property, especially land and slaves (which were the two most economically important kinds), and much of their legal system was devoted to defining and protecting owner-ship. Economists have long emphasized the economic role of free markets, but market economies as we know them today could not exist without elaborate systems of property rights, which are legal inventions. A quirk of the Roman code—which has long caused confusion for struggling law students around the world—is that property is defined as a relationship between a person and a thing, which gives the person absolute power over the thing. This definition is strange, because while it is possible to have relationships between people, we don't usually think of relationships with inanimate objects. I don't think I own my car because I have a relationship of unlimited power over it (which clearly isn't the case, otherwise it would always start).

A plausible answer to this conundrum, according to sociologist Orlando Patterson, is that Roman property law is based on the ownership of slaves.[48] A slave, after all, is a property that is also a person, so it makes sense to say that the owner has a relationship of power over it. As the historian Jerry Toner notes, "Wealthy Romans saw slaves as being necessary for a high standard of living, just as we view modern domestic appliances."[49] At the height of the empire, even "middle-class" Roman households could expect to have a person or two from a recently conquered region helping out with chores. This link between money and power is written into our legal system and coded like DNA into the fabric of our lives. Its echoes appear in the modern idea of powerless "wage slaves" who only earn enough to pay for their upkeep, or for that matter the actual slave labor that forms part of many global supply chains (11 percent of British businesses believe that their supply chains are "likely" to include slavery, according to the *Guardian*).[50]

As with its money, the Roman system of civil law outlasted the empire and—after something of a falling off during what is often referred to as the Dark Ages—was by the sixteenth century forming the backbone of law in most European countries. Its great attraction, according to historian C. F. Kolbert, "was not so much the technical apparatus . . . but its clarity, simplicity and orderliness."[51] As Edward Gibbon noted in *The Decline and Fall of the Roman Empire*, "The hunter, the shepherd, the husbandman, may defend their possessions by two reasons which forcibly appeal to the feelings of the human mind: that whatever they enjoy is the fruit of their own industry; and that every man who envies their felicity may purchase similar acquisitions by the exercise of similar diligence."[52] Romans may not have been able to trust their coins, but their legal system was the real thing.

Hard Money

To summarize the story so far: credit systems such as that of ancient Mesopotamia far predated the use of coins. When coin money did emerge, it was not a natural and spontaneous process, as recited in mainstream economics, but was instead the result of government policy. The Greek and Roman Empires were both built on a military–financial complex that obtained bullion and slaves from conquered lands, paid soldiers using the minted coins, and collected taxes in said coins. Money was therefore a tool to transfer resources from the general population to the well-armed state. Once established, money created its own dynamic, as the use of money created a need for money. Its role was enforced not just through military conquest, but also by laws. The idea of value is inherently fuzzy and hard to quantify, but legal systems such as that of the Romans required clarity, straight boundaries, and exact calculations. Everything had to be convertible into money.

The standard story from Economics 101 therefore has it the wrong way round. Coin money did not supersede barter; rather it was predated by state-backed systems of credit. And rather than emerging naturally, with government and its legal system only stepping in at the last moment to claim credit by putting its stamp on everything, the use of coin money was imposed by government in the first place. It was forced on the population, just as a coin's stamp was forced onto metal. This changes the way we see money. Menger's idea that state sanction is "alien" to money applies better to some of the new cybercurrencies—which get their authority from their network of users—but even these don't emerge naturally, they are very carefully planned and designed by computer scientists and programmers. There is a parallel with the currencies used in online gaming, which are usually imposed in a top-down fashion by the game's designers.[53]

So why has the Aristotelian story endlessly been repeated? One reason is that in order for economics to present itself as an objective discipline, it must cast the modern economy as being the logical endpoint of a historical process in which alternative types of exchange or interaction are seen as just imperfect approximations of the real thing. If money has emerged naturally from commerce rather than been imposed by government, then economics can be seen as a kind of natural science, divorced from its social and political context.[54]

The economics version also reflects an inbuilt assumption that there is essentially no trust between parties. Exchange therefore has to be immediate, in the form of goods or some form of money. An IOU would be right out of the question, even if it were wrapped in an envelope made of clay and stamped with a seal. Economics can therefore ignore the complex web of human relationships in which the economy is embedded. In this picture, notes Geoffrey Ingham, "the natural economy does not possess a complex social-economic structure; it is essentially simple barter with a monetary veil."[55]

Above all, though, the idea that money replaced barter by making transactions more efficient allows one to see the economy as something in which money is nothing more than a passive intermediary—a "lubricant in exchange." Money objects such as coins are not fundamentally different from commodities such as weights of gold: the stamp is merely something to "save the trouble of weighing" (Aristotle) and "a great convenience" (Ragan and Lipsey) but has no unique importance of its own. The Canadian economist Todd Hirsch quipped that "you could use chickens as money" as long as people are ready to accept them as a means of exchange.[56] However, the fact that many things can serve as money does not tell us much about money, any more than the number of actors who have played Hamlet tells us about Shakespeare's play. What counts is the properties of objects at the time when they are used as money, not when they are offstage.

An example of this view of money as passive intermediary is the famous (in monetary circles) paper "Money Is Memory," by Narayana R. Kocherlakota of the Federal Reserve Bank of Minneapolis.[57] The paper begins by noting that "fiat money consists of intrinsically useless objects that do not enter utility or production functions" in economic models, and goes on to provide a quasi-mathematical demonstration that the role of these "barren tokens" is to act as a kind of memory substitute and keep track of who owes what to whom in what amounts to a barter economy. The conclusion is that "money is technologically equivalent to a primitive version of memory." The argument relies on standard ideas from economics such as "perfect public equilibria" and the existence of well-defined utility functions (i.e., mathematical measures of value) to give "a rigorous notion of what outcomes are possible" (such assumptions are explored further in chapter 7). Obviously money could therefore never lead to irrational responses or have a destabilizing effect on the economy, because it is nothing more than a memory crutch, a convenient reminder system.

This idea of money as something that is inert, sterile, and boring is consistent with the mainstream economics view of the economy as a stable, self-regulating, logical machine in which money plays no special role, other than as a metric for economic activity. As economist Stephanie Kelton notes, "Money, debt and finance don't even fit into many economic models."[58] Former Bank of England governor Mervyn King observes that "most economists hold conversations in which the word 'money' hardly appears at all" (which is particularly strange given the way the financial community hangs on every word of central bank governors).[59] As shown in chapter 7, this leads to the curious situation in which the powerful dynamics of money have traditionally been all but excluded from mainstream economic models—as if the subject is too grubby to touch—and alternatives are not taken seriously.

The central, founding myth about the origins of money is one of the reasons why economists still, despite the countless number of books written on the subject, seem to be in denial about its true nature. And it shows that, far from representing the perfection of a logical process, our current version of money is only one of the possibilities. In chapter 3, we will discuss the emergence of private virtual currencies that used strings of information instead of precious metal to convey value—in the Middle Ages. Before that, we first take a brief philosophical diversion, as we ask what magical property it is that makes money, *money*.

2

The Money Magnet

Money is a singular thing. It ranks with love as man's greatest source of joy. And with death as his greatest source of anxiety.

JOHN KENNETH GALBRAITH, *THE AGE OF UNCERTAINTY*

As all things change to fire, and fire exhausted falls back into things, the crops are sold for money spent on food.

HERACLITUS, FRAGMENT 22

The question "What is money?" never has a fixed answer because money is not stable; it would be answered differently by an accountant in ancient Sumeria, a nineteenth-century banker, a teenager at a mall, or someone in the future. Some people will argue that the only real money is gold; others, that all money is a collective illusion with no reality of its own. Some believe that the production of money is the prerogative of government; others, that we need government to get out of the way of private currencies. Money is the root of all evil, or (George Bernard Shaw) lack of money is the root of all evil. But everyone will agree that money holds a magnetic appeal. In this chapter, we adopt an approach inspired by modern, non-Newtonian physics to investigate the basic properties of money and show how such an apparently simple thing can evoke such strong and varied responses, while remaining in many respects our central point of reference: our true north.

In *Nicomachean Ethics*, Aristotle wrote that money "makes all things commensurate, since all things are measured by money."[1] Money therefore acts as a kind of map from the real world to the abstract world of numbers.

It projects the messy plurality of objects and services onto a uniform metric that is easily compared and referenced.

This role as an economic weigh scale is reflected by the association between units of money and units of weight. The word "shekel" is based on the Sumerian root word for "weighing." Similarly the British pound sterling originally referred to 1 pound of silver. The Latin word for "pound" is *libra*, which is why the English pound symbol is £. *Libra* also appears in Italian as the lira. A difference between units of weight and currency, of course, is that even if the names of coins are stable and enduring, their value is shifting and fluid—a dollar isn't what it used to be (or actually it is, but it doesn't buy as much). Also, value doesn't actually weigh anything.

While many things have been used as means of payment throughout history, an implication of the idea that "all things are measured by money" is that, in principle at least, all things are measurable by *one kind* of money. In the same way that we can translate between imperial pounds and metric kilograms without any loss of accuracy, we can translate between units of currency by using an accepted exchange rate—so why have more than one? As we will see, keeping two currencies on the go at the same time—such as silver and gold under a bimetallist regime—adds flexibility to the money supply but can be confusing and unstable, because market prices tend to shift for one metal relative to the other, raising the question of which is the proper unit of account. Furthermore, the power of a currency depends on its range of acceptance. The greater the number of people who recognize a single currency, the more useful it becomes for trade. Finally, governments prefer to have monopoly power over currencies.

In 175 B.C.E., the Chinese emperor Wen decided to address a monetary crisis by an unconventional strategy: he allowed anyone to mint money at will. While this did accomplish the aim of providing more money for circulation, it also led to some unwelcome competition. As the ancient *Records of the Grand Historian* observed, "The King of Wu, though only a feudal lord, was able, by extracting ore from his mountains and minting coins, to rival the wealth of the Son of Heaven."[2] In 113 B.C.E., the monopoly on minting coins was reclaimed by the emperor, with his economic adviser noting, "If the currency system is unified under the emperor's control, the people will not serve two masters."

Money therefore has within it a tendency toward unification, homogenization, and the development of a single common standard (such as gold). A modern example of this trend was the establishment of the euro, which is the monetary equivalent of the metric system. A principal aim of the euro was to unite the continent of Europe and help prevent the kind of military conflicts that dominated much of its twentieth century. At the same time, though, the adoption of a single currency exacerbated the differences between its member states. Critics described it as a top-down project imposed by bureaucrats who were detached from economic and social realities. In 2012 and then again in 2015 (most likely not for the last time is the consensus at the time of writing), this tension came to a head when Greece, unable to pay its debt without massive aid from its neighbors, came perilously close to exiting the common currency.

The story of the euro is just one example of how money is driven by two conflicting impulses. On the one hand, it wants to unify messy reality; but on the other, it seems that it can achieve this only by separating itself from the real world. To understand the sources and nature of this conflict, we need to go back once again to the ancient Greeks, particularly the schools of philosophy that took root at the same time that coins were invented.

Unity

The first Greek city to produce its own coins in the sixth century B.C.E. is believed to have been Miletus, a commercial hub located in what is now Turkey, adjacent to the kingdom of Lydia. However, Miletus is most renowned in history for its minting of not coins but great minds. It would be no exaggeration to view the city as the birthplace of Greek philosophy. Just as its money provided a way to unify the world of material transactions, Milesian philosophy provided a way to unify the universe.

According to Bertrand Russell, "Western philosophy begins with Thales."[3] Thales was born in Miletus around 624 B.C.E. and is credited with a number of mathematical discoveries; it is said that he used his knowledge of geometry to compute the height of the Pyramids and the distance of a ship at sea. He is supposed to have predicted an eclipse of the sun in 585 B.C.E. And he also proposed the original (and often copied) theory of everything. Today, many physicists think that everything is made from infinitesimally small strings vibrating in a ten-dimensional space. According to Thales, everything was made of water. The earth, which was made of one form of water, floated on an infinite ocean. Earthquakes were caused when the earth sloshed around in this pool.

Thales's water-based theory might not seem like a huge advance over then-prevalent ideas that everything was controlled by gods. But as Aristotle later pointed out in *Metaphysics*, it did answer a logical conundrum, which is how things change from one form to another: they didn't really, because they were all made of the same thing.

The choice of water may have reflected the fact that Miletus was a coastal city, where life and commerce were dominated by the sea. But other Milesian thinkers soon chipped in with their own versions. Thales's student Anaximander pointed out that water could not describe all the opposites found in nature—for example, it could be wet but not dry—and therefore a special type of material was called for, which he called *apeiron* (having no limit). His student Anaximenes, in turn, argued that there was no need to invent some new, invisible substance. Everything in the universe was made of air. After all, when water is heated it evaporates, which seemed proof that it turned into air; and when air is cooled, water condenses out of it.

The idea, known today as material monism, that matter was made of one primordial substance was later picked up by Heraclitus (who thought it was fire) and Xenophanes (earth). Eventually the Greeks settled on a kind of compromise, championed by Aristotle, which was that matter was made up of the four elements of earth, water, air, and fire, with the fifth element, the ether, being reserved for the heavens. The idea that all things—including land, clean water, fresh air, and energy—are measured by money, though, never went away. The reason is related to another strand of Greek thought, which we could call "immaterial monism."

Immaterial Monism

The most influential of the pre-Socratic philosophers was Pythagoras. According to his biographer Iamblichus, as a young man Pythagoras visited Miletus, where he met with Thales (who was by then an old man) and Anaximander.[4] Pythagoras is famous today for the theorem concerning right triangles that bears his name, but the most significant discovery attributed to him is actually about music—he found that harmonies, as played, for example, on the lyre, are related by simple mathematical ratios. If you fret a string halfway up, then it produces a note that is an octave higher. Fretting two-thirds of the way up produces a musical fifth; three-quarters of the way up a fourth; and so on.

This discovery led Pythagoras to develop his own theory of everything—based this time not on a specific material, such as water or air, but on the abstract concept of number. Music, after all, was considered the most subtle and mysterious of art forms, so if it could be reduced to number, then—so it seemed—could anything else. The Pythagoreans, as his followers were known, therefore believed that number was the ultimate reality, the stuff of which the universe is made. According to the Pythagorean version of the big bang theory, the universe began in a state of unity, which then divided into two opposite components, the Limited (*peiron*) and the Unlimited (*apeiron*). These mixed together to form numbers, which made up the structure of the cosmos.

The Pythagorean enthusiasm for number was undoubtedly influenced by the development of money. His followers believed that Pythagoras was a demigod descended from the god Apollo, but he was also the son of a gem engraver, and according to classicist W. K. C. Guthrie, he "derived his enthusiasm for the study of number from its practical applications in commerce." He was likely also involved in the design of coinage for his region in what is now southern Italy. As Guthrie noted, "The impact of monetary economy . . . might well have been to implant the idea that one constant factor by which things were related was the quantitative. A fixed numerical value in drachmas or minas may 'represent' things as widely different in quality as a pair of oxen, a cargo of wheat and a gold drinking-cup."[5] Just as a coin tied an abstract idea (numerical price) to a material structure (metal), so the Pythagorean philosophy tied the concept of number to material monism.

The Pythagorean, number-based theory of everything was powerful because it promised a way to understand and control the world. The use of mathematics, which it championed, advanced hand in hand with the use of money, since both are ways of thinking about the world in terms of number and computation. The Pythagoreans may not have been the first economists, but they certainly helped to prepare the ground. And their belief in the mystical power of number is reflected today when we obsess over figures such as gross domestic product (GDP).

Mind Versus Body

As shown in box 2.1, the Pythagoreans saw the universe as governed by opposing principles, and so their philosophy was fundamentally dualistic. They also had a preferred side that defined a kind of aesthetic; for example, limited was better than unlimited, linearity was better than nonlinearity, stability was better than change, and symmetry was preferable to asymmetry (the most perfect and beautiful shape was the sphere). This duality can be viewed in part as a way to resolve a fundamental disconnect between numbers and the natural world, by dividing the world into things that are

Box 2.1
Duality

To the Pythagoreans, each number had its own mystical meaning. The number 1 stood for the initial, unified state of the universe. Two represented the polarization of unity into duality and was associated with mutability and the feminine. Three signified all things that have a beginning, a middle, and an end. Four represented completion, as in the four seasons that make up a year. The greatest and most perfect of all numbers was 10, the sum of the first four numbers, which symbolized the universe.

In line with their belief that 10 was a very important number, the Pythagoreans also produced a list of ten opposites that represented the organizing principles of the universe. These were:

Limited	Unlimited
Odd	Even
One	Plurality
Right	Left
Male	Female
At rest	In motion
Straight	Crooked
Light	Darkness
Square	Oblong
Good	Evil

The list is somewhat similar to the Chinese yin–yang system of opposites, with the left column yang-like and right column yin-like; but rather than seeing these as part of a whole, the Pythagoreans explicitly associated the left side with good and the right side with evil.

Pythagorean thought has been highly influential for generations of philosophers and scientists, from Aristotle to Newton to modern physicists, so it is not surprising that its legacy is also apparent in mainstream economics—with its emphasis on things like scarcity (Limited), stability (At rest), linearity (Straight), symmetry (Square), and rationality (the Light of reason).

consonant with simple numerical analysis (good) and things that don't quite fit with the grid (evil). For example, there is only one way to draw a straight line between two points, and it is easily described by a mathematical equation. But if the line is crooked, it can follow an infinite (unlimited) number of different paths. Similarly, things that are stable and symmetric are more amenable to mathematical treatment than are things that are oddly shaped and don't stay still. In natural organic systems, there aren't many straight lines or other regular shapes—as the mathematician Benoit Mandelbrot observed, "Clouds are not spheres, mountains are not cones, coastlines are not circles, and bark is not smooth, nor does lightning travel in a straight line."[6]

The split between good and evil properties, between number and the living world, was related to a broader split in Greek culture between mind and body (or between virtual symbols and physical realities). The former was associated in Greek culture with the male principle, and the latter with the female principle. There were no female philosophers to argue against this, because schools such as Plato's and Aristotle's did not admit women.

Plato took this split to its logical conclusion with his theory of forms. According to Plato, any real-world object, say a chair, is an imperfect version of a form, in this case the Chair form, which exists in some higher plane of reality. Such forms can be known only through the intellect, because our poor plodding bodies are seated in the real world—on chairs, not Chairs. Forms are static and unchanging, while real things move and decay. Mathematical equations live in the world of forms—as does the virtual aspect of money, which obeys mathematical rules and exists outside time and space. As we'll see, that is both its main advantage and the fatal flaw that leads it into conflict with natural systems.

Perhaps unsurprisingly, given the time and place of its emergence, money is a lot like Greek philosophy: it begins with the idea of unifying the world, like the euro, but this leads to a kind of schism between ideas and reality, because the only way it can achieve unification is by imposing abstract rules. The production of coins by stamping a metal blank can be seen as the physical manifestation of this conflict. The stamp represents the abstract, "male" world of virtual forms from Greek philosophy (not to be confused with gender reality), while the metal represents the material, "female" body (the word "matter" is from the Latin *mater* [mother]). It is the Greek philosophical divide, in your pocket. The process of stamping coins resembles the Aristotelian view of procreation: "The female always provides the material, the male provides that which fashions the material into shape; this, in our view, is the specific characteristic of each of the sexes: that is what it means to be male or female."[7] It is no coincidence that the materials for the first coins, gold and silver, were also used as ornamentation for women's bodies.

Money is frequently described as a symbol, but it is more accurate to say that money objects such as coins incorporate a specific type of symbol. The stamp on a coin typically consists of two parts that merge the ideas of power and number. The obverse or "heads"—which often features, for example, a portrait of the head of state—represents the mint's authority, and the reverse or "tails" expresses the numerical value of the coin in chosen units. However, coins in Lydia were originally stamped on only one side, and for metaphorical convenience we can associate the stamp with heads and the physical matter with tails.[8] Money functions as a link between these two things—the heads and the tails, the abstract idea and the embodied reality—which have very different properties.

In the case of a coin, the link appears more direct because the metal has a physical worth that is always a positive amount. The U.S. "Jefferson nickel," for example, has recently tended, subject to price fluctuations, to contain more than 5 cents worth of copper and nickel (but it is illegal to melt it down).[9] Quarters contain about the same value of metal but are worth 25 cents, so no one melts them down. More serious forms of physical money, such as weighted gold, grant the holder a kind of independent, anonymous power. As a physical object, money can also be damaged, lost, stolen, hoarded, and liked or not for its aesthetic properties, and the material from which it is made can become plentiful or scarce. Above all, it can be valued.

In contrast, the stamp is a symbol of abstract debt, which represents not real wealth but a contract between two parties, the creditor and the debtor. Its meaning relies on a banking system and a legal system, on mints and on merchants, and above all on trust (the word "credit" is from the Latin *credere* ["trust" or "belief"]). Debts correspond to negative quantities, which (as physicist-turned-economist Frederick Soddy pointed out) don't exist in the real world—it is impossible to have a negative house, even if you have an underwater mortgage. Numbers such as prices or net worth are additive, can be compared on a numerical scale, and obey unyielding mathematical laws; for example, compound interest means that abstract debts can grow without bounds, while real objects tend not to. Along with conquest by more conventional means, this particular feature of debt has historically been a major cause of people falling into slavery or peonage.

Money always combines these ideas of negative debts and positive value; like a magnet, it contains opposing poles that are in a state of tension and stored energy. Most state currencies today are fiat currencies that represent government debt (the word is from the book of Genesis: *fiat lux*, [let there be light]); cybercurrencies exist only in electronic form, but even they retain a link to physical worth in two senses. First, any kind of money object is a valuable thing to be physically possessed—even if only in electronic form. Patterns formed by electrons on a computer are as "real" as the patterns of atoms that make up a metal. Numbers do not become scarce, but money objects can, because there are rules surrounding their production. Second, even virtual currencies retain a link to physical worth through the markets they create. A dollar is no longer officially redeemable for a set quantity of gold, but the use of dollars has led to an institution called the London Gold Fixing, wherein the current price is set (literally fixed, as it turned out, by corrupt bankers) in dollars.[10] When we transfer funds electronically from one account to another, it might seem that we are just sending a number, but the number is attached to a currency unit, which is what makes it money and connects it to markets. Anyone with the right skills can invent a new cybercurrency, but it has no worth until markets emerge that make it tradable for other things (or a significant number of people believe it will happen).

One way to think of a virtual money transfer is as a transaction that has the same effect as if cash had physically changed hands, except the cash doesn't exist. In ancient Mesopotamia, a payment in shekels was registered only as a credit for one party and a debit for the other, but it represented a weight of virtual silver. The transfer might take place in the imagination, but the effects are real enough, which is why ownership of virtual currency still evokes a powerful, physical sense of possession—we will fight for ownership over our "money points" as much as for any desirable object. The virtual and the real are bound together by money.

An exception of sorts to this need for a physical connection is the currencies used to buy imaginary goods in online games: a pretend sword to kill a pretend dragon. As economist Edward Castronova writes, these can be used to purchase "a bewildering cloud of things, all of which are definite, distinctly identifiable things as such, and some of which have clear economic value. Yet none of them has a physical manifestation. The physical traces these things leave—and they're only traces—are electrical signatures on memory chips."[11] While the situation "would have thrilled Plato," such currencies are of wider interest only when they become tradable for nonimaginary things outside the gaming environment (as many of them do) and thus establish a link with the real world.

The Power of Number

By assigning an exact number to value, money offers a kind of clarity. As the Victorian scientist Lord Kelvin put it, "When you can measure what you are speaking about, and express it in numbers, you know what you mean; but when you cannot measure and express it in numbers, your knowledge is of a meagre and unsatisfactory kind."[12] In *Principles of Economics*, Alfred Marshall wrote, "Just as the chemist's fine balance has made chemistry more exact than most other physical sciences; so this economist's balance, rough and imperfect as it is, has made economics more exact than any other branch of social science."[13] However, this apparent exactness is often an illusion—after all, just because we or the markets can assign a precise figure to something, say $103.58 for a barrel of West Texas Intermediate crude oil, doesn't mean it is some uniquely correct or stable price (the price has varied by more than a factor of 4 just during the writing of this book). Value is an inherently fuzzy concept that, according to the Indian philosopher K. R. Srinivasiengar, "finds its locus in the interrelation between subjective need and objective quality" and therefore depends on many vague, changeable, and socially negotiated factors.[14]

When you buy a house or a car, the official price is just a starting point in a negotiation. With something like fashionable clothes, it might be impossible to haggle over price, but you can wait a few weeks and maybe see the same item in the clearance rack. Gold is considered by many to be the ultimate store of wealth, but its value in dollars is highly unstable, as we will show in chapter 7. It is impossible to put an exact price on qualities such as natural beauty, but with a coin we know exactly what it is worth because it has a number on it.

The split between exactness and fuzziness mirrors the division of the human brain into two hemispheres. According to psychologist Roger Sperry, who pioneered this field of research in the 1960s, the left side of the brain (which controls the right side of the body; recall the Pythagorean concept of duality from box 2.1) is "highly verbal and mathematical, performing with analytic, symbolic, computerlike, sequential logic," and the right side (which controls the left side of the body) specializes in tasks that are "nonmathematical and nonsequential in nature."[15] As psychiatrist Iain McGilchrist observes, the hemispheres are like two distinct personalities that complement each other but are also involved in a kind of struggle. In particular, "the left hemisphere is competitive, and its concern, its prime motivation, is *power*."[16] (Note this is distinct from the popular idea of a split between "creative" and "logical" personalities being based on hemisphere function—barring physical damage, we all use both sides of the brain.) Money shapes our behavior in many ways, but the most obvious is that it encourages us to think analytically. The historical shift toward left-brained attributes such as numeracy and literacy in Western society coincided with the expanding use of money. McGilchrist describes money as a consequence rather than a prime mover of "deeper change in hemisphere balance."[17] However, this perhaps gives money too little credit. It is hard to imagine a more potent technology for mental programming than money, with its constant referral to abstract number.

Money may encourage analytical, computational thinking, but as discussed in more detail later, it also provokes strong emotional responses, leading to conflicted behavior. Point-scoring systems are a highly effective tool for providing motivation in everything from parenting to professional sports, and in Western society money is the ultimate way of keeping score, with other people and even with one's self. "Nothing had an effect on people like money—not naked bodies, not corpses," noted Stanford University neuroscientist Brian Knutson of his experiments. "It got people riled up. Like food provides motivation for dogs, money provides it for people."[18]

Money favors certain kinds of exchange over others (gifts don't really compute, unless they are vouchers). The affiliation between money and number also means that the use of money prioritizes things that can be accurately measured in terms of money, such as GDP. The concept of net worth as a measure of wealth is not about how much stuff a person owns but about a number and a rank: what that stuff can be exchanged for, in dollars or some other unit, and how it compares in magnitude with the wealth of other people. And when markets assign prices that are essentially arbitrary, as we will discuss later, to things such as precious resources or pollution, we act as if those numbers are real and meaningful. Like a weighted coin, money contains an inbuilt bias.

The concept of money, like the Chinese yin–yang symbol, therefore holds together two contrasting aspects—virtual number and concrete reality, quantity and quality—in a single package, as a marriage of opposites. The two poles can never be separated, any more than the north and south ends of a magnet (monopoles have never been observed in nature) or the two sides of a coin. But as with the good/evil Pythagorean list of opposites, money has a polarity, a direction; the lines of force run from the world toward number. When we consider the value of a personal possession, say a treasured heirloom, and its price, we have to hold two fundamentally incompatible ideas in our mind at the same time; the result is a cognitive dissonance that we have learned to mostly ignore. When it comes to seeing and interpreting the world, number is our dominant eye.

The inherent tension between these poles, which never reaches equilibrium, may explain why money has remained so mysterious and protean, constantly shape-shifting and taking on new forms and appearances as the balance between its two sides realigns and adjusts. As discussed in chapter 1, standard economic definitions of money concentrate on its roles as a "medium of exchange," a "store of value," and a "unit of account."[19] Economists such as Paul Samuelson have focused in particular on the first, defining money as *anything that serves as a commonly accepted medium of exchange* (his emphasis, as if to squash further discussion).[20] Or from a book by the nineteenth-century publisher Effingham Wilson (you can guess the title), money is "the something that serves to get something else for somebody from some one else."[21] Our interest in this chapter, though, is the inherent nature of this "something" called money: What properties does it contain that make it acceptable for fulfilling those roles? What, in other words, *is* money?

The Money Thing

Throughout history, answers to these questions have tended to fall into one of three camps.[22] The first, known as metallism or bullionism (from the Latin *bullire* [to bubble or boil]), holds that only the metal in a coin is real money. So money should either consist of scarce, precious metal or at least be backed by it. Fiat money of the sort cranked out by the U.S. Federal Reserve and other central banks is a dangerous kind of play money that is destined to eventually blow up. This viewpoint was once orthodox (see chapter 4 on the gold standard) and still has its support, especially among economists from the hard-money Austrian school and conservatives who are suspicious of government's role in finance. To bullionists, the cuneiform system of Mesopotamia was only a form of proto-money.

The second camp is chartalism (from the Latin *charta* [record]), which holds that only the stamp is real.[23] Coins and other money objects are just tokens that society collectively agrees to accept as currency. As Georg Friedrich Knapp wrote in *The State Theory of Money* (1905), "Money always signifies a Chartal means of payment. . . . The State as guardian of the law declares that the property of being the means of payment should be inherent in certain stamped pieces as such, and not in the material of the pieces."[24] In this view, the government is extremely important, because it issues the money and requires it back for payment of taxes, which is what keeps money spinning around. Independent schemes such as Bitcoin need not apply. Chartalism tends to find support among liberals, who think the state should have an active role in the money system.

Finally, there is the dominant, hands-off school of thought, with which most mainstream economists would agree, which says that money has no unique or special qualities but instead is defined by its roles—for example, as a medium of exchange. It could be gold; it could be a dollar bill, who really cares? What matters is not money, but exchange. Bullionists (tails) and chartalists (heads) therefore emphasize a different side of money, while most economists treat it as an inert chip. But strangely, none of them have much, if anything, to say about the most glaringly obvious aspect of money—that it is based on number. In bullionism, the role of number is subsumed into the weighing of metal; in chartalism, it appears as a unit of value; in mainstream economics, it is summarized by the idea of a unit of account—but the idea that we can attach numbers to value in the first place is taken for granted.

Consider, for example, a U.S. dollar bill. Sure, there is the portrait of George Washington on the front, and the weird iconography on the back with an eye on top of a pyramid, and something going on with an eagle, and various stamps and signatures and statements about trusting in God, legal tender, and so on. But the most important thing—at least if number is a guide—is the number. The first function of a currency is to establish the meaning of one unit, and here it is drummed in by repetition. The back of a dollar bill has the word "ONE" and the number 1 in each corner. In addition, "ONE DOLLAR" is written along the bottom, and there is a large "ONE" in the middle, for a total of ten ones on that side. There are also four 1's and two "ONE"s on the front, giving a total of sixteen ones. The designers are being very insistent about the fact that this note is a one. The number on the money is more than a convenience; it's the entire point.

So to address the question "What is money?," maybe we should start with number. Our own answer to this question is that money is a technology that does for value what the Pythagoreans did for music (and the universe): it converts value to number. Money is transmitted by money objects such as coins, notes, or electronic transfers, which have both a physical aspect and a virtual number aspect. A useful way to understand money is to analyze the properties of these objects. The magic quality in money does not reside in its heads or its tails or neither, but in both, working in dynamic opposition.

Now it is often pointed out, especially by those sympathetic to the chartalist school, that money is not actually a "thing" but a kind of abstract credit system, a form of debt management, and that it is a distraction to focus on material objects such as coins or notes. Alfred Mitchell-Innes pointed out in 1914 that "the eye has never seen, nor the hand touched a dollar," in the same way that it hasn't touched a square inch.[25] According to the economist Felix Martin, "The great temptation has always been to think that coins and other currency, being tangible and durable, are money—on top of which the magical, incorporeal apparatus of credit and debt is constructed. The reality is exactly the opposite."[26] Anthropologist David Graeber: "What we call 'money' isn't a 'thing' at all."[27] Economist Bernard Lietaer: "We should now dissipate a key illusion in the magic about money: money is not a thing."[28] However, while such comments capture the rather nonphysical and ethereal properties of money, we would argue that it is actually both weirder than that and more corporeal. In fact, this partitioning between the mental system and the physical object, between ideas and things, can be an obstacle to comprehension.

We first need to distinguish between money and its units. For example, while economics textbooks may routinely state that money serves as "a unit of account," this is like saying that length serves as a unit of measurement. What they really mean is that monetary *units*, such as dollars, serve as units of account, which is not the same thing as money itself. The concept of an "ounce" does not have physical presence, but the thing it describes—the mass of an object—does. In the same way, the concept of a "dollar" may live in the world of Forms, but any monetary transaction does have a physical dimension, because it involves a transfer from one party to the other (even if that transfer is over a phone). You cannot pay someone with a unit.

So the question then becomes "What are these units measuring?"[29] As discussed further in chapter 7, economists have usually answered this, when pressed, by saying that it measures some ill-defined quantity such as "utility" or "intrinsic value." But another approach is to say that it measures—money. After all, when we say that electrons have a fixed electrical charge whose value is approximately $1.60217657 \times 10^{-19}$ coulombs, we don't necessarily try to parse "electrical charge" down to some finer description. In the same way, we can treat money as a fundamental quantity. Monetary value is a measure of money in currency units, where here we use "value" in its quantitative sense, as in a value provided by an instrument reading.

Money, it is true, is therefore not really a thing but is better described as a conserved, transferable stuff, or quantity, like electric charge. However, it is informative, as Marshall McLuhan noted, to think of money, or more accurately the money system, as a kind of social medium, a means of communication.[30] And just as in physics it is sometimes easier to understand the concept of electric current in terms of electrons or light in terms of photons, so we can analyze currency in terms of the actual things exchanged in transactions—such as coins or notes or money transfers of any kind. This bottom-up perspective is in a sense dual to the top-down, systems-level perspective. When people treat money as if it were a kind of stuff they can accumulate, it isn't because they are confused about the true nature of money.

Now an amount of virtual money being transferred electronically may not resemble the Newtonian, mechanistic picture of a *thing*—that is, a self-contained lump of matter—but then neither does matter when viewed from the perspective of modern physics. For example, according to quantum theory, subatomic entities such as electrons behave in some ways like a particle and in others like a wave. They exert forces on each other by the exchange of "virtual particles" that flash into existence from the ether before being annihilated almost immediately. The electromagnetic force, for example, is transmitted by massless virtual photons whose ghostly presence is nonetheless sufficient to hold atoms together. In quantum physics, the distinction between real and virtual becomes blurred, and so it is with money. Saying that money is not a thing is like saying that light is not a thing, which sounded sensible until physicists discovered they could count the photons in a beam of light (see box 9.2).

Quantum Coin

In this quantum spirit, we define money objects as transferable entities, created by a trusted (or simply obeyed) authority, that have the special property of a *defined monetary value*, specified by a number and a currency unit. They can be a coin or a mark on a ledger, a piece of paper or a piece of electronic information, $1.23 counted out by hand or 0.00784581 bitcoins sent from a computer. Money is a fundamental quantity (from the Latin *quantum* [as much as]). Its unit specifies the currency framework, which involves political and legal factors such as the range of acceptance and other rules, and its smallest quantum amount, such as a penny ($0.01) or a satoshi (0.00000001 bitcoin). The authority (the author of the piece) might be a sovereign, a government, a company, a designed system, or just the collective will of a network of users, but it has the ability, through law or coercion or general consent, to create the objects and define their worth in the specified units.

These money objects are the carriers of the money force, in the same way that photons are the carriers of the electromagnetic force. The first time a Sumerian accountant scratched some numbers specifying a payment into a clay tablet, he was creating a technology whose puzzling behavior—and potential power, for both creation and destruction—mirrored that of the dualistic forces that control the subatomic world. The trade of money objects for goods or labor in a market means that those things attain a numerical value (in the money's units) as well—the price—by contagion, just as the atoms in iron spontaneously align in a magnetic field. In other words, market prices are ultimately attained from the use of money objects; this is how money spreads its numbers around. Market prices are therefore an emergent property of the system, in the sense that they emerge from the use of money objects. Rather than money being backed by something of monetary value, such as gold or labor, it is the other way round—market value comes from the use of money.

As discussed further in chapter 7, the overall price level can be controlled to an extent by the money's issuer. At its simplest level, a Roman soldier's base pay of a denarius per day, coupled with the requirement for suppliers to pay fixed taxes, would imply certain approximate price bounds for food, shelter, and so on, and these prices would in turn propagate through to any goods that were traded. Markets and payment systems that accept a certain currency unit therefore act as an extension or appendage of that currency; they are what allows it to work on the world and have to be fostered and managed for money to be of use. Tapping a credit card in a store to send an electronic transfer is not much use if the card reader is broken.

While markets assign prices to all kinds of things, money objects are unique in that their value is designed to be objectively fixed and stable: like subatomic particles, they are characterized by exact, unchanging, numerical quantities. The values of other goods are indeterminate until the moment those goods are exchanged for money (just as, according to quantum mechanics, the position or momentum of a particle is fundamentally undetermined until it is measured, at which point it "chooses" a value).[31] You might think that your house is worth $728,000, but you don't know until you sell it, and if the buyer tried to flip it, she could find that its value had changed again. The main difference in this respect between a commodity-based currency and a virtual currency is that the former assigns, or tries to assign, a price to one commodity in the market (which, as seen in chapter 4, tends to create an interesting dynamic around that commodity), so other goods and services have to find their own level; with the latter, everything has to find its level. Another difference is that with a commodity-based currency, there is a direct link between numerical price and the amount of the particular commodity (2 ounces of gold is worth twice as much as 1 ounce), so the connection between money and weight is more tangible, while in a virtual currency the numbers just relate to the currency itself.

As another example, if you have a $20 bill, then its most basic property is that it will have the number 20 on it today and tomorrow and the day after tomorrow. Its dollar value is something you can bank on. If, however, you exchange it for some groceries, then their price will change with time—they will no longer be worth exactly $20. The difference is that money is designed to be permanent and does not have a best-by date. Inflation can erode the purchasing power of the note, but it cannot change the number that is written on the note (although, as discussed in chapter 3, some currencies are designed to simulate this effect). The equality between numerical price and value is actively, if not always perfectly, enforced by the issuing authority—a dollar is a dollar; a shekel, a shekel.

This special status makes money objects desirable in themselves. They live partly detached from the world of space and time. It is often said that money is just a medium of exchange and therefore needs to have no value itself. But by attaching numbers to money objects, in a kind of alchemy, we make them golden. If a society decides that cattle must be used for payments, then cows suddenly become more valuable—one cause of overgrazing.[32] Conversely, gold has long been favored as money, in part because its qualities of stability (it doesn't rust), fungibility (1 ounce can be substituted for another), and divisibility make it rather like number.

The central concept of money—the irreducible nut of the matter—is therefore that it is a means to attach exact, timeless, Pythagorean numbers to the fuzzy and transient concept of real-world value. The point of doing this is to facilitate certain transactions (e.g., tax payments, exchanges, settling of scores, rewards, motivating people) by shifting them to the mathematical space, with its addition, subtraction, and compound interest. A property of such transactions is that when a money object changes hands, the total amount of money stays the same—one person gains, and the other loses. This is obvious when the money object is a coin, but cyber-currencies such as Bitcoin must be carefully designed to avoid double spending, where a person tries to use the same bitcoin more than once. An exception occurs when money is freshly produced. Banks currently have a special license to create new funds, so their loans do not obey this conservation rule. Counterfeiting, of course, must be discouraged, which is one reason the first coins were made from precious metal rather than ordinary pebbles.

While such a definition—money objects are things with a fixed monetary value—may appear obvious to the point of truism, the objects thus described have some remarkable properties that feed into the economy as a whole. In particular, money objects have one foot in the physical world and one foot in the world of number. The dualistic, two-sided nature of money means that, as already discussed, it frequently shows paradoxical behavior and can seem both real and unreal at the same time (it is fitting that many early Roman coins featured the two-faced god Janus). In the early 2000s, the cheap availability of credit in the United States meant that even low-income people could afford their own homes. Some became rich by selling their houses at the top of the market, and for them the money had real, tangible effects. But after the credit crunch of 2007/2008, most of the new money disappeared into the ether, as if it had never existed.

As one of the authors, Orrell, who has studied and taught quantum mechanics, argued in his previous book *Truth or Beauty*, much of our difficulty in understanding topics such as money relates to our failure to absorb, or dismiss as flaky, the equally paradoxical teachings of quantum physics.[33] We remain rooted in our philosophical tradition of hard, yes/no reasoning, and the idea, as Aristotle wrote in *Metaphysics*, that "it is impossible for anyone to suppose that the same thing is and is not." The dislike of duality can be traced to the Pythagoreans, who saw the number 2, or dyad, as representing the initial division of the universe, and a symbol of discord and dissent. However, this type of logic breaks down at the quantum level—as Niels Bohr argued in his theory of complementarity, neither the wave nor the particle description of matter is complete by itself; instead, together they represent two sides of the same phenomenon. Fuzzy logic, in which statements can be partly true and partly false at the same time, is now routinely used in areas such as computing science (not to mention our own thought processes). In the same way, money has a dual nature, with complementary aspects that seem to confound traditional logic. It is credit and debit, mind and matter, virtual and real, all at the same time.

The Emergent Economy

Because concepts such as value and authority are socially negotiated, it is not always clear-cut whether something should be considered a money object or not. For example, a check is an instruction to debit one account and credit another with a certain amount, but its value may be in the eye of the beholder. As one bank writes: "The reason we have a hold funds policy is that a cheque is not the same as cash—it is a promise to pay by one party to another party. If the first party doesn't have sufficient funds in their account at another financial institution, or if the cheque is fraudulent, that other financial institution can refuse to pay the item and return it unpaid to us."[34] In this case, we would define the money object to be the amount that is actually transferred virtually through the banking system when the check is cashed. However, if the check is endorsed and is itself exchanged between people and accepted as payment, then it becomes a kind of quasi-money object in its own right, with the difference that it is backed less by the state than by the credit of the writer, with the spread between these reflected in a possible discount rate. As shown later, banknotes got started in a similar way, but they fully became money only when they were guaranteed by a central bank. Financial instruments such as stocks, bonds, and options sometimes look like money, because they are valued in currency units and are tradable, but they are better described as assets whose price is variable. A bond, for example, can be viewed as an instruction to make certain money payments in the future in return for an initial investment, but it isn't money itself, and its market price at any time will depend on factors such as prevailing interest rates.

Perhaps the best way to measure the "moneyness" of an object—its ability to hold money—is to ask how well its market price corresponds to its designated numerical value and how well equivalence is maintained. In general, this will depend on the authority of the issuer, which varies both geographically and with time. An example is the case in which the value of a coin equals its stamp value in the region where it is issued but elsewhere reflects its metal content, or the case in which a substandard coin trades for less than its face value. This price equivalence also depends on the existence of markets that will accept the object as payment. Private moneys, such as the medieval bills of exchange discussed in chapter 3, are limited not by region but to a circle of users who accept them in exchange. Air Miles are a kind of money backed by airlines, which accept them for flights, but you can't use them to pay taxes. Fiat banknotes don't usually get discounted for being substandard, but they are worthless if the state stops supporting the currency. (It is no coincidence that today the world's reserve currency is backed by the world's largest military.) Currencies based on credit sharing, discussed in chapter 8, rely less on a central authority than on the mutual trust of a network. Bitcoin transactions are kept honest by constant, automated network surveillance.

Money could in principle emerge naturally without top-down design or intervention, but the evidence shows that it is better described as a planned social technology, and statements to the contrary are usually based on dogma rather than facts. Instead of money emerging from markets, it is historically more accurate to say that money-based commercial markets emerged from money, after some pump priming from the state. Governments in ancient Greece and Rome issued coins, used them to pay soldiers and other people, and demanded the coins back in the form of taxes; the development of sophisticated markets that fully exploited those coins came later. Money's behavior depends on its design and its context and is shaped and controlled by a variety of forces, such as social customs, power structures, financial institutions, market regulations, physical and intellectual property rights, and so on, but its distinguishing if rarely mentioned feature is its connection to number (box 2.2).

As we'll see, money objects—and the links they forge between mental heads and physical tails—can take myriad forms, from weights of precious metal, to *pointers* to precious metals like warehouse warrants or gold standard banknotes, to account transfers stored in an electronic wallet; but money's essence is most graphically displayed by the physical action of minting a coin, where the abstract number is literally stamped into the metal. The fact that number and real-world value have different and complementary properties—one is exact and enduring, the other fuzzy and changeable— makes the union complex, dynamic, anxiety inducing, inherently fragile, sometimes volatile, often rewarding, and always interesting. It comes presuffused in rich overtones of power, gender, and mind–body duality. Its structure resonates with the deepest properties of brain function, with profound consequences for human behavior. It is inherently political and reliant on a kind of faith, and as a result its workings are usually shrouded and obscured in layers of pomp, intrigue, duplicity, secrecy, deception, deliberate vagueness, and blandly recited misinformation. Like a glamorous and desirable character in a good story, money is alive with energy, contradictions, and a backstory of its own—which is why treating it as a passive placeholder, as in mainstream economics, is so dangerous. For example, the right to create and

Box 2.2
Number Versus Reality

The mysterious and oft-paradoxical properties of money arise from its dual nature, and in particular the incompatibility between numbers and the real world:

- Numbers are stable and unchanging—the number 3 was the same in ancient Greece as it is today—however, physical things change and decay. A house gets old, but the debt owed on it endures.
- Numbers are linear and additive ($2 + 2 = 4$), but the world is often nonlinear—working twice as many shifts may not give twice the results, having twice as much money (as seen in chapter 7) does not give twice as much pleasure. Weights and measures, on the other hand, are linear, which explains the affinity, made explicit in commodity currencies, between money and weight.
- Numbers can grow without limits, while natural processes tend to be subject to bounds. This point was illustrated in 1850 by the American lawyer John Whipple, who did the math and calculated that five English pennies, invested at 5 percent compound interest since 0 C.E., would have accumulated to 32 billion spheres of pure gold, each equal in size to the earth.*
- You can't own numbers or stop others from using them, but you can own things.
- Numbers can be negative, as in debts, but you can't have a negative number of objects.
- Numbers are not intrinsically small or large—everything is relative—but can be arranged on a linear scale and ranked in order. That is not possible for most things in the real world (though we often try, for example, by measuring intelligence with IQ tests).
- Numbers are universal and exact (even where they represent exact probabilities), while qualities such as perceived value depend on the person and the context.
- Numbers can be calculated using equations and are amenable to mathematical analysis, unlike many things of importance in the real world (there is no equation for romance, though again, people have tried).
- Numbers are hard and fixed, like the particle aspect of matter. Concepts or judgments such as worth or value are fuzzy, like the wave aspect of matter.
- Number is a human invention, and so is money—it is not a simple extension of the exchange processes seen in nature.

*John Whipple, *The Importance of Stringent Usury Laws: An Answer to Jeremy Bentham* (Boston: Wentworth, 1857).

control money, which is currently mostly held by private banks, is one of the greatest powers of all—but as discussed further in chapter 6, just try to find the section on power in a standard economics textbook.

Rather than defining money in terms of its roles as a means of exchange, a store of wealth, an accounting device, a signifier of debt, a measure of labor or utility, a symbol for something else, a memory substitute, a kind of social interaction, or a vector of human desire (even though it is all these things and more), or insisting that it can be made only from metal (bullionism) or through government edict (chartalism) or is not fundamentally different from other goods and is really nothing special (mainstream economics), it makes more sense to see money as a quantity in its own right whose roles emerge, deliberately or not, from its use in society. Money is useful for accounting, because it is based on number and has well-defined units. Its roles as store of value and means of exchange are conflated: it is a store of value because money objects are designed to be exchangeable for other things in the economy; it is exchangeable because it is seen as a store of value. We often think of value as being an inherent quality of an object— for example, the metal content of a gold bar—but it can also be socially assigned. With money, the value is assigned by the stamp (real or digital). The question of real-world value is highly subjective, but the numerical value of money is precisely defined, and this is both the central dichotomy at its heart and the delicate balancing act that keeps it aloft.

To say that money is a highly charged subject would be an understatement. The only things to come close are sex and power, and, of course, the topics are related. In Sumeria, temples served as a storehouse for wheat, and one of the shekel's original uses may have been for payment for sacred sexual intercourse with priestesses at the temple of the goddess Inanna as part of a fertility ritual.[35] Coin money, when it was invented in Lydia, was as suited for anonymous sex as it was for war. According to Herodotus, "It is a fact that in Lydia, all daughters of the common people work as prostitutes; they accumulate their dowries while they work in this profession until they get married."[36] The accuracy of such accounts might be disputed, but money and sex have clearly been seeking each other out for millennia. The equally torrid relationship between money and power is explored in chapter 6.

Quantifying Value

The word "quantum" has been applied to all kinds of thing outside physics and is often misused to evoke a vague sense of spooky, nonmechanistic behavior.[37] However, we think the use of the term, and more generally the comparison with non-Newtonian physics, is constructive here for the following reasons:

- Money is seen as a fundamental quantity (quantum), a word that captures both the numerical aspect of money and its existence as a kind of stuff.
- Money objects contain a fixed amount of monetary value, in the same way that an electron contains a fixed amount of charge. It is fitting that the first coins were made from electrum, named after the Greek word *electron* (for amber, a material that also holds static electricity).
- Money objects bind the virtual to the real, and abstract number to the fuzzy idea of value, paralleling the particle–wave duality in quantum physics.
- Just as a substance's properties emerge from the quantum interactions of molecules, so prices emerge from the use of money objects.
- Money serves as a means to quantify value, in the sense of reducing it to a mathematical quantity—but as in quantum measurement, the process is approximate.
- Finally, economics is often accused of physics envy—so why not go all the way!

By attaching numbers to our idea of value in order to quantify it, the money system binds together two very different things, and it is this fusion that gives rise to its complex behavior. Money objects are our contribution to the quantum universe; and as with quantum physics, the problems in interpretation seem to appear when we try to reduce a system to exact numbers. Money objects are unique in that they have a forced equivalence between number and value. For anything else, confusing the numbers with reality can be a huge mistake, in economics or in life.

Of course, the comparison of economics with physics should not be taken too far, and our aim here is by no means to further mathematicize the subject or produce a quantum mechanics of the economy—but at least if we are going to draw on physics, we should draw on the right kind of physics. The wave–particle duality of subatomic particles is mirrored in the mind–body, heads–tails duality of money objects, where it leads to confounding effects. Economists have traditionally handled money by assuming that market prices and value are the same thing, which is equivalent to collapsing the two aspects of money to a single point. Money objects therefore have no special properties, they just happen to be convenient for exchange. But as discussed further in chapter 7, this Newtonian, mechanistic approach fails in economics in much the same way that it breaks down in physics. Particles are not just self-contained billiard ball–like objects, and neither is money; both embody dual properties that need to be taken into account. In particular, our failure to recognize the charged, two-sided, dynamic nature of money contributed both to the 2008 financial crisis and the ensuing eurozone crisis by blinding us to the importance of debt.

As David Graeber describes in his book *Debt: The First 5000 Years*, the history of money involves an "alternation between periods of virtual and metal money."[38] For chartalists, or bullionists, these phases reflect our attitudes about money, as they oscillate between clarity and confusion (though the two camps disagree on which phase is which). But another way to see it is that this behavior of money is a direct reflection of its inherently dualistic nature, and in particular the unstable relationship between number and value. During a virtual phase, money is seen primarily as mathematical debt—a score in a ledger—while in a physical phase, money is seen primarily as material wealth. However, the two sides cannot be separated, so money always retains the essential characteristics of each. The process is like a monetary equivalent of geomagnetic reversal, in which the earth's north and south poles spontaneously swap places, which happens on average about twice every million years: the world stays the same, but the directions change.

These reversals are written like strata in the historical record, and each layer shows money in a different aspect. As we have seen, early agrarian empires were dominated by virtual credit, where the value of a clay tablet lay in the inscription and not so much in the clay (although silver was there too, out of sight). So in our scheme, that era was primarily heads. The Axial Age (800 B.C.E.–600 C.E.) saw the widespread adoption of coinage made from precious metals, so we'll call it tails. And we will see in the next chapter, the Middle Ages, which lasted for almost the next thousand years, saw a swing back toward negative, virtual credit (heads). The reason was not because gold and silver went out of fashion but because there was just not enough to go round.

3

Virtual Money

People are often reproached because their desires are directed mainly to money and they are fonder of it than of anything else. Yet it is natural and even inevitable for them to love that which, as an untiring Proteus, is ready at any moment to convert itself into the particular object of our fickle desires and manifold needs. . . . Money alone is the absolutely good thing because it meets not merely one need in concreto, but needs generally in abstracto.

ARTHUR SCHOPENHAUER, "THE WISDOM OF LIFE"

Credit alone is money. Credit and not gold or silver is the one property which all men seek, the acquisition of which is the aim and object of all commerce.

A. MITCHELL INNES, WHAT IS MONEY?

A basic question of economics is how to manage the money supply. Following the collapse of the Roman Empire, for example, gold and silver were suddenly in short supply. But money could still function as an accounting device—and an advantage of numbers is that they never run out. This chapter explores the dual role of money—as an abstract signifier of debt and as a valuable physical object in its own right—and shows how, with some help from mathematicians, the balance between these two aspects shifted in the Middle Ages. Our generation is not the first to struggle with the concept of a virtual currency.

Money, as discussed in chapter 2, represents both debt and wealth at the same time. Debts are represented mathematically by negative numbers, and wealth by positive numbers. A modern banknote, for example, is created by monetizing government debt, and so is like an IOU to someone else from the state (perhaps they should carry minus signs). At the same time, while the paper itself is of no value, the note is still an object that can be physically possessed and is valuable because it can be traded for other things. Having it is a definite plus. The same is true of other types of money. In the Axial Age, though, this dual nature of money would have been less obvious, for two reasons. The first was that coins were made of precious metals that you dug out of the ground, so they obviously represented wealth (though the fact that the state handed them out, then demanded them back as tax, hinted that debt was involved as well). The second was that negative numbers hadn't been invented. Both of these factors changed in the Middle Ages, when money rediscovered its virtual roots.

The collapse of the Roman Empire put an end to the forced mining of silver and gold that had kept the army in coin and to trade routes between East and West. Cities shrank in size—the population of Rome fell from a peak of about 1 million in the second century C.E. to only about 30,000 by 550—and the markets they had nourished followed suit.[1] At the same time, the religions of Christianity and Islam rose in power and influence. The precious metals that had earlier been used to pay soldiers now ended up in churches, monasteries, or other religious establishments, where they were hoarded, often after being melted down, or transformed into sacred symbols. The economy also came under increasing regulation from religious authorities. A similar pattern unfolded even earlier in India and China.[2]

One result of this transformation was that money became increasingly virtual—an abstract means of account rather than a piece of metal you can weigh in your hand. Money was mostly used as way to keep score, and loans were often in the form, not of a temporary transfer of physical material, but of a mark on a ledger. The leader in this process was the Islamic world, centered again on Mesopotamia. As today, Islamic finance forbade usury but allowed a range of fees, so moneylenders could still make money. Markets there flourished, but rather than being based on cash transactions, they relied on credit instruments, including the promissory notes known as *sakk*, or "checks." Since transactions were backed only by a signature, rather than a government-endorsed currency, a person's reputation—his credibility—was as important in business as his wealth.

As in ancient Greece, these financial developments both influenced and were themselves driven by advances in mathematics, the most important of which was the invention of negative numbers. When the Pythagoreans thought of numbers, they would demonstrate their ideas by arranging pebbles into different shapes. For example, the numbers 4, 9, and 16 were called "square numbers" because they could be formed into squares with sides of 2, 3, and 4 pebbles, respectively. Since there were no negative pebbles, there were no negative numbers; and for centuries afterward, negative numbers were thought to be absurd—even when they popped up as answers to equations.

The rules concerning how to deal with negative numbers, and the number 0, appeared for the first time in a book called *The Opening of the Universe* (628), by the Indian mathematician Brahmagupta. For example, a problem that had stumped the Greeks was equivalent to the equation $4x + 20 = 4$, which has the answer $x = -4$. Brahmagupta thought about such seemingly nonsensical answers by putting them in monetary terms. Positive numbers he called "fortunes," and negative numbers were "debts." He was also the first to write about the number 0, the unique number whose negative is itself.

These concepts spread to the Islamic world through translations of Brahmagupta's work but continued to be resisted by most European mathematicians. One of the first to accept them, along with the idea of arabic numerals (which actually originated in India), was the Italian mathematician Leonardo Fibonacci. He is best known today for the Fibonacci sequence, which is used to describe everything from the arrangement of sunflower petals, to (less reliably) patterns in the stockmarket.[3]

Fibonacci, the son of an Italian merchant, grew up in Bugia (now in Algeria), where he was first exposed to the Arabic number system. Until then European mathematicians had labored under the Roman system, which made calculations such as division or multiplication almost impossible for anyone without a large amount of training. In his book *Liber abaci* (*Book of Calculation*, 1202), Fibonacci popularized the Arabic system by showing how much it aided not only mathematicians but also business people in their computations.[4] Many of the examples involved activities such as money-changing, the calculation of interest, bookkeeping, and so on. For centuries, the Arabic system was viewed as less prestigious than the Roman system, and universities continued to teach the latter until the late seventeenth century. Even today, dates on important buildings are often expressed in roman numerals.

Progress of this type in the field of accounting reached a climax with the development of double-entry bookkeeping. This was codified by the mathematician, Franciscan friar, collaborator with Leonardo da Vinci, and part-time magician Luca Pacioli, in his book *Summa de arithmetica* (1494), but by that time it had already been in use for over a century.[5] The technique got its name from the fact that every transaction was entered in two different accounts, once as a debit and once as a credit. Thus an asset in one account appeared as a liability in another. The method helped detect errors, since the sum of credits over all accounts should be balanced by the sum of debits, as positives are balanced by negatives. It also gave a quick snapshot of profitability, with enduring consequences for our view of the world. As Mr. Micawber said in Charles Dickens's novel *David Copperfield* (1849): "Annual income £20, annual expenditure £19.19.6, result happiness. Annual income £20, annual expenditure £20.0.6, result misery."

Keeping Tally

During the early Middle Ages, Christian Europe was organized in the static and rigidly hierarchical system now known as feudalism. Under this system, what counted was not money, but land and power, and the ultimate source of both was God's representative on Earth—that is, the Crown.[6] The king granted land to his lords, who in turn granted plots to their vassals in exchange for loyalty, military service, work on the estate, and a portion of the land's agricultural yield. Large areas were reserved as collectively managed commons and were used for purposes such as animal grazing and collecting firewood. The most powerful landlord was the Church, which also dominated most of the thinking about money and economics. Usury was strictly forbidden (although loopholes existed), and the pursuit of wealth for its own sake was considered a capital sin. These restrictions put a further damper on the widespread use of coins. Feudal estates were therefore relatively closed and self-contained communities in which money played little role, apart from as an accounting device, and rents and taxes were usually paid in kind or through labor rather than in cash.[7] Society was bound together by a connection to the land, rather than to money.

Medieval coinage was on the whole a motley collection (box 3.1): each king and lord wanted to produce his own version, so that he could collect the "seigniorage" (from the Old French *seigneur* [lord]), which is the difference between the face worth of the coin and its cost of production—that is, between the coin's numerical worth (heads) and its bodily value (tails). Unlike in Roman times, there was no central authority, with some jurisdictions covering only a city and its surrounds (an exception was England, where the king maintained a monopoly). The tendency for money to spread and unify was therefore frustrated, and its lines of force were scattered and weak.

Box 3.1

Sun and Moon

In Europe during the Middle Ages, low-value coins, known as black money and usually made of copper, served for small transactions. A more valuable but still common coin was the silver denier, denoted "d," whose name was derived from the Roman denarius. Twelve deniers made up 1 sou, and 20 sous made up a livre. The sou and livre were units of account—no actual coins were minted—with the livre (lira in Italy) nominally equal in value to 1 pound of silver. In fact, inflation meant that the unit of account was worth much less. The livre system was originally set up by the emperor Charlemagne during his reign from 800 to 814, and deniers were minted in France and Italy through the Middle Ages. The system was later emulated by a number of European currencies. For example, the British version of the denier was the penny, denoted in the same way by the symbol "d." Twelve pennies made up 1 shilling, and 20 shillings made up 1 pound sterling. This system remained in place until decimalization in 1971.

For larger transactions—such as international trade, financing of wars, or military ransoms—silver ingots or gold coins such as the florin and ducat were preferred. The Florentine florin was first struck in 1252 and contained 3.5 grams of gold (about $150 at current gold prices), which equated to the value of 1 lira; the similarly sized Venetian ducat (duke's coin) was introduced in 1284. At its peak, the mint in Florence was cranking out about 400,000 gold florins per year, with most of the gold being imported from Africa.* Both coins had a number of local versions, and ducats were still in use until the early twentieth century. The French version was the gold *écu*, minted during the reign of Louis IX (no relation to the European Currency Unit or ECU, which was used as a unit of account before the adoption of the euro). To protect against clipping, gold coins often circulated in leather pouches that were sealed by the mint. This again raised the question of whether the value was in the gold, which you couldn't verify without breaking the seal, or in the seal itself.

The relative worth of gold and silver coins needed to be kept in balance to reflect the prices of the two metals, but in Europe at least remained fairly constant at a price ratio of about thirteen, as it had since ancient times. The reason is probably that gold has long been associated with the sun and silver with the moon—as Geoffrey Chaucer wrote, "Sol gold is and Luna silver we threpe"—and thirteen corresponds to the number of lunar periods in a solar year. The number also corresponds roughly to the relative abundance of the two metals in the earth's crust. However, the price ratio varied with location—in Asia, for example, silver tended to be valued more highly than gold—which created profitable arbitrage opportunities and helped to power East–West trade.†

*Jacques Le Goff, *Money and the Middle Ages* (Oxford: Polity, 2012), 86.

†Andrew Watson, "Back to Gold—and Silver." *Economic History Review*, 2d ser., 20 (1967): 1–34; Joel Mokyr, *The Oxford Encyclopedia of Economic History*, vol. 2 (Oxford: Oxford University Press, 2003).

Around 1100 in England, King Henry I introduced a payment system that was based on wooden sticks, about ten inches long, known as tallies. The sticks, which were made of polished hazel or willow wood, were carefully notched to indicate their worth and split lengthwise; the creditor kept one half, which was known as the stock (from which "stock market"), and the debtor the other part, called the stub. As described in the twelfth-century treatise *The Dialogue Concerning the Exchequer*, the manner of cutting was as follows: "At the top they put 1000 pounds, in such way that its notch has the thickness of the palm; 100 pounds, of the thumb; 20 pounds, of the ear; the notch of one pound, about of a swelling grain of barley; but that of a shilling, less; in such wise, nevertheless, that, a space being cleared out by cutting, a moderate furrow shall be made there; the penny is marked by the incision being made, but no wood being cut away."[8] When the debt was retired, the stock would be matched with the stub to verify the amount and protect against tampering, and the tally would be destroyed. The system was therefore similar to ancient cuneiforms, except there the security was supplied by the clay envelope.

Such tallies, as historian Michael Clanchy notes, were "a sophisticated and practical record of numbers. They were more convenient to keep and store than parchments, less complex to make, and no easier to forge."[9] They were initially used as receipts for taxes but soon expanded into a general form of debt that circulated as money objects. For example, the state could use its half of a tally to pay a supplier, and that person could then collect from the debtor or use it to pay taxes or sell it at a discount to a goldsmith or another broker who would collect the debt when it came due. In China, most accounts during the Middle Ages were apparently handled by a similar technique, with the difference that the tallies were made of bamboo.[10]

The use of tallies in England peaked in the second half of the seventeenth century, by which time they had become a general tool for raising revenue (as receipts for a loan rather than just taxes) and remained in use until 1826.[11] In the history of money, however, they seem destined to remain in the shadows; old sticks lack the glamour of precious coins, and they are also easily destroyed. In 1834, the remaining sticks were collected up and burned in a stove under the House of Lords. However, the money gods had the last laugh: the fire ran out of control, resulting in what is known to history as "The Great Fire of 1834." The existing palace of Westminster was built on its ashes in the Victorian-Gothic style.

Borrowed Time

In the twelfth and thirteenth centuries, Europe was unified not by a single currency but by the quest to capture Jerusalem from the Muslims. One of the compensations for Christian knights joining the Crusades was that it offered a way for them to plunder some of those hard-to-find coins. While these were a transportable form of wealth, they were also easy to steal, which posed a challenge given the long distances involved. Money also had to flow in the other direction to fund the Crusades, which for the states and organizations involved were a highly expensive enterprise. These security issues were addressed by the Knights Templar—a secretive, ascetic, warrior order of monks—who, stealing a leaf from their Islamic foes, set up what amounted to an early version of travelers checks. A departing pilgrim or warrior could deposit his valuables at one of its castles, pick up a letter of credit, and use it to withdraw funds from another branch along the route. Usury was officially forbidden by the Church; however, the Knights Templar managed to make money by other methods. For example, a lord could take a mortgage on one of his properties and sign the right for the rent on the property over to the Templars.

The castles eventually morphed into banks for the nobility. At its peak, the group had 870 "branches" and employed about 7,000 people.[12] However, their success soon turned them into a target for the state. When debasing the currency by 75 percent didn't solve his financial problems, King Philip IV cracked down on the Knights Templar, sentencing their leaders to death and confiscating their immense riches.

Apart from the Crusades, another expense that was stretching the finances of the Church was the building of magnificently expensive cathedrals. Notre-Dame in Paris, for example, was paid for by a combination of grants from the Church, bequests from rich bishops and burgesses, and a head tax known as the *taille*. Many towns such as Amiens took out large loans to finance their building. Construction often went on for centuries; in part this was because financing was sporadic, but it also tells us something about the attitude toward money in the Middle Ages. Most modern governments, obsessed as they are with the scarcity of money, would be loathe to commit to such enormous projects that stretched over generations—even if they did promise an enormous payoff in the long run. Cathedrals were the tourist attractions of the day, attracting huge numbers of pilgrims, and even today they continue to boost their local economies.

One reason for the more relaxed attitude toward timescales was that usury was considered a sin, so in principle at least there was less hurry to pay debts. The main argument against usury was that it was considered to be a form of the mortal sin of avarice; however, it was also considered to be a type of theft—of time. Usury made money out of the time it took to repay a loan, and time—including the time it took to build a cathedral—belonged only to God.

A similar argument, interestingly, was levied against intellectuals and teachers who took on students in return for payment. As Saint Bernard noted, such people were "sellers and merchants of words"—and knowledge, like time, was the property of God.[13] Partly in response, intellectuals organized themselves into that new institution known as the university. These provided academics with a reasonable standard of living, while allowing them to distance themselves from the need to charge fees. The first recognized universities were in Bologna (1088), Paris (ca. 1150), and Oxford (1167). At the center of the university curriculum were the works of Aristotle. A Paris-based school of economic thought, known today as Scholastic economics, aimed to reconcile Aristotle's ideas about money and property with Christian theology.

As with Aristotle, money was seen as no more than a social convention, which certainly made sense in an era when most transactions were carried out without the use of coins.[14] According to Aristotle, monetary profit of any kind amounted to theft, and "the most hated sort, and with the greatest reason, is usury, which makes a gain out of money itself, and not from the natural object of it. For money was intended to be used in exchange, but not to increase at interest. And this term interest, which means the birth of money from money, is applied to the breeding of money because the offspring resembles the parent. Wherefore of all modes of getting wealth this is the most unnatural."[15]

The synthesis of Aristotelian and Christian doctrines reached its highest point with the Dominican friar Thomas Aquinas, who taught in Paris and Cologne. According to Aquinas, money was "the one thing by which everything should be measured."[16] Money was seen not as an end in itself—the pursuit of wealth was un-Christian—but "was invented chiefly for the purpose of exchange." The most important virtue, and the glue that held society together, was *caritas* (charity), which was an expression of love.

Aquinas put great emphasis on the rationality of Greek philosophy and agreed with the ancient Greeks that man was a "rational animal." His concept of a "just price" corresponded to the conventionally accepted price that would hold when neither the buyer nor the seller was under duress. Aquinas allowed that the price for a good could be agreed between two parties by haggling, but it was unjust for one party to take advantage of the other—for example, by charging a starving person more during a famine. Economics (the name had not yet been invented) was therefore part of a larger framework based on ethics and rationality.

The root of the word "rationality" is the Latin word *ratio*, which refers to both reason and calculation. Aquinas and the Scholastics may have emphasized the former, but money was all about the latter. As historian Jacques Le Goff points out, "Money was a tool of rationalization," and its growing use would have profound effects on the medieval mind-set.[17]

Arte de Cambio

The discovery of new mines, along with technical improvements in minting, led to a spread in the use of metal money during the thirteenth century. Perhaps counterintuitively, this increase in money supply was accompanied by a huge rise in indebtedness for all classes of society, but especially the peasantry. One reason was that institutions, including the Church and nascent states, with their growing demands for taxation, began to demand payment in coin rather than in produce or a set number of days of labor.[18] Society was once again aligning itself with the pull of money.

The rise in indebtedness made moneylending a very profitable activity—in this world at least, if not the next. While it was taboo for Christians to lend money for interest—in his *Inferno*, the Italian poet Dante Alighieri described usurers' existence in the seventh circle of hell, and it didn't make for easy reading—no such restriction applied to Jews, with the result that Jewish communities became the financial services centers of their time. But as the economy grew in size, and money played a more important role, a wider debate began in the universities and elsewhere about the restrictions on usury.

One argument in favor of the practice was that the interest charged on a loan was compensation for the risk of not being repaid. Another was that the interest represented payment for a kind of opportunity cost, since the money loaned could not be put to another use. And finally, there was the idea of justice: like anything else, money should surely have a just price (typical rates at the time were actually around 20 percent, which is high by our standards).[19] Therefore, while theologians continued to condemn usury, it gradually became more acceptable in practice to introduce charges for loans. In Italy, for example, Christian moneylenders would loan money for free but insisted that the debtor pay insurance against default, rather like a modern credit default swap. The growing link between time and money was mirrored by the development of mechanical clocks, which originated as a prompt for bell ringers in monasteries and cathedrals but were soon put to use in regulating the workday.

The economy was also becoming increasingly complex, as the manufacture of crafts was broken up into specialized trades and guilds—many of which were reflected in surnames such as Smith in English and Schmitt in German—and businesspeople formed themselves into associations that later became known as companies. In response to the growing need for finance, moneylenders and changers themselves evolved into the precursors of modern insurance companies and banks.[20] The nascent financial industry was centered in the major northern trading cities of Italy, such as Venice, Genoa, and Florence. These cities had become wealthy through trade with Asia in goods such as silks and spices, which was carried out along the famous 4,000-mile caravan track known as the Silk Road. Unlike the now-defunct Knights Templar, the new banks catered not just to nobility or the church but also to the needs of landlords, vendors, and merchants like the fictional Antonio in William Shakespeare's *The Merchant of Venice* (Elizabethan playwrights were beginning to incorporate money into their works). Expansions in trade meant that merchants had to borrow money to finance their expeditions, and moneychangers, who had their own guild called the Arte de Cambio, did a thriving trade swapping between the multiplicity of coins available.

Money for Nothing

When the Venetian explorer Marco Polo returned from China in 1295 via the Silk Road, one of the many marvels he described was how the government of Kublai Khan had compelled the Chinese population to accept money made from sheets of paper, signed and stamped with the royal seal, instead of metal (part of the trick was that counterfeiters were put to death). As he noted: "All these pieces of paper are issued with as much solemnity and authority as if they were of pure gold or silver . . . everybody takes them readily, for wheresoever a person may go throughout the Great Kaan's dominions he shall find these pieces of paper current, and shall be able to transact all sales and purchases of goods by means of them just as well as if they were coins of pure gold." The scheme was very successful—the Chinese economy was thriving at the time—and of course it meant that the government could hang on to its silver and gold instead of releasing it as currency. Damaged notes could be returned to the mint, where they were replaced for a charge of 3 percent (a kind of negative interest).[21]

Inspired by this example, European bankers and goldsmiths (who needed a working supply of gold) began issuing paper promissory notes in exchange for deposits that were payable to anyone who had them in their possession. The notes could therefore be traded, rather like the banknotes of today (the term originates from the fourteenth-century *nota di banco*). The innovation that really disrupted the existing money system, however, was the bill of exchange. These were essentially letters instructing a banker or an agent in another country to make a payment on the writer's behalf. For example, suppose a merchant in Venice wanted to import some goods from a supplier in France. He could purchase a bill of exchange, paid for in coins (or on credit), that allowed him to withdraw the same amount, at a set exchange rate, from a bank or an agent in France.

The banker's fee, of around 10 percent, would be incorporated into the exchange rate. In fact, the amount of the bill was usually denominated in virtual units of account such as sous, or the imaginary unit known as the *écu de marc*. This acted as a kind of single, unifying money for all the different moneys and meant there would be two exchange rates, one for each of the real currencies. Unlike checks, which didn't appear until the late fourteenth century, bills of exchange could be deposited or cashed only in person. Since the bill represented a loan for a certain time, the commission included what amounted to an interest charge.

The main advantage of bills of exchange was that they allowed international business to be carried out without having to deal with coins. These were slow to transport (it could take a month to move a stash a few hundred miles), easily stolen en route, and expensive to exchange. Coins were also often of questionable quality and were subject to clipping or devaluations. (In 1529, when Francis I of France paid 12 million escudos to ransom his two sons who had been substituted for him as hostages after his capture, it took the Spanish four months to count and test the coins, and 40,000 coins were rejected.)[22] As discussed later, similar arguments are today made for cybercurrencies such as Bitcoin—the *écu de marc* of our time—which sidestep government currencies and radically reduce the cost of international currency transfers.

Bills of exchange soon became the favored payment system for the emerging class of European merchants who needed to make international transactions. Huge trade fairs, such as the one in Lyon that happened each quarter, could be carried out almost without the need for sovereign coin.[23] Once the trading had been completed, the bankers would huddle together to reconcile their books, agree on a set of exchange rates, and settle outstanding balances. The bankers would also trade the bills between themselves to balance their obligations in different currencies. If someone were short of cash, he could borrow some by selling a bill of exchange, drawn on himself and payable at the next fair. In practice, this amounted to a loan with the effective interest rate of around 2 to 3 percent per quarter.[24] The currency exchange aspect offered many opportunities for speculation, especially during times of war when currencies were unstable.

By arranging their affairs in this way, bankers were collectively acting as a central node between buyers and sellers and creating a mechanism for the creation and transmission of money. A merchant's credit with his local banker was transferred into a bill of exchange that represented a temporary loan. Because it could be traded between bankers, it was a money object in its own right, though only within this private system. As with many other forms of financial innovation, a side effect of the use of bills of exchange was therefore an expansion in the money supply. The bills also boosted the circulation of money by substituting written letters for real coins and putting money to use in new ways. In 1317, for example, the pope arranged for money collected from Catholic churches in England to be deposited with the local London representatives of the Florentine banks of Peruzzi and Bardi. The bankers shipped a bill of exchange to the banks in Italy, which paid the pope in cash but used the deposits in London to buy English woolen garments, which they sent to merchants in Europe. Money was effectively circulating between London and the Continent, but the actual cash did not need to cross the channel.[25]

Trust

As discussed in chapter 2, money objects have the special property that their market value is defined to be equal to their numerical price. The price of gold in dollars goes up and down, but a dollar is a constant unit. This relationship is enforced by the issuing authority, so it relies on both power and its more passive relative, trust. This is especially true for virtual currencies, since an IOU has value only if the creditor knows the debt will be repaid. In ancient Mesopotamia, the primary creditor and backer of the system was the government. In the Middle Ages, the bill of exchange payment system was run by bankers. As mentioned earlier, part of the latter's attraction was that it bypassed to an extent the use of national currencies, which were liable to be debased at any time in order to pay off some royal debt. Trust was therefore provided not by the endorsement of a government but by the mutual support of the banking network.

Another feature of an IOU, such as a loan or bill of exchange, is that it has a time dependence. Cash is ready right now, but an IOU is a promise to repay at some time in the future. Again, this is related to the issue of trust, since the longer the time period, the more likely it is that something can go wrong. Banks, then as now, also have to balance the needs of long-term borrowers, such as mortgage holders, with depositors who might want their money back at any time. As discussed in chapter 1, one of the defining features of money is that it acts as a store of value over time and place. In a bullion-based currency, this feature is provided by both the inherent worth of the coin and the sovereign's stamp. In a virtual instrument such as the bill of exchange, it is the centralized banking system that holds and maintains value. With cybercurrencies, trust is maintained by a decentralized network of users in concert with a defined computer protocol.

The bill of exchange system worked because, unlike merchants, bankers were part of a small clique who knew each other personally or through reputation. Their money network was a private network that operated in a kind of shadow economy. It was controlled by an exclusive and secretive elite and was resistant to both competition or government interference. As head Jesuit Diego Laynez noted in the sixteenth century, the merchants and bankers "have so many tricks for inventing ingenious practices that we can hardly see what is going on at the bottom of it all."[26] However, the need for exclusivity also limited the network's power and meant that the sovereign maintained the upper hand over monetary matters—at least for a while.

New currencies often become popular when the state loses its financial authority and trustworthiness, as during the collapse of Soviet Union, when around 40 percent of company debts were handled through thousands of private systems;[27] or following the 2012/2013 Cypriot financial crisis, when government confiscation of savings accounts suddenly boosted interest in alternative currencies. Rather like modern cybercurrencies, bills of exchange represented a new type of money object that offered direct competition to conventional money and allowed merchants to operate semi-independently of debt-laden and financially unreliable monarchs. The role of private banks in the parallel payment system naturally made them important economic players and was the start of a shift in power from the state to the private sector. The state could (and did) try to regulate the system, but as discussed in the next chapter, sovereign money and private money only reached an accommodation with the founding of the Bank of England, which effectively bundled them together and shared the proceeds.

The Rise of the Bankers

As the feudal system broke down with the spreading use of money, so did people's connection with the land and, therefore, the organizing principle of society. In England, for example, tenants were increasingly evicted from common land as part of the privatization process known as enclosure (a similar process is at work today as wealthy hedge funds or national governments take over arable land around the world).[28] Soldiers and serfs were paid in cash instead of produce. Rather than live off their lands, feudal lords could live as *rentiers* in cities such as Paris (whose population in the fourteenth century reached 250,000, before the plague arrived), while investing their capital in business, city bonds, or real estate.[29] As Marx later wrote, "The medieval proverb *nulle terre sans seigneur* [There is no land without its lord] is thereby replaced by that other proverb, *l'argent n'a pas de maître* [Money knows no master], wherein is expressed the complete domination of dead matter over man."[30]

Indeed, while finance was booming in the fourteenth and fifteenth centuries, it did not seem to translate into a general improvement in living conditions for the masses. Up until about 1300, the quality of life for common people, especially women, had attained something of a peak, at least by certain metrics.[31] Women played an important role in many crafts and industries and formed associations with monopolies in cloth production, brewing, dairy, cooking, and so on. Workers of all kinds had ample supplies of food, decent working conditions, and far more holidays than we have today (from 90 to as many as 170 in some regions). This began to change in the fourteenth century, for a number of reasons. Power became more centralized under strong monarchs. Chivalric knights were replaced with massive armies, now armed with muskets and gunpowder, who clashed in increasingly expensive wars. Governments debased their currencies to pay the bills (box 3.2), or simply defaulted. Construction of cathedrals came

Box 3.2
Debase or Recoin?

Although one of the main functions of money is to act as a store of value, coins have often been subject to debasement in their metal content. As discussed in chapter 1, for example, the decline in the silver content of the Roman denarius mirrored the decline of the Roman Empire. In the sixteenth century, Henry VIII of England was known by his subjects as "Old Coppernose," because his portrait on his "silver" coins turned to copper with use (higher-quality gold coins were used for foreign trade). In 1920, the silver content of all British coins was reduced from 92.5 percent to 50 percent; the silver vanished altogether in 1947.

France saw 123 debasements in the period 1285 to 1490, with one in 1349 responsible for almost 75 percent of the king's takings. This abuse led to a Tea Party–like anti-inflationary protest from the philosopher and mathematician Nicolas Oresme (1320–1382): "I am of the opinion that the main and final cause why the prince pretends to the power of altering the coinage is the profit or gain which he can get from it . . . every change of money, except in the very rare cases which I have mentioned, involves forgery and deceit, and cannot be the right of the prince."*

By issuing new coins with the same face value but less precious metal, the seignoirage earned by mints is boosted accordingly. Debasement, as Oresme noted, therefore acts as a kind of stealth tax on the population. A less subtle way of doing the same thing is the practice known as "recoinage," in which old coins are exchanged for a smaller number of new ones.

As an example of this approach: in England around the end of the tenth century, before the adoption of sterling, every six years all existing coins were declared invalid and were recalled to be replaced with new ones at the rate of three new for four old. The seignoirage therefore amounted to 25 percent every six years. Unlike with debasement, though, the new coins contained the same amount of metal, so recoinage did not cause inflation (new coins could be introduced to maintain the money supply). In fact, inflation appears to have been very low during this period.

One coin that was explicitly designed for recoinage was the bracteate, which was the main coin type in large parts of northern Europe, including Germany, Austria, and Scandinavia, in the twelfth and thirteenth centuries. These were local currencies, so the coins would circulate only in a small area, such as a town or region. The pieces were typically made of a wafer-thin sheet of silver, and the impression was made by stamping on one side over a soft surface so it appeared as a negative on the reverse. Because of their fragility, the coins lasted for only a short time, but that wasn't a problem, because once or twice a year they were called in to be replaced.[†]

Recoinage came to an end in the fourteenth century, as some rulers abused the practice with frequent recalls, and local currencies yielded to powerful national currencies. However, the practice has its advantages, which have since been exploited in the design of some alternative currencies. The fact that such currencies effectively earn negative interest deters hoarding, encourages the spending of money, and boosts the economy. As the German economist Silvio Gessel argued in 1913, "Only money that goes out of date like a newspaper, rots like potatoes, rusts like iron, evaporates like ether is capable of standing the test as an instrument for the exchange of potatoes, newspapers, iron and ether. For such money is not preferred to goods either by the purchaser or the seller . . . we must make money worse as a commodity if we wish to make it better as a medium of exchange."[‡] The greatest impediment to negative interest is that money gains its power from its association with number—and numbers don't rust.

[*]Nicole Oresme, *The De Moneta of Nicholas Oresme, and English Mint Documents*, trans. Charles Johnson (London: Nelson, 1956), 24.

[†]Roger Svensson, "The Bracteate as Economic Idea and Monetary Instrument," IFN Working Paper No. 973, Research Institute of Industrial Economics, Stockholm, 2013.

[‡]Silvio Gesell, *The Natural Economic Order*, trans. Philip Pye (London: Peter Owen, 1958).

to a halt. The most shocking change was in the status of women. A widespread hysteria about satanic witches meant that as many as 100,000 (mostly female) accused witches were put to death.[32]

The descent toward chaos was accelerated by the Black Death. The outbreak, which peaked in 1348, killed an estimated one-third or more of Europe's total population. The microbe that caused it is believed to have been imported from the Silk Road. The lethality of the outbreak was due not just to the virulence of the disease but to the fact that it arrived at a time when many people were malnourished and therefore vulnerable.[33] The staggering damage inflicted by the plague on medieval Europe led to societal changes—including a doubling of many wages due to labor shortages—that paved the way for the Renaissance.[34]

In Italy, banking was initially dominated by the Bardi and Peruzzi families of Florence, but these fell into bankruptcy in the 1340s. The temporary demise of Florentine banking has been blamed on factors such as

King Edward III's default on war loans and was capped by the appearance of the Black Death. Into the gap entered the Medicis: the most famous and powerful banking family of history. The Medicis started off as money-changers but soon branched out into other areas of finance, including bills of exchange, and over the course of the fifteenth century expanded from a single office to branches in fifteen cities across Europe. They were involved not just in banking but also in trade, organizing shipments of every kind of product (at one point they even had a sideline in castrated choirboys).

Cosimo de Medici was anointed ruler of Florence, and together with his grandson Lorenzo commissioned buildings and artwork that made the city into the tourist attraction it is today. Even now, people like Michelangelo Buonarroti (whose Sistine Chapel was funded by the Medicis) and Leonardo da Vinci (who cryptically wrote in a notebook, "The Medici made me and destroyed me") remain the brightest stars of the art world. The artists repaid their patrons by immortalizing them in their paintings. Perhaps the most famous example is Sandro Botticelli's *Adoration of the Magi* (1475), in which, under close inspection, all the Magi turn out to be Medicis. Instead of being portrayed as evil usurers, bankers had taken their place next to the gods. Of course, the way in which the art market has since effectively morphed into part of the luxury goods business, with the finest works battled over by oligarchs and hedge fund managers, would have amazed a person from the Middle Ages, when the word "art" still referred to skill at crafts, and beauty was not valued in monetary terms.

Caritas

While metal money did play an important role in the Middle Ages, and many developments such as bills of exchange can be viewed as precursors to modern finance, it can be misleading to view the period through a modern lens. As Jacques Le Goff notes, those interested in finance were "no more than tiny isolated islands in a vast medieval sea, the majority of people remaining remote from sophisticated practices in the case of everything we would put under the heading of money. At most we may accept that money, however limited its role in the Middle Ages, acted as a stimulus in the spheres of writing and commercial bookkeeping and in arithmetic applied to the necessities of daily life."[35]

Rather than a kind of emerging proto-capitalist economy, it is probably more correct to see the medieval period as being based on a version of a gift economy.[36] The economy, to quote Karl Polyani, "was embedded in the labyrinth of social relations."[37] And the core principle of social relationships, as taught by both the universities and the Church, was the idea of *caritas*. It was this, rather than money or "net worth," that a person's quality was measured against. It was this that defined relationships between people and also relations with God. The greatest gift of all was the free gift of life from God, and everything else—including money—could be seen as an extension of that. As Thomas Aquinas wrote, "Charity is the mother of all virtues, inasmuch as it informs all virtues." If time is money, then interest sets the exchange rate, and the ban on usury reflected a static worldview in which everything had its place in God's scheme.

The Middle Ages certainly saw a gradual monetizing of many aspects of life, including the payment of rents and taxes; however, most of this monetization involved gifts, such as almsgiving and bequests, which represented much larger sums than anything raised by taxation.[38] Economic theories and ideas also seemed to be more related to the exchange of gifts rather than the hard calculation of commercial value. The concept of the "just price," for example, was in some respects the opposite of the law of supply and demand, since it implied that prices should be stable even if conditions change. Saint Francis told his followers that "we ought not to have more use and esteem of money and coin than of stones."[39]

Also, the fact that money was relatively unimportant did not imply that the period was an economic disaster. We often tend to think of the Middle Ages as a bleak time in which progress ground to a halt, but in many respects the opposite is true, at least for the period until around 1300 known as the High Middle Ages (before the plague, witch-burning, etc.).[40] There is much that we can learn from antihoarding coins such as the bracteate or an economics with ethics at its core or the willingness to plan for future generations; and there are lessons too in the later, heady rise of a secretive, elite banking class and the link between wealth and power personified by the Medicis. One might also wonder how our own financial system would hold up in the event of a modern-day plague.

Above all, the idea of a society that was based on *caritas* and saw avarice as a deadly sin is in stark contrast to our money-based system, which replaces charity with the invisible hand and ethics with the unbridled pursuit of wealth. As the Scholastics knew, money has profound effects on human behavior, and those effects are not always positive. The U.S. psychologist

Paul Piff, for example, has shown through a series of experiments that feelings of monetary wealth can lead to a psychological syndrome that he unromantically calls the "asshole effect." In one experiment, his team monitored the behavior of drivers at crossroads, and found that drivers of high-status cars behave like feudal lords surrounded by serfs. They are four times more likely to cut off other drivers and three times more likely to not yield at pedestrian crossings. "While having money doesn't necessarily make anybody anything, the rich are way more likely to prioritize their own self-interests above the interests of other people. They are more likely to exhibit characteristics we would stereotypically associate with, say, assholes."[41] According to neuroscientist Keely Muscatell, wealth calms the part of the brain associated with empathy (or *caritas*): "As you move up the class ladder, you are more likely to violate the rules of the road, to lie, to cheat, to take candy from kids, to shoplift, and to be tightfisted in giving to others. Straightforward economic analyses have trouble making sense of this pattern of results."[42] Even mentioning the word "money" has been shown to prompt people to act in a less ethical manner (slightly concerning about this book, then!).[43]

Aquinas saw man as a rational animal, whose narrow self-interest was subservient to a broader ethos of charity. In fact, the Middle Ages seem to have been a period of great emotional intensity—from the romance of chivalric knights, to the hysteria against witches. But it was also the time when rational man, led by the mathematicians, became very good at counting and calculating. In a predominantly gift economy, where one of the gifts happened to be money, these two aspects of rationality—like the two sides of coin money—were in a state of tension. The balance between them would change when Christopher Columbus discovered the New World—and claimed as his prize one of the largest monetary gifts of all time.

4

New World

What greater stupidity can be imagined than that of calling jewels, silver, and gold "precious," and earth and soil "base"? People who do this ought to remember that if there were as great a scarcity of soil as of jewels or precious metals, there would not be a prince who would not spend a bushel of diamonds and rubies and a cartload of gold just to have enough earth to plant a jasmine in a little pot, or to sow an orange seed and watch it sprout, grow, and produce its handsome leaves, its fragrant flowers, and fine fruit.

GALILEO, *DIALOGUE CONCERNING THE TWO CHIEF WORLD SYSTEMS*

Money is gold, and nothing else.

J. P. MORGAN, TESTIMONY BEFORE THE BANK AND CURRENCY COMMITTEE OF THE HOUSE OF REPRESENTATIVES

What gives money its value? What backs the dollar or, for that matter, the bitcoin? Even today, many people think that bullion is still the "gold standard" for money. But as the Spanish discovered in the sixteenth century, a currency's value is not just a question of metal content. This chapter shows how too much of a good thing can upset the financial system; how a Newtonian approach to money helped to build the British Empire; how paper came to be seen as valuable as gold; and how the invention of "fractional reserve" banking boosted economic growth, while introducing into the world of finance a term that we still write about—the bubble.

"In passed days I wrote very fully to you of my return from new countries, which have been found and explored with the ships, at the cost and by the command of this Most Serene King of Portugal; and it is lawful to call it a new world, because none of these countries were known to our ancestors and all who hear about them they will be entirely new." Thus began a letter written in 1503 from the Florentine explorer Amerigo Vespucci to his former patron, the Medici banker Lorenzo di Pierfrancesco de' Medici. The letter was later published with the Latin title of *Mundus Novus* (*New World*). For his troubles, Vespucci had the continent in question named after him—America.

Since at the time even Christopher Columbus thought that the "New World" was part of Asia, the fact that it was an entirely new continent was exciting news—particularly to the Castilian monarchy, which had funded the search for new trading routes to the Far East, and people like the Medicis who had given financial backing to a number of trips, including Columbus's third voyage. More explorers soon followed in the wake of Vespucci and Columbus.[1] One of them was the Spaniard Hernán Cortés, who took part in the conquest of Cuba and was rewarded for his service with a grant of land and slaves. After seven years, by which time he was one of the wealthiest men on the island, he was chosen by the governor of Cuba to head an expedition to the interior of Mexico.

When the governor changed his mind at the last moment (part of a long-standing feud), Cortés—in an apparently reckless toss of the coin—mortgaged his estate to help pay for the voyage himself. After a few stops and skirmishes with the natives along the Mexican coast, Cortés and his army of several hundred reached what is now Veracruz. In order to eliminate any possibility of retreat, and in another display of there-is-no-plan-B confidence, he ordered his men to scuttle their ships.

Of course, the New World was new only to Europeans, being as it was the home of sophisticated civilizations such as the Mayans, Incas, and Aztecs, who had developed their own systems of agriculture, writing, mathematics, law, religion, and trade. These systems were in some ways similar to their European equivalents, but there were also key differences—one of which was their attitude toward precious metals. Gold and silver were abundant, and perhaps for this reason were valued primarily for their beauty and were not made into coins (thus destroying the theories of generations of economists about the inevitable emergence of coin money based on precious metals). The Incas thought that gold represented the sweat of the sun and silver the tears of the moon, and used the metals to line their temples.

Aztec society, like those of the Incas and Mayans, was based primarily on a tributary system, with goods and produce flowing into the capital

Tenochtitlán from various far-flung provinces. Markets were relatively small and local and were closely supervised by the government. Cacao beans were used for smaller purchases. Alternatively, the beans could be dried, roasted, and used to make a very bitter version of a chocolate drink (the Europeans later added sugar), which is more than you can say for most forms of money. Cotton capes of standardized length known as *quachtli* served for larger transactions. For example, merchants who wanted to "sponsor" a human sacrifice during the midwinter festival known as Panquetzaliztli could purchase a captured enemy soldier for up to 40 *quachtli*.[2] Precious metals were not used as a form of currency, as in Europe; however, they were widely displayed as jewelry and ornamentation, reports of which further fueled the interest of people such as Cortés and his men.

Sweat of the Sun, Tears of the Moon

According to the Spanish account (the Aztec one has been lost to history), the rulers of Yucatán had predicted the appearance of a blond, bearded deity known as Quetzalcoatl, which translates roughly as "Feathered Serpent." When Cortés arrived with his blond hair and sporting a beard, the Aztecs believed their forecast had come true and greeted him—not as an invading enemy, but as a god.

In any case, the Aztec emperor Moctezuma II met Cortés peacefully, and allowed him and his men to enter Tenochtitlán, a city with a population of more than 200,000 people. There he presented the Spaniards with lavish gifts of gold and silver, presumably in an attempt to placate them. Unfortunately, his gifts seemed to have the opposite effect. As recorded in the *Florentine Codex* (an account from the Aztec perspective by Bernardino de Sahagún): "They picked it up and fingered it like monkeys. It was as if their hearts were satisfied, brightened, calmed. For in truth they thirsted mightily for gold; they stuffed themselves with it; they starved for it; they lusted for it like pigs."[3] Even Cortés himself reflected that his soldiers were stricken by a "disease of the heart which can only be cured by gold."[4] Perhaps he was thinking about that mortgage.

The ensuing battles between the Spanish and the Aztecs ended with the death of Moctezuma, the sacking of Tenochtitlán, and eventually the conquest of the entire continent. The fight would not have been so one-sided had it not been for the fact that one of Cortés's men was carrying smallpox, to which the native populations had no prior exposure or immunity.

It hit them like the Black Death. Millions also died laboring in gold and silver mines; from exhaustion, hunger, disease, accidents such as rockfalls and cave-ins, or exposure to the mercury used in the refining process. The population of the Americas decreased by about 90 percent, and the sudden halt in farming—followed by regrowth of forests—was so large that it led to a noticeable dip in global carbon dioxide levels.[5] As author Mark Cocker wrote, "When viewed as a single process, the European consumption of tribal society could be said to represent the greatest, most persistent act of human destructiveness ever recorded."[6] And it was motivated entirely by the lust for riches: the "asshole effect" writ large.

Both slavery and the use of metal money had declined during the Middle Ages, but were now back with a vengeance. The strategy of the conquistadors was essentially a repeat of that used during the Axial Age by the Greek and Roman Empires: invade foreign lands; destroy their armies; set the survivors to work as slaves in mines digging up precious metals; turn these into coins to pay the army and finance further adventures; and tax the population in those same coins so they have to play along.

One difference was that the operation was on a much grander scale. The amount of gold and silver completely dwarfed anything the world had seen before. From 1500 to 1800, American mines produced about 150,000 tons of silver and 2,800 tons of gold, amounting to about 85 percent of the world's silver supply and 70 percent of the gold.[7] A single mountain in Peru, known appropriately as Cerro Rico (rich hill), gave the Spanish some 45,000 tons of pure silver—an amount that would have kept Alexander the Great's huge army in pay for a couple of hundred years (the mountain is still being mined by the locals but is in danger of total collapse).[8] Gold production in the Portuguese colony of Brazil produced more than 16 tons a year, with labor supplied from about 150,000 slaves. Because of high death rates among the locals, most of the slaves were imported from Africa as part of the newly globalized slave trade.

Another important difference was that the process had now been partly privatized. Cortés arranged the funding for his own mission, and he was also responsible for dividing up the loot afterward. The Crown retained rights over the land and charged a 20 percent fee called the *quinto real* (royal fifth) on any treasure extracted. Together with other taxes, this meant that most of the conquistadors made little money, and some even ended up in the red because they were forced to pay for their own equipment and expenses from government suppliers. Hence their insatiable appetite for new conquests—the big payoff was always on the horizon. Even Cortés found himself broke, after betting it all (again) on a failed venture in California.

The biggest difference, though, was in the power and status of money. Money was no longer primarily an instrument of state power, as it had been in the Axial Age, or a component of a social order dominated by the Church, as under feudalism, but was itself a dominant force that was finding its own balance and creating its own patterns. This shift in the standing of money was part of a larger shift in thinking during the Renaissance, which was again related to developments in science and mathematics. And the sudden influx of precious metal would lead, paradoxically, to an emphasis on scarcity that persists in economic thinking to the present day (box 4.1).

New World Order

Christian cosmology had long been based on the Aristotelian idea that the heavenly bodies circulate around the earth, encased in crystalline spheres. The first cracks in this model appeared in 1543, when the Polish astronomer Nicolaus Copernicus—who had spent several of his formative years studying science and the humanities in Italy—proposed that the earth might go around the sun, rather than vice versa. In 1577, the Danish astronomer Tycho Brahe observed a comet that passed between the planets, so if Aristotle's crystalline spheres had actually existed, it would have broken through them. In the early seventeenth century, supported by his Medici patrons, Galileo mapped out the heavens using his telescope; on discovering that Jupiter had moons, he named the four he could see after Medici children he had tutored—thus immortalizing them not in a painting but in the sky itself. The Christian image of the universe, with man safely ensconced at its center under the eye of a watchful God, was being replaced by a rational, scientific worldview in which the universe was governed by mechanistic forces and mathematical laws. Following in the footsteps of money, scientists were reducing the physical world to number.

As money became an increasingly important part of everyday life, it began to be seen not just as a sterile, static medium of exchange, as Aristotle had viewed it, but as something with a dynamism of its own. The ban on usury, which had been debated in the Middle Ages but had never gone away, was finally dropped. In England, King Henry VIII's Act Against Usury (1545) was more of an act *for* usury, since it permitted the charging of commercial interest rates up to 10 percent.[9] The Scholastic idea of a just price was also modified by an understanding of inflation. It had always been known that coins could lose value if their metal content was reduced,

Box 4.1
The Silver Dollar

In the early sixteenth century, precious metals, including silver, were discovered in the Czech town of Joachimsthal, near the German border. Silver coins minted from the area were known as Joachimsthalers. This was later shortened to "thalers" or "talers," pronounced in English as "dollars." The large silver coins were popular, with more than 10 million put in circulation, and were copied throughout Europe.

The most famous version, known as the Maria Theresa taler, was named after the Austrian empress. After she died in 1780, an estimated 800 million coins were minted until 1975, all with the same 1780 date.

However, it was the Spanish version of the dollar, also known as the *peso de ocho* (piece of eight) because it was worth 8 *reales*, that became the first truly international currency. Minted in Spain but also in Mexico and Peru, it served as the basis for the U.S. dollar, the Canadian dollar, the Chinese yuan (from the word for "round things," which referred to Spanish dollar coins), the Japanese yen (an abbreviation), and so on. In Spanish, it became known as the peso.

The U.S. version was first issued by the U.S. Mint in 1794 and was discontinued for domestic use in 1873 as the country moved toward the gold standard. The silver coins had an eagle on one side, and a Native American or

The silver peso (Spanish dollar) of Philip V, minted in Mexico in 1739. (https://en.wikipedia.org/wiki/Spanish_dollar#/media /File:Philip_V_Coin.jpg)

mythological figure on the other (George Washington objected to having his image on the coin because he didn't want to be perceived as casting himself in the mold of an English monarch).* Unlike European currencies such as the Spanish dollar and British pound, the U.S. dollar was based on the decimal system. A dollar could be divided into dimes, cents, and even mills (one-thousandth, though such coins were never minted).

*Only in the early twentieth century did the faces of presidents make an appearance on coins.

but inflation could also be a problem if the money supply was increased, for example, after the discovery of a new continent packed with massive quantities of gold and silver.

Before Copernicus set about rewriting the model of the universe, he published a small treatise called *Monetae cudendae ratio* (*On the Minting of Coin*, 1526). As he wrote: "Innumerable though the evils are with which kingdoms, principalities and republics are troubled, there are four which in my opinion outweigh all others—war, death, famine, and debasement of money . . . in the States which make use of degraded money, reigns cowardice, laziness and indolence."[10] To protect the value of a currency against such depredation, he advised—in what is perhaps the first statement of what is now known as the quantity theory of money—that "money usually depreciates when it becomes too abundant."[11] The flow of precious metal into Spain and its dispersal to other countries meant that more money was chasing the supply of goods and services, which bid up their prices in what historians now refer to as the "price revolution." (Of course, metal by itself is not money—money objects are created from metal objects by stamping them with a number. But if the international currency system is based on metal coins, that tends to set the price of the metal; and if the metal supply expands, the effect is similar to increasing the money supply, even if it is not converted into coins. In a sense, the stamp is extended to quantities of the metal by weight.)

Money and wealth also showed a different form of dynamism, which was a distinct tendency not to stay in the same place. People have long speculated about what happened to all the treasure that flowed into Spain. A portion was lost to theft, piracy, or shipwreck, but most of it ended up leaving the country because of trade. As Voltaire noted, much of the wealth "entered the pockets of the French, English, and Dutch," with another part going "to the East Indies to pay for spices, saltpeter, sugar, candy, tea, cloths, diamonds, and monkeys."[12] Price and wage inflation meant that Spanish goods became relatively expensive compared with foreign goods. The wealth also tended to concentrate with the state and nobility, who squandered it on gold-plating their palaces, coaches, books, and anything else they owned (as with the Aztecs, the ornamental value of gold seemed at this point to be prized more than its use as money). Spain from the mid-fifteenth century became a net debtor nation, borrowing from creditors in Italy, Holland, and Germany at interest rates as high as 18 percent. Gold shipments peaked in the mid-sixteenth century; silver, a few decades later.[13] In the space of 150 years, between 1550 and 1700, the country defaulted on its debt fourteen times. One problem was that gold inflamed the country's ambitions, leading to costly military ventures such as the failed invasion of England by the Spanish Armada in 1588. It also didn't help that in 1492, the Spanish monarchs had expelled the Jews and Muslims, who made up much of the merchant, administrative, and intellectual classes.

The main problem, though, was that gold boosted the money supply but had no such effect on the productive activity that underlies an economy. In a 1730 essay, the Irish-French banker and political economist Richard Cantillon described what today we would call the resource curse:

When the excessive abundance of money from the Mines has diminished the inhabitants of a State, accustomed those who remain to a too large expenditure, raised the produce of the land and the labour of workmen to excessive prices, ruined the manufactures of the State by the use of foreign productions on the part of Landlords and mine workers, the money produced by the Mines will necessarily go abroad to pay for the imports: this will gradually impoverish the State and render it in some sort dependent on the Foreigner to whom it is obliged to send money every year as it is drawn from the Mines. The great circulation of Money, which was general at the beginning, ceases: poverty and misery follow and the labour of the Mines appears to be only to the advantage of those employed upon them and the Foreigners who profit thereby. This is approximately what has happened to Spain since the discovery of the Indies.[14]

Or as Gonsalez de Cellorigo put it in 1600, "Spain is poor because she is rich."[15] (As discussed in chapter 8, local currencies are designed to keep money circulating within a specific city or region for just this reason.)

The trade with Asia—which was again dominated by merchant bankers from Italy, Holland, and Germany—turned out to be the real source of wealth. China had ceased its innovative experiment with paper currency after bouts of hyperinflation, coupled with the discovery of new mines, made metal again popular as money.[16] A booming economy, the opening of new trade routes, and a tax system based on silver all fueled growing demand. By the late sixteenth century, China was importing 90 percent of its silver (almost 50 tons a year), which was paid for by exporting enormous quantities of goods such as silk and porcelain (often called "china" in English because it usually came from there). Gold came too, but it was valued and hoarded for its beauty rather than being used as money.

So if China was inundated with silver, why didn't prices go up there as in Spain? The most likely reason is that output was expanding along with the money supply, so instead of more money chasing a fixed supply of goods and services, more money was chasing an increased supply of goods and services, and Copernican inflation was held at bay. But when bullion imports declined in the mid-seventeenth century, the result was a drastic economic contraction, as inflation went into reverse.[17]

The Age of Mercantilism

Gold may appeal to dictators, but it also boosts a sense of individual power and liberty. In sixteenth-century Europe, the flood of gold and silver into Europe meant that even the lower classes had access to coins. As in ancient Greece, this acted as both an individuating and a democratizing influence by allowing more people to participate in the money economy.[18] Something similar was happening at the macro level, where the feudal system was being replaced by centralized and militarily powerful nation-states. These were organized economically around an emerging doctrine, today known as mercantilism, that aimed to build and maintain a nation's military reach and power not so much by increasing economic activity as by accumulating as much "treasure" as possible.[19] Underlying mercantilism was bullionism: the idea that wealth is measured by a weight of precious metal. In this sense, Spain was both a good and a bad example—it was good at getting the stuff, less good at holding onto it.

The first economy to fully organize itself along these mercantilist/bullionist lines was England under Queen Elizabeth I. Not well endowed with gold and silver mines, it compensated through trade, exploration, and hard labor, which was supplied in part by colonial slaves. As with the Spanish conquistadors, the actual gritty work was largely privatized, in this case to companies such as the British East India Company. Founded in 1600, this was a joint-stock company that was granted a royal charter for trade monopolies, but whose shares were owned by wealthy investors rather than the government. The company eventually mutated into a quasi-military organization that virtually ruled India with its private armies for a century, even minting its own silver rupee coinage, which became the Indian standard.[20] It also played a major role in the slave trade, sending African slaves to work in the colonies.

Other countries launched their own East India Companies, the largest of which was established by the Dutch in 1602. Its shares were tradable on the Amsterdam Stock Exchange, a new institution whose invention galvanized the Dutch economy and gave the country a significant advantage over its competitors. The fact that investors could easily buy and sell shares was very attractive and made it easy for a company to raise capital. The Dutch East India Company soon dominated the spice trade and grew into the world's first multinational corporation. Other businesses, including shipbuilding, were similarly boosted, with the result that Holland's navy for a period ruled supreme, and the country's coins became the dominant world currency.

While economic thinking in the Middle Ages was dominated by monastic scholars who had taken an oath of poverty, the mercantilist era saw new economic ideas being developed by a range of public officials, journalists, and businessmen like Thomas Mun, who was a director of the East India Company. Just as the production of money was being privatized to an extent, so was the production of economic ideas. Under mercantilism, the total amount of wealth in the world was treated as fixed, so the economy was a zero-sum game: as Mun succinctly put it, "One man's loss is another man's gain."[21] The government should therefore use its money-fueled military power to find and control new resources, while employing trade tariffs, monopolies, and subsidies to encourage exports: "We must ever observe this rule; to sell more to strangers yearly than wee consume of theirs in Value." The power of private banks and foreign exchange markets acted as a check on monetary policy and government profligacy, since depreciations of the sort that had characterized the Middle Ages would be punished by a loss in international purchasing power.

By acting as a kind of superbusiness, the state also became dependent on the business world to maintain its credibility. According to Sir James Steuart, whose tract *An Inquiry into the Principles of Political Oeconomy* (1767) introduced the phrase "supply and demand" into English, this relationship was "the most effective bridle ever was invented against the world of despotism." It was less good at promoting what today we would call corporate ethics: the main trading pattern during Steuart's lifetime was the "trading triangle," which consisted of shipping weapons, iron, and textiles from Britain to Africa; swapping them for African slaves, who were taken to North or South America; and exchanging them in turn for gold, silver, sugar, and tobacco, which returned with the ships to Europe.

A License to Print Money

In the seventeenth century, European investors had access to many of the banking services that we enjoy today. They could buy and trade bills of exchange or pieces of paper that gave them a share in a company or government debt bonds. Establishments such as goldsmiths and notaries (which often functioned also as bankers) gave receipts in exchange for coins and bullion deposited with them.[22] After a while, they realized that rather than let the gold sit there, they could lend most of it and charge interest on the loan. Alternatively, they could just lend receipts for the gold, in the form of notes.[23] The borrower could use the note to pay someone else. That person could either redeem the note or use it to pay a third person, and so on. At some point, the note might be redeemed as cash, or it could just circulate indefinitely as a money object (in which case, the initial deposit would be left untouched). The original loan would continue to earn interest until it was repaid, in cash or in notes. Issuing notes was therefore a profitable business and meant that goldsmiths could pay interest on deposits, thus attracting more deposits. As Sir Dudley North observed, "Merchants kept their money with Goldsmiths and Scriveners [notaries or legal clerics], whose accounts show ten thousand cash, but they seldom have a thousand in specie."[24] Since 1609, the Amsterdam Exchange Bank had allowed merchants to set up accounts and transfer money, and therefore conveniently and safely carry out transactions on paper; from 1656, the Swedish Riksbank in Stockholm explicitly allowed loans that exceeded its reserves.[25]

Europeans had also known about the possibility of paper currency since the times of Marco Polo, and the idea had been anonymously pumped in 1650 in a British pamphlet called *The Key to Wealth, or, a New Way for Improving of Trade: Lawfull, Easie, Safe and Effectual*. It therefore seems strange that paper banknotes were not adopted as money until the end of the seventeenth century, even though they were obviously much cheaper to make than coins. The reason, perhaps, is that during this period money was viewed both economically and psychologically not as a virtual instrument of exchange, as in the Middle Ages, but in terms of bullion. The moment that New World gold and silver began flowing into Spain, the dual nature of money had flipped from its virtual head to its bodily tail, and paper didn't have the same physical appeal as coins. Mercantilism was about stockpiling material wealth, and when Colbert said that "it is simply, and solely, the abundance of money within a state that makes the difference in its grandeur and power," he was not talking about the ability to print paper.

While the idea had already been floated a number of times, the use of state-sponsored banknotes in Europe properly dates to the creation of the Bank of England in 1694. After military defeat by France in the Battle of Beachy Head, King William III found himself in urgent need of £1.2 million to rebuild the navy. The first idea—a state lottery known as the Million Adventure—did not do the trick. The second idea was to start a bank, along the same lines as state banks like the ones in Holland (William was born Dutch) and Sweden, but with a twist: it would be a public–private partnership, with the funds coming from businessmen. The bank would give the government a permanent loan of gold in return for notes against this debt. The bank would therefore operate like a goldsmith, but on a much larger scale. It would receive 8 percent interest in perpetuity on the original loan, plus a service charge of £4,000 per year, plus whatever it could make from banking services.[26] The subscription was sold out within twelve days to forty London and Edinburgh merchants. It was a huge success for the government and so much easier than raising taxes.

Nothing in the Bank of England's original charter mentioned banknotes, but they turned out to be the most important part of the enterprise. Like other banks, the new corporation gave notes in return for deposits and also lent them out at interest. Such notes, which were handwritten by a cashier, included a promise to pay the bearer the sum of the note on demand, so anyone could redeem them in full or in part (in which case the note was suitably endorsed) for metal coins. Supported as they were by royal approval, they soon began to circulate as money.[27]

As mentioned in chapter 1, new inventions often result from a collision between existing technologies and cultural practices. The founding of the Bank of England represented a melding of the financial technology of the banking network with the power of the state. The new money system of bills and notes was certified, like a coin, by the sovereign's stamp. There was therefore a transfer between the sovereign and the private system of credibility for cash. For the first time, private businessmen were directly involved in issuing and controlling the government's money. Instead of acting as a check on the state's power, as described by Steuart, they now had their hands on the controls.

The bank was originally sited in a small office in Walbrook in the City of London, the square mile of the financial district, which lies within the remains of the walls surrounding the Roman town of Londinium. Archaeologists later discovered on that site the remains of a Roman temple of Mithras, the god of contracts (the bank moved to its current location in Threadneedle Street in 1734). Perhaps the contract between the government and the newly formed corporation had the god's blessing, because it was certainly fortuitous for all concerned. The effort to rebuild the navy had knock-on effects on the rest of the economy and set the newly revitalized country on its way to becoming the dominant power for the next century and a half, with the largest empire in history. England ruled the waves—and driving it, like the core of a nuclear-powered submarine, was the quantum power of money.

Intrinsic Value

The Bank of England was the first independent central bank and, as discussed later, served as a template for other central banks around the world. While the development of paper money would eventually reshape the world financial system, it didn't seem to represent much of a revolution at the time. The reason was that banknotes were just a receipt, a pointer to something else, and it was understood that the real money—the gold bars and coins—existed in a vault somewhere. The banking system has since been described as "perhaps the most astounding piece of sleight of hand that was ever invented," and certainly this move appears to have tricked the audience.[28] (The exact size of the reserves, which consisted of both bullion and government securities, was kept deliberately vague by the corporation. When later questioned on this point by a royal commission, Lord Cunliffe said the reserves were "very, very considerable." Asked to expand on that, he said he would be "very, very reluctant" to do so.)[29]

A much more serious matter, in the minds of intellectuals, politicians, and the public alike, was the so-called silver crisis. As discussed earlier, a feature of coin money is that if the face value of a coin falls below the market price of the metal it is made of, then it will tend to be melted down or sold abroad as bullion. England at the time operated under a bimetallic regime, with both low-denomination silver and high-denomination gold coins that could be exchanged at a set rate. This meant that the Royal Mint in the Tower of London had to maintain a tricky balance between the market rates of the two metals and the formal exchange rate, since otherwise it would open up arbitrage opportunities. For several decades, the face value of silver coins had tended to dip a few percent below the metal value—with the result that there weren't enough silver coins to go round.

The problem was exacerbated by the widespread practice of "clipping" coins—that is, removing a tiny amount of the valuable metal from the edges, to be melted down and sold. The coins that remained in circulation were therefore often but fragments of their former selves, with many containing only half their original silver. Merchants began to discount such coins, valuing them on weight rather than stamp, which resulted in inflation. Money was losing its most basic property, which was that market value should be designated by the stamp. By 1694, the economy was in serious trouble. The government therefore decided to issue new coins, but was unsure whether to restore them to their former level of silver or keep them at the new lower level. The latter option was favored by mercantilist economists, who argued that a cheaper coin would result in a low exchange rate. This in turn would make goods cheaper to produce relative to those of other countries, and thus maximize exports.

On the other side of the debate was the philosopher John Locke. In his *Two Treatises on Government* (1689),[30] he argued that the role of the state was to protect the rights and freedoms of its citizens. One of the key rights was property rights, which Locke believed are generated when people mix their labor with the material world. For example, an apple on a tree is of no use to anyone; but by picking it, a worker mixes his or her labor with the apple, thus giving it value: "His labour hath taken it out of the hands of nature . . . and hath thereby appropriated it to himself." Money was a way of crystallizing these gains and a means of asserting and guaranteeing one's freedom.

Locke's work therefore countered the mercantilist idea that the economy was at the service of the state. It also provided political justification for the sanctity of private property and the accumulation of money, and later served as one of the main influences on the Constitution of the new American government. Above all, it meant that the government should protect the integrity of the money in people's pockets, not try to dilute it or allow it to be debased by coin-clipping thieves or force people to exchange their old coins for new, smaller versions. According to the rational, scientific, materialistic perspective of the Enlightenment, it made sense that the value of a coin should be determined by its physical qualities, that is, its precious metal content rather than the sovereign's stamp, which after all was just a stamp. The answer to the question "What is money?" was a set weight of metal. Money's "intrinsic value" was measured by its precious metal content, and you could no more change it than you could "lengthen a foot by dividing it into Fifteen parts, instead of Twelve."

Locke therefore won the argument over the silver coins, and they were restored to their former level of content, but this time with milled edges to discourage clipping. Instead of a flexible exchange rate, the worth of money would be firmly tethered to the price of metal. An unexpected result, however, was that people hoarded the new silver coins and spent the old ones. This is an example of "Gresham's law," known to Copernicus, Oresme, and others, which states that "bad money drives out good."[31] (Here "good" can refer to either metal weight or even the appearance of a currency—shiny new coins with a nice design are preferred to old, beaten-up ones.)[32] The shortage of money, coupled with the inflexibility of the monetary standard, created a deflationary disaster that was only alleviated as paper money and cheaper-denomination coins slowly became available for everyday transactions. Perhaps the stamp was worth something after all.

The Alchemist

Locke was acting as an adviser for none other than Isaac Newton, who had career-shifted from physics into a position as warden (later master) of the Mint. The job was intended as a sinecure—Newton had recently suffered a mental breakdown, perhaps caused by mercury poisoning from his alchemical experiments (the same problem suffered by many New World slaves, only this time self-inflicted). But Newton took his role seriously, devoting a surprising amount of energy to chasing down clippers and counterfeiters, a number of whom were sent to their deaths. He was also inadvertently responsible for putting England, and eventually much of the world, onto the gold standard.

The guinea coin—named for the region of West Africa where the material was sourced—was the country's first gold coin to be struck by machine instead of by hand. It weighed about ¼ ounce of gold, bore an image of a small elephant (the logo of the Africa Company), and was originally worth 1 pound sterling, equal to 20 silver shillings. However, the actual market exchange rate tended to be somewhat higher. In 1717, Newton announced in a report that in England, "a pound weight of fine gold is worth fifteen pounds weight six ounces seventeen pennyweight & five grains of fine silver, reckoning a Guinea at 1£. 1s. 6d. in silver money" (1 pound, 1 shilling, and 6 pence). He calculated the European price ratio to be a little different, so for purposes of harmonization Newton recommended that the price of a guinea be set to 1 pound and 1 shilling, or 21 shillings. The Treasury therefore issued an order announcing that to be the official exchange rate.

This number 21, which fixed the relationship between gold and silver coins, was the monetary equivalent of a fundamental physical constant. As discussed in chapter 2, though, the concept of real-world value is fuzzy and uncertain, tends to vary with time and place, and has ways of confounding exact calculation. Because Newton's ratio—in the eyes of merchants and traders around the world—still slightly favored gold over silver, gold coins were used to buy silver coins, and these were melted down and exported to places like India, where the British East India Company did a roaring trade. In a kind of reverse Gresham's law, if money is underrated, it tends to leave, like a jealous lover. (A similar problem can occur when one country tries to peg its currency against that of another—not everyone may respect the peg.)

In theory, according to what is now known as the "law of supply and demand," the market price of gold would fall as it became relatively abundant compared with silver; and Newton predicted that any discrepancy would be erased over time. Instead, what happened was that the market price of silver adjusted to a degree but remained volatile, and the price of gold stayed the same. Perhaps this was because the attractive, machine-produced gold coins were seen as superior to the more shopworn silver currency.[33] Or maybe it was just that gold had more gravitational pull over the collective monetary consciousness. Either way, guineas therefore retained their face value of 21 shillings, even though the unit referred to a weight of silver. Newton may not have been able to turn lead into gold through alchemy, but in a sense he turned gold into silver. The result was that the pound sterling switched de facto from a bimetallic standard to a gold standard, with the Mint price of gold set at £3 17s 10½d an ounce (which made a guinea 21 shillings). There it remained, with wartime interruptions, for the next 200 years; a frozen Newtonian accident.[34] In 1821, a new coin, the sovereign, was introduced, containing 20/21 of the gold in a guinea, thus making it worth exactly 1 pound sterling.

The inherent and unavoidable tension between money's material value (tails) and stamp value (heads), which is complicated by bimetallism, later prompted a similar argument in the United States. Thomas Jefferson had recommended that the U.S. currency be based on a bimetallic standard so as to "abridge the quantity of circulating medium."[35] The Coinage Act of 1792 therefore defined a dollar to be 371.25 grains (24.1 grams) of silver, with gold worth fifteen times as much by weight. By the late nineteenth century, however, the country had essentially adopted what was fast becoming the international gold standard. The silver dollar stopped being coined in 1873 (see box 4.1), and the money supply shrank. This self-imposed, deflationary scarcity boosted the wealth of anyone holding gold and led to an intense political debate—with Populist politician William Jennings Bryan famously arguing that its effect was to "crucify mankind upon a cross of gold"—that is believed to have inspired the themes behind L. Frank Baum's children's novel *The Wonderful Wizard of Oz* (1900).

Rich bankers (the Wicked Witches of the East and West) wanted to control the money supply and keep with gold. Indebted farmers (the Scarecrow), who wanted a cheaper silver currency, were not helped by either industrialists (the Tin Woodsman) or fearful politicians (the Cowardly Lion). In real life, the wicked witches won, the country stayed on the yellow brick road, the value of the dollar was still measured in ounces (oz, get it?) of gold until 1971, Dorothy's silver slippers were turned into ruby slippers for the movie, and the wonderful wizard at the central bank kept his job. The argument ended with the discovery of new supplies of gold in Alaska and Colorado—but the novel/play/film ran and ran.

The Madness of People

The gold standard was Newtonian in the sense that it prescribed an exact mathematical relationship between a currency and a weight in metal. The desire for Enlightenment scientists and philosophers, discussed further in chapter 7, to place the study of money and the economy on a solidly rational and mechanistic footing was no doubt also related to the fact that the economy itself had for a while been showing some rather footloose behavior. Financial innovations such as joint-stock companies and stock exchanges had boosted economic activity but had also magnified the possibility of adverse events, such as everyone losing all their money.

Leaders in this area, as in many other monetary developments, were the Dutch, who in the "tulip mania" of 1637 saw the price of the newly introduced bulb soar to incredible heights before suddenly wilting. The collapse created an economic chill that took some of the shine off what is known as the Dutch golden age, when the country was a dominant power in everything from art to warfare. A number of similar "manias" followed in other countries, with even more disastrous consequences. In England, what became known as the South Sea Bubble was driven by speculation in shares of the South Sea Company—a kind of South American version of the East India Company—which had been granted a monopoly to trade with Spain's colonies there in exchange for helping to fund the national debt.

The company's apparent success, which turned it into a competitor to the Bank of England, inspired many others to cash in on the trend for stock market flotations. One person set up a company whose Internet-like prospective famously consisted of "carrying on an undertaking of great advantage, but nobody to know what it is." Others offered a "wheel of perpetual motion" and a method for "extracting silver from lead." In 1720, the South Sea share price soared within a few months from £175 to more than £1,000—despite the fact that not much trade was actually occurring. Directors sold some shares, investors began to suspect a scam, and by the end of September the price had deflated to £135. The ensuing crisis caused a record number of bankruptcies at every level of society. In 1721, the English government passed what became known as the Bubble Act, which forbade the founding of joint-stock companies without a royal charter. This protected the South Sea Company, which had such a charter, but unfortunately did not succeed in making bubbles illegal.

The problem, it seemed, was that while under the gold standard a coin or banknote might have a well-defined value corresponding to a physical quantity of gold, the same could not be said of a share in a company or a futures contract to buy a tulip bulb at the end of the growing season, because these represented bets on future prospects, which are inherently uncertain. One of the victims of the South Sea Bubble was Isaac Newton, who lost a large part of his fortune and concluded: "I can calculate the motions of heavenly bodies, but not the madness of people." As discussed in chapter 5, his losses paled in comparison with those of the Paris-based Scotsman John Law—who in the space of a few years may have made (in the literal sense of created) and lost more money than anyone in history.

Lender of Last Resort

The Bank of England's founding as a public–private merger may have been a shotgun marriage; but it worked, and endured, in large part because of the way in which it separated out responsibility for the dual heads–tails aspects of money. The state (heads) supplied the official government stamp that specified value. The private sector (tails) put up the store of precious metal that backed the currency. The balance between the need for stable money and sufficient supply was skillfully managed by the Bank. It recovered from the damage of the South Sea Bubble and gradually expanded its role by establishing a near monopoly (and in 1844 a full monopoly) in the issuance of notes and becoming a clearinghouse for settling transactions between other banks such as London & Westminster, Lloyds, and Barclays. By 1776, Adam Smith could write that paper money outnumbered the total coin in circulation and "the stability of the Bank of England is equal to that of the British government."[36] As the hub of the "fractional reserve" system (box 4.2), it also became what the financial journalist Walter Bagehot called the "lender of last resort," responsible for bailing out smaller banks that became the victim of bank runs or South Sea–like crises.

Under the fractional reserve system, banks maintained only small reserves with the central bank. In theory, rational customers would assess this risk, and banks that did not maintain adequate reserves would go out of business. As Bagehot noted, however, trade was "largely carried on with borrowed money" and was backed by only a sense of trust and confidence that eluded rational analysis and that financial crises had repeatedly shown to be fragile: "No abstract argument, and no mathematical computation will teach it to us."[37] Bank runs were an inevitable feature of the system, and the only way to treat them was for the central bank to pump credit and liquidity into the system when it threatened to run dry by lending at high rates against collateral. (Another approach, used in 2014 by banks in China's city of Yancheng following rumors they had run out of cash, was to display piles of notes in the window.)

This role of the central bank was not, as Bagehot pointed out, explicitly acknowledged either by the bank or by Parliament. And perhaps this was part of the reason it worked, for to officially accept the responsibility would

Box 4.2
The Multiplier

One of the most mysterious arts of finance is how money is created in the first place. The basic idea, as traditionally described in most economics textbooks, is similar to the way in which the Bank of England was founded: a central bank buys a government bond (initially with gold, later by fiat). The government then pays this amount into the accounts of its creditors, and the new money enters the larger economy.

Under fractional reserve banking, however, these payments are just the first stage in a process. Suppose, for example, that one such payment from the government is for £1,000. The bank that receives the deposit has a new asset worth that amount. If the bank's reserve requirement is 10 percent, that means it can lend out up to 90 percent of the deposit, so £900. Say that the £900 is lent to a customer, who in turn deposits the £900 into the account of a merchant. That bank can now lend out 90 percent of that amount, or £810, which again ends up in another account. The original deposit of £1,000 therefore creates a cascade of further deposits, and the total amount of money thus created is £1,000, plus £810, plus £729, and so on, which sums (in the limit) to £10,000. Of course, only the first £1,000 can be traced back to the central bank, so the other £9,000 has been created out of thin air (though loans are backed by things like property titles). The original deposit has therefore been "multiplied up" by a factor of 10.

The central bank can also destroy money by selling its government securities for cash and/or raising the interest it charges for loans. Either of these reduce the amount of cash held by private banks, and therefore the amount they in turn can loan out.

This, at least, is the conventional picture.* As discussed further in chapter 7, the system doesn't work that way in practice—in fact, it is the other way around. In most countries reserve requirements have been diluted or eliminated—in Canada, for example, they were phased out in the 1990s—and private banks are effectively free to lend as much money as they want, with only indirect restrictions, such as the interbank lending rate that is controlled by the central bank.† Therefore the bulk of the money supply is really set not by the central bank but by private banks in response to demand for loans. "Fractional reserve" no longer seems quite the right name, since there are no set fractions or reserves. Alternative currencies, of course, need not rely on central banks at all.

However you name it, the system has obvious risks (such as the possibility of a bank run), but it also has advantages. For example, it makes deposits more valuable to banks, which means savings accounts can earn interest, and it allows money supply to scale easily to the demand for loans.

*According to Michael McLeay, Amar Radia, and Ryland Thomas, "The reality of how money is created today differs from the description found in some economics textbooks" ("Money Creation in the Modern Economy," *Quarterly Bulletin* [Bank of England], no. 1, March 14, 2014, 1).

†The U.S. Federal Reserve does set some reserve requirements, one example being for checking accounts at depository institutions, but they can be funded using loans with nonreservable liabilities and play only a small role in the money creation process. See Ed Dolan, "Whatever Became of the Money Multiplier?," September 23, 2013, *EconBlog*, www.economonitor.com/dolanecon/2013/09/23/whatever-became-of-the-money-multiplier.

have encouraged smaller banks to take risks (so-called moral hazard). Money is based on the fragile and uncertain relationship between number and value, which seems more comfortable in the shadows and doesn't always respond well to attempts at transparency. Nonetheless, an implication of its position at the pinnacle of the monetary system was that the central bank, even if it was nominally a privately owned, independent institution, was no longer a normal company, but one that required considerable political oversight.

The power of the bank expanded with the world economy as the Industrial Revolution took hold. Money and industry grew in concert: the new steam engines of Andrew Boulton and James Watt powered trains and industrial plants, but also the screw presses at the Royal Mint, which cranked out shiny new copper pennies. By the end of the nineteenth century, the Bank of England was firmly ensconced as the go-to financier and backstop for the British Empire, as well as the unofficial guardian of the international gold standard, which had gradually won out over bimetallism to create a unified global currency.[38] The model of a dominant central bank, acting as the central hub for an ecosystem of private and commercial banks, was also adopted in other wealthy countries. Each country maintained large gold reserves, which were thought to act as a kind of automatic stabilizer on the world economy. In theory at least, if one country had a trade deficit, gold would flow out of the country to pay for it; the money supply would decrease; prices would fall; there would be a curative spell of austerity and belt-tightening, making the country more competitive; and exports would improve, bringing the deficit back into balance. In practice, it was found that correlations between things like prices and exports were not so neat—but as always in economics, the story counted as much as the reality.

As John Kenneth Galbraith noted, the Old Lady of Threadneedle Street, as the bank became known, "is in all respects to money as St. Peter's is to the Faith. And the reputation is deserved, for most of the art as well as much of the mystery associated with the management of money originated there."[39] The separation between bank and state was symbolized by the historic quasi-independence of the City of London from the rest of London and the country. The Bank of England was eventually nationalized by a Labour government in 1946—when the visage of the queen began to appear on banknotes—but even today, the City has its own lord mayor, with whom the ruling monarch needs to ceremonially check in before entering.[40]

During this time of unprecedented rapid economic change, the gold standard provided a number of advantages, including predictable exchange rates, a degree of stability, and a brake on the tendency of governments to print money to pay off debt. Above all, it gave money a reassuring sense of credibility, by rooting it in gold, and endowed nations with pride in their currency. The economist Joseph Schumpeter described it as a "badge of honor and decency."[41] The system particularly benefited England, which as ruler of the largest empire in history could control much of the international money supply. As the nineteenth-century economist David Ricardo noted, "Neither a State nor a bank has had the unrestricted power of issuing paper money, without abusing that power; in all States, therefore, the issue of proper money ought to be under some check and control; and none seems so proper as that of subjecting the issuers of paper money to the obligation of paying their notes, either in gold coin or in bullion."[42] According to Baron Overstone, "Precious metals alone are money. Paper notes are money because they are representations of metallic money."[43] Of course, the Chinese were several centuries ahead of the English in discussing this issue, as when the medieval historian Ma Twan-lin argued that "paper should never be *money* (but) only employed as a representative sign of value existing in metals or produce. . . . When the government . . . wished to make a real money of paper, the original contrivance was perverted."[44]

The sense of stability granted by the gold standard was captured by the Austrian writer Stefan Zweig in his autobiography *The World of Yesterday*

(1942, translated into English in 1943), in which he wrote about how "the Austrian crown circulated in bright gold pieces, an assurance of its immutability. Everything had its norm, its definite measure and weight."[45] Despite these advantages, the maintenance of the gold standard was vulnerable to the trade disruptions that occurred at times of war. In Austria, the hyperinflation that occurred after World War I—and which Zweig said "struck the word 'security' from our vocabulary"—appears also to have marked the worldview of many Austrian economists, including Ludwig von Mises, who urged a return to the gold standard.[46] The desire for an inflexible standard also lives on in the form of German ordoliberalism, a rule-based approach to economics emphasizing things like monetary stability, low inflation, and balanced budgets, which has influenced the European Union and the European Central Bank (as Greece discovered during the Grexit crisis).

While the gold standard helped protect the currency from the vagaries of politicians, linking the quantity of money to a finite commodity also meant that the money supply did not adjust appropriately to the size of the economy and left it vulnerable to changes in gold supply. After a large find or improvement in mining technology, the money supply might become too large, causing inflation. Alternatively, it might not keep up with the pace of economic growth, with the result that gold became too expensive, causing deflation and recession. As discussed in the chapter 5, those conditions, as experienced in France and America, led to the next financial revolution, whose implications are still unfolding today.

5

A Wonderful Machine

Real talers have the same existence that the imagined gods have. Has a real taler any existence except in the imagination, if only in the general or rather common imagination of man? Bring paper money into a country where this use of paper is unknown, and everyone will laugh at your subjective imagination.

KARL MARX,

"THE DIFFERENCE BETWEEN THE DEMOCRITEAN

AND EPICUREAN PHILOSOPHY OF NATURE"

The study of money, above all other fields in economics, is one in which complexity is used to disguise truth or to evade truth, not to reveal it. The process by which banks create money is so simple the mind is repelled. With something so important, a deeper mystery seems only decent.

JOHN KENNETH GALBRAITH,

MONEY: WHENCE IT CAME, WHERE IT WENT

There never seems to be enough money to go round. This is especially a problem when the money is either made of precious metal, or is backed by it, as under the gold standard. One idea—which was proposed in eighteenth-century France by John Law, but later found more fertile soil in the United States—was to create a new currency whose value was maintained only by the support of the government. This chapter discusses the history and properties of fiat currencies and shows that money might not grow on trees, but it grows faster if it is printed on paper—and faster still if it is produced electronically.

When King Louis XIV of France (the Sun King) died in 1715, he left his country in an appalling financial condition. The country had enormous debts, both from funding his wars and from underwriting the costs of his extravagant lifestyle, including the construction of the palace of Versailles. The next in line for the throne, Louis XV, was only five. Control of the country therefore passed to the regent, the duc d'Orléans. Somewhat overwhelmed by too many financial problems on his already-full plate, he did what someone in a similar position would do today: he hired a consultant.

John Law came highly recommended by the regent's brother-in-law, Duke Victor Amadeus of Savoy, to whom Law had pitched his ideas for financial reform. In a letter to the regent, Law outlined a similar proposal that would cure France's financial problems in a single stroke: "I will devise a scheme that will astonish Europe by the alterations it will make in France's favor, alterations more radical than those procured by the discovery of the Indies or the introduction of credit."

Law's personal history was complicated. He came from a well-off Scottish family—his father was a goldsmith—and was a trained mathematician with a great aptitude for mental calculation. In 1694, at the age of twenty-three, he killed another man in a duel in London. He was arrested and sentenced to death but somehow escaped to Holland. He took up with a married woman, had two children with her, and traveled around Europe supporting his family by gambling.

He then returned to Scotland and tried to convince the government to adopt a new monetary system inspired by what he had seen in the Bank of Amsterdam and the Bank of England, but with an improvement. Instead of issuing banknotes backed by loans of gold from private bankers, the government could issue notes backed by land—which Law argued was the ultimate source of all wealth. A banknote would therefore be like a mortgage against a piece of Scotland.

Law's idea was turned down. Instead, Scotland united with England, and its financial system was folded into the purvey of the Bank of England. Worse for Law, this legal union meant he would be wanted for murder in his home country, and he again had to flee to Europe, which is how he ended up in France. (One imagines that very little of this was on his CV when he first approached the regent.)

In direct opposition to Locke and Newton, Law believed that money had little meaning other than as a kind of casino chip: "Money is not the value for which goods are exchanged but the value by which they are exchanged; the use of money is to buy goods, and silver, while money, is of no other use." It made no sense for a country to use silver or gold as a currency, especially if it were not blessed with the mines to supply those metals. France's problem, he told the regent, was that it did not have enough money. The solution, therefore, was to print some.

Like the Scottish government, the regent balked at the idea of reinventing the entire monetary system. However, he did allow Law to set up a small bank, so long as he funded it himself. The Banque générale, which issued banknotes against coin deposits, was so successful that the notes actually traded at a small premium, since they were easier to handle than coins and could not be clipped or otherwise degraded. In 1718, the bank was nationalized, becoming the Banque royale. With the currency now backed by the power of throne, Law did a sleight of hand that outdid even the Bank of England: he delinked the banknotes from reserves of precious metals, turning the money into a fiat currency. No one seemed to mind, because the easing of the monetary drought meant that the French economy was suddenly coming alive.

At the same time, Law established the Mississippi Company. This was run along the same lines as its competitor the South Sea Company (which had not yet gone bust) but had exclusive trading rights over the enormous area of the Mississippi River basin, including its tobacco plantations and its rumored huge deposits of gold. Law's "system," as he called it, was truly coming together. The company's share price soared as people used the freshly created banknotes to buy stock in the venture. The money supply doubled within a year, with much ending up in real estate; the resulting price increase meant that land that had earned 4 to 5 percent per year, according to the eighteenth-century French economist Nicolas Dutot, now yielded only 1.2 percent.[1] Law, who by this point was the richest man in the world, invested in a number of grand chateaux and a couple of blocks of Paris. The duc d'Orléans had a city named after him (New Orleans).

Clearly on a roll, Law arranged for the company to buy the national debt and take over the collection of taxes. This expansion required more shares, and more banknotes to pay for them. Unfortunately, the massive increase in money supply was feeding into inflation, with food bills soaring. At the same time, Law's opponents in the business community spread rumors that the Mississippi might be a gold-free zone. The system unraveled as quickly as it had come together, with the share price of the Mississippi Company dropping peak to trough by almost a factor of 20. In the panic to offload shares, fifteen people were crushed to death in the crowd outside the exchange, and a run on the bank meant that Law's banknotes became effectively unusable. As Voltaire is supposed to have remarked: "Paper money has now been restored to its intrinsic value."

Again on the run, Law fled to England, then to Venice, where he died a poor man. In 1803, Napoleon needed money to pay for his wars and sold Louisiana to the United States for $15 million. A few years later, Law's story served as inspiration for the character of Mephisto in Goethe's *Faust*. The word "bank" was hardly used in France again until the late nineteenth century, with institutions preferring to call themselves a *caisse, crédit, comptoir,* or *société*.[2]

Today, of course, fiat currencies are the norm, even if in many respects we seem to be in denial about that fact. As we'll see, financial institutions such as central banks, as well as mainstream economic theories, were shaped under the gold standard and—in an example of what Marshall McLuhan called "culture lag"—have changed surprisingly little since. The reasons can be found in the 200-year American struggle between proponents of "paper" credit money—championed by figures such as Benjamin Franklin and Abraham Lincoln—and conservative forces that supported the gold standard—Baum's "Wicked Witches of the East and West"—for the right to determine what counts as money.

New World II

Law's system was brilliant, innovative, ahead of its time, and (with the benefit of hindsight) fatally flawed. One problem was that it relied on the power of the throne to give the paper money its credibility and set its value. Unlike the Bank of England scheme, the business and private banking community had no direct role except as a competitor. This made the system unstable. It didn't help, of course, that the Mississippi Company, like its South Sea counterpart, was basically a Ponzi scheme. Perhaps Law's biggest error, though, was that he was taking his show to the wrong country. John Law may have been Scottish by birth, but at heart he was surely an American.

In America at the time, as in France, there was a shortage of coin. There were few mines for local production, and the mercantilists in London forbade the export of gold or silver to the colonies. Settlers often relied instead on commodity money (tobacco, beaver skins, and wampum beads all found use) or foreign coins, particularly the Spanish dollar, many of which ended up being exported in exchange for goods. The imperial system of pounds, shillings, and pence acted as a common unit of account.[3] In 1690, the Massachusetts

Bay Colony had funded a military campaign (to invade Canada) using paper "scrip" money. Other colonial governments adopted similar schemes as emergency measures during wartime, often with inflationary results. In the 1720s, though, legislatures began to introduce more permanent schemes.

A leader in this area was Pennsylvania, which in 1723 issued a paper money that was backed by future taxes and the land assets of people who borrowed from the government.[4] The scheme was therefore similar to Law's idea of a land bank. One of its main promoters was Benjamin Franklin, a Pennsylvania printer who at the age of twenty-three wrote (and printed) a pamphlet titled *A Modest Enquiry into the Nature and Necessity of a Paper-Currency*. Echoing Law, whose work he had read, Franklin argued that a shortage of money leads to a shortage in trade.[5] The money supply therefore had to be adjusted to match the needs of the economy, which was impossible if the material used to make it was controlled by other countries, but easy if the money was printed on paper. Of course, the supply had to be carefully limited to ensure that the money not sink in value.

The new paper money, which was issued by using it to pay public expenses, had the desired effect of stimulating economic growth, and Franklin was influential in having the currency enlarged and extended (he also won a contract to print it). The British Parliament was less impressed, and soon passed a law making it illegal for colonial governments to produce their own money. Only gold and silver would be accepted for payment of taxes. The resulting contraction of the money supply, according to Franklin, meant that within a year the streets were full of unemployed people, just like back in England. This unemployment, he believed, was the real cause of the American Revolutionary War (1775–1783). In general, while the value-retaining properties of gold and silver were appreciated by tax collectors, rich creditors, and merchants—that is, those in positive credit—they were less admired by people like farmers or the unemployed, who often ended up in negative debt (perhaps this is why inflationary paper money has since been associated with a number of revolutionary movements, including the French and the Russian Revolutions).[6]

Debts from the war were paid by the Continental Congress using "Continentals." However, so many were printed, some by British counterfeiters, that over the course of the war they collapsed in value from a value of 1 silver dollar to more like 1 cent—thus turning them, as Franklin noted somewhat sarcastically, into a "wonderful machine" to pay for the conflict without using either hard currency or taxes.[7] The result of this hyperinflation was a backlash against paper money, which again gave gold the upper hand (box 5.1).

Box 5.1
Hyperinflation

As shown by John Law's experiment in France or the Continentals during the Revolutionary War or the German mark after World War I or many other cases around the world, an episode of hyperinflation can make money less valuable than the paper it is printed on (especially because the paper is now full of dyes). In 2009, at the height of Zimbabwe's hyperinflation, the *Zimbabwean* newspaper actually started running ads on banknotes saying, "It's cheaper to print this on money than paper." In 2015 the central bank officially retired the Zimbabwean dollar, allowing people to exchange the 100 trillion (100,000,000,000,000) notes for US$0.40.

Hyperinflation is caused by a feedback loop in which an overstressed state or central bank prints money to pay off debts, but this has the effect of devaluing the currency. If the debts are in foreign currencies, devaluation makes the debts bigger. Currency speculators abandon or even short-sell the currency, which drives it down further. Since the money is only paper, the short-term solution is just to print some more, which creates more devaluation, and so on, until the process eventually burns out, and the currency has some zeros removed or is renamed as something else.

To visualize how hyperinflation can affect one's personal savings, fans of the TV show *Breaking Bad* will recall the episode in season 5 in which it is shown that former chemistry teacher Walter White's crystal meth operation has generated an impressive pile of cash, which his wife, Skyler, has put in a storage locker: "I rented this place and I started bringing it here because . . . I didn't know what else to do. I gave up counting it. I had to. It was just so much, so fast. . . . I just stack it up, keep it dry, spray it for silverfish." A ballpark estimate from a still image is that the pile contains about 850,000 bills.[*] Assuming that none are smaller than $20, that would translate to a minimum of about $17 million. A lot of money—but a dose of hyperinflation could reduce it to less than the locker rental fee. In 1922 Germany, for example, the largest denomination note was 50,000 marks. The next year, the exchange rate was about 4.2 trillion marks to US$1, and a locker full of notes would have been worth only 1 cent. That is worse than silverfish. (Though perhaps a better comparison for the drug trade is Bolivia in 1985, when most of the country's income came from exporting cocaine to the United States. A spike in inflation turned the same number of 10,000-peso notes into about US$5,000.)

[*]Tom Cook, "What Is a Good Approximation of How Much Money Skyler Had in the Storage Unit When She Showed Walt How She Stopped Counting It?" *Slate*, September 6, 2012, http://tinyurl.com/cby36g8.

What Is Coin?

After the Revolutionary War, the Founding Fathers were in the same position as many a former European monarch: they needed a way to pay off a
substantial national war debt. The collapse of the Continental meant that,
while it had helped win the war, there was little appetite to risk the atten-
tions of speculators and counterfeiters by issuing more paper currency. Secretary of the Treasury Alexander Hamilton therefore decided to imitate the
Bank of England by bringing in the private sector and monetizing the debt.
After all, while the Constitution specifies that only the government can
mint *coins*, there was no such restriction on the printing of *banknotes*. The
Bank of the United States was duly founded in 1791.[8] However, the scheme
reached more resistance than it had in England. When the bank's twenty-
year charter ran out, Congress failed to renew. A second attempted Bank of
the United States lasted no longer (1816–1836).[9]

In the meantime, private banks were proliferating under a chaotic array
of regulations that varied from state to state. The 1859 edition of *Hodges
Genuine Bank Notes of America*, for example, listed some 9,916 notes issued
by 1,365 banks. Counterfeiting was big business.[10] The frontier needed cash,
and quality was a secondary concern.

The good money in the form of banking reserves tended to congregate
in New York, and by the end of the nineteenth century some 75 percent of
the country's reserves were held by that city's six largest banks.[11] A number
of legislators and presidents, including Thomas Jefferson, Andrew Jackson,
Martin Van Buren, and Abraham Lincoln, attempted to limit what Van
Buren referred to as the "money power." Jackson famously remarking that
if left unchecked it would be "more formidable and dangerous than the
naval and military power of the enemy."[12] In 1862, in the middle of the
American Civil War, President Lincoln signed into law the first Legal Tender Act, which authorized United States notes as legal tender. These paper
notes, which soon became known as greenbacks, were not backed by gold
or silver, did not add to the national debt, and did not earn interest, but
could be used for any transaction apart from paying custom duties. As
Lincoln told the Senate in 1865, just a few weeks before being assassinated
(and conspiracy theorists have long seen a connection): "The government
should create, issue and circulate all the currency and credit needed to
satisfy the spending power of the government and the buying power of
the consumers. . . . Money will cease to be master and become servant of
humanity. Democracy will rise superior to the money power."[13] A leading

advocate of the greenback program was the politician Benjamin Butler, who in 1869 told the House: "I stand here therefore for inconvertible paper money, the greenback which has fought our battles and saved our country. . . . I stand here for a currency by which the business transactions of 40 million people are safely and successfully done. . . . I stand for that money therefore which is by far the better agent and instrument of exchange of an enlightened and free people than gold or silver, the money alike of barbarian and despot."[14]

At its peak in 1878, the Greenback Labor Party, whose platform called for full-scale adoption of the paper currency, won more than 1 million votes.[15] Although the party was defeated and the greenbacks in circulation were gradually phased out (they remained legal tender as late as 1971), the issuance of money, which had long been the preserve of elites, was now a major topic of debate for the general public. William Jennings Bryan campaigned three times for president on a Populist platform that called for the end of the banking cartel. Part of his argument revolved around the wording of the Constitution, which gives the government the right to "coin money" and "regulate the value thereof"—but does not define what is meant by money. So here the answer to the question "What is money?" took on a rather important legal significance. In a famous speech in 1896, Bryan argued that "the right to coin money and issue money is a function of government. . . . Those who are opposed to this proposition tell us that the issue of paper money is a function of the bank and that the government ought to go out of the banking business. I stand with Jefferson rather than with them, and tell them, as he did, that the issue of money is a function of the government and that the banks should go out of the governing business."[16] (It has since been argued, so far unsuccessfully, that the U.S. government could issue a number of $1 trillion coins and pay off the national debt; most recently in 2013 during the debt ceiling debate when Republicans and Democrats could not agree on the issue of U.S. indebtedness and the Twitter hashtag #MintTheCoin became the rendezvous point of the idea's supporters.)

One consequence of the general suspicion of the "money power" was that there was no real central bank to act as the lender of last resort and general hub of the banking system until, after a number of financial crises such as the Panic of 1907, the Federal Reserve was set up with the cooperation of financiers in 1913.[17] Its dollar bills were similar in appearance to the greenback but, in the manner of Bank of England notes, represented a debt to the quasi-private Federal Reserve. Even then, the banking system

remained highly fragmented, and the first interstate bank was not established until 1976 in Maine. The history of banking in the United States
has therefore been chaotic, but that does not seem to have held back economic growth—perhaps because in a rapidly growing country, a degree of
flexibility, rather than anal control over the money supply (Freud associated our interest in gold with a baby's interest in feces),[18] are exactly what
you need.

In keeping with the opaque nature of modern monetary systems, the
Federal Reserve is confusingly named. No one wanted to call it the Bank of
the United States, because that would have sounded like a central bank, and
two of those had already been rejected. While the Fed is commonly assumed
to be part of the federal government, and certainly plays an important role
in governing the country's money supply, it is actually an independent not-
for-profit corporation consisting of twelve regional Federal Reserve banks,
each of which in turn is owned by a consortium of commercial banks. The
question of who actually "owns" the Fed is so complicated that it seems
to have no real answer, but it doesn't seem to be the people of the United
States.[19] It is one example of what Galbraith called the "deeper mystery"
that seems to be deliberately cultivated around the financial system. This
sense of intrigue is further heightened by the fact that policy decisions are
made in private meetings, with only limited minutes released three weeks
later, and by Delphic mutterings of the sort epitomized by former chairman
Alan Greenspan, who reportedly said at one point, "If I have made myself
clear then you have misunderstood me."[20] Efforts at transparency have
since increased somewhat, but as always with money, part of the aim is to
keep people guessing.

The Nixon Shock

Throughout this debate, the Newtonian gold standard remained in force
internationally. It was suspended at the onset of World War I, when countries abandoned it en masse to manage their balance of payments. From
then on, gold coinage mostly disappeared from use, but bullion still served
as a money object for central banks. In Britain, when Winston Churchill
decided as chancellor of the exchequer in 1925 to restore the gold standard to its prewar level, an overvaluation of about 10 percent, the resulting pay cuts led to a general strike.[21] Adherence to gold is also believed
to have exacerbated the Great Depression in the United States, since the

government could not boost money supply to stimulate the economy. In 1933, President Roosevelt tried to address this situation by mining a new source of gold—private citizens. With some exceptions, people were given three weeks to hand in all gold coins, bullion, and gold certificates (except for an allowance of $100 for things like jewelry) and were paid cash in return at the current rate. The gold was melted down, added to the gold reserves—the Fort Knox depository was built for the occasion—and used to back more paper money.

At the Bretton Woods conference held in July 1944, the U.S. dollar was set as a kind of reference currency. As discussed earlier, money has always been important in war, not just for paying the bills but also as a way for the victor to enjoy the spoils. In a watered-down version of the gold standard, exchange rates between currencies were fixed, and dollars earned through international trade could be redeemed for gold bars at a rate of $35 per ounce. This was highly advantageous to the United States because, like England in earlier times, it essentially controlled the world money supply. Its indebted allies had little say in the matter. Britain's representative, the economist John Maynard Keynes, argued for a new, truly global reference currency, but his proposal was blocked by the Americans.

In the early 1960s, though, the growing private market for gold began to show a tendency to lift the price above $35, in part because there was a shortage of gold to back the expansion in international trade but also because the U.S. government was printing money to fund its military programs. The largest of these was the Vietnam War, which had an estimated total cost of about $111 billion.[22] The Cold War was also a significant drain on the national budget. Even the Apollo space program was a sizable expense, with a total budget of about $24 billion.[23] It too could be considered a war expense, since its main aim was to develop missile technology and acquire a technological and psychological advantage over Russia. Rome had its far-flung colonies, America had the moon. So the dollar was losing its luster as a reserve currency—and gold was losing its status as a money object with a stable price.

Perhaps as a kind of warning, in 1963 the words "PAYABLE TO THE BEARER ON DEMAND" were removed from newly issued dollar notes, to be replaced with "IN GOD WE TRUST." In 1968, the economist Milton Friedman wrote a letter to Richard Nixon urging him to abandon Bretton Woods and let exchange rates be determined by markets.[24] The gold system finally collapsed completely on August 15, 1971, when Nixon unilaterally imposed wage and price controls and an import surcharge and halted the dollar's direct convertibility to gold—an event that became known as the "Nixon shock." As he told his TV audience on that day:

> We must protect the position of the American dollar as a pillar of monetary stability around the world. In the past 7 years, there has been an average of one international monetary crisis every year. . . . I have directed Secretary Connally to suspend temporarily the convertibility of the dollar into gold or other reserve assets, except in amounts and conditions determined to be in the interest of monetary stability and in the best interests of the United States. Now, what is this action—which is very technical—what does it mean for you? Let me lay to rest the bugaboo of what is called devaluation. If you want to buy a foreign car or take a trip abroad, market conditions may cause your dollar to buy slightly less. But if you are among the overwhelming majority of Americans who buy American-made products in America, your dollar will be worth just as much tomorrow as it is today. The effect of this action, in other words, will be to stabilize the dollar.[25]

By November of that year, the price of gold had reached $100. Soon after, the Bretton Woods currency system ended, and exchange rates between major currencies were allowed to float freely, unburdened by the effects of Newtonian gravity, like astronauts in space.

Money 5.0

The Nixon shock effectively transformed the dollar, and every other currency linked to it, into fiat money. In one of its magnetic reversals that happen only once or twice a millennium, money had completed a switch from being based on scarce supplies of metal to being based on the word of the state. However, because all the components of the machine were kept in place, it didn't appear from the outside as though anything had changed. Unlike John Law, Nixon had made sure that the bankers were onboard. And as Galbraith noted, language was carefully controlled: "Men did not speak of the final abandonment of the gold standard. Instead it was said that the gold window had been closed. No one could get much excited about the closing of a window."[26] So the new system was superficially the same as the old one. The only difference—which no one liked to draw attention to in case it harmed the stability of the dollar—was that now there was no connection to gold. There was still plenty of gold in the vaults of Fort Knox or the Federal Reserve, but in theory it had nothing to do with the monetary system. The Federal Reserve was not renamed the "Public–Private Non-reserve," which would have been more accurate, since the only "reserves" it can produce to back up its banknotes are bookkeeping credits on an electronic ledger.

Of course, these changes had repercussions (including inflation which climbed to 11 percent in 1974). As nervousness was growing about the dollar, the International Monetary Fund (IMF) decided in 1969 to create its own reserve asset, known as special drawing rights (SDRs), which were handed out to members in proportion to quotas. Initially an SDR was valued at 0.888671 gram of gold, but this too was abandoned in 1973, and since then its value has been computed with reference to a basket of major currencies. Since an SDR can be swapped for hard currencies, it provides liquidity to the global banking system, even if it can't be used to buy anything directly. As the IMF's deputy managing director Min Zhu put it, "They are fake money, but they are a kind of fake money that can be real money."[27] SDRs have since played a growing role in the global economy, especially following the Great Financial Crisis (GFC) of 2007/2008.

At the same time that money was losing its connection with precious metal, new forms of electronic money such as credit cards were emerging (box 5.2). The automated teller machine, or ATM, made it possible to use a bank card to withdraw money. In 1971, the NASDAQ was the first electronic stock market, allowing traders to buy and sell stocks using computers. The growth of this electronic system was enabled, and ensured, by the development of the Internet. It was only a matter of time before people were having their salaries deposited electronically, managing their finances online, and shopping at e-commerce outlets such as Amazon and eBay. Once again, money was going back to its virtual roots, as a score in a ledger, a digital record this time rather than cuneiforms.

All of this activity was dwarfed, however, by the massive growth in currency trading that occurred after currencies were free to float against one another. In one sense, currency trading is the most pure form of economic activity in that it only involves money—no actual goods change hands. It is unbounded by time zones or geographical location, is highly liquid and leveraged, and—like the financial equivalent of a superconductor—is mostly untroubled by regulatory friction or resistance. Average turnover on a typical *day* is now about $4 trillion, which compares to an annual world GDP of $71 trillion. Much of the trading is carried out by high-frequency automated

Box 5.2
Paying with Plastic

The first charge card, made out of cardboard, was introduced by Diners Club in 1950. The idea came to company founder Frank McNamara after he forgot his wallet while dining out in New York. The card allowed customers (mostly well-off businessmen) to purchase meals at the restaurants listed on the back and settle the bill at the end of the month. In 1961, Diners Club switched to a plastic card.

Competition arrived only in the late 1950s, when American Express launched its charge card, and the Bank of America introduced the BankAmericard (renamed Visa in 1977). This last was a credit card, which meant the debt could be rolled over with an interest charge. In the 1960s, Barclays Bank in the United Kingdom joined in with its Barclaycard, and the City Bank of New York came up with the Everything Card, later renamed MasterCard. American Express introduced its gold card, which was soon copied by other issuers, showing that gold still held psychological appeal at least. The list of participating outlets no longer fit on the cards. In Nigeria, a 2014 scheme to give every citizen an ID card with an embedded MasterCard debit card and share biometric data with the firm was protested by local groups that said the branding was similar to the branding of people during the nineteenth-century slave trade.*

Just as subatomic particles exert forces on each other by the exchange of transient, virtual particles, so shoppers exert forces on the economy using credit cards, which create pulses of virtual money that are annihilated when the monthly bill is paid. This virtual money adds up—the current total credit card debt in the United States amounts to more than $10 trillion. Processing the transactions is a complex task, and fees—which amount to 2 to 3 percent— are a major source of profit not just for the credit card companies, led by Visa and MasterCard, but for a range of intermediaries such as banks, payment processors, and clearinghouses.

*Patrick Jenkins and Tom Braithwaite, "New Platforms Vie to Take Finance to the Masses," *Financial Times*, January 29, 2015.

computer algorithms. This frenetic, twenty-four-hour, globalized activity is driven not so much by news or information but by the actions of other traders and investment firms that not only follow and react to one another but, as shown by a U.S. Department of Justice investigation, sometimes collude to rig prices.[28]

Because floating currencies are linked through the markets, which quickly exploit and remove any opportunity for arbitrage, a change in the exchange rate between any two currencies, say the yen and the dollar, is quickly reflected in other exchange rates, such as the yen versus the pound. However, the fact that currencies are linked in this way does not mean that they are driven to equilibrium, only that their motions are closely coupled, so shocks or fluctuations immediately propagate through the system. Rather than accurately reflecting economic "fundamentals," the market is mostly reacting to itself. This feedback means that, like turbulent flow, price changes are characterized by sudden spikes of intense volatility.

As in other financial makets, much trading in currencies is done not through spot transactions but through derivatives such as options (contracts to buy or sell at a particular date and price). As discussed in more detail later in the chapter, complex derivatives can be used to bet on anything from stock prices to mortgage defaults. The nominal value of all such derivatives—that is, the amount potentially at risk—has been estimated at $1.2 quadrillion.[29]

On the surface at least, central banks are still responsible for managing the money supply. According to the conventional picture, as discussed in box 4.2, the "fractional reserve" system means that deposits from the central bank are multiplied, through the private banking system, by an amount set by the reserve requirements.[30] However, as the Bank of England noted in a recent paper, this is misleading, because it makes it seem that the central bank initiates the process and is in total control of the money supply. In most countries, there is no formal reserve requirement, and banks are free to lend as much as they want. "In normal times," therefore, "the central bank does not fix the amount of money in circulation, nor is central bank money 'multiplied up' into more loans and deposits."[31] To back up their loans, banks do want to hold some central bank money, on which they pay interest at a rate set by what is known as the interbank interest rate—the rate at which banks lend to one another. The central bank controls this rate by, for example, using made-up funds to buy bonds on the open market from preferred suppliers—which adds reserve money to the system, thus making it cheaper—or by selling those bonds—which does the reverse. So money creation is the job of banks, and the central bank's main lever of control—apart from emergency measures such as quantitative easing—is limited to tinkering with the interbank interest rate.

As Adair Turner notes: "Economic textbooks and academic papers typically describe how banks take deposits from savers and lend the money on to borrowers. But as a description of what banks actually do this is severely inadequate. In fact they create credit money and purchasing power. The consequences of this are profound: the amount of private credit and money that they can create is potentially infinite."[32] In other words, while we usually think of the money for a bank's loans being generated by the deposits of its customers, that is really the wrong way around. Instead, the money in the system is created in the first place when the bank makes a loan. The money supply is therefore almost completely detached from the physical actions of minting coins or printing banknotes and is only indirectly influenced by government policy. In fact, in countries like the United States and the United Kingdom, currency in the tangible form of coins or notes makes up only around 3 percent of the total money supply.[33] Since the entire economy is funded by these interest-bearing loans, it has been estimated that about half the cost of everything we buy can be traced back to interest payments.[34] Turner adds: "To a quite striking extent, the role of banks in creating credit, money and purchasing power, was written out of the script of modern macro-economics." More on this in chapter 7.

Because this bookkeeping money is created when a loan is made to businesses or individuals, and destroyed when the loan is repaid, the money supply is like a bathtub full of water with both the tap on (money creation) and the plug out (money destruction). The amount a bank can lend is limited by the interest rate it needs to pay the central bank for reserves and regulations that loosely tie it to government policy, but the real source of money is not the government but private banks. The government has to borrow money from a central bank and pay interest on the loan like everyone else. This helps counteract the impulse to print money with abandon, but as discussed later it is a rather expensive approach. Even were the government to run a surplus, it cannot pay off the debt, because it is exactly those securities that back the debt and therefore the money supply.

Governments are therefore *supposed* to be in deficit, as neochartalists such as L. Randall Wray point out, because they need to supply citizens with money (which puts the lie to austerity politicians who compare national budgets with household budgets).[35] It is hard to grow the economy if there isn't enough money in circulation to buy more goods and services.[36] And if the government does not borrow the extra money by issuing bonds, then it has to come from somewhere else—the private sector or other countries—and usually at a higher rate of interest. So there is always a trade-off between public and private borrowing. Of course, this is not to say that governments should attempt to artificially boost GDP by borrowing even *more* money—debt helps to fuel short-term growth but is not in itself sufficient for long-term growth, because what counts in the end is how the money is used.

Since the dollar is the global reserve currency, the United States also has to run a trade deficit to supply currency to the rest of the world. As Federal Reserve governor Marriner Eccles explained to Congress in 1941, "If there were no debts in our money system, there wouldn't be any money."[37] Whether the country needs quite so much debt is less obvious: since the Nixon shock in 1971, its credit card has developed an impressive balance, with the ratio of federal debt to GDP roughly tripling from 35 percent to 103 percent. Private debt, which is of greater concern (as will be discussed in chapter 7), has followed a similar trajectory, going from 144 percent to 367 percent of GDP.[38]

Aftershock

Of course, these developments that began in the 1970s did raise the question: If the U.S. dollar, which was still the main reserve currency for the global economy, was not backed by gold, then what was it backed by? Perhaps it was backed by the seal (or electronic equivalent) of the government. But if governments were now free in principle to produce as much electronic money as they wanted, and only had indirect control over the money supply anyway, then how much was the seal worth?

One alternative was to say it was backed with oil instead of gold, which is essentially what happened in the early 1970s when OPEC countries agreed to price their product in dollars. The fact that countries needed dollar reserves to pay their fuel bills certainly supported the currency; but the value of oil is a slippery quantity that lacks the reassuring (if largely psychological) stability of precious metal. Or perhaps dollars were backed by military force—which would help to explain all those U.S. military bases in far-flung destinations around the world.

Today, the term "virtual currency" is usually reserved for cybercurrencies, but (and this hasn't quite sunk in yet) even traditional forms of money such as the U.S. dollar have now gone virtual. This was illustrated in a 60 Minutes interview with Ben Bernanke in 2009. When asked whether it was "tax money that the Fed is spending," Bernanke replied: "It's not tax money . . . we simply use the computer to mark up the size of the account."[39] No wonder personal and sovereign debt in many rich countries is at record highs, when money itself has lost any sense of tangible reality. Just as music lovers are rediscovering the tactile experience of playing vinyl records, and studies show that we recall text better when it is read from a physical book than a screen, so money seems less real when it exists only on a computer and payments are made using contactless terminals. It seems bizarre to think that less than a century ago gold and silver coins were a regular part of everyday commerce.

In the 1990s, the trend toward virtualization accelerated with the spread of complex new financial derivatives such as the credit default swap (CDS) and collateralized debt obligation (CDO). The CDO allowed banks and financial intermediaries to bundle up large numbers of loans, such as mortgages, and divide them up into tranches with different risk levels. The CDOs could then be sold off to other institutions, so a mortgage on a house in California might be held by a bank in Germany. Mortgages were no longer an arrangement between a person and his or her local bank but were a commodity that was passed between a large number of brokers and intermediaries. The CDS, meanwhile, was a kind of insurance against default. If a bank lent a company some money, then the bank could insure its loan by taking out a CDS. Alternatively, it could take out a CDS as a bet that another company would go bust. These derivatives were traded over the counter rather than in public exchanges, so there was little transparency. A consequence of these developments was that banks had many ways to reduce their perceived exposure to risk. This meant they could lend out even more money, boosting the money supply in a manner very similar to John Law's scheme in eighteenth-century France. And like Law's scheme, it revealed one of the dangers in virtual money, which is that its validity rests on the authority and stability of its issuer—and private banks proved to be no better equipped for this role than was the French monarchy.

While financial innovations had appeared to reduce risk, all they had done was to conceal it, by making the system more complicated and opaque.[40] And instead of helping to safeguard the value of the currency as at the start of the gold standard, the private-banking sector had been using it for rampant and uncontrolled speculation. The collapse of these schemes meant that the banks had to be rescued by the public sector. In the United States, 4.5 percent of GDP was spent on recapitalizing banks, an amount almost equivalent to its massive defense budget. The United Kingdom spent 8.8 percent, and Ireland 40 percent (about eighty times its defense budget). This went rather beyond Walter Bagehot's idea of the lender as last resort, since the problem was not one of bank liquidity but of solvency—the loans were no good. The Bank of England's public–private template made sense when the private sector supported the credit of the state but not when it needed to be *rescued* by the state during the Great Financial Crisis.

The GFC can be seen as a kind of delayed aftershock from the Nixon shock, and the reverberations continue to the present day. Money had switched to a virtual phase, and—surprised by its new power—the first thing it did was blow up a giant multidecade global credit bubble, which the crisis only partly deflated. Just as the GFC revealed problems in the fiat currency system, it also exposed the flaws in our economic theories of the financial system. Risk models used by credit-rating agencies to price instruments such as CDOs were based on the "gold standard" theories of neoclassical economics, which assumed that price changes were random perturbations to an underlying equilibrium. They therefore failed to take into account the unstable nature of the monetary system or the possibility of a general financial crash (when equilibrium is not a useful concept). As discussed further in chapter 6, the implications were felt especially keenly in the eurozone, where the fledgling euro currency proved to be both an asset and a liability.

Transmoney

To summarize the story so far: money objects, like quantum particles, have two contradictory aspects. There is the abstract "heads" of virtual money, which the Greeks associated with the male principle, and the embodied, female-principle "tails" of physical wealth. Money gains its power by binding these two sides together, but the union is unstable and at times fractious. This is shown by the evolution of money, which can be viewed as a series of flip-flops between virtual and physical money, with one becoming dominant only to yield to the other. By necessity, this is a broad-strokes history that concentrates on mainstream Western currencies; however, we believe it is the one that best explains how the international finance system reached its current state. Today, currencies such as the dollar and pound, with their Federal Reserve and Old Lady of Threadneedle Street, are in a state of transition. They retain many of the trappings and pretensions of their old scarcity-based, gold standard versions, but in fact are completely virtual. They are male-principle virtual currencies dressed up as female-principle physical currencies—money in drag. Cybercurrencies, meanwhile, have shed their associations with either physical matter or government authority; and the head–tail duality has merged into a string of os and 1s. Like a coin flip in outer space, it no longer makes sense to say that one side is up.

The dual nature of money is profoundly connected to Greek ideas about gender; in particular, as Jack Weatherford notes, "from very early classical times, money showed a close relationship to the divine and to the female."[41] The goddess Juno Moneta, from whom the name derives, was the protector of women and family (*moneta* is from the Latin *monere* [to warn], because it was said that the honking of the sacred geese around the goddess's temple in Rome warned the city of a night attack by the Gauls). The denarius was originally minted in her temple and bore her name and image. Interestingly, though, the gender aspect of money (which again refers to traditional designations based on Greek duality) appears to be out of phase with the rest of society, in that the use of what we have termed "female" currencies corresponds to periods when women were particularly oppressed. The role of money is therefore like a shadow version or negative reflection of social values.

The adoption of gold and silver as money, rather than ornaments for women, in ancient Greece took place at a point in history when patriarchy— and especially warfare—was in the ascendant.[42] One of the slogans at the temple of Delphi was "Keep women under rule." According to Xenophon, "It is better for a woman to stay inside the house, and not show herself at the door." During the virtual currency period of the Middle Ages, particularly the twelfth and thirteenth centuries, the role of women in the economy expanded to include crafts such as spinning, baking, brewing, and so on, and the Virgin Mary was as important a symbolic figure in Christianity as was Jesus. Nearly all cathedrals built at the time, such as Notre-Dame in Paris, were dedicated to Mary. The switch to coin in the sixteenth century coincided with the peak number of witch hunts in Europe—an extraordinary period of repression that can be seen as a backlash against the growing power of women. Conversely, the birth of our latest version of "male" credit money in the early 1970s coincided with that of the women's liberation movement.[43]

The psychology of money, it seems, has much to do with our attitude toward femininity. For example, it is often said that market behavior is driven by the twin emotions of greed and fear. These responses both shape and are programmed by our scarcity-based money system. But while they have been treated as normal by economists—the English economist Lionel Robbins even defined economics in 1935 as "the science of scarcity"—psychologists might argue that there is something else going on. In his book

The Mystery of Money, Bernard Lietaer points out that this fear, which affects so much of our economic life, is related to our repression of the life-giving abundance of the feminine principle.[44]

Indeed, it is ironic that the bloodthirsty, hypermasculine conquistadors were driven by their obsession for a shiny metal that has traditionally been valued because it looks pretty on women. Or that perhaps the most famous financial crash in history, the Dutch tulip crisis, was about men betting on the price of flowers. Even the subprime crisis, in which the vast majority of financial players were male, had its roots in the domestic, traditionally female realm of people's homes. Perhaps this inverse correspondence isn't so surprising, since the desire to possess gold bears resemblance to the desire for sexual possession. (Gold is usually identified as a "hard" or "yang" currency, but this is based on the behavior of the people who use it rather than the money itself—we would argue that this softest of metals is yin, but has a way of bringing out the yang.)[45] Viewed this way, the gold standard begins to seem related to a rather strict attitude toward female sexuality, which may explain its popularity among certain types of social conservatives—an extreme case being the Islamic State.[46] The Grexit crisis in 2015 at times resembled a marital dispute, with advocates of the euro comparing its strict gold-inspired rules to the public declaration of wedding vows.[47]

The question of what gives money its value is therefore almost as mysterious as the question of what makes a person attractive or a marriage stable. Gold has value not because of its industrial uses, which are limited, or even its beauty, but because people think it will *remain* valuable. It is a statement about future attractiveness, based on extrapolation from the past, and the fact that supplies are finite. In our era of virtual money and cyber-currencies, perhaps the closest thing to gold is Bitcoin. The future supply of bitcoins, as discussed in chapter 9, is strictly limited to a cap of 21 million; for comparison, the total amount of mined gold in the world is estimated to be about 6 billion ounces. Like gold, bitcoins offer a degree of anonymity and are hard to trace. Of course, bitcoins exist only on computers, don't have a track record stretching back millennia, and lack the pleasingly physical presence of gold—but at least they are easier to transport. Bitcoin is gold in a virtual world.

Most central bankers (former and current) would hesitate to describe bitcoins as real money. Alan Greenspan recently described the entire Bitcoin phenomenon as a "bubble." The People's Bank of China concurred that it isn't a currency with "real meaning" and backed up that statement by banning financial companies from making Bitcoin transactions. But central banks don't like gold much either, vastly preferring paper notes with their own messages and numbers stamped on them. The main problem with modern currencies is not that they are insufficiently "real" but that they are not true to their own nature.

For fiat "let there be cash" currencies, an important part of their "meaning" is the story that surrounds them. The U.S. dollar, the British pound, the euro, the yuan, all carry with them, and are supported by, associations about their countries and their economic systems. And as always, power is at the heart of the matter, because money's validity—which is always fragile and liable to evaporate—relies on the authority of its issuers. Conversely, the ability to coin a region's dominant currency is itself a source of great power. If money is the thing that imposes number on the world, then the first question is "Whose numbers, and in what units?" That is the topic we turn to next.

6

The Money Power

What is it that causes most conflict at every level of social interaction, from the family, to the village, up to the management of the city, the state or international organizations? It is the control of money. . . . Who gets to spend it and under what constraints.

SUSAN STRANGE, "WHAT THEORY?
THE THEORY IN *MAD MONEY*"

Money is the crowbar of power.

FRIEDRICH NIETZSCHE, *THUS SPOKE ZARATHUSTRA*

If money were just an intermediary for barter, then messy issues such as power and politics wouldn't come into the analysis. But this chapter shows that power and money are entwined at every stage—and particularly at the moment when currency is issued. Money does not exist in some abstract space, removed from the concerns of the world, but is highly political. We explore the complex relationship between money and power, show why the two seem so inseparable, and consider the dynamics between major currencies as they face off against one another on the world economic stage.

After being awarded a Nobel Prize in 1921 for his work on the basic properties of radiation, which he carried out at McGill University with Ernest Rutherford, the English chemist Frederick Soddy decided to switch fields. From then on, he devoted himself to economics, his theories of money, and the need for what he called a "radical restructuring of global monetary relationships." One of the first to foresee the development of nuclear weapons, he was motivated by his belief that only such a restructuring could prevent their eventual use. In his book *Wealth, Virtual Wealth, and Debt* (written three years before the Wall Street crash), Soddy argued that many economic problems of the sort that lead to social conflict—including crashes—are created by the confusion between real wealth and virtual wealth, by which he meant bank money.

Real wealth, according to Soddy, can be calculated by adding up the values of objects. To use one of his examples, a farmer might have two pigs, which is twice as good as having one pig. Paper money, in contrast, has no value in itself, but only represents a debt, so it is a negative quantity that does not exist in the real world. As Soddy patiently explained, "The positive physical quantity, two pigs, is something anyone may see with their own eyes. It is impossible to see minus two pigs. The least number of pigs that can be physically dealt with is zero."[1]

According to Soddy, "The Virtual Wealth of a community is not a physical but an imaginary negative wealth quantity. It does not obey the laws of conservation, but is of psychological origin." What we consider to be wealth, in other words, is actually a kind of fragile group illusion that can be shattered at any time. Soddy argued that, under fractional reserve banking, the stock of virtual wealth balloons with time and soon exceeds real wealth. During a crisis, people want to swap virtual wealth for the real thing and cash in their chips; but because virtual wealth is bigger than the real wealth, this can't happen. In the absence of inflation, the only remedy is wealth destruction through stock market collapses, housing crashes, bankruptcies, foreclosures, bond defaults, forced taxation, and so on, possibly leading to social unrest or worse.

Soddy's concerns about the instability of the financial system and the societal risks of collapse were not welcomed or recognized by economists who saw him as a crank, but were borne out by the Great Depression, the rise of Nazism in Germany, World War II, and the use he had foreseen of nuclear weapons. And the tension between virtual and real wealth, which as discussed in chapter 2 is not just a symptom of an unbalanced economy but is intrinsic to all forms of money, has not eased since. In 2014, according to a study by the McKinsey Global Institute, global debt reached the heady heights of $199 trillion, up by $57 trillion in the seven years following the most recent crisis.[2] For perspective, that is almost three times the total capitalization of the world's stock markets, or twenty-five times the value of the world's above-ground gold supply. The Chinese "growth miracle" has been fueled by a quadrupling of debt since 2007, half of it related to real estate.

But what debt gives, it can later take away, and the ability to borrow our way forward seems to be coming to an end. As financial manager

Bill Gross notes, we "issued one giant credit card for the past 30 years. Now the bill is coming due."[3] According to the IMF's Global Financial Stability Reports, ultra-loose monetary policy following the crisis has encouraged excessive risk taking and the rapid credit growth that caused the collapse in first place.[4] Is the power of money once again going to blow up in our face?

Stable Money

The economy is infused with power relationships. As Norbert Häring and Niall Douglas wrote in their book *Economists and the Powerful*, there is "the power to abuse informational advantage, the power to give or withhold credit, the power to charge customers more than it costs you to produce, and the power to change the institutional setting to your advantage. There is the power of the corporate elite to manipulate their own pay and to cook the books, the power of rating agencies to issue self-fulfilling prophecies, the power of governments to manipulate the yardsticks that voters are offered to judge their economic policies."[5]

It may therefore be surprising that "all these types of power, which were important in bringing about the global financial crisis, are defined away by standard assumptions of most mainstream economic models. These models feature perfect competition, efficient financial markets, full information and eternal equilibrium." The economists M. Neil Browne and J. Kevin Quinn have similarly noted what they call the "almost complete absence of power from the toolkit employed by mainstream economists." In a survey they performed of sixteen introductory textbooks, they found a total of zero pages dealing with topics directly related to power.[6] We explore this curious power vacuum at the heart of economics—which is matched by an equal lack of interest in money—in chapter 7. But here we consider what Soddy identified as the greatest form of economic power: the power to issue money.

Money objects such as coins are created by an authority forcing a stamp onto a physical thing and calling it money. The power that binds the virtual with the real, and thus attaches numbers to the world, is therefore the power of the authority. The stamp on coins and the decorations on banknotes has always served as an impressive display of power and order— from the lion on the coins in ancient Lydia to the profiles of Roman emperors to the images of saints on medieval coins to the all-seeing eye on U.S. dollar bills (box 6.1).

Box 6.1

The Eye of Providence

The idea that the economy is inherently rational is captured by the all-seeing "eye of providence" that adorns the back of every bill. As Joseph Campbell noted, the United States was "the first nation that was ever established on the basis of reason instead of simply warfare," and the iconography of the bill showed how "the mind of man, cleansed of secondary and merely temporal concerns, beholds with the radiance of a cleansed mirror a reflection of the rational mind of God."[*] The design element was originally proposed in 1776 by the Swiss-born Pierre Eugene du Simitiere and was incorporated in 1782. Simitiere also came up with the idea for the U.S. motto *E pluribus unum* (Out of Many, One).

According to Iain McGilchrist, schizophrenic subjects also "often depict a detached observing eye in their paintings."[†] He sees this as evidence for the dominance of left-brained, objectifying thinking in such patients.

Somewhat worryingly in the age of Internet surveillance, the all-seeing eye was also adopted by the U.S. government's Information Awareness Office, which promised to track threats to national security by achieving something they called "total information awareness." The office was set up in 2002 but was defunded the next year. However, it is a warning that the tech-utopian vision of cybercurrencies, discussed in chapter 9, could easily turn into a dystopia, wherein every transaction is electronically tracked by an all-seeing, one-eyed state (though it would be an eye-opener if the books of governments and corporations became similarly visible).

[*]Joseph Campbell and Bill Moyers, *The Power of Myth* (New York: Doubleday, 1988), 31.

[†]Iain McGilchrist, *The Master and His Emissary: The Divided Brain and the Making of the Western World* (New Haven, Conn.: Yale University Press, 2009), 224.

Under the fractional reserve system, the power to issue money is largely delegated to private banks. Soddy saw the power of this private banking system as a direct challenge to the state. As he wrote in *The Role of Money*:

The "money power" which has been able to overshadow ostensibly responsible government, is not the power of the merely ultra-rich, but is nothing more nor less than a new technique designed to create and destroy money by adding and withdrawing figures in bank ledgers, without the slightest concern for the interests of the community or the real rôle that money ought to perform therein. . . . To allow it to become a source of revenues to private issuers is to create, first, a secret and illicit arm of the government and, last, a rival power strong enough ultimately to overthrow all other forms of government.[7]

Soddy was hardly alone in issuing such warnings. As mentioned in chapter 5, American politicians, including Abraham Lincoln, had long railed against the strength of the "money power." However, the money power has remained remarkably robust—even as the economy itself has been through wrenching changes.

When the Federal Reserve was founded, it was with the collaboration of American and European families of financiers, primarily the Morgans, Rockefellers, Kuhns, Loebs, and Warburgs.[8] At the time, the top representatives of the House of Morgan (a predecessor of JPMorgan Chase and Morgan Stanley), the First National Bank of New York (now part of Citibank), and the National City Bank of New York (acting in the Rockefellers' interests, now also part of Citibank) occupied 341 directorships in 112 corporations with resources exceeding the assessed value of all property in the 22 states and territories west of the Mississippi River.[9] While some of the names have changed in the past 100 years, the underlying power structure—and particularly the concentration of power in the world economy—has not. An analysis of 43,000 transnational corporations undertaken by a trio of complex systems theorists at the Swiss Federal Institute of Technology showed that 1 percent of the companies were able to control 40 percent of the network. This small group consisted mostly of financial institutions such as Barclays Bank, JP Morgan Chase, Merrill Lynch, and Goldman Sachs.

Note that the stability of the power structure does not translate into stability of the economy. The data set, which dated to 2007, included Lehman Brothers, which was ranked at number 34; and its collapse the next year, along with the subsequent domino effect that destabilized the global financial industry, graphically illustrated how complex and interdependent the system is. Thus, calls to break up those institutions deemed "too big to fail" were understandable. Instead though, the crisis—like many before—yielded the opposite result.[10]

In Great Britain, the financial sector was still an oligopoly, with the four biggest banks controlling some 75 percent of the retail banking market in 2013. This was a 10 percent increase from the precrisis levels that regulators criticized and were fighting for almost a decade. At the same time, the proportion of assets controlled by the six largest U.S. banks reached 67 percent, which means an increase of 37 percent from 2009 to 2014. The biggest bank in the nation, JP Morgan, has $2.4 trillion in assets, which equals the size of England's whole economy. (The original J. P. Morgan, who began his career during the American Civil War buying defective rifles from an arsenal and selling them back to the army at six times the price, would have been pleased.)[11] "They [the commercial banks] are still too big to fail, too big to jail, and too big to manage well," says Robert Reich, a Berkeley economics professor and former U.S. Secretary of Labor.[12]

Since at least the time of the Medicis, banks have been at the heart of the global financial system. Only banks are granted the unique power to produce money and then charge interest for it. The question then is whether one can expect a change without a crisis that would really shake the world. (The one of 2007 and beyond clearly did not.) Bloodless revolutions do occur but are quite rare; and here the possibilities for change are conditioned by the fact that the monetary and political power structures are so intertwined that they often resemble a single organism.

Big Politics of Big Money

The so-called revolving-door phenomenon, in which Wall Streeters end up with government jobs and vice versa, is often traced back to 1934, when President Franklin Delano Roosevelt appointed the former head of the Columbia Trust Bank, Joseph Kennedy, to be the first chairman of the Securities and Exchange Commission. Since then, many bankers have gone to work for the government and at the same time talented and well-connected bureaucrats have been hired by top banks. The most visible in this sense is Goldman Sachs, number 18 on the Federal Institute of Technology's list of companies that exercise huge global influence.

Sometimes dubbed "Government Sachs," Goldman is "a political organization masquerading as an investment bank," according to Christopher Whalen, the managing director of Institutional Risk Analytics.[13] While in the spotlight for quite some time, its visibility only increased during the crisis. Former Goldman executive Henry Paulson led the Treasury when the idea to bail out the big banks was formulated. Later on, Paulson appointed Goldman ex–vice president Neel Kashkari to oversee the $700 Troubled Asset Relief Program (TARP) fund, which was created to prop up financial institutions. For many, the climax came when the bank hired former

Securities and Exchange Commission chairman Arthur Levitt right when it was about to get $10 billion in TARP funds.

Under pressure from those that perceived these deeds—and in more general terms, banks and the entire power structure—as arrogant and ignorant of people's will, Goldman's chief executive Lloyd Blankfein stunned everyone when he said that he is merely a banker "doing God's work." This lack of empathy (or a misunderstood joke, as Blankfein later presented it) was supposed to defend the ways politicians and financiers were dealing with the crisis and, above all, to vindicate the highly controversial bonuses paid out to bank executives—including those at Goldman—that were getting massive government support.

Blankfein sees himself as "a relentless apostle of efficiency," explains Joris Luyendijk, an anthropologist who was hired by the *Guardian* to research bankers in London, adding that the city is full of these types.[14] They perceive themselves as teachers who have to discipline their pupils, who have to cause pain, because it is for the greater good, for the sake of the world as God intended it, says Luyendijk. Of course, the same conviction of uniqueness is exercised by many professionals, for instance representatives of political parties, and often for a good cause; however, the problem arises when those who are supposed to function as a counterweight—the government and its institutions in the case of bankers—share the same worldview or ideology and render the system of checks and balances void. The result is to reinforce groupthink, or in other words the belief that the way the current system operates, with finance at its very core, is natural and thus right.

Moreover, as an examination of the sector's expenditures shows, personal connections and like-mindedness are supported by intensive lobbying that aims at the general population and decision makers alike. According to the Bureau of Investigative Journalism, the City of London, fearing stricter regulation in the immediate aftermath of the financial crisis, spent £92.8 million lobbying government in 2011 alone. Its donations to the leading Conservatives totaled 51.4 percent of their funding. And at the same time, it could rely on the goodwill of 124 Lords (16 percent of the House of Lords) who have direct links to City firms. These statistics, as well as 800 full-time staff working and lobbying on behalf of the financial industry, led Andrew Simms of the New Economics Foundation to talk about "full-scale mobilization for an economic war."[15] One that, as box 6.2 indicates, the banks are winning.

The Center for Responsive Politics similarly scrutinized the financial industry's lobbying over the course of an entire decade. Its extensive research shows that the sector spent $5 billion on "political influence purchasing"

Box 6.2

The Success of City of London's Lobbying

Some of the more impressive examples of the bank lobby's influence over the British government include

- Slashing British corporation and overseas subsidiaries taxes following an intense lobbying campaign
- Blocking European legislation aimed at limiting commodity speculation through a strategy devised jointly in closed meetings between the Financial Services Authority and finance industry bodies
- Constraining a nationwide not-for-profit pension scheme that had the potential to benefit millions of low-paid workers
- Killing government plans for a new corporate super-watchdog to police quoted companies

Source: Nick Mathiason, Melanie Newman, and Maeve McClenaghan, "Revealed: The £93m Lobby Machine," July 9, 2012, Bureau of Investigative Journalism, www.thebureauinvestigates.com/2012/07/09/revealed-the-93m-city-lobby-machine/; Nick Mathiason and Melanie Newman, "Finance Industry's Multimillion-Pound Lobbying Budget Revealed," *Guardian*, July 9, 2012.

---

from 1998 to 2008. Some $3.3 billion ended up in the pockets of officially registered lobbyists; $1.7 was then spent on campaign contributions. Goldman Sachs, for instance, spent $46 million (still less than Citigroup at $108 million or Merrill Lynch at $68 million).[16]

As Luyendijk says, these numbers only prove that the Anglo-Saxon model involves legal corruption. While this is called campaign contributions in the United States and Great Britain, it would be labeled corruption should it happen in developing countries, argues Luyendijk, adding that the financial lobby manages to steer attention away from crucial issues. Thus we argue about the financial transaction tax while the way money is created and distributed—and the structural power that comes with it—remains largely ignored by those who can change the order of things peacefully—politicians.

As finance became globalized, the "money power" became increasingly international. Monetary arrangements consisting of a powerful state and a powerful financial industry could suddenly exercise influence across borders. Money thus became de facto one of the weapons of choice for twenty-first-century warfare. Ian Bremmer, president of Eurasia Group, the world's largest political risk consultancy, considers the weaponization of finance (i.e., creative use of access to capital markets or sanctions that deprive a country of foreign funds, among other things) to be a top political risk.[17] Global and regional financial behemoths are able to change the direction of entire economies, both intentionally and accidentally. Central and eastern Europe learned this the hard way at the beginning of the GFC. The foreign headquarters of banks that have near monopoly in most of these countries all but stopped lending in order to build capital reserves for potential losses in the West, with the result that the crisis in the East came faster and was deeper than necessary.

This illustrates how the current setup benefits a group of powerful states and financial corporations that on a structural level have tight connections and a common interest to preserve the status quo they underwrite. Being in charge, they can "discipline," to parallel Luyendijk's terminology, individuals as well as states that "misbehave." This can be for better, meaning for the sake of momentary order that enables coexistence, or for worse.

It is thus no wonder that experts such as Albrecht Ritschl at the London School of Economics predict that the next global crisis may be caused by speculative attacks on states.[18] Given that the late global power structure is breaking down, with no agreed framework or global-policing agency, attacks launched by sovereigns, corporations, or interest groups simply cannot be excluded. Money may not seem like much of a weapon, but as Soddy knew, it contains within its bonds more power than any number of thermonuclear devices.

The Rise and Fall of the Dollar Empire

The battle for supremacy between the world's mega-currencies, which shows the money power in full display, is reminiscent of the battle between rival empires that characterized the gold standard era—with the difference that in a virtual currency era, strength can be a form of weakness and vice versa. Consider, for example, that (mostly) virtual cybercurrency, the U.S. dollar. If money is "like any other language through which people communicate," as American author Kent Nerburn says, the greenback has to be considered lingua franca. Along with English—which only reconfirms the overarching influence of the Anglo-Saxon culture—it is understood almost universally.

The U.S. dollar is the ultimate choice for central bankers shopping for reserves, despite dropping from 70 percent of total share in the year 2000 to a 61 percent share at the beginning of 2014.[19] At the same time, it is the world's most used currency in international trade and finance and a currency in which key commodities such as oil are overwhelmingly priced. Whether one is a backpacker looking for a warm bed and meal in a remote corner of our planet or a high-flying businessperson negotiating a mega-deal in one of its financial centers, one can rely on the greenback. This holds despite all the tricks Washington has played on both.

Historically, those who issue money tend to abandon their promises to uphold the value of these IOUs when it suits them to do so. Ancient Romans, for instance, kept adding an ever-smaller amount of silver into their coins, with the eventual result that people lost faith in Roman money and, by extension, the empire. The United States is following a path that is strikingly similar. Since the establishment of the Fed in 1913, the dollar has lost 96 percent of its value. Measured against the currencies of U.S. trading partners, it lost 25 percent of its value since the floating system was introduced after the shock of 1971 (though it made an impressive comeback in 2015). In this context, it seems all the more relevant that currencies have held onto their prime positions for approximately a century since 1450; the dollar has been in charge for ninety-four years.[20]

Rome, concluded fifth-century Christian priest Salvian of Marseille, collapsed because it deserved to collapse; because it had denied the first premise of a good government, which is justice to the people.[21] Sixteen centuries later, the same goes for the United States, as both foreign and domestic critics of American policies argue. They point out that Americans have seen their savings inflate away, making the greenback fail to deliver on the promise that currencies store value. The international community, as described earlier, has seen Washington taking advantage of the fact that it owns the Fed—a world bank—and controls the World Bank that globally promotes the gospel of neoclassical economics and thus reinforces the status quo.

It was the possession of the printing press of the world currency that enabled Nixon to shock the globe in 1971. As political economist Susan Strange put it, "The U.S. government was [thus] exercising the unconstrained right to print money that others could not (save at unacceptable cost) refuse to accept as payments."[22] And it is because of this very possession—along with the belief that there is no alternative—that the dollar remains the most important currency, despite the gradual loss of value, which reached its climax at the beginning of the financial crisis in 2007, and despite the rhetoric that was flying high even before the implosion of the U.S. real estate market and became even fiercer thereafter. Russian president Vladimir Putin, for instance, has characterized Americans as "living like parasites off the global economy and their monopoly of the dollar"; both Brazil's finance minister Guido Mantega and Indian prime minister Manmohan Singh mentioned the currency wars and the United States in the same sentence; and other more or less respected leaders have chimed in. They all called for a rearrangement of the global monetary order in a way that would correspond with reality and not the distribution of powers in the immediate aftermath of World War II.

Such calls should not be expected to yield results any time soon. First, the United States will most certainly do all it can to preserve its privileged position for as long as possible, as discussions with China about the strengthening of the role of SDRs within the global structure reconfirmed.[23] Second, monetary regimes and their particularities tend to have a rather robust momentum, as shown by the overweight role of the British pound within the current structure. Third and foremost, currencies need to be backed by sovereigns that appear strong, stable, and predictable enough to uphold their promise to preserve (at least some of) the value of the currencies.

When it comes to credibility, the intangible quality that decides how much the currency is really worth (meaning whether its face value or the currency itself is accepted), the United States still enjoys a relatively strong position compared with its (potential) challengers: given the size of the global economy and the resulting demands made on its principal currency, the moneys of smaller powers such as Australia, Switzerland, and Canada will not suffice. That leaves the world with the euro, which is dealing with its childhood diseases, and the yuan, which is not even at that stage. Thus, "the dollar may be our currency but it's your problem," claim made by Nixon's Treasury secretary John Connally rings true for now and the near future.

Yuan: Power Within, Power Without

Beijing commands the second-largest economy in terms of nominal GDP and purchasing power parity, and might be number one by the time this book is published.[24] This would be only a natural climax of thirty years of growth that averaged 10 percent a year and made it the fastest-growing major economy. Yet while China is both the world's largest importer of many key commodities and the world's largest exporter of manufactured products, the yuan only came to officially play a role in its international dealings in 2008. The reason? Chinese growth had relied on boosting exports by keeping the yuan undervalued, which in turned caused a significant inflow of the globe's prime currency—the U.S. dollar.

When Chinese manufacturers sell American consumers their goods, the dollars received are converted to yuans (through intermediary banks) by the People's Bank of China. Because China sells more products to America than vice versa, the result is that the central bank ends up with a surplus of dollars and a shortage of yuans. In a freely floating currency, the normal action would be for it to sell those excess dollars for yuans on the foreign exchange markets, thus lifting the yuan and narrowing the trade gap. But instead, the bank has used the dollars to buy U.S. Treasuries and has acquired the yuans it needs to pay the manufacturers by creating them. The central bank can therefore control the exchange rate, rather than leaving it in the hands of the foreign exchange markets. Another side effect is that the demand for Treasuries has kept U.S. interest rates low (though China sold some of those Treasuries in 2015 in order to defend the yuan against a resurgent U.S. dollar).

One danger is that the printing of yuans could lead to inflation. However, as when China imported massive amounts of silver from Spain in the sixteenth century, the rapidly growing economy has meant that the excess flows are absorbed (though note the expanding credit bubble in things like real estate).[25] Another flaw in the strategy became apparent in 2007, when Beijing's holding of $1.5 trillion of U.S. financial assets, including the disastrously overleveraged Fannie Mae and Freddie Mac, proved a rather disappointing investment. (The two institutions, which were to support stable funding for the housing and mortgage markets, proved to be a black hole that Washington was forced to fill with the total cost to the parties involved yet to be determined.) This was a wake-up call for the Chinese, who became "obsessed" with the extent of their national power vis-à-vis the other great powers in the mid-noughties.[26]

In 2008, Chinese president Hu Jintao called for "a new international financial order that is fair, just, inclusive, and orderly." Shortly afterward, Beijing started encouraging the use of its currency in trade, swap arrangements, bank deposits, and bond issuances in Hong Kong, which became the yuan's prime offshore center.[27] China thus began to address the mismatch between the fact that it is a power that can afford to violate the global rules when it comes to foreign trade but is in a far less comfortable position when it comes to the monetary issues that power that trade.

The question now is how quickly will Beijing be able and willing to come out from behind the U.S. dollar and bring its currency onto the global stage. Some economists such as Arvind Subramanian, the chief economic adviser to the government of India, claim that the yuan "could become the premier reserve currency by the end of this decade, or early next decade."[28] Subramanian and others usually cite rapid expansion in areas such as international trade, where the value of cross-border transactions in yuans totaled $78 billion in 2010, the first full year these were allowed. In 2014, Deutsche Bank expected this number to reach $988 billion, which would represent 50 percent year-on-year growth and would amount to 20 percent of China's global trade volume.[29] Moreover, the yuan surpassed the euro to become the second-most-used currency in international trade and finance in October 2013.[30] In November 2015, the IMF decided to add it to its SDR basket of reserve currencies, where it joins the dollar, euro, pound, and yen. However, despite these milestones, most economists and political economists argue for a more distant horizon.

Beijing has already encouraged domestic exporters and foreign exporters to China to price in yuans, University of California professor Barry Eichengreen notes. But to become truly internationalized, the Chinese currency needs to enjoy a stable and transparent institutional arrangement that international investors will trust, Eichengreen continues, adding that the final step will be to encourage—or convince—central banks to hold reserves in yuans. It is the second step, having the Chinese currency adhere to the code of conduct of global markets, including for it to float, that many experts believe may prove difficult for Beijing to accept.

The Chinese had long resisted U.S. pressure to revalue their currency—or more generally to allow the market to determine its value—letting everybody know that they would deal with it on their own terms. Besides having a rather symbolic dimension, this stance also reflects the long-held conviction, reminiscent of the mercantilist era in Europe, that an economy driven by exporters needs the institution of an undervalued currency. And while the crisis of 2007 and beyond pointed out the flip side of this model, a weaker yuan still yields a clear short-term benefit given the ongoing turbulences on the global stage and the jump-started reform of the Chinese economy. Moreover, in the battle between those who advocate fast internationalization of the currency and those who oppose it, political clout is evident within the former group that consists, among others, of state-owned banks and politically connected borrowers and exporters.[31]

China "is leading the charge toward the next monetary order," as global strategist Parag Khanna suggests, but this next arrangement is not expected to revolve around the yuan or any other national currency.[32] Instead, Beijing seems to be aiming for a multilateral arrangement that would prove more stable than the current dollar-centered world—and that may serve as a transitory period on the way to the next monetary order. This is why China brought back the idea of the SDRs, and why it has been slowly divesting away from the dollar and has been buying gold as well as euros during the time when the eurozone crisis was far from over. While seemingly not in concert, these moves, in the short term, allow China to keep all doors open, to lessen the power Washington exercises vis-à-vis Beijing, and to utilize every opportunity to extend the reach of its own currency, all at the same time.

One complicating factor in this strategy is that any shift in policy, such as cutting back on U.S. Treasury purchases, could have destabilizing effects on the U.S. dollar and other currencies (the yuan is China's currency, but it could become America's problem). Another is China's need to dismantle its own debt bomb, a task that, as in other countries, may be for future generations. As a Chinese proverb puts it: "Father's debt, son to give back."

Euro Gold

The idea for a common European currency was first proposed at the League of Nations in 1929. After the long process of cultural and economic integration and convergence that followed World War II, it finally came to fruition on January 1, 1999, when eleven European countries, after appearing to satisfy convergence criteria on things such as inflation, interest rates, and government borrowing, officially adopted the euro. At first, exchange rates between currencies were fixed in terms of euros, which were purely virtual and existed only as digital assets in bank accounts. The first coins and notes were issued in 2002, replacing the legacy currencies, which were removed from circulation.

One of the architects of the euro was the Columbia economist Robert Mundell, who was awarded the Nobel Prize in Economics in 1999 for his work on the idea of an "optimal currency area." It wasn't clear that the new European Union met the optimality conditions, which related to things like high labor mobility and shared economic drivers, but to Mundell and other economists the euro's main attraction was that—like the gold standard—monetary constraints would impose fiscal discipline on politicians.[33]

Monetary unification also offered many advantages, such as elimination of the need for currency exchange and a strengthening of European identity. Society aligns itself with the field lines of money, so unifying the money is a way to promote political union as well. Germans did not like the idea of giving up their "flag . . . the fundament of our post-war reconstruction" as Chancellor Helmut Kohl called the D-mark, but representatives of other continental powers were more concerned with political goals such as "Europeanizing" Germany.[34] Europe's aim to enhance its might via economic and political unification acquired further momentum in the noughties when long-dormant developing powers made their impressive entrée onto the global stage. More countries lined up to join the union, with the latest entry being Lithuania in 2015.

The European Union has been described by political scientist John Ruggie as the world's "first truly postmodern international political form" because of the way in which, like a postmodern architect jumbling design elements and references, it reinvents classical concepts such as sovereignty and territoriality.[35] The designers of euro notes also took a postmodern approach. The front of the bills feature idealized representations of windows, doors, and archways in various historical styles. The reverse side shows structures such as bridges and viaducts. There are no human figures at all, perhaps to avoid offending anyone.

In spite of the theories describing hybridity—that is, the ability to extend multiple loyalties—as being common to (post-)modern women and men, it became clear with time that it would be hard to find something with which the mosaic of European nationals could identify.[36] This is even more true if the unifying object is as sensitive a subject matter as money—the ultimate measurement of one's well-being in our society. This partially explains the depth of the euro crisis that unfolded in the aftermath of the GFC, when the scale of the Greek, Irish, Spanish, Portuguese, and Italian problems—and the drawbacks of the euro itself—became clear.

There is a sense that, like an unconvincing example of a postmodern building, the whole euro project has been patched together from old currencies and gold standard–inspired ideas, retaining some parts but dispensing with others. And like the design of its notes, it leaves out the messy dynamics of people and democracy. The European Central Bank (ECB), for example, is unique in that it has no fiscal branch and no sovereign or powerful central government to back it up. Instead, these functions are handled at the national level. As economists, including L. Randall Wray, warned, this effectively means that member countries "operate fiscal policy in a foreign currency; deficit spending will require borrowing in that foreign currency."[37]

The euro is more flexible than the gold standard, because the central bank can adapt the money supply to tackle inflation or deflation. However, the gold standard had a safety valve in that countries could temporarily exit during emergencies. This is not easy with the euro, because the national currencies no longer exist, and resurrecting one would take several months. Perhaps the biggest difference between the two systems is that, as discussed in chapter 4, the gold standard had a stabilization mechanism—gold would tend to flow out of countries running a trade deficit, driving down wages and prices, while countries outside the core borrowed only at a premium. But in a financial world driven by private credit rather than finite stocks of metal, the dynamics are a little different—credit growth prior to the crisis in Greece, which was viewed as safe because it was in the eurozone, was considerably higher than in Germany.[38]

In 2012, it was widely assumed that the eurozone was on the brink of collapse, with Harvard professor Martin Feldstein proclaiming the euro to be "an experiment that failed."[39] The shock and awe that forced the market to backtrack on its skepticism has been epitomized by the now famous "whatever it takes" speech by ECB president Mario Draghi. Draghi reminded the world that there is a difference between an "*optimal* currency area" and what politicians and bureaucrats deem to be an area that *should* share a currency. While there might be a discrepancy between the two, the aim to construct and preserve the latter could prevail, at least momentarily, thanks to ECB ammunition. "Believe me, it will be enough," Draghi said. The power of money was in naked display during the 2015 negotiations between the European Union and Greece, when the European Union—in the face of its refusal to write off unpayable Greek debts—was accused of everything from attempted regime change to financial war on the Syriza government.[40] Most of the bailout money went to bailing out European banks, who needed to hold government bonds for regulatory purposes and had chosen Greek ones because of their higher yield.

Despite the euro's problems, it seems clear that it is not (just) Washington that will be calling the shots; and that it is not (just) the dollar that is going to be the lingua franca of global finance and trade. The rules of the game are being rewritten and none of the European countries alone are relevant enough to participate. And since the choices are either to be at the table or to be on the menu, the political will to hold the European Union together is expected to be strong.[41] The project of a common Europe—and the euro by an extension—shall therefore remain at the edge of the politician's sword for some time to come. Whether it will last as long as the gold standard is another question.

Us Versus Them, Our Money Versus Theirs

While on a reportage in Estonia in 2011, it became apparent to one of the authors of this book, Chlupatý, that the idea of belonging is as important as a common monetary arrangement with the major trading partner. Top politicians, foreign diplomats, and ordinary people considered accession to the eurozone to be yet another symbolic as well as strategic step to integrate the country deeper into Western structures and thus lessen the influence Russia, the former occupying power, extends over it. A shared currency, in other words, enables an emphasis of the "we" versus "them" distinction, indirectly confirming the premise of Benedict Anderson's "imagined communities" constructed around symbols people (more or less voluntarily) embrace.[42] Money is as much about soft power as about hard power.

The symbolic dimension of the euro was only reconfirmed in the course of the Ukrainian crisis. "It is very important for countries to stick together and with the European Union. We will be more integrated and protected in case of troubles, and we can see what is happening in Ukraine today . . . That is one reason why the Baltics and Finland were so eager to go to all institutions including NATO. It's not easy for small countries to deal with these issues; we need help," is how Latvian finance minister Andris Vilks explained why the monetary demarcation line is so important.[43] It then only follows that the Russians briskly made the ruble the only official currency in Crimea shortly after they gained control over it, labeling the Ukrainian hryvnia "a foreign tender."[44]

The Europeans and Russians thus mirrored what has become the norm on the ever-shifting stage of cross-border politics: in the same way Roman emperors used coins to communicate their victories and policies from the British Isles to Turkey, Brussels, and Moscow let their influence be known via legal tender. Historically, this could be as much an exercise of a power by a center as a matter of expediency for the periphery.

Both the West African CFA and the Central African CFA franc, for instance, are relics of colonialism (CFA stands for Communauté financière d'Afrique [African Financial Community]). Both were introduced mainly to facilitate trade with the colonies and had a fixed exchange rate to the French franc; once France joined the eurozone, the African francs became fixed to the euro. Such an arrangement, critics say, deprives fourteen countries with a combined population of 147.5 million inhabitants and a GDP of $166.6 billion of economic planning, since their monetary policies are effectively constructed in Frankfurt.[45] However, its proponents point out that the CFA (also) "helps stabilize national currencies of Franc Zone member-countries and greatly facilitates the flow of exports and imports between France and the member countries."[46]

It is this conundrum of sovereignty loss versus the promise of stability that comes with numbers that is at the core of common monetary arrangements. This is why in the early stages of the global crisis of 2007 and beyond the appetite to join the eurozone spiked even in the Czech Republic, Denmark, Iceland, and other countries where European structures—or the euro as such—were traditionally shown the cold shoulder. The feeling that a robust institution consisting of many economies can function as a shield was suddenly stronger than the sympathy for a national currency and what it represents. And while subsequent eurozone troubles resulted in a retreat into the national(istic) shell, it was an episode the world watched very carefully.

What some have dubbed the great European monetary experiment, while criticized, is considered a testing ground for the next step being mulled by many other regions.[47] Europe has its problems, but there is simply no other model to follow, as Tatiana Valovaya of the Euroasian Economic Commission (Putin's attempt to revive the Soviet Union) put it bluntly at the annual meeting of the European Bank for Reconstruction and Development (EBRD) in 2012. As the panel went on, the discussion only reconfirmed that the issues of any union are twofold: on the one hand, there is the theory of an optimal currency area that seems to explain the troubles being experienced by the heterogeneous economies of the eurozone; on the other hand, there is the political will and intent that could lead to the structural shift necessary for such an area to be created or at least approximated. The latter might have to do more with politics and strategic goals than with short- to mid-term economic realities.

In a world where the monetary order seems to be collapsing, efforts at stability are ever more pressing. This is why there are many plans to construct common monetary arrangements all around the world. "I think that the GCC [Gulf Cooperation Council] countries should benefit from the euro experience and continue with the GCC monetary union project without delay," Khalid Alkhater, director of research and monetary policy at the Qatar central bank, told Reuters in 2012.[48] And while the idea of a pan-Arab currency still seems far-fetched, it is being considered by the powers in the region. "A monetary union is a strategic long-term project for these countries, not only economically, but it should be also politically," explained Alkhater, adding that "the costs of not establishing it could be very high for the GCC countries . . . in the future."

It is the very same strategic concern, rooted in the uncertainty of what might come next on the global stage and the desire to deepen regional ties (which is related but not exclusive to the former), that is pushing or sustaining common monetary arrangements in many parts of the world. These are being discussed in Latin America (the Bolivarian Alternative for the Americas seems to be the furthest developed), in East Africa (shilling) and West Africa (the newly minted currency area should merge with the West African CFA), and even by some members of the Association of Southeast Asian Nations—Indonesia, Malaysia, the Philippines, Singapore, and Thailand—that perceive it as a possible hedge against a repetition of the 1997/1998 currency crisis. However, these are not the only regional—or pan-regional—monetary arrangements that are in motion today and that will influence how and with what people will be paying tomorrow.

Moneys Within, Moneys Without

Many economies formally or informally accept the moneys of established powers for the sake of stability and predictability for domestic households and businesses as well as for international trade and finance partners. The American dollar is thus used not only in insular areas such as Puerto Rico but also in Ecuador, El Salvador, and other Latin American states, where it has either replaced a fallen currency or created a parallel monetary universe that coexists with the official one. A great degree of dollarization can also be found in Asia and Africa, where the greenback is widely accepted by Michelin-starred restaurants and street vendors alike.

The same then goes for currencies of other first- and second-tier powers. The euro, for instance, seamlessly circulates through the veins of those EU economies that have yet to adopt it, such as the Czech Republic, and is in use in many non-EU countries in the region such as Serbia; the Chinese yuan is readily accepted by Nepalese or Cambodian vendors, while many

North Koreans consider it a hedge against the permanent instability of their own won;[49] the Indian rupee is widely used in Nepal; and the South African rand is one of the eight official currencies of Zimbabwe, which resembles a monetary laboratory after abandoning its own hyperinflated dollar in 2009.

The Zimbabwean case shows the elasticity of people and business when it comes to monetary arrangements. If Zimbabwe can deal with the U.S. dollar, yuan, euro, and rand, among other legal tenders, other countries can surely deal with multiple currencies, should this benefit their individual agents and the economy as a whole. The question remains whether there is the will to democratize the monetary regime(s) in an orderly manner, meaning before the implosion demands it, such as in Zimbabwe. We discuss the case for multiple currencies in chapter 8.

Clearly, the demand for new moneys and a regime that would safe-guard them is growing. First, this came as a direct response to the economic crisis of 2007 and beyond, when both finance and politics lost the trust of people and businesspeople alike. Second, this came as deepening regional integration, erosion of the late global order, and modern technologies, among other issues and trends, began to compromise the existing order and codes of conduct. This is why both preexisting and new alternatives are being discussed so passionately. The magnetic lines of the money force are reconfiguring into new patterns, and, as will be seen in chapters 8 and 9, the possibilities are not limited by the constraints of traditional currencies. The results, as always, will both shape and be shaped by the global power structure. In its role as a medium of exchange, money is a means of communication that builds ties and fosters collaboration. But its reliance on hard-edged number makes it both a formidable weapon and a potentially destructive and self-destructive force. Far from being passive, money has the power to reshape the world.

If there has been one dominant monetary theme since money went virtual in the 1970s, it is debt. Public or private, in developed countries or emerging markets, debt has been on a steady upward climb, nourished by an expanding financial sector and interrupted only briefly by the recent crisis. Never since the time of its invention have people become so familiar with the concept of negative numbers. In the United States, according to Pew, eight out of ten Americans carry debt, and seven out of ten said debt was a necessity in their lives, with mortgages the most common form, even though they preferred not to carry any debt.[50] Debt is the engine of economic growth, but its now-overpowering presence—for a Shanghai stock investor trading on margin, a Vancouver homeowner with a borrowed down payment, an American graduate saddled with a student loan and a car loan, an overleveraged hedge fund, or a bankrupt nation—has stretched the distance between debtors and creditors, the many and the few, to breaking point. The gap dividing money's two sides fills the financial air with a crackling electromagnetic tension; the loaded calm before the next storm.

Only to a completely linear mind-set, which sees money as neutral, debits as canceled by positive credits, and prices at stable equilibrium, could such levels of debt appear benign. So in the next chapter, we turn to another kind of power that is central to the topic of money—the power of economic ideas. We begin with the development of neoclassical economics in the Victorian era. This highly rational theory, with its emphasis on stability and efficiency, still forms the basis of the mainstream theory taught in universities today. It is also informative about our attitudes toward money—not for what it includes, but for what it leaves out. It might seem ridiculous, in our money-obsessed society, to say that we are as squeamish about money as the Victorians were about sex. But as we'll see, the subject of money has been sterilized to a point where it seems that we are in denial about its true nature.

7

Solid Gold Economics

In economics, money has traditionally been viewed as static, neutral, inert substance, rather like gold (which is an inert metal). Models of the economy don't usually include things like banks—which makes it hard to predict events such as banking crises. This chapter traces the development of economics from Adam Smith to the present day, asks where the money went, and shows how new ideas from areas such as complexity science and psychology are reshaping the field. The shift is from seeing the financial system as a kind of utility-optimizing machine, to seeing it as one part of a living system. Different forms of money are like biologically active agents that can work to help or hinder the health of the system. In the future, the new currencies discussed in the final chapters will play an important role in reconfiguring the economy.

Anthropologists say that a good way to understand a society is to listen to its myths. The central myths of economics are the stories, discussed in chapters 1 and 2, that money emerged naturally as a means for facilitating barter and is nothing more than a medium of exchange. While economists clearly agree that money is an intriguing subject and have produced a voluminous literature about it, one manifestation of these underlying beliefs is that money, as a thing in itself rather than an accounting metric, is largely excluded from macroeconomic models, which is one reason the GFC of 2007/2008 was not predicted (it involved money). To the general reader, untrained in the ways of orthodox economics, this will seem a remarkable situation. How can money be both central to economics and somehow excluded where it really counts? Why are its mysterious properties left unfathomed in both the textbooks presented to students and the models used by policy makers? Our aim in the first part of this chapter is not to give a survey of economic thought but to address these specific questions. The reason, as we'll see, is that mainstream economics is based on a belief set in which money can only be allowed a very limited and repressed role.

Beginning with Adam Smith—who is considered the founding father of economics—the aim of economists has been to build a kind of Newtonian cosmology for the economy, one that, as Thomas Pownall wrote to Smith in 1776, "might become Principia to the knowledge of political operations; as Mathematics are to Mechanics, Astronomy, and the other Sciences."[1] Just as we can compute the motion of the moon around the earth, so economists have attempted to model and predict interactions in the economy. The topic of money, however, was glossed over from the start.

In his *Wealth of Nations*, Smith first of all asserted that the value of money was determined only by its weight in precious metal, with the numerical stamp playing no role other than proof of inspection: "By the money-price of goods, it is to be observed, I understand always the quantity of pure gold or silver for which they are sold, without any regard to the denomination of the coin. Six shillings and eightpence, for example, in the time of Edward I, I consider as the same money-price with a pound sterling in the present times; because it contained, as nearly as we can judge, the same quantity of pure silver." So money is metal, a commodity like any other, and the denomination is not important. This approach was consistent with the story, discussed in chapter 1, that metal money emerged as a replacement for barter.

Smith then defined the exchange value of a good as being "equal to the quantity of labour which it enables [a person] to purchase or command." Just as John Locke associated property rights with the labor needed to obtain it, so Smith associated a property's value with the labor for which it could be swapped: "If among a nation of hunters, for example, it usually costs twice the labour to kill a beaver which it does to kill a deer, one beaver should naturally exchange for or be worth two deer." In a market economy, this value would be discovered by the quasi-spiritual "invisible hand" that was the centerpiece of Smith's theory (though the term was only later popularized by Paul Samuelson).[2] If the price (relative to other goods) were too high, more suppliers would enter the market, driving the price down; and conversely, if the price were too low, suppliers would cut back, thus restoring the price.

Smith's theory was in part a response to the mercantilist economists who had confused value with bullion. According to Smith, money might be metal, but value is the energy-like quantity of work. There was furthermore a distinction to be made between what Smith called the "real" and "nominal" prices of goods. Like any other commodity, the cost of gold or silver depended on the labor needed to produce it, which in turn depended on factors such as the "fertility or barrenness" of mines. An excess of money therefore translated into higher nominal prices. But the role of the economist was to focus on real prices, which stripped out such distracting effects. In psychological terms, we may care about numerical prices, but in mathematical terms, what counts is relative prices. Smith therefore interpreted the economy in terms of ideas such as the division of labor and the mechanics of exchange, rather than of money, which dropped out of the equation like an unneeded variable: "The real price of every thing, what every thing really costs to the man who wants to acquire it, is the toil and trouble of acquiring it." Value is labor, and the real price is labor, so they are one and the same. Money is just a medium of exchange. The economist Jean-Baptiste Say, who popularized Smith's work in France, summed this up in his statement that "money is a veil."

Smith's chain of reasoning was not backed by empirical evidence: for example, he did not check whether the price of gold actually reflected the labor required to obtain it, or explore the fact that much of the bullion in existence had been produced by slave labor. And it neatly sidestepped the difficult question about what it means for money to assign number to fuzzy qualities such as value or labor in the first place. In both respects, his work set a precedent that would be followed by future economists. Karl Marx's own labor theory of value, for example, was heavily influenced by Smith (he added the capitalist's markup). And when Victorian economists such as William Stanley Jevons, Leon Walras, and Carl Menger attempted to put economics on a sound mathematical footing, they similarly focused on the exchange of goods in idealized markets. But instead of relating value with labor, they related it to the subjective quality of utility—defined by Jeremy Bentham, the English philosopher and social reformer, as that which appears to "augment or diminish the happiness of the party whose interest is in question." As Jevons put it in the second paragraph of *The Theory of Political Economy* (1871): "Repeated reflection and inquiry have led me to the somewhat novel opinion, that *value depends entirely upon utility*" (his emphasis). More precisely, according to this theory, exchange prices are determined by marginal utility, which takes into account whether you already have what is being offered—you will pay less for a loaf of bread if you already have as much as you can eat.

According to these neoclassical economists, as they became known, the purpose of exchange—and of the market economy as a whole—was to maximize overall happiness. People trade what they have for what they want, and everyone involved becomes happier. While utility was highly subjective and could not be measured directly, Jevons argued that it could be inferred from prices: "Just as we measure gravity by its effects in the motion of a pendulum, so we may estimate the equality or inequality of feelings by the decisions of the human mind. The will is our pendulum, and its oscillations are minutely registered in the price lists of the markets." His theory was therefore similar to Smith's, with the difference that the quantity revealed by the market was utility rather than labor. Explicitly inspired like Smith by Newton's rational mechanics, the aim was to reduce the economy to a set of elegant laws and equations. As Jevons put it, these laws were to be considered "as sure and demonstrative as that of kinematics or statics, nay, almost as self-evident as are the elements of Euclid, when the real meaning of the formulae is fully seized."[3]

Just as the economy was based on the Newtonian gold standard, so economics was to be based on a version of Newtonian physics. To make their program consistent, though, economists had to make multiple further assumptions, none of which were based on empirical observations. These included:

- Agents make decisions on a purely rational basis (no shows of emotion).
- Their aim is to optimize their own utility, as described by a utility function that reflects their fixed preferences (no one can change their minds).
- Agents act independently of one another (no talking allowed).
- Agents are of equal power and have access to the same information (no powerful banking networks).

- Variations in behavior are assumed to average themselves out over a large number of people, so what counts is the opinion of the "average man."
- Economic forces are transmitted in a mechanical way courtesy of Smith's invisible hand, which acts like an economic force of gravity and gently guides prices to their natural place.
- The result is that markets tend toward a self-regulated and stable equilibrium that balances supply and demand (Walras attempted to demonstrate this using a mathematical model of an idealized economy).
- Money is treated as a commodity like any other, that happens to also serve as a medium of exchange.[4]

In the same way that the force of gravity exerted by an object depended on its mass but not its color or appearance, so money was just a distraction that could safely be ignored by the serious economist. As John Stuart Mill wrote in *Principles of Political Economy*, which served as a standard text for more than sixty years, "There cannot, in short, be intrinsically a more insignificant thing, in the economy of society, than money."[5]

The Money Illusion

Orthodox economists, according to Gilles Dostaler and Bernard Maris, "wanted to create a science that ignored money."[6] In particular, they wanted to draw attention away from the awkward incompatibility between exact number and fuzzy value (and therefore between economics and reality) that is at the beating heart of money, and focus purely on the math. Of course, this is not to say that mainstream economists neglected the subject of money completely—even Mill followed up his dismissal of money with a number of chapters about its mechanics—only that they treated it in a mechanical, sterilized way that deprived it of any kind of life or power.

As discussed in chapter 1, speculation from economists including Smith, Jevons, and Menger on the emergence of money as an intermediary for barter was key to the subject's self-mythologizing. During much of the twentieth century, the dominant theory about how money actually functioned in the economy was the quantity theory of money, as formulated by Irving Fisher. After receiving Yale University's first doctorate in economics, Fisher went on to develop or popularize many of the key ideas of modern economics. The so-called Fisher identity, which reads $MV = PT$, states that the amount of money in circulation M, multiplied by the average rate (or velocity) at which the money changes hands V, is equal to the average transaction price P multiplied by the total volume of transactions T.[7] The left-hand side, MV, represents the flow of money through the economy—if a dollar bill changes hands three times in a year, then it represents $3 in total transactions. The right-hand side, PT, aggregated over a country, amounts to what today is called the gross domestic product, or GDP. So the equation says that GDP equals money times velocity. A typical rate for velocity is about two, meaning that money changes hands about twice a year, but there is considerable fluctuation around that number, both in time and from place to place.[8]

The Fisher identity has a clear analogue in Newtonian physics, where an object's momentum P is equal to its mass M times its velocity V. Mercantilism saw wealth as being the sum of money (in the form of bullion), but the Fisher equation shows that what counts is the economy's momentum. Money changes hands whenever an economic transaction takes place, and the faster the flow, the more the products and services being sold. "If the coin be locked up in chests," observed David Hume in the eighteenth century, "it is the same thing with regard to prices, as if it were annihilated."[9] As Fisher pointed out in 1934, some of the scrip currencies that emerged in the Depression needed a stamp added once a week to remain valid, which had the effect of boosting the velocity of the money, since people tried to spend the notes before the stamp was due.[10]

The equation is just an accounting statement, but Fisher applied it by arguing that velocity V and volume of transactions T are fixed with respect to the money supply, so if the supply of money is increased by, say, 5 percent, then prices will also increase by 5 percent. The money supply can therefore be used by the central bank as a lever: if it wants to reduce inflation, it can just trim back on the money supply. According to Fisher, inflation was harmful because of the "money illusion," which was our tendency to think in terms of nominal values rather than "real" values. This made it hard to connect past costs with present costs (e.g., to understand whether selling your house for double what you paid was a great deal) or for businesses to raise prices without losing customers.

Fisher's equation later formed the basis of the theory known as monetarism, whose best known exponent was Milton Friedman. As Friedman said in 1970, "Inflation is always and everywhere a monetary phenomenon in the sense that it is and can be produced only by a more rapid increase in the quantity of money than in output."[11] Monetarism was essentially a more refined version of Copernicus's observation that the value of money depends on its scarcity, so governments should try to keep the amount in circulation stable. As Friedman told EconTalk: "What you want—if possible—is a mechanical system." He suggested that the quantity of so-called high-powered money—currency plus bank reserves—should simply be kept the same. "I would freeze that and hold it constant and have it as sort of a natural constant like gravity or something."[12] This doctrine was adopted by Ronald Reagan and Margaret Thatcher as a means to tackle inflation, with decidedly mixed results (Friedman later admitted the experiment had not been a success). In Britain, inflation hit 18 percent at one point. Its influence was also evident in the design of the European Union, with the central bank's strict mandate on controlling inflation.

Despite its enduring attractions, the theory is an example of the kind of linear, mechanistic thinking that so often leads us astray when thinking about complex systems. One problem is that terms such as velocity V are not constant, as assumed, but change along with other economic variables in a highly complex and unpredictable manner. For example, a major contributor to inflation is expectations of future inflation, which creates a nonlinear feedback loop: a worker who thinks prices will go up next year will (1) spend his money before it is devalued, which increases the velocity; and (2) demand a higher pay settlement, which in turn drives up prices of the firm's products. These actions, when replicated over a large number of people, lead to more inflation, which creates the expectation that prices will go up in future, and so on. Conversely, in a depression, deflation may mean that people are afraid to spend and businesses are afraid to invest, and again this behavior exacerbates the situation.[13] Such feedback loops are discussed in more detail later in the chapter.

Furthermore, velocity varies across the economy, so the average may not be very informative—any more than the average wind speed in your country tells you about the local weather. The link between money supply and economic output is also spongy and complicated, as shown for Canada in the figure in box 7.1. By concentrating on high-powered money, the theory downplays the role of private bankers, who adjust their lending based on their predictions of the future. It sees private debt as just a temporary imbalance between debtors and creditors that cancels out in the aggregate, and has little to say about the credit crises that periodically emerge. Above all, like mainstream economics in general, it treats money as an inert placeholder rather than an active substance with its own dynamics. Monetarism is less a way of thinking about the behavior of money than a way to stop thinking about money by assuming it can be made stable.

Box 7.1
Moneyfication

The literal meaning of "mortgage" is "death-pledge" or "death grip." However, in the years following the financial crisis, this has not dissuaded borrowers in many countries from taking advantage of record-low interest rates to invest in real estate, driven by the promise of gains and a fear of being locked out of the market. In Canada, the government is heavily involved in this process, since apart from maintaining a relaxed monetary policy it also offers cheap mortgage insurance to banks, which means they can lend out more money. In 2008, it even instituted a program to buy mortgage securities that was similar in nature to the TARP in the United States but received much less public notice or debate.*

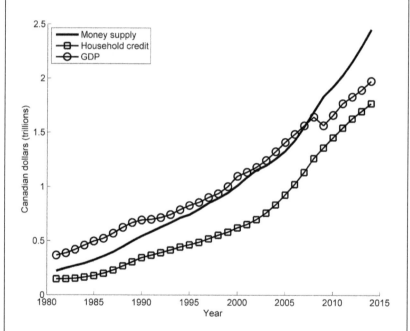

The growth of the money supply (*solid line*) in Canada, compared with credit and GDP (in trillions of Canadian dollars). Since 2005, the growth in the money supply has outpaced GDP (*circles*), even though inflation has been low, contrary to what one might expect from quantity theory. This growth is largely due to household lending, which as a fraction of GDP increased from 32 percent in 1971 to 90 percent by 2015. (Statistics Canada)

All this lending led, as intended, to an unprecedented boom in prices. Houses have come to be so aligned with money—so *moneyfied*—that they are seen as investments (i.e., numbers) as much as homes (i.e., physical places with roofs); and the housing stock—with its graphite kitchen counters and renovated basement suites—has become a kind of physical representation of money supply. While selling mortgages is a profitable activity for banks, homes are unproductive assets, and the new lending appears to have contributed little to either velocity or inflation (the calculation of which excludes asset prices). The growth in money supply has therefore outpaced GDP, creating what looks like a dangerous credit bubble that leaves borrowers—and the economy as a whole—highly exposed to an economic shock or rise in interest rates (as graphically illustrated by the real estate decline in Alberta that started in late 2014, after the price of oil collapsed).[†] This is part of a wider phenomenon in advanced economies, in which credit creation tends to go not toward business investment but toward household consumption or (especially) real estate.[‡]

This type of private debt has traditionally been viewed as benign by economists for a number of reasons. One is that, unlike public debt, it is driven more by market forces and so—according to theory—should self-regulate. Another reason is that the debt is backed by assets—what can be more "real" than real estate?—but this breaks down in a crash, when home prices fall but debt levels remain high. Debt is also seen as something that cancels out between borrowers and lenders, but this ignores the money creation role of banks: when a bank loans money, it gains a new asset on its books, so the net money creation is positive instead of canceling out. Finally, this view of debt ignores the asymmetry between lenders (banks) and borrowers (households). The latter may drive economic growth, but they can't rely on bailouts when things go wrong.

---

[*]Hilliard MacBeth, *When the Bubble Bursts: Surviving the Canadian Real Estate Crash.* (Toronto: Dundurn, 2015), 90.

[†]This increase in mortgage lending is symptomatic of a real estate bubble, according to David Orrell, "The Problem with Predictions," *World Finance*, November 6, 2013.

[‡]Martin Wolf, "Hair of the Dog Risks a Bigger Hangover for Britain," *Financial Times*, February 13, 2014.

Animal Spirits

An alternative to monetarism was provided by John Maynard Keynes, whose ideas were especially influential in the period following World War II and were back in vogue after the GFC. Keynes trained as a mathematician but was aware of the limitations of mathematical models and emphasized the importance of psychological factors in propelling the economy: most "decisions to do something positive," he wrote, "can only be taken as the result of animal spirits—a spontaneous urge to action rather than inaction, and not as the outcome of a weighted average of quantitative benefits multiplied by quantitative probabilities."

Keynes was also fond of pointing out the economy's paradoxical qualities. These included the so-called paradox of thrift. During a recession, people save more and consume less. Rather than being used as a medium of exchange, the physical quality of money as a seemingly secure store of wealth reasserts itself. As John Law had earlier noted, people "hoard up those Signs of Transmission as a real Treasure, being induced to it by some Motive of Fear or Distrust."[14] While the act of saving seems sensible and even virtuous, the fact that no one is spending money has the effect of making the recession worse—in quantity theory terms, the velocity of money grinds to a halt. Monetary policy in itself cannot address this problem, since making money cheaper does not help if no one wants to borrow it. Keynes therefore argued that during recessions the government should actively intervene by spending money on public projects like railways or other infrastructure to boost consumption. In other words, fiscal policy is more important than monetary policy. (The IMF made similar recommendations in 2014 to boost growth in the eurozone.)

Friedman complained that, as a result of Keynes's influence, "It became a widely accepted view that money does not matter, or, at any rate, that it does not matter very much."[15] Indeed, Keynes seemed to treat money in a rather idealized manner, and again downplayed the power of financial intermediaries such as banks, and of money itself. In "Economic Possibilities for Our Grandchildren" (1930), for example, he wrote: "The love of money as a possession—as distinguished from the love of money as a means to the enjoyments and realities of life—will be recognised for what it is, a somewhat disgusting morbidity, one of those semi-criminal, semi-pathological propensities which one hands over with a shudder to the specialists in mental disease."[16] But could the Spanish lust for New World gold or phenomena such as financial bubbles really be put down to bizarre cases of psychological morbidity when they affect such a large proportion of the population? As Glyn Davies notes, "The Keynesians . . . tended to ignore or play down the importance of money, while the monetarists focused their monocular vision solely on the narrower ranges of money."[17]

A dissenting viewpoint was provided by the Austrian economist Friedrich Hayek, who was based at the London School of Economics and later the University of Chicago, and who argued that the economy was so complicated that the government should avoid dabbling in it altogether. "The curious task of economics," he wrote, "is to demonstrate to men how little they really know about what they imagine they can design." In his book *The Denationalisation of Money*, he argued that the state should give up its "age-old prerogative of monopolizing money"—which he described as "the source and root of all monetary evil"—and allow multiple private currencies to coexist. This would allow market forces to correct relative values in cases in which "the national monetary authorities misbehaved."[18] Today, when the vast majority of currency trading is purely speculative, we are concerned at least as much with the misbehavior of traders. An example was the recent scandal in which it turned out the London Interbank Offered Rate (LIBOR), used as a marker for interest rates, was being manipulated by a cartel of bankers.

As discussed further later, other "heterodox" economists offered a range of opinions about the role of money, but their contributions were marginalized, and mainstream economics in the mid-twentieth century solidified into a fairly unified approach with neoclassical theory and assumptions at its core. Keynesian ideas were amalgamated into the model by equations that attempted to relate quantities such as money supply, savings, investment, and so on into a single package. This approach was exemplified by Paul Samuelson, whose textbook *Economics*, first published in 1948, sold in the millions of copies to students all over the world and was translated into more than forty languages. Samuelson's aim was to express the core economic theories in a self-consistent mathematical framework, based on the two related principles of maximization and equilibrium. Firms and individuals, he believed, act rationally to maximize utility, and this drives markets toward a stable equilibrium. The balance is perturbed only by occasional shocks, such as new technologies, and a steady background rate of economic growth. Again, money was not important to this analysis because "if we strip exchange down to its barest essentials and peel off the obscuring layer of money, we find that trade between individuals and nations largely boils down to barter."[19] (This did not stop Samuelson from exploring the properties of money in his academic work; for example, his "overlapping generations" model provided a theoretical argument for how money can serve as a store of value between generations.)[20]

The English economist Joan Robinson famously called the neoclassical synthesis "bastard Keynesianism" because of the way in which it effectively neutered those ideas of Keynes that did not fit easily into the neoclassical mainstream—especially his emphasis on the type of uncertainty that resists mathematical quantification.[21] Critics also noted that the preference for complicated mathematical models had a profound effect on the type of questions that economists addressed. Issues such as social justice or power relationships that had once concerned classical economists, but were hard to quantify, were dropped from the mainstream. The fact that money itself was left out of the model also made it less than useful for people like future Bank of England governor Mervyn King, who noted: "The basic New Keynesian model . . . lacks an account of financial intermediation, so money, credit and banking play no meaningful role. Those omissions obviously limit the ability of the model to help us understand the trade-offs between monetary policy and financial stability." (As economist Steve Keen pointed out, the model is not really new Keynesian; it is better described as new Samuelsonian.)[22]

Weaponized Theories

Gold is valued because it is beautiful but also (being chemically inert) extremely stable and resistant to decay. The same might be said of mathematical equations, with their combination of strength and sterility. With its heavy emphasis on mathematics, neoclassical economics was seen as the gold standard of the field—and the Arrow–Debreu model, created by Kenneth Arrow and Gérard Debreu in the 1950s, was often called its jewel in the crown.[23] This model was a mathematical description of an idealized economy, similar to that proposed by Walras in the nineteenth century, whose basic components are lists of goods, firms, and households. The model computed the total supply and demand for the available products at the specified prices. Money was not explicitly included because this was essentially a simulation of a barter economy, but one in which barter is perfectly efficient in the sense that buyers are always matched to sellers. There was no need for banks or loans or finance.

The authors of the model managed to show that, under certain idealized conditions, the model economy had a stable fixed point that was optimal in the sense that nothing can be changed without making at least one person worse off. This finally appeared to justify both Walras's assertion that idealized market economies would have a stable equilibrium and the idea going back to Adam Smith and before that the invisible hand would lead to an optimal arrangement of prices. It also had clear political implications. During the Cold War, a mathematical "proof" that the invisible hand of capitalism rather than the state fist of communism was the best guide to organizing society was a useful result.[24] Like the Apollo space missions, which beat the Russian competition to the moon in another Cold War showdown, it seemed to show that the American model was supreme. The model may not have included power, but it certainly had power.

The Arrow–Debreu model was in fact funded by grants from the Office of Naval Research, and the authors had also worked at the Pentagon-affiliated consultancy firm Rand.[25] During this period, the Department of Defense was pumping funds into all kinds of scientific programs in an attempt to gain technological supremacy over its Soviet rival, and one of these recipients was the subject of mathematical economics. In 1965, Rand created a fellowship program in economics at the following institutions: Harvard, Stanford, Yale, University of Chicago, Columbia, Princeton, and University of California. Ever since, these institutions, along with MIT, have tended to dominate battles for funding, publication, and deciding what constitutes "good economics."[26] Economic theory became an intellectual tool of American might that—coupled with the need for countries to obtain dollars to pay for oil, and therefore open their markets—helped U.S. corporations gain unfettered access to world markets, all without the need (mostly) for military conquest.[27]

Of course, it was not just the military that subsidized the development of mainstream economics. The primary lesson of neoclassical economics is that markets set prices correctly—which is very attractive for the portion of society that controls most of the wealth, including banks. Frederick Soddy observed in 1934 that "orthodox economics has never yet been anything but the class economics of the owners of debts."[28] Such work doesn't need to be funded directly, but can be favored and promoted in all kinds of ways—which may explain why Adam Smith's theories, which extol the self-regulatory properties of free markets while ignoring the role of money, have proved so popular over the years. The close connection between Wall

Street firms and university economics departments was more recently documented in the film *Inside Job* (2010).

Superrational

The Arrow–Debreu model was impressive because it managed to prove its conclusions using only a minimalistic set of assumptions. Unfortunately, these assumptions included not only things like rational utility-maximizing behavior, negligible transaction costs, money-free trade, and so on, but an even more demanding requirement: everyone in the economy had to compile a list of all the available future states of the world and figure out the prices in all of those worlds. This was of course highly unrealistic, since the future is completely uncertain and we all have different ideas about what will happen.

One might imagine that such unrealistic requirements would have led to the abandonment of equilibrium theory, but instead the opposite happened: the idea that market forces drove the economy to an optimal equilibrium became increasingly well entrenched as the main result of neoclassical economics. This equilibrium approach was exemplified by the Chicago school of economics, based at the University of Chicago. The group, which was headed by Milton Friedman, became famous for its free-market ideology, opposition to taxes, and a confidence in the ability of markets to self-regulate their way to optimal efficiency. As Gary Becker wrote in his book *The Economic Approach to Human Behavior*: "The combined assumptions of maximizing behavior, market equilibrium, and stable preferences, used relentlessly and consistently form the heart of the economic approach."[29] Friedman and Becker's colleague Robert Lucas pushed the idea of rational economic man to its limits with his theory of rational expectations, which says that people are not just rational but also have a perfect mental model of the economy in the sense that they don't make systematic errors. Markets have to be at equilibrium, because disequilibrium can be caused only by irrational behavior. If people are unemployed, it is not because they are the victims of circumstances, but because they have rationally chosen not to work at available wages.

This Chicago school model was soon being rolled out to countries around the world from Chile to South Africa. Even today, tools developed by neoclassical economists remain the gold standard, especially in the realm of macroeconomics. For example, policy makers continue to rely on so-called dynamic stochastic general equilibrium (DSGE) models, which are similar in design to the Arrow–Debreu model but incorporate shocks to equilibrium to assess how a change in government policy will affect the economy. As the Bank of England's Andrew Haldane observes, these models enjoy a number of "aesthetically beautiful properties." In particular, they typically encode an equilibrium that is "unique, stationary and efficient," a view of the economy that is "ordered and rational," and result in dynamics that are "classically Newtonian, resembling the damped harmonic motion of Newton's pendulum." Unfortunately, as we have argued elsewhere, this "simple and beautiful" elegance comes at the expense of realism.[30]

In particular, as former deputy governor of the Bank of Canada William White points out, "An important practical aspect of [DSGE] models is that they make no reference to money or credit, and they have no financial sector."[31] The model used by the Bank of England to simulate the economy before the recent banking crisis, for example, had the singular disadvantage of not including banks. In fact, as White observes, "such crises were literally ruled out in DSGE models by the assumption of self-stabilization."[32] The result, according to Haldane, is that DSGE models "have failed to make sense of the sorts of extreme macro-economic events, such as crises, recessions and depressions, which matter most to society."

Intrinsic Value II

For most scientists, the acid test of a theory is not its mathematical elegance but its ability to make accurate predictions. Newtonian physics has been deemed a success because it can predict things like the course of a spaceship. In contrast, the predictive ability of general equilibrium models has been shown to be little better than random guessing.[33] Forecasts of important indicators such as GDP or oil prices are routinely made, and routinely miss. In the words of economist Alan Kirman: "Almost no one contests the poor predictive performance of economic theory. The justifications given are many, but the conclusion is not even the subject of debate."[34] So how did economics manage to avoid this test? The answer was a theory that said markets were inherently unpredictable—not so much because they were too complex or messy, but because they were too perfect.

Eugene Fama's 1965 efficient market hypothesis assumed that markets are made up of "large numbers of rational profit-maximizers" who have access to perfect information.[35] The theory claimed that market forces would drive the price of any security to its correct "intrinsic value." Because changes were random, or driven by unpredictable news, it was impossible to beat the market: all the information was already priced in. The theory, which was essentially an updated version of Smith's argument that market price equals intrinsic value, cemented the idea that markets are inherently rational, efficient, and optimal, with no role for the often-explosive dynamics of money and finance. While the Bubble Act had failed to outlaw bubbles, mainstream economists outlawed them in another way, by saying they had never existed. As Fama later told the *New Yorker* magazine, "I don't even know what a bubble means."[36]

The efficient market hypothesis soon became the cornerstone of the risk-management and financial-engineering techniques used by banks, firms, and regulators. An example is the widely used value at risk (VaR) formula, which is used to estimate the worst-case loss that an institution could face on a given financial position. Risk can be calculated by taking historical data over a time window ranging from a few months to several years, depending on the case, and estimating the likelihood of a particular loss in the future. The model is based on the efficient market idea that prices are drawn to a stable equilibrium but are perturbed randomly by the actions of independent investors or by unexpected news. The risk of an asset can therefore be reduced to a single number based on its historical variation (the future is assumed to be statistically the same as the past). It can also be counterbalanced or "hedged" by financial derivatives that represent bets on future price changes.

Risk can therefore in theory be engineered away: there is no need to worry about collapsing bubbles or the effect of a credit crunch or the activities of hedge funds or contagion from other markets or investor psychology or other obscure and unquantifiable risk factors or even the whole disconnect between number and fuzzy reality. In mainstream economics, the price (relative to other prices) always corresponds to the true value, and money, whose fluctuating and unpredictable force field permeates the economy, is just a distraction. As physicist J. Doyne Farmer and economist John Geanakoplos observed, "Economic theory says that there is very little to know about markets: An asset's price is the best possible measure of its fundamental value, and the best predictor of future prices."[37] As we have noted, money objects are *designed* to have price and value be equivalent, and this equality is actively enforced by the issuing authority, but economists granted this property to everything else as well; rather than being special, money was just another tradable good.

Model Risk

The legitimacy of economics as a quantitative science was enhanced in 1969 when the Swedish central bank—in what is perhaps the ultimate example of the capture of economic thought by the finance industry—created the Sveriges Riksbank Prize in Economic Sciences in Memory of Alfred Nobel. It soon became known by the media, and economists, as the Nobel Prize in Economics. Winners would include Simon Kuznets, Kenneth Arrow, Gérard Debreu, Friedrich Hayek, Paul Samuelson, Milton Friedman, Robert Lucas, and Tom Sargent. In a classic exhibition of fence-sitting, the 2013 prize winners included both Eugene Fama, who invented the efficient market hypothesis, and behavioral economist Robert Shiller, who in 1984 famously called it "one of the most remarkable errors in the history of economic thought."[38]

Indeed, those risk models developed by economists, and given the Nobel gold medal stamp of approval, have turned out to be rather unreliable. The VaR model, for example, has failed on a regular basis, often to disastrous effect. In 2007, the CFO of Goldman Sachs complained that they "were seeing things that were 25-standard deviation moves, several days in a row."[39] A 25-standard deviation event is something that is not expected to happen even once in the duration of the universe—so if it happens several days in a row, you begin to realize there is a problem. The damage created by exploding financial derivatives the following year was enough to throw the world into a global depression.

As Adair Turner noted in 2014, "Modern macroeconomics and finance theory failed to provide us with any forewarning of the 2008 financial crisis."[40] That was the case even at the actual time of the crisis—in 2008, according to a study by IMF economists, the consensus of forecasters was that not one of seventy-seven countries considered would be in recession the next year (forty-nine of them were).[41] James Heckman of the University of Chicago said, "Everybody here was blindsided by the magnitude of what happened. But it wasn't just here. The entire profession was blindsided."[42] Central bankers, who were heavily influenced by mainstream economic theory, were caught equally unawares.[43] According to Alan Greenspan, the crisis was "almost universally unanticipated."[44] Even worse than this failure of prediction, though, is the fact that these theories and models helped cause the crisis in the first place by creating a false illusion of confidence. Modeling the economy as an inherently stable system had the perverse effect of making it unstable.

This failure has been disputed by leading economists. Tom Sargent said in 2010 that such criticism displayed "woeful ignorance or intentional disregard for what much of modern macroeconomics is about and what it has accomplished. . . . It is just wrong to say that this financial crisis caught modern macroeconomists by surprise."[45] In contrast, Robert Lucas said that the reason the crisis was not predicted was because economic theory predicts that such events cannot be predicted.[46] According to Fama, the efficient market hypothesis "did quite well in this episode," and when asked whether the crisis would lead to any changes in economics, he replied, "I don't see any."[47] But such protests and assertions sound like denial of the damaging role that economic theories played in the crisis. There is a growing awareness, at least among students and heterodox economists, that the basic concepts and assumptions of the mainstream theory are flawed—which is why, according to Cambridge University economists Ha-Joon Chang and Jonathan Aldred, their subject "is the only academic discipline in which a significant and increasing number of students are in an open revolt against the content of their degree courses."[48]

Traditional economics has long been dominated by a Pythagorean fascination with number. As Thomas Piketty wrote in his book *Capital in the Twenty-First Century*: "To put it bluntly, the discipline of economics has yet to get over its childish passion for mathematics and for purely theoretical and often highly ideological speculation, at the expense of historical research and collaboration with the other social sciences. . . . This obsession with mathematics is an easy way of acquiring the appearance of scientificity without having to answer the far more complex questions posed by the world we live in."[49] In particular, it means that money is treated as a passive placeholder, so objective number and subjective value are the same. At the heart of mainstream theory is an ideology—a sort of received consciousness—that takes money at face value, that with willed blindness doesn't want to see what's on the other side.

Martin Wolf, chief economics commentator for the *Financial Times*, echoed Say when he observed at a 2013 conference on the teaching of economics that students are left thinking we operate in a "barter system where money acts as a veil"—as if economics exists in a Platonic world of Forms, where there is no need to dirty your hands with cash.[50] This lack of interest in money might seem strange—isn't that what economics is supposed to be about?—but it is perfectly expressed in the origin myth from economics (chapter 1), in which money is seen as just a way of facilitating barter, and by the desire to collapse the dual nature of money (chapter 2) to nothing more than an inert medium of exchange. It is particularly ironic, given that economic principles such as rationality and optimizing behavior only make sense when transactions can be reduced to number, which of course is the job of money. Mainstream economists are fond of describing people who propose alternative monetary schemes as "cranks," but with their sanitized ideas about the origins and nature of money, coupled with Victorian notions of a social pseudo-physics based on the energy-like idea of utility and dreams of pristine rationality and equilibrium, they might want to look in the mirror (the main difference is that they write the textbooks).

According to Chang and Aldred, "Part of the self-image of most academic economists today is that the core of the subject is an established, settled science." However, while mainstream assumptions such as stability and rationality may have appealed to the subject's Victorian founders, they are out of step with recent developments in science which show money and the economy in a very different light.

It's Alive

In the preface to his *Principles of Economics*, the neoclassical economist Alfred Marshall wrote that "the Mecca of the economist lies in economic biology." However, he did not pursue the metaphor very far. He continued, "Biological conceptions are more complex than those of mechanics; a volume on Foundations must therefore give a relatively large place to mechanical analogies, and frequent use is made of the term equilibrium which suggests something of a static analogy."[51]

Instead, economists built up a model of the economy in which people or firms acted like inert atoms, deprived of any life or individuality or power relationships or connection with one another. While these assumptions may have seemed reasonable at the time, as mathematical simplifications, they have found less use in life sciences such as biology and ecology. For one thing, living systems show so-called emergent behavior, which means that the macro-behavior cannot be predicted from a knowledge of individuals. An ant colony is not simply a larger version of a single ant, because ants do not behave as atomistic individuals but are embedded in a complex social organization, are in constant communication with one another, develop specialized roles, experience group dynamics, and so on. The same can be said, on a grander scale, of the human economy. When people are seen as living beings that are part of larger groups (families, communities, nations, etc.), it makes no sense to describe their behavior in terms of static utility functions, because their preferences will change with time and context.

Nor are living systems homogeneous. As Charles Darwin knew, diversity, along with competition, is one of the drivers of evolution. If everything were the same, "survival of the fittest" would result in a draw and nothing would change. The same dynamic explains why markets are often dominated by a small number of successful firms, instead of a large number of essentially indistinguishable firms as assumed by neoclassical economics. The result of this evolutionary process is not equilibrium, but a state of dynamic change and continuous adaptation. And while competition plays an important role, so does cooperation. Diversity means that people and firms can often do more when they function as part of a team than they can individually. Ecological niches appear as a result. In this world, money is not an inert placeholder or a passive lump of metal, but a vital, active medium that circulates through the economy, changing it as it goes (box 7.2).

Prices can never perfectly reflect value, because value is a fuzzy quality that changes with time and context and cannot be reduced to number. It does not come down to energy-like measures of labor (Smith) or utility (Jevons). It is not objective (classical economics) or subjective (neoclassical economics), but a mix of the two. It is largely a product of culture, which means that it can change—sometimes very quickly. We do not value gold so much for its beauty, but because we are told it is valuable. If we collectively decide that unexploited forests and oceans are extremely valuable, say, for their role in maintaining the biosphere, even if we don't perform work on them or exploit them or even see them, then they will be valuable—but that doesn't mean their price will go up by just the right amount in some imaginary market. There is certainly feedback between prices and value— if something is expensive, then we tend to value it for that reason, and vice versa—but the two can never be equated, any more than the two sides of a coin can merge to one. The process by which market forces such as supply and demand determine a price is similar to the delicate process of measuring a quantum system—the measurement changes the system, is susceptible to distortion, and gives only an approximate description of the state. And market dynamics do not resemble the gentle, linear dynamics of a guiding hand, where everything is *just right*, but rather the nonlinear dynamics of a turbulent system, with states of apparent calm interrupted by moments of chaos.

Box 7.2

Small Money

While money is a human invention, the idea of a medium of exchange is not. A biological version is the molecule known as adenosine triphospate, or ATP, which transports energy within cells. Food energy is stored transiently in ATP and then released for such tasks as the fabrication of larger molecules such as proteins or DNA. By donating energy to certain chemical reactions, ATP makes them orders of magnitude faster. It also plays a role as a kind of signaling device, for example, for opening or closing channels in the cell wall. After use, in which it is converted to a different molecule, ATP is recycled for future use. A person's body only contains around 50 grams of ATP at any one time, but because of the recycling we go through nearly our own weight in the stuff every day.[*]

The ATP molecule has been selected by evolution as a kind of molecular currency because it has various properties, including the ability to store a large amount of energy through the arrangement of its chemical bonds; but nature could have chosen some other molecule. The system is an example of what biologists call a bow-tie network, in which multiple inputs (one side of the bow) feed into a central control unit (the knot) to produce multiple outputs (the other side of the bow). Here the knot is ATP: many components can be used as inputs to make ATP, and all cells use ATP to transport energy. The advantage of this structure is that it gives great flexibility, while allowing for a high degree of control.

In economic exchange, money plays a similar role. In the Middle Ages, the bankers who arranged bills of exchange acted as the central control node in the network. With Bitcoin, as with the Internet, the central control comes from the operating protocol. With fiat currencies, system control of money production is dispersed to private banks rather than being centralized.

What distinguishes money from natural systems such as ATP, though, is that money is based on number, which gives it special properties. ATP is not completely stable (it has a life span), does not multiply exponentially forever (cells can't get rich by hoarding it), and does not have a number stamped on its side. Money is not a simple extension of natural processes, but maybe it can be redesigned to behave more like one.

[*]Reginald H. Garrett and Charles M. Grisham, *Biochemistry* (Fort Worth, Tex.: Saunders, 1995).

A useful comparison is with the behavior of water, whose complex thermal, biological, mechanical, and chemical properties are essential for life (our bodies are about 60 percent water). At a molecular level, water is just an oxygen atom connected to two hydrogen atoms. However the molecule's electrical polarization means that it is in a constant, intricate, quantum mechanical dance with its neighbors, resulting in emergent behavior which could never be deduced from a knowledge of the molecular properties alone. Ditto for our human currency.

All of this complexity and ambiguity poses something of a problem to conventional models, because it is no longer possible to make the simplifying assumptions of the Newtonian, mechanistic approach. Just as the dualistic, quantum-like nature of money mediates between exact number and fuzzy value, the quantitative and the qualitative, so economists need tools that mediate between mathematics and the living economy. In recent decades, a number of mathematical techniques such as nonlinear dynamics and complexity theory have become increasingly popular in the life sciences and are now also providing new ways to understand and visualize the flows of money that course through the economy.

The Uncertainty Principle

Underlying the Newtonian gold standard system was the idea that money, and through it the entire economy, could be made stable by linking it to gold—as if the establishment of a numerical link between a currency and a physical mass would in itself turn the human economy into a mechanistic system, understandable by physical laws. The belief that markets, including currency markets, are fundamentally stable is also axiomatic to neoclassical economics. It therefore came as a major psychological blow to all concerned in 1971 when the world currency system suddenly went chaotic.

The assumption of stability is reminiscent of Aristotelian physics, which asserted that moving objects slowed down and stopped because they were drawn to a state of equilibrium. However, living systems from the earth's biosphere to the human economy are better viewed as operating in a state that is *far* from equilibrium, in the sense that the contents are constantly being churned around. Equilibrium, where it exists, is an emergent property that depends for its maintenance on the presence of self-regulating feedback loops. The key insight of James Lovelock's Gaia theory, for example, was that what makes the earth discernibly alive, compared with other planets, is that its atmosphere is far from chemical equilibrium, but feedback loops maintain the temperature and so on in a zone suitable for life.

In general, positive feedback amplifies perturbations, while negative feedback reduces them. Biological systems are characterized by complex networks of interacting feedback loops, which face off against one another in a kind of tug-of-war, with positive feedback allowing for rapid reaction, and negative feedback providing control. Periods of apparent stability represent a temporary truce between these opposing forces. The economy is similarly full of feedback loops. Economists have traditionally focused on the stabilizing role of negative feedback—an example is Smith's invisible hand, which is supposed to drive prices to an equilibrium level—but positive feedback is equally important.

Consider, for example, the price chart of gold shown on the top in figure 7.1. Pre-1968, under the Bretton Woods agreement, the price was maintained at US$35 per troy ounce. The price was stable, because gold was still used as a money object by central banks and therefore had a defined price. This arrangement first came under stress in 1968, and when it collapsed completely in August 1971 the price of gold began a highly nonlinear, chaotic-looking path. In the first two business days of 1980, the price of an ounce of gold went from $110 to $634, as people lined up to swap dollars for gold. It peaked at $850 on January 21, and fell the next day by $145, as the same people queued to sell.[52] This shows the difference between a money object and a metal object: prices for gold were stable under government control, but the invisible hand of the market apparently has a bad case of the shakes.[53]

The volatility in this case is caused by the feedback loops leading to unstable behavior. If the price of gold is going up, then "momentum buyers" who follow the trend tend to get excited and buy more. That acts as a positive-feedback mechanism that drives the price even higher. The same thing happens in reverse on the way down, as investors dump their holdings. Alternatively, "value investors" may sell their holding if the price gets too high or buy when it goes too low, which acts as negative feedback. If the positive feedback outweighs the negative feedback, then the outcome is boom followed by bust, with the price lifting to extreme heights before suddenly collapsing.

At times when the price of gold is high, it is often debated whether it is in a bubble. But is more accurate to say that gold is always in a bubble, a bubble of human desire, which inflates or deflates in unpredictable ways. Newtonian calculations aside, gold doesn't have a constant value—it doesn't

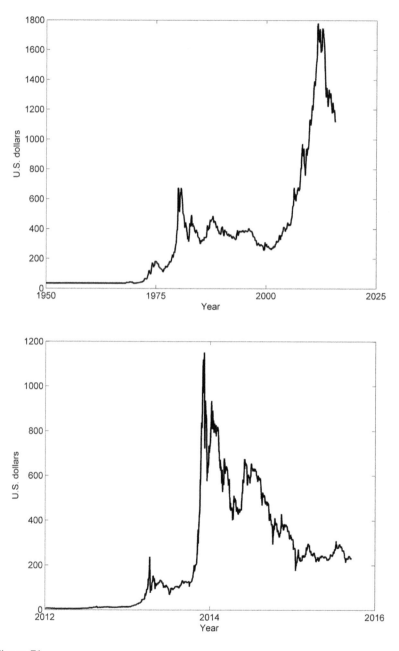

Figure 7.1
(*Top*) The price of gold was stable when gold bars were used by central banks as a money object, with a defined price, but was unstable under the control of the invisible hand; (*bottom*) the price of a bitcoin shows similarly nonlinear behavior.

come out of the earth with a number stamped into its side. Money objects are designed to have a fixed numerical value, but for other things, including gold, the tether that ties numerical price to fuzzy conceptions of value is highly flexible and influenced by investor psychology. The price of gold therefore has its own dynamic, which depends to a large extent on what is happening with the price of gold. The same is seen in any speculative bubble, be it for tulips in seventeenth-century Holland or bitcoins in the fall of 2013 (see the bottom graph in figure 7.1), when the price increased by a factor of 100 in a matter of weeks. Nout Wellink, the former president of the Dutch central bank, compared media interest in Bitcoin at the time with tulip mania and pointed out that "at least then you got a tulip at the end."[54] If the behavior of money can be described to an extent by mathematics, then it is the mathematics of nonlinear dynamics and chaos rather than stability. And to deny the existence of bubbles—which neoclassical economists such as Fama are wont to do—is to deny the role of money and emotion in the economy.

In general, while markets tend to reduce arbitrage opportunities, this acts more as a consistency check on prices than as a stabilizing force. As discussed in chapter 6, currencies are linked together through the activities of traders, but instead of reducing volatility, this activity just means that currencies are in a kind of synchronized dance, with changes in one place propagating quickly through the system. To borrow a phrase from Jevons, the unstable, bipolar nature of money is "registered in the price lists of the markets," with their oscillations from peaks to troughs and from optimism to pessimism. The reason market prices—the numbers attached to investments—are hard to predict has nothing to do with efficiency; it is because prices are inherently unstable. Such effects can be simulated using the so-called agent-based models from complexity science, which are designed to capture the nonlinear behavior caused by interactions between individual agents.

In quantum physics, the uncertainty principle, which is related to the wave/particle duality of matter, puts a fundamental limit on our ability to accurately measure both the position and momentum of an object. So, for example, we can put an exact number on a particle's position, but momentum is known only to within a certain bound. A similar principle could be said to exist for markets—we can measure prices at the instant something is sold but remain uncertain about how it will change. And because markets are part of a closely coupled system, this uncertainty is further magnified through feedback loops. Market volatility is an expression of money's fragile and uneasy link between objective number and subjective value, reason and emotion, reality and perception, order and chaos, precision and ambiguity; and it is fueled by the same energy—and the same quantum chaos—that binds heads with tails. Note that this wild uncertainty is very different from the tame sort of randomness assumed by traditional economic models, in which the system is treated as being at equilibrium, with price changes being due to small, random perturbations to the steady state.

The Money Moment

The most important market in the economy, of course, is the market for money; and as heterodox economists, including Frederick Soddy and later Hyman Minsky, pointed out, its supply is also affected by destabilizing feedback loops. According to Minsky's financial instability hypothesis, the desire for money, and therefore credit creation, tends to increase during an expansion.[55] This raises asset prices, which provides collateral for further loans, and so on, exaggerating the expansion, as "success breeds a disregard of the possibility of failure." Much of the investment goes into unproductive assets such as real estate or excess industrial capacity. The last people to join the party are those, such as the famous NINJA borrower with "no income, no job, and no assets" of the U.S. subprime crisis, who can't service interest payments but relies on the borrowed asset increasing in value. On the surface, everything seems to be going well, but only if you ignore the mounting and destabilizing levels of debt. At some point—since dubbed the Minsky moment—debts become unsustainable, asset prices stop rising, speculative borrowers fail to make payments, and the process reverses, with the economy sliding into a recession whose depth is exaggerated by a rapidly contracting supply of credit.

The role of the central bank is to control this process; however, its power is limited by the fact that most of the money supply is created by private institutions, which it can influence only indirectly. There is also a tendency to ease conditions during a recession (e.g., quantitative easing) rather than to withdraw stimulus during an expansion (let the good times roll!). The result has been a credit boom/bust cycle on top of an upward-trending level of total debt, which finally started to turn over in 2007. As his former student L. Randall Wray put it: "This wasn't a Minsky moment. It was a Minsky half-century."[56]

Minsky was considered something of a maverick in the economics profession; one assessment, published a year after his 1996 death, concluded that his "work has not had a major influence in the macroeconomic discussions of the last thirty years."[57] According to mainstream economics, as summarized by Ben Bernanke, the debt cycle "represent[s] no more than a redistribution from one group (debtors) to another (creditors)."[58] Or as Paul Krugman explains: "Think of it this way: when debt is rising, it's not the economy as a whole borrowing more money. It is, rather, a case of less patient people—people who for whatever reason want to spend sooner rather than later—borrowing from more patient people."[59] In this linear view of the economy, debts and credits cancel each other out in the aggregate, just as the two sides of money are assumed to merge into a neutral chip. However, this ignores the pivotal money creation role of private banks, who act as a kind of amplifier on the system.[60] As Steve Keen notes, the main reason central banks were surprised by the crisis was because their DSGE models include "neither money nor banks nor debt."[61] Again, this omission will seem bizarre to noneconomists but is consistent with the assumption that money is just an inert medium of exchange; its consequences are a graphic illustration of how our ideas about the nature of money have influenced economic outcomes.

While subjects such as nonlinear dynamics and complexity are beginning to influence economics, this does not mean that economists are abandoning the equilibrium approach, as epitomized by DSGE models, en masse. As Wolfgang Munchau wrote in the *Financial Times* in 2015, "The mainstream invested a life's work in developing their DSGE models. They will not let go easily, but continue to tinker with their models, and hope that no policy maker will ever use them. Unfortunately, many institutions already have. An example is the European Central Bank's use of a DSGE model that has produced persistently too optimistic forecasts." He predicts that "the successful challenge will come from outside the discipline, and that it will be brutal."[62] Economics may be about to experience some disequilibrium of its own.

Happy Yet?

Money's volatility is, of course, not limited to just the markets. One of its most obvious features is that it is a highly emotional subject. Married couples—not to mention countries—have more arguments over money than probably any other topic, and it has been called the leading cause of divorce.[63] Words used to describe spending habits include "greed," "generosity," "miserliness," and "extravagance." As discussed in chapter 2, the dualistic structure of money resonates powerfully with the dualistic structure of our thought processes. We value it both as an idea and as a thing in itself. It is therefore amazing that orthodox theory, by focusing only on the numerical, left-brained side of money, somehow managed to strip economics of all its psychological and societal implications.

The fact that people are prone to make all sorts of irrational judgments about money was demonstrated in a long series of experiments, starting in the 1970s, by the psychologists Daniel Kahneman and Amos Tversky, whose work helped create the field of behavioral economics.[64] For example, we tend to underestimate the possibility of extreme events like crashes and overestimate our ability to cope with them. We put more value on things that we can see now, and discount the future.[65] It is perhaps not surprising, then, that most people find it hard to get excited about planning for retirement. Marketers and advertisers have always known that reason is only sparingly applied when making buying decisions, which is why they target our emotions through images, music, and so on (one study, for example, showed that gamblers spend more if slot machines smell nice, which doesn't seem to involve rationality at any level).[66]

While economists have traditionally modeled people as independent atoms, we are affected by people around us, and emotions are particularly contagious. In markets, this often leads to a herd mentality, with everyone stampeding into or out of positions at the same time—confidence is highest when everyone is doing the same thing, which is exactly when risk is highest. And at its core, money relies for its function on trust and power, which have a complicated relationship (power inspires obedience, which isn't quite the same thing as trust). As Walter Bagehot (chapter 4) knew, trust is not produced by a purely rational calculation but, again, is also influenced by emotions and the influence of others. Runs on banks, or runs on currencies, occur when trust evaporates.

Money is a source of pleasure, and we associate its pursuit with the pursuit of happiness. This connection was made explicit by neoclassical economists such as Francis Edgeworth, who went so far as to imagine a "psychophysical machine" called a hedonometer that would register "the height of pleasure experienced by an individual."[67] Other economists preferred to assume that utility could be measured by prices. However, happiness can also be measured in other ways—for example, by asking people how happy they are. The results appear to show that in rich countries happiness actually peaked some time back in the 1960s and has been stable or in slight decline ever since—even though per capita GDP has soared in the same time.[68] One reason for this discrepancy is that GDP is a purely monetary measure of economic activity and was never intended to be a measure of welfare. Confusing it with well-being is like confusing price with value.

Also, while wealth certainly affects our happiness, we tend to be more concerned with relative wealth, as compared with one's peers, than with absolute wealth. Because money is based on number, it doesn't have any inbuilt sense of scale—it doesn't really make sense to say that a number is big or small, because it's all relative ($1,000 is just noise to a billionaire). However, numbers can be ranked in order, and we therefore tend to assess our wealth not in absolute terms, but by comparing it with those around us. As John Stuart Mill put it: "Men do not desire to be rich, but to be richer than other men."[69] This was illustrated by a U.S. Gallup poll that asked, "What is the smallest amount of money a family of four needs to get along in this community?" The answer simply tracked the average income. As other people get richer, we feel we must do the same just to maintain the same relative position.[70] A survey by Boston College of superwealthy people with net worth in excess of $25 million found that most still reported anxiety about their finances, and to achieve full financial security would require on average 25 percent more than whatever they had.[71] Of course, if they got that then they would need another 25 percent, and so on. The hedonic treadmill is an expensive ride.

As Daniel Kahneman points out, there might even be a negative correlation between money and happiness beyond a certain point, since those with a higher income usually spend more time on doing things that evoke negative feelings.[72] But the perverse effect is that we just want even more of the stuff. According to Jeffrey Pfeffer from Stanford Graduate School of Business, the more money we are paid, the more we tend to value that money. His research was inspired by a remark from Daniel Vasella, the former CEO of pharmaceutical giant Novartis AG, who turned down a $78 million severance package after a public outcry. "The strange part is, the more I made, the more I got preoccupied with money," he told *Fortune* magazine in 2002. "When suddenly I didn't have to think about money as much, I found myself starting to think increasingly about it."[73]

Money has become a way of keeping score, in a game that we no longer play for its own enjoyment. It is what Peter Singer, professor of bioethics at Princeton, calls "an end in itself, a way of measuring one's status or success, and a goal to fall back on when we can think of no other reason for doing anything, but would be bored doing nothing."[74] We mark our position and display our wealth through what Thorstein Veblen called in 1899 "conspicuous consumption." In a recent study of American households, University of California, Los Angeles, anthropologists found that a typical family works hard so it can spend hard and even goes into debt in a "vigorous show of consumerism."[75] Working parents are able to spend four hours or less with their kids on a weekday, feel guilty, and are trying to make up for it with bought stuff. The subsequent stress is then treated via so-called shopping therapy, meaning more shopping and bills. The outcome, as the UCLA team noted, could be epitomized by 2,260 visible possessions they found in three bedrooms of one of the researched households along with the admission that these things do not really make their owners happy.

While it makes sense to accumulate some possessions for pleasure or reserves for whatever might come, there is a difference between a sensible purchase and a hamster wheel, with many clearly following the latter path. As Bournemouth University's Donald Nordberg notes: "Greed incentivized a lot of people to do a lot of good things. However, once it is without context it creates an illusion that the ultimate goal is to scrabble. And there is certainly no virtue in that."[76] Because we tend to compare ourselves with those of our peers who are better off, any increase in social inequality—of the sort seen in most rich countries over the past few decades—can have the effect of decreasing overall happiness.

Cowboy Capitalism

Money has two poles, the abstract mental and the embodied physical. The split between these two is acted out on a global scale in the split between the economy and the planet; just as money contains a bias toward the numerical, so our economy has becoming increasingly virtual and disembodied. When we refer to Western materialistic, capitalistic culture, it isn't really materialism we are talking about: it is the numerical representation of the material world, which is enabled by money. It is a kind of immaterialism, a final realization of the Pythagorean dream of reducing the universe to number. We boost GDP by liquidating the planet (a different measure known as the "genuine progress indicator," which accounts for resource depletion, apparently peaked some forty years ago, according to a study in the journal *Ecological Economics*).[77] But the environmental ethos that emerged in the late 1960s reminded us that human well-being is linked to that of the bio-sphere. This point was perhaps best expressed in a 1966 paper by economist Kenneth Boulding, who—inspired by the Apollo missions—compared two versions of what an economy could look like: a cowboy economy and a spaceman economy.[78]

Boulding's cowboy economy was driven by a frontier mentality. Like the pioneers who first settled the open plains of America, or sixteenth-century Spanish conquistadors, or an oil worker in what journalist Laura Gottesdiener called the "Wild West" of the U.S. fracking industry, cow-boys see the universe as a landscape ready to be plundered.[79] There is no need to worry about the availability of resources or pollution sinks, because they are effectively infinite, and with cheap nuclear energy per-haps not even necessary.[80] The world is seen as property, and the job of the cowboy is to convert it all into money. As the inventor of the steam engine and the steam-powered screw press, James Watt wrote: "Nature can be conquered, if we can but find her weak side."[81] It is fitting that capi-talism, whose name refers by root to heads of cattle (*capita*), is based on this idea of subduing nature and branding it with number; like a cowboy tackling an unruly calf and sinking a firebrand, or more recently a scan-nable microchip, into its side.

In a cowboy economy, the scarcity of money drives the thirst to acquire more. The spaceman economy, in contrast, is seen as an explicitly open sys-tem, in the sense that it takes in food energy at one end and outputs waste at the other. Growth is therefore constrained not by a shortage of precious metal or the actions of a central bank, but by the capacity of the natural sys-tems in which it is embedded. In one economy scarcity is primarily mental, in the other it is primarily physical. Of course, with a fiat currency, it might seem there is no shortage of money, since it can be easily created. But when the money is created through interest-paying loans to people or firms, the interest component has to be actively taken or borrowed from someone else—so either the money supply must inflate, or someone has to go broke. We are therefore all drawn into a high-stakes competition for resources to pay our interest bills. As economist Bernard Lietaer notes, "The job of central banks is to create and maintain that currency scarcity. The direct consequence is that we have to fight with each other in order to survive."[82] While scarcity is a fundamental feature of life (as is its opposite, plenty), our monetary system has elevated it to a kind of defining principle. Where it does not exist, corporations artificially create scarcity to protect profits (e.g., through patents, intellectual property laws, and similar mechanisms).

Money is a way of stamping number onto the world, but (since the planet is not a head of cattle or a frozen chicken in a supermarket) there is a fundamental inconsistency between the artificial constraints of our money system, which are designed to foster continuous growth, and the real constraints of the biosphere. The result is two kinds of debt: one the numerical type, the other physical, to the planet and to future generations. Money has an inbuilt tendency toward the abstract and mental: to restore some balance, we need to align not with money, which points always toward number, but with the kinds of environmental impulses that money seems to erode. This requires new economic thinking, but especially new ideas about money itself: a kind of monetary yoga, which yokes (the root meaning of yoga) together the mental and physical aspects of money.

The Virtual Economy

Viewed from a complexity perspective, the world economy seems less a mechanical system operating at a state of maximum efficiency than an organic process dominated by a financial industry that demands constant growth to sustain itself with interest payments and other profits. Since these profits flow to a small number of asset-rich people, they have contributed to growing levels of income inequality. In most jobs, salaries have remained stagnant for the last few decades, while the wealth of the top 1 percent has soared.[83] The magnetic fields of money are polarizing society— while a degree of inequality is natural, money amplifies the differences. Another consequence is that the economy has to grow just to keep the system rolling, which brings it into conflict with natural systems—just as cancers come into conflict with our bodies. As Boulding famously pointed out, "Anyone who believes exponential growth can go on forever in a finite world is either a madman or an economist." In particular, an economist who confuses numbers with the real world.

Just as money is experiencing a transition between its real and virtual sides, so is the economy itself. In external appearances, our countries and cities are still based on infrastructure, natural resources, and human labor—the world of physical things. But much of the economy is concerned not with things but with information. A pharmaceutical company, for example, may employ thousands of people in sites and laboratories around the world, but much of its worth will be tied up in intellectual property for a handful of drugs—remove that and the rest falls apart. Commuters in a modern city such as London or Toronto still navigate a transit system that looks rather like the one their grandparents used fifty years ago, but they are consumed by their smartphones. As with money, the virtual sometimes seems more real than the reality.

The problem from the perspective of traditional economics is that, as Stewart Brand famously observed, "Information wants to be free."[84] Unlike land, commodities, labor, or energy, something like computer code can be duplicated and transmitted at near-zero cost. Our scarcity-based money system, which was designed for an earlier era, therefore struggles to cope. As mentioned earlier, scarcity can be maintained to an extent through legal means, but the system is leaky. Some protected workers in the knowledge economy, such as those in the financial sector, are very well compensated, while others, such as journalists, face shrinking incomes. Much knowledge work, for example, writing open-source code, is done for free, on a volunteer basis.

The impact of the virtual knowledge economy extends also to the real economy, as more and more tasks are handled by robots. As the Boston Consulting Group's Michael Zinser notes, "The price and performance of automation are improving rapidly. Within five to ten years, the business case for robots in most industries will be compelling, even for many small and midsized manufacturers."[85] According to Harvard's Justin Reich, "Robots and AI will increasingly replace routine kinds of work—even the complex routines performed by artisans, factory workers, lawyers and accountants."[86] A study by Bruegel, a Brussels-based research organization, for instance suggests that 54 percent of jobs in the twenty-eight member states of the European Union are already at risk due to advances in computerization.[87] One of the explicit aims of the cybercurrencies discussed in chapter 9 is to remove the need for human intermediaries—that is, jobs. Algorithmic trading systems are already responsible for most of the activity in stockmarkets, and they don't ask for bonuses. Robot armies are just a matter of time. But this leads to an inherent contradiction: If value is increasingly a measure of information, but information wants to be free, then what is the role of money? We return to this question in chapter 10.

Quantum Economics

The transition from seeing the economy as a mechanical system to seeing it as one part of a living system amounts to an aesthetic shift that has profound implications for the way we think about money and the economy.[88] Instead of speaking about "linear," "mechanistic," "rational," "predictable," and "efficient" behavior, the relevant terms are "networks," "complexity," "nonlinearity," "contagion," "emergence," "health," and "uncertainty." We can also learn from properties such as redundancy and modularity, which lend stability to natural systems such as ecosystems. For example, William White observes that the study of such systems "might lead to the conclusion that our current 'fiat money' system invites complexity with all its associated dangers. . . . We urgently need to rethink the foundations of our current international monetary (non) system."[89]

Our gold standard economic theory is based on the idea that the economy is made up of individual agents who act rationally to optimize their own utility. The result is supposed to be a stable system that maximizes overall happiness. But as discussed earlier, none of these assumptions stand up to critical analysis. Prices are not the optimal result of a rational, mechanistic process governed by deterministic laws but are an emergent phenomenon influenced by myriad complex processes. In recent years, groups such as Rethinking Economics (with branches in seven countries), Manchester University's Post-Crash Economics Society, and many others around the world have sprung up to demand urgent reforms in the way that economists work and teach.[90] These call for an approach that incorporates

Pluralism. Students from Quebec wrote a petition in 2014 noting that the field leaves "little room for ethical, epistemological, philosophical, political and historical reflection, which would allow the discipline to reflect on itself and renew continuously."[91] Instead of being shoehorned into a unified, consistent approach, models should be seen as imperfect patches that capture some aspect of the system. University textbooks could be replaced by anthologies of economic thought.

Humility. A consistent theme is that mainstream economists are not receptive to new ideas. As Keith Harrington from the activist group Kick It Over told *Yes!* magazine in 2015, "Despite its enormous failings in the face of the financial crash, the mainstream of the profession has by and large failed to embrace self-criticism or open itself up to different approaches."[92]

Empiricism. Economists such as Smith and Jevons based their theories on imagined villagers trading beaver pelts rather than on actual observations. While these ideas are still taught as timeless mathematical truths in some textbooks, the social sciences—including economics—are being transformed by the flood of empirical data that has become available in recent years. At the same time, economic theories should be put into historical context, since the economy is changing and adapting over time.

Science. The subject needs stronger interactions with areas such as biology, ecology, complexity, network theory, and nonlinear dynamics.[93] A first step will be to unlearn the Newtonian model that has persisted in economics long past its use-by date.

Money. Above all—and implicit in the foregoing—money needs to take its rightful place at the center of economic thought.[94] Money is not an inert substance but an active medium. We may therefore be able to shape its form to achieve certain outcomes—even if this means inverting some of the sacred tenets of economics.

As we have argued, money objects—with their dualistic, contradictory aspects—have much in common with quantum objects. Now, it is something of a cliché to say that quantum physics is so weird that it is beyond human understanding; and indeed, many of the properties of quantum objects do seem to defy everyday logic.[95] This appears to back up the view, frequently expressed, that money is an impenetrable mystery, comprehensible only to a privileged elite. It might be tempting to throw your arms up in the air and conclude, as one medieval churchman did, that

> Money and currency are very strange things.
> They keep on going up and down and no one knows why;
> If you want to win, you lose, however hard you try.[96]

But perhaps the respective problems are less to do with quantum reality, or with money, than with classical logic, which is based on Aristotelian yes–no, true–false dualities; and perhaps these properties and behaviors aren't as foreign or bizarre as we tend to believe.

For example, behavioral economists have shown that we make economic choices based on a range of cognitive processes, which then "collapse" to a single decision, in a manner similar to the process in which wave-like quantum properties collapse to a single value when measured.[97] However, if queried, we then tend to justify the decision based on a logical argument. Quantum physics is context sensitive, so the act of interrogating a system changes its behavior. We can even modify the behavior of a particle just by checking to see if it has moved. Context is equally important in economic questions: the answer we get will depend on time, place, and our own stance. We can modify the behavior of something just by putting a price on it. The behavior of quantum objects or money objects is often paradoxical, but then so is that of humans—"If you want to win, you lose" describes more than just money. As physicist Diederik Aerts notes, "People often follow a different way of thinking than the one dictated by classical logic. The mathematics of quantum theory turns out to describe this quite well."[98] Money is only truly perplexing if you view it from the abstract viewpoint of classical logic—as an inert, dead thing, rather than something with a life of its own. No wonder mainstream economics tries to ignore it.

To summarize, economics is on the verge of a revolution that in a more modest way resembles, or at least can draw inspiration from, the quantum revolution that rewrote the laws of physics a century ago. As then, a first step is to acknowledge the quantum nature of money—that is, the notion of money as a fundamental quantity and the dualistic properties of money objects—and the effect of this on the system as a whole:

- Prices are an emergent phenomenon that arise from the use of money objects. They do not necessarily optimize utility, efficiency, or anything else (they don't always need to make sense).
- Money objects have a fixed, defined value, but other values are fuzzy, indeterminate, and variable.
- Prices and values are coupled because we value something when it has a high price, and vice versa, but the two have a complex relationship, because price is numerical and value is not. The link breaks down completely for digital goods that can be freely copied and distributed.
- The money system is not a veil over the true workings of the economy, as assumed in mainstream economics—it is the driving force of the economy, and its design affects societal outcomes.
- Our money system boosts economic activity, which feeds into cultural and technological development, but its negative effects—which include obsession with numerical measures such as net worth or GDP, wealth polarization, financial instability, and environmental damage—reflect the innate tension between number and the real world: money's quantum contradictions writ large.
- The two sides of a ledger—positive credit and negative debt—are in a kind of oppositional balance but do not simply cancel one another out, either in a coin or in the economy as a whole. In particular, while moderate levels of debt boost economic activity, excessive levels are destabilizing.[99]
- To mathematically model these effects, we need to use techniques that have been developed for living, organic systems, such as nonlinear dynamics and complexity science.

• The design and function of money has evolved throughout history and is evolving now.

Reforming economics will, of course, not just come down to a kind of economic Manhattan Project, in which genius scientists solve the problems of mankind. Economics is as much about human behavior as it is about number, so it is both a science and an art. And while the reform process is already under way in many institutions and university campuses and activist organizations around the world, one should not underestimate the resistance of economists to adopting new ideas.[100] The impetus from change will come from people outside the profession and is likely to be driven and overtaken by developments in finance. Neoclassical economics made money irrelevant, and now money is returning the favor.

Since its invention, money has been through a number of phases in which it has flipped back and forth between being primarily virtual and physical. The shift currently taking place, though, is a bifurcation point that promises to completely upend everything we know about money. Just as the monoculture of economic thought is being replaced by a range of new ideas, so monopolistic national currencies are being challenged by a diverse ecosystem of alternatives. In chapter 8, we see how the currency system is changing as we abandon gold standard ideas and learn to exploit the power of money in new ways.

8

New Money

Since the 1970s, the world economic system has been based on virtual fiat currencies. As many critics have pointed out, that means cash no longer has intrinsic value, so it can be printed at will, unlike under the gold standard. Psychologically, though, we seem to still have one foot in that previous era. Like a king short of funds, the government borrows money at interest from central banks. The private banking system clings on to its Victorian traditions and prestige. Money is scarce, even though it is made of electrons, instead of electrum. In this chapter, we look at how developments, including new alternative currencies, are reinventing the basic design principles behind money, subverting our gold standard mentality, and pushing the economic system toward something that may look very different.

One of the defining features of money is that there is never quite enough. As discussed earlier, even the wealthy always seem to feel a little short. At the same time, though, we have strong moral rules and codes about how money is handled. Our monetary and economic system is based on the concepts of scarcity and competition. Life is a game, and money is a way of keeping score. During exchange, the net amount of money stays the same, so trades involve winners and losers. We have to fight for our lucre, and it seems morally wrong to get something for nothing. This principle is encoded in the oft-quoted statement that economics is the science of scarcity and is based on the idea that money is, like gold, a kind of limited commodity.

It therefore came as a surprise to many when, following the Great Financial Crisis, the U.S. Federal Reserve under Ben Bernanke decided to embark on the procedure known as quantitative easing (QE), which seemed rather like bending the rules. The aim was to stimulate the economy in a top-down fashion by using newly created money to buy assets such as government bonds from private sector banks. The theory was that this would flood said banks with money, which they would then lend out to companies, and this would boost the economy, just as the discovery of new sources of gold did in olden days. After a period of time, in theory, the bonds are sold back to the private sector, so the effect is only temporary.

The name was an example of the deliberate obfuscation that has been perfected by central banks over the years. To use the words of the journalist Ed Conway, "Central banks have been able to carry out such radical policies without inciting public unrest comes down to the oldest trick in the economic textbook: jargon."[1] (What was being eased? What would nonquantitative easing look like?) Many critics saw it as a disguised form of money printing that would inevitably lead to inflation or even threaten the dollar's role as a key pillar of the financial system.[2] Others argued that the new money was just filling a void left by the implosion of credit instruments during the financial crisis, so inflationary effects would be muted.

The latter appears to have been the case in the United States and Great Britain (so far), though the long-term effects have yet to be seen. A more damaging critique, as discussed in chapter 6, was that the banks ended up hoarding much of the money or channeled it into unproductive activities such as boosting house prices and paying themselves bonuses. This is why some suggested circumnavigating commercial banks—the middlemen who benefited from central bank easing en masse—and give money directly to the people. Australia, for instance, sent every taxpayer a paycheck of AU$900 in December 2008. The aim was to prevent contagion at the very early stage of the unfolding global crisis caused by the collapse of Lehman Brothers in September of the same year. This bet on the consumer rather than the financial industry paid off, as Australia was the only big, high-income country that did not experience a recession in the aftermath of the collapse of 2008.

In fact, Australia approximated a scheme suggested earlier by Bernanke, back when he was a professor of economics at Princeton, as a way to treat the chronic malaise of the Japanese economy in 1998. And it is a variant of a much older idea, known as basic income, that has been around for some time and has been tested on a small scale in a number of countries but has never caught on.

QE for the People

Unlike QE, the idea behind unconditional basic income can be divined from its title—give people an income, without conditions. Amounts vary depending on the proposal, but a typical sum is in the range of $10,000 per year. People wouldn't have to work (or not much as they do now) unless they truly wanted to. The government could also avoid micromanaging tax allowances and different benefits for housing, food, and other basics. Although it is often presented as socialist, its appeal is broad based. Even Milton Friedman thought it was a good idea (though his version was called negative taxation), since he thought it would shrink the size of government and therefore pay for itself. It would have the largest impact on low-income people, who tend to spend their money rather than hoard it, and therefore boost economic activity directly. Of course, they might spend it on things like drink, drugs, gambling, socially inappropriate body piercings, or whatever, but empirical evidence from a number of pilot studies shows that the money is usually spent quite sensibly.[3] And how much of the QE money was spent on champagne?

Current benefit systems tend to stigmatize the poor while incentivizing them to not seek paid work, because if they get jobs their benefits are cut. This makes it hard to wean them off state support (rather like certain banks). A basic income, in contrast, could boost risk taking and entrepreneurship by giving people the time and space to experiment and potential customers some money to spend. As record label owner Alan McGee has pointed out, the unemployment benefit system in England certainly helped to incubate the music industry until it was cut back—most musicians in the 1980s and 1990s seem to have honed their skills while on the "dole."[4] The author Geoff Dyer wrote: "I couldn't have learned my trade (if one can dignify writing with that word) and become a respectable tax-paying citizen without the support of the dole."[5]

At the time of this writing, the idea appears to be gaining widespread interest: Switzerland is planning a referendum on the subject; Finland is considering it; the Dutch city of Utrecht is launching an experimental version; and in the Canadian province of Alberta, the mayors of Edmonton and Calgary have spoken in favor of the idea.[6] Perhaps the biggest impediment to a basic income is psychological, our aforementioned obsession with scarcity and competition. But much of the wealth in the economy is generated from public goods such as natural resources or land values, and what the father of Social Credit, the British engineer C. H. Douglas, called the "cultural inheritance" of society, which today would include inventions such as the Internet or mobile communications.[7] So it makes sense that some of these proceeds be considered a birthright rather than something that can be captured by a small group (e.g., Facebook shareholders).

The fact that central banks have been willing to take a huge risk on QE, but not on something like basic income, points to a fundamental contradiction in our attitude toward money (and of course is not unrelated to the fact discussed in chapter 6 that banks are powerful). As shown earlier, financial systems have historically oscillated between the twin poles of credit and physical money, and we are still currently experiencing a transition between a gold standard system and a fiat system. Our gold standard economic ideas have not caught up, and neither have our financial institutions. To use McLuhan's words, we are "trying to do today's job with yesterday's tools—with yesterday's concepts."[8] But being in a virtual currency phase opens up a number of possibilities.

QE for the State

For example, if we continue the QE thread a little further, could we not have QE for the state as well? If the government can print money to give to banks, could it not print money to give to itself?

In our current monetary system, governments borrow money at interest from quasi-private central banks, which sell bonds via private banks to the public. This model is based on the gold standard system and originated when the private Bank of England lent gold to the sovereign. But today, if the government wants to add money, it could in principle just produce it afresh—after all, it's not gold. For example, the U.S. government could revive Lincoln's greenbacks. Would that not be quantitatively easier on future generations than burdening them with massive debt payments?

For example, after the financial crisis, the United States and other countries chose to boost demand by lowering interest rates. The net effect was to soften the recession but also to create a credit bubble as households and companies leveraged themselves up. But another way to boost the economy, instead of borrowing money and paying interest on it, would be to just create the money as a permanent addition to the supply. As Adair Turner points out, "Money-financed deficits would increase demand without creating debts that have to be serviced. This would lift either real output or inflation and allow interest rates to return to normal more quickly. True, banks might amplify the stimulus by creating additional private credit, but they can be restrained with higher reserve requirements. There are no technical reasons to reject this option, only the fear that once we break the taboo, money-financed deficits will be used on too large a scale."[9]

Indeed, with a fiat currency, the entire role of the private sector in the money creation process becomes less clear. The Bank of England originally rescued the king because the king was too big to fail. But now the roles seem to have reversed: the state has to rescue the banks, because the banks are too big to fail. As Nicolas Oresme pointed out centuries ago, there are dangers in leaving control of the money supply to the state. There will always be a temptation for the government to print too much money and generate inflation. But as shown in figure 7.1, the private sector can do a good job of printing massive amounts of money as well, with little risk to itself, because it can always rely on a bailout. And we trust the state with other important and dangerous things, including nuclear weapons. Moreover, in democracies, there is a safety mechanism in the form of elections, meaning that should the mismanagement of a particular issue become perceived as gross the electorate has a power to act.

The other main function of private banks is to scale up the money supply through the mechanism of "fractional reserve" banking. Again, this made a certain amount of sense under the gold standard. But today banks are free to generate pretty much as much money as they like. This pivotal role is very well compensated; and as discussed in chapter 6, the banks end up with undue influence over government decision making, so rather than checking it, they are directing it.[10] A 2014 Princeton study claimed that the United States, for example, was essentially run by an economic elite, with the general public wielding "near-zero" influence over policy decisions (which rather undercuts the aforementioned advantage of democracies).[11]

An alternative system, known as 100 percent banking, or full-reserve banking, has been proposed (for different reasons) by people including Frederick Soddy, Henry Simons, Irving Fisher, Milton Friedman, Herman Daly, and Frank Knight. In a 1927 review of Soddy's *Wealth, Virtual Wealth, and Debt*, Knight wrote: "In the abstract it is absurd and monstrous for society to pay the commercial banking system interest for multiplying severalfold the quantity of the medium of exchange when a) a public agency could do it all at negligible cost, b) there is no sense in having it done at all, since the effect is merely to raise the price level, and c) important evils result, notably the frightful instability of the whole economic system."[12] To avoid deflation during the transition, new money would be created by the government and lent to the banks to bring their reserves up to par. Full-reserve banking would create a new separation of powers between the state and the private sector: the former in charge of money creation, and the latter responsible only for arranging finance through loans of the existing supply.[13] Because banks would be out of the business of money creation and would only recycle existing funds, seigniorage profits from the creation of new money would go directly to the government. As Martin Wolf explained in the *Financial Times*, the amounts are significant: the British government, for example, could potentially "run a fiscal deficit of 4 per cent of GDP without borrowing or taxing."[14] In Iceland—where the GFC led to the complete collapse of the banking sector—the prime minister recently commissioned a plan for monetary reform along these lines.[15] The Swiss are also planning a referendum on it (though they do that a lot). From the viewpoint of complexity science, another advantage of 100 percent banking is that it would simplify the monetary system and remove some of the positive-feedback loops that destabilize the economy.

Why One Currency?

As discussed in chapter 2, money has an inbuilt tendency to unify, just as power has a tendency to try and become absolute. The government, with its private sector partners, has therefore long enjoyed a monopoly over money creation. But would a number of complementary currencies be more resilient and help to address problems such as scarcity of the main currency? Ecosystems tend to be broken into separate modules, rather than a single highly connected network, and a similar structure may also be useful in finance.

Parallel currencies have been called upon repetitively as possible saviors throughout periods of financial turmoil. Given that, according to the

IMF, the world has experienced an average of about ten systemic financial crises—including banking crises, monetary crashes, and sovereign debt crises—per year since the floating exchange regime was introduced in the early 1970s, it is clear that the system needs some fine-tuning.[16] As complexity scientists point out, in complex systems there is a trade-off between efficiency and resilience.[17] Today, the financial system—or its guardians, the apostles of efficiency, to employ Joris Luyendijk's rhetoric introduced in chapter 6—stresses too much of the former and neglects the latter, which explains the system's fragility and volatility.

To have but one currency might seem simplifying and thus "right," especially given the rather chaotic transition of the world order we are living through. However, such a one-dimensional approach corresponds with neither the demands of a complex, globalized economy fueled by mutual dependencies and exposures nor the opportunities the current state of affairs offers. By giving up on the possibility of mixing and matching existing problems with multiple monetary solutions we deprive ourselves of what is called the edge effect in nature: one can find the most diversity as well as the greatest new life-forms in the transition zone where two ecological communities meet and influence each other. The same should be expected of a monetary order that forgoes the one-size-fits-all paradigm.

History, after all, delivers multiple examples of economies that benefited greatly from the introduction of a parallel legal tender. Some of these supporting pillars that propped up collapsing monetary regimes were created in a bottom-up fashion, as we shall see, meaning that they were community driven and often tolerated rather than accepted by the currency monopoly centers. Some of the parallel currencies were constructed in a top-down manner and were considered solid albeit temporary scaffolding by the representatives of respective governments and central banks.

In Russia, for instance, the golden chervonet was reintroduced by the government as a parallel to the floating fiat ruble in 1922. Both currencies were part of the system until the ruble was pegged to gold, at which time the second currency lost its meaning and was retired in 1947. Until then, the chervonet did its job quite well, stabilizing the economy and thus a society disturbed, among other things, by rampant inflation. Once the faith in the dominant currency—its stability and thus its future—is lost, the introduction of a trustworthy supplement can either provide for a stabilization of the original monetary order or for an ultimate orderly opt out.

The euro was founded on the idea that a single currency would make Europe stronger. However, the GFC led some to question this premise and suggest that the best way to ease monetary stress would be to have more currencies, old or new. One such proposal, suggested by former Deutsche Bank chief economist Thomas Mayer, was the creation of the geuro. The idea worked with the premise that Greece does not want to leave the eurozone and does not have the means to quickly put its fiscal house in order. The Greek government should thus issue IOUs to its creditors who—short of cash—would have to use them to settle their own bills. As a result, geuros would start circulating within the domestic economy, settling at a rate of circa two geuros to one euro, Mayer said, adding that this would give Greece both a chance to recapitalize domestic banks and to devalue with a second boosting of its competitiveness and thus its economy.

Bernd Lucke, a founding member of the Alternative for Germany political party and a professor of economics at the University of Hamburg, suggested that the countries of highly indebted southern Europe should bring back the drachma, the peseta, the lira, and so on. This would allow them either to leave the currency union without a bang or to stabilize and regain full membership in the club. Of course, it is difficult to unscramble the scrambled egg, says Parag Khanna, a global strategist, summing up all the technical as well as psychological issues tied to a possible eurozone breakup or split.[18] But as history shows there are a number of exceptions that prove that it is difficult, yet not impossible. Great empires collapse, and big (and small) currencies disappear. The demise of the Soviet Union, for instance, brought about a messy albeit brief, in some instances, transitory period with fifteen new currencies—including the Russian ruble, a successor to the Soviet ruble—at the end. Similarly, the Czechoslovakian koruna split into two tenders after the breakup of the country, causing only minor turbulence and proving that it is possible to have an egg where once there was a scramble. What is needed is political will to drive the change—or, alternatively, a lack of will to stop it.

Corporate Money 101: In Ones and Zeros We Trust

A return to the drachma or lira would represent a return to traditional currencies. However, these are not the only choices available. As mentioned earlier, since the time of the gold standard, money creation has conventionally been managed by a public–private consortium involving private banks and a centralized state. But just as modern virtual currencies don't necessarily need the private banking system to prosper, so there may be less need for the state, there is no rule to say that the only way to create money is to monetize government debt. And politicians, when willing, can enable potent parallel monetary schemes not only to exist but also to thrive. One of the oldest and certainly most successful examples is the Swiss WIR Bank, formerly the Swiss Economic Circle, which was founded in 1934 by two businessmen, Werner Zimmermann and Paul Enz, as a direct response to issues faced by small and medium-sized businesses.

A typical problem for such businesses is that they are pressured to pay quickly, within a month or so, even though the delivery horizon might be three to four times longer than that. The resulting cash-flow problems complicate their development, operations, and—during crises such as the Great Depression—existence. Commercial banks are mostly disinterested in helping and of course charge interest on loans. This creates bureaucratic obstacles and financially burdens the borrowing firm.

WIR is short for *Wirtschaftsring* (economic circle), but is also the German word for "we," which symbolizes the sense of community. The system solves the cash-flow problem by creating a mutual credit network of businesses, suppliers, and clients, which eliminates the need for financial middlemen. The WIR currency has a value equal to the Swiss franc (CHF), but mutual loans are arranged at zero interest. The currency can also be borrowed directly at a low interest rate. It is therefore a mix between a mutual credit system (which just keeps track of who owes what to whom) and a fiat currency system (where money can be created by loans). The loans must be repaid in WIR, and if a company wishes to leave the system, then its surplus WIR must be spent within the system. These measures protect the currency by making it more difficult to switch out of.

What started with only 16 members is now a network of some 62,000 small and medium-size enterprises (large corporations are not allowed to join) that announced a turnover of almost 2 billion WIR in 2012. Moreover, since the transactions typically involve both WIR and CHF, the real turnover generated by this currency might be up to three times higher. Companies experience an average 5 percent increase in business when they join the network, due to loyalty effects.[19] The system has also proven to be quite countercyclical, and helps to fill in for the national currency during times of economic stress.[20]

Negative Interest

Historically, people often seek alternatives when the currency of choice, deliberate or forced, is in short supply or is otherwise losing its footing. The situation is akin to a cardiac arrest: money stops flowing, and unless something takes its place, parts of the economy can wither and die. The Great Depression saw the invention not just of the WIR but also of some more radical monetary experiments that proved very successful, at least while they were allowed to continue, and paved the way for the later development of local currencies,

In 1929, the owner of a small Bavarian coal mine offered to pay his workers in a script that was redeemable in coal (the alternative was to close the mine). The notes, called Wära, had a monthly fee of 1 percent—a kind of negative interest—that paid for the storage costs. As the economist Silvio Gessel had shown, this meant that people spent the bills as quickly as possible, instead of hoarding them (see box 3.2). The effect—as with the bracteate coins from the Middle Ages—was to boost the velocity of money and, therefore, economic activity. Wara quickly gained popularity, first among local businesses, which accepted it in exchange for goods and services, and then nationally, as some 2,000 companies from all around Germany joined the scheme. Shortly afterward, in November 1931, the German central bank prohibited the use of wara, and the coal mine that backed it closed down.

It therefore met the same fate as the equally short-lived worgl money (1932–1933), which was backed by Austrian schillings rather than a commodity. Worgl, a small town in the Austrian Alps, decided to cope with the failing economy and rising unemployment via "certified compensation bills." Each month, a stamp worth 1 percent of the face value had to be applied, which again amounted to a negative interest rate, and created an impetus to spend (if people didn't want to buy anything, they could always pay their taxes early). The town's economy thrived and attracted the attention of economists, including Irving Fisher, and mayors of 170 communities that started exploring the possibility of adopting the worgl. At that point, the Austrian National Bank issued a prohibition order against this tender and made the issuance of "emergency money" a criminal offense.

Scrip currencies were also popular in many other countries during the Great Depression. In the United States, they were championed by Fisher, who wrote a book on the subject called *Stamp Scrip*, and suggested the slogan "Stamp Your Scrip to Stamp out the Depression."[21] Instead, Roosevelt stamped scrips out in 1933, by making them illegal. In 1936 the Social Credit government in the province of Alberta issued prosperity certificates to civil servants as part of their pay. Each dollar certificate needed a 1-cent stamp to be added every week to remain valid; at the end of the week there was a rush to spend the certificates, with the result that merchants were often left with the task of affixing the stamps. The federal government outlawed the program after one year (matters weren't helped by the fact that the stamps tended to fall off).

It is not clear how sustainable schemes such as the wara or worgl would have been, since the experiments were artificially cut short, but it is notable that their closure coincided with the rise of unemployment, and later fascism, in Germany and Austria in the period leading up to World War II.[22] And of course it was the preparation for that war that finally lifted countries such as the United States and Canada out of depression. Scarcity-based currencies, which were invented to pay war debts, have war in their DNA.

(Hyper)local Currencies for Local Wants and Needs

The idea of local currencies did not of course die out, and indeed their popularity has steadily gained in recent decades, propelled by the monetary uncertainty that followed the Nixon shock, the rise in community activism and environmental/antiglobalization groups, and the advent of personal computers and the Internet, which made administration much easier. As with liquidity networks such as WIR, they gained a further boost in the fall-out of the GFC, when people again became understandably keen to explore alternative monetary avenues. Greece, for example, has seen a resurgence in local currencies since the debt crisis created a sudden shortage of euros.[23] Estimates vary, but it is believed there are up to a few thousand alternative currencies of various sizes in operation around the world. Many (though certainly not all, as we will see later) are explicitly motivated by community activism or ecological principles and an attempt to move away from the conventional currency system, which is seen as socially and environmentally damaging.

The model for many such schemes is Ithaca Hours, which was first introduced by community organizer Paul Glover in Ithaca, New York, in 1992. Each Hour is valued at $10 and is generally considered to be a reward for an hour of work, though rates are subject to negotiation. While not directly convertible to dollars, they are backed by a network of businesses that agree to accept them as payment at that rate. Users were originally matched through advertisements in a bimonthly newspaper and received four Hours when they placed an ad. Today the printed notes can be purchased from a local credit union and are currently accepted by more than 900 participating local businesses.[24] Because the currency needs to be used locally, this gives an advantage to small businesses with local supply chains (or put another way, it counterbalances the advantage of large companies that source globally and have no attachment to the community). As Glover said in an interview: "We would like to change the trading process so that it's more equitable, more welcoming, more fair, opens doors between people, builds bridges, allows people to trade on a more fair basis, and get compensated doing what they like to do. Especially, the environment is a consideration in the market place for us."[25]

The Canadian city of Calgary's version, known as Calgary Dollars, has been operating successfully since 1996. San Francisco's Bernal Buck, unlike most other local currencies, relies on plastic and is thus a local Visa, based on an account at a local credit union. When used at participating venues, consumers get back 5 percent of their next purchase, which resembles the scheme that frequent-flier or rewards cards—corporate money we shall discuss further—employ.[26] In England, the seaside city of Bristol got a lot of attention in 2012 with its launch of the Bristol Pound, a local currency backed (in pounds sterling) by the Bristol City Council and the Bristol Credit Union, and endorsed by firms including the local bus company and the electricity provider Good Energy. Users of the currency are charged 3 percent to convert back into sterling, which incentivizes them to stock with local providers. A critical feature is that council taxes can now be paid in local currency, which is a direct challenge to the main currency's monopoly. The mayor of Bristol, George Ferguson, takes all of his income in Bristol pounds. The project is run by the nonprofit Bristol Pound Company, whose Stephen Clarke says: "We're not really just an economics project, we're a social project. One of the big things we've done is we make people talk about money and think about money."[27]

Most community currencies are still fiat currencies that need to be administered by a central authority—even if it is now a local authority. An alternative approach is Local Exchange Trading Systems (LETS), which act as a kind of WIR-like exchange network for labor. The name was coined in 1983 by Michael Linton, who initiated a LETS system in Courtenay, British Columbia. Under this system, a babysitter, for example, can swap time for a credit and use it to pay someone for a haircut. The credits don't become scarce, because they can be created at any time by doing work, and interest is not charged. It is therefore not necessary to manage the money supply as with a centralized currency. LETS and related Time Dollar schemes, which are valued in terms of labor time, now exist in many countries, but tend to be rather small-scale, perhaps because that makes it easier to identify and deal with freeloaders (a problem with any form of credit sharing is that people can go into debt, and some decide to stay there).

A unique advantage of alternative currencies is that they can be tailored to incentivize users not just to shop locally but also to shop or otherwise behave in a particular way. As just one of many examples, the Torekes currency from Ghent in Belgium, created by a team led by Bernard Lietaer, was explicitly designed to revitalize the deprived Rabot-Blaisantvest area of the city. Participants earn Torekes by performing tasks such as caring for their street, participating in community events such as cleanup days, coaching sports, signing up for green electricity, and so on. The Torekes can be spent in local shops and are the only accepted means of payment for renting a plot in community gardens.[28]

Similarly, Equal Dollars of Philadelphia is based on the idea that a good deed should not go unrewarded. Accepted by more than 100 local businesses, Equal Dollars can be earned largely by helping neighbors and volunteering. "The U.S. dollar is fine to feed the upper one percent, but we are missing something that gets people to work for each other and for the community. . . . This helps regular people exchange goods and services in an economy that is in deep trouble," explained Bob Fishman, the executive director of Resources for Human Development (RHD), a nonprofit that launched the project in 1996.[29] Successfully, one might argue, since the crisis-driven spike in interest enabled RHD to offer a $50,000 grant to the first state government that will try out its baby. The EU similarly decided to back projects such as Community Currencies in Action, which aim at understanding the purpose and function of local moneys and at subsequent explanation of these to the public sector.

Japan, too, has developed a number of innovative schemes. Hureai Kippu (Caring Relationship Tickets), launched in 1994, are earned by helping to look after seniors, so are like Time Dollars but are tailored for a particular type of work. The credits are transferable, so for example, a person can send them to their parents in another town. Another complementary currency known as WAT, which started in 2000, operates on the same principle as bills of exchange or tally sticks. A WAT is reckoned as 1 kWh of electrical current generated by natural forces (e.g., wind or solar), and equates to about six minutes of unskilled labor or around ¥75 to ¥100. Any participating business can write a WAT ticket, which circulates within the network of users until it returns to the original issuer, who then cancels it.[30] And anyone can join this peer-to-peer network just by accepting a ticket as payment; transactions and participants are not centrally tracked or controlled.

Box 8.1

Of a Pensioner's Private Currency

In 1999, retired law professor Giacinto Auriti persuaded people as well as forty retailers from the Italian village of Guardiagrele to dump liras and adopt his very own currency, the simec. He offered an unbeatable deal, since the simec was pegged to the lira but Auriti paid two simec for every lira received. This experiment was supposed to prove his theory about money and a vast banking conspiracy in which central banks, instead of giving money to the people, lend through the banking system at interest and thus are robbing the common man.

A chance to double one's purchasing power, rather than the reasoning behind it, inspired a shopping spree that generated an estimated 5074.6 million liras ($2.74 million) in turnover, with Auriti claiming that at one point there were 2.5 billion liras in circulation. That is when Italy's Finance Guard, a militarized police force that usually deals with smuggling or tax fraud, came in. One hundred guardsmen invaded the town, confiscating the simec banknotes— only to be later ordered by a judge to release both the notes and the professor. Auriti, as tax police investigators found out, funded the scheme from his very own savings, and thus no criminal offense had been committed.

This could have been the end of the story but it was not. In 2002, before European states were about to adopt the euro, Auriti returned to the stage, warning that global central bankers were about to provoke an artificial crunch, adding that the simec provided a necessary safety net. At the same time, Italy's anti-immigrant, anti-euro Northern Party announced its interest in replicating the Guardiagrele monetary experiment. Since then, nonconformists and fringe politicians alike occasionally reintroduce the idea.

Because the system is based on mutual trust, rather than deference to a central authority, it helps to foster business relationships.

The success of these currencies proves there is a tectonic shift going on at least in certain pockets of society and shows how specific niches—meaning groups that identify themselves with a particular idea—can be served well by an appropriate monetary tool (box 8.1). Local currencies are also perceived as being somehow warmer and more friendly than cold hard cash and help to build community spirit and social capital, and their use is associated with an increase in reported well-being.[31] Money operates at the nexus between number and value, between calculation and spirit, and its design affects that relationship. Just as scarcity-based currencies foster a sense of individuality, competition, and power, so complementary currencies can foster a sense of connection, cooperation, and trust, and be used to incentivize desired social outcomes.

Alternatively, of course, the same effects can be harnessed by corporations to improve profitability. Tiring of branding commodities and experiences, some are now turning to branding money itself.

Corporate Money 201: In Brand (Loyalty) We Trust

Which is the biggest currency of all? While most would probably guess the U.S. dollar, the reality is slightly different, should we allow for a broader definition of money. In 2005, the *Economist* weekly calculated that there are $700 billion Air Miles in circulation worldwide, making it the globe's number one currency. Quite a trip for what started as the loyalty program of Texas International Airlines in 1979. Along the way, the number of people who belong to the scheme grew to over 100 million. More than half of the Air Miles were collected on the ground, since airlines sell points to phone operators, credit card companies, and other retailers.

Naturally, Air Miles did not stop at conquering the global reserve currency and grew further. In 2005, there were 14 trillion frequent-flier miles outstanding. Seven years later, the amount doubled according to the *Economist*. Such an expansion comes at a price. "Airline miles are the most rapidly depreciating currency in the world," the news site Zero Hedge said, pointing out the steep increase in the number of miles needed to get places in 2013.[32] The "prices" went up by as much as 87 percent, which only underlined the gradual erosion of the miles' value. At the beginning, an upgrade to first class on a supersonic Concorde cost 20,000 points; today, on a normal airplane, it is 50,000 points plus $900 in fees.

Needless to say, while consumers suffer from this erosion of wealth—Orrell even had his Air Canada miles confiscated after being out of the country for a few years, so now scrupulously avoids that airline—those in charge reap a hefty profit. United Continental, for instance, brought in some $3 billion from its frequent-flier program in 2010. Moreover, while its revenue per passenger was $20.59, its revenue per member was $32.97, showing that these programs offer both an interesting marketing tool and also "piles of cash from sales of miles."[33] No wonder, then, that some economists compare the system to current central banking: miles can be bought, sold, held, and traded, just like (supra)national currencies, with airlines being at the center of it all, resembling central banks, controlling the rates by an increase or decrease in supply. An important advantage of miles is that the airline can control how they are spent, for example, by limiting their use to off-peak times, so that they complement rather than cannibalize conventional sales.

A wide range of companies of various backgrounds have introduced similar loyalty programs. Canadian Tire money, for example, is issued to customers of the country's largest hard-goods retailer when they make a purchase. It serves as a scrip currency that can be redeemed at the store (some other businesses also accept them). Introduced in 1958, it came into its own in the early 1960s when the store was involved in a gas price war with competitors. Each note was printed with the rousing message that "together we will defy the giants and win the gas war. . . . Our mutual cause is morally and economically right."[34]

While loyalty schemes have always offered the possibility to boost revenues and open up a communication channel with users, they more recently have also made it easy to spy on consumers. Given that a loyalty card follows spending patterns, and given the improving ability to crunch big data, the potential these schemes have exceeds by far what could had been expected of them when the concept was introduced in the 1980s. Because the legislation lags behind the practices used, "this is a Wild West period of personal data harvesting," as one person working in the area put it to us.[35]

Empowered by modern technologies and faced with a natural limit to growth within their own sectors, a loyal community of trusted—and trusting—consumers can open up a gate to a brand new potential. Coffee chain Starbucks, for instance, could also become tomorrow's bank. It is estimated that its Stars system accounts for up to 30 percent of all transactions, meaning that every third customer buys into the scheme that allows them to buy food and drinks with a card on which they collect points by paying with it, using the Starbucks app, or entering Star codes collected at participating retailers. Every third customer is a "good old friend" to Starbucks—and the Starbucks' barista is their good friend.

It is the latter that can enable the coffee company (and many others) to expand into the territory that has long been occupied by banks only. "You probably haven't seen a bank teller since the Bush administration, but you're on a first-name basis with the barista at your neighborhood," notes Marcus Wohlsen of *Wired* magazine. A growing list of corporate nonbank heavyweights such as PayPal, Wal-Mart (through its Bluebird partnership with American Express), and Google Wallet now offer alternatives to debit cards, checking accounts, and money transfers.[36] No wonder, then, that consultancy Accenture predicts that nonbanking competition will deprive banks of one-third of their revenues by 2020.[37]

Be it Starbucks Stars, Amazon Coins, or Nike's Sweat, big firms are offering alternative monetary worlds that, like fiat currencies, rely mainly on brand recognition and trust. Given that the fan base of some of the brands compares in size to large countries (Real Madrid, for instance, has 450 million fans worldwide, making it the third largest "nation" on the planet), the potential is certainly there. Moreover, as some experts argue, an interesting opening exists to create hybrids that will exploit the possibilities of two or more parallel monetary universes (box 8.2).

"Private banks issued gold backed currency a hundred years ago for ease of use in everyday transactions. Corporates will be issuing Bitcoin backed rewards/loyalty/gamification tokens in the near future," predicted Jack Liu, head of institutional development of OKCoin, which used to be the largest Chinese Bitcoin exchange, adding that in this way companies large and small would explicitly guarantee the stability of one's investment.[38]

Box 8.2

Time Is Money

In the early 2000s, a sort of alternative currency became popular for making money transfers in a number of African countries: airtime on mobile phones. If a person wanted to send money to another, he could transfer (by text message) some of his airtime to the other person's phone. That person could either use it or sell it to someone else. In areas where more people had mobile phones than bank accounts or credit cards, the ability to transfer funds in this way was extremely useful. And migrants living abroad could send funds home as easily as texting, rather than using intermediary institutions that charged exorbitant rates.

Once mobile phone companies got wind of this, some of them decided to branch out into financial technology—instead of sending time, phones could be used to send money directly. M-Pesa (for mobile-money, in Swahili) was launched in 2007 by Vodafone. Users make a lump-sum payment to the mobile operator through agents such as retail outlets. They can then make purchases by typing in the merchant's account number (even street vendors have them) followed by a PIN. Each party receives a text message confirming the transaction. The system is very secure, and one of its benefits is that crime rates have fallen because businesses can have less cash on their premises. The service was later extended to allow for things like savings accounts and loans and spread to other regions, including India, Afghanistan, and parts of eastern Europe.

An area with one of the highest rates of digital transactions in the world—most of which are carried out in U.S. dollars on a system called Zaad—is Somaliland. Adan Abokor, who is a local scholar and democracy activist, says "I don't even carry money any more."* It might seem surprising that this revolution in financial technology (or "fintech") is bigger in a breakaway region of Somalia than in Silicon Valley, London, or Berlin. But the need for handling remittances, combined with lax regulation of the telecommunications sector, a weak local shilling, and the fact, as Abokor puts it, that "Somali society is an oral culture, so everyone needs a mobile phone," turned the area into a perfect laboratory for innovation. A switch to a purely digital currency, such as the proposed pan-African impala currency, would be a natural next step.†

Similar mobile payment systems are now also taking off—even in the developed world. In Britain, for example, Paym and Barclay's Pingit link mobile phone numbers to bank accounts. China has Alibaba's AliPay and Tencent's WeChat messaging app, which allow digital payments. And then there is Apple's iPhone, which has its own digital wallet. If money is a means of communication, the phone may be the ideal payment device.

*Geoffrey York, "How Mobile Phones Are Making Cash Obsolete In Africa," *Globe and Mail*, June 22, 2013.
†Jonathan Ledgard and John Clippinger, "How a Digital Currency Could Transform Africa," *Financial Times*, October 29, 2013.

Diversity for Better, Diversity for Worse

It is not just nonbanks that are branching out. Some commercial banks have decided to explore the uncharted waters as well. As discussed in the chapter 9, JP Morgan and others are closely monitoring the latest developments related to Bitcoin and the technology at its heart. At the same time, large banks such as Russian Sberbank are considering their own currencies. Any bank "could create its own currency, with all of the accompanying services such as bank deposit accounts, payment services, checks, credit cards, debit cards, electronic transfers via smartphone or whatever, and also physical banknotes and coins," argues Nathan Lewis, adding that banks in Hong Kong already issue their own money based on the U.S. dollar.[39]

This only confirms that after a period of centralization, when money creation and distribution largely became the domain of central and commercial banks, the time of decentralization has come, propelled by the instability of the environment on the one hand and new technologies on the other. This momentum yields a potential for the creation of a richer and thus more robust as well as accommodative environment, but it also constitutes a threat of too much fragmentation, which would be harmful. The pendulum, in other words, can swing toward an extreme the world has already experienced. In Japan, for instance, there were 1,694 paper moneys based, among other things, on precious metals, rice, potter's wheels, and umbrellas in the 1850s. Friedrich Hayek's idea of "denationalized money" with a free-for-all of multiple competing currencies suffers from the same problem as denationalizing railways—sometimes an integrated system works best. Just as a transport system can be improved by integrating different types of transport—walking, bicycle, car, bus, rail, plane, and so on—so the monetary system can be improved by integrating moneys that operate on different scales, from local to global.

Many people all around the world already use various moneys every day, but fully exploiting their potential requires a changed attitude not only of policy makers but also of the general public. As Bernard Lietaer puts it, "We are boxed, trained to believe that the only way to manage the economy is with a single currency."[40] The change of perception, one must add, should then not be necessarily confined within the realm of the economy where (almost) everything is monetized, where money functions as the glue that holds the whole structure together. Historically there were moneyless societies and economies and, as discussed later, this idea has its followers even today.

To summarize, we have seen in this chapter that alternative currency arrangements usually arise when the official currency begins to lose its status or luster. The ultimate such breakdown, which remains to be fully processed by the collective monetary consciousness, was the Nixon shock of 1971, when mainstream gold-backed currencies were suddenly converted to fiat currencies. The conditions that justified the cozy public–private partnership of the gold standard no longer applied. The arrangement came under further stress in the GFC, which in turn laid the ground for eurozone crisis. It is not surprising that during this time a plethora of new currencies has emerged, being offered by anyone from community organizers to airlines. Their development has been abetted by new technologies such as the Internet and smartphones. In the process, the basic assumptions of money—that is, that it must be created by monetizing government debt in concert with the private sector—have been completely overturned, along with foundational economic concepts and the emphasis on scarcity and competition.

Once we accept that money is virtual and can exist in a variety of forms, we are free—at least in theory—to mix and match between the different possibilities. For example, as mentioned earlier, the strongest impediment to basic income is psychological—it seems unfair to give scarce funds away for nothing. But if basic income were delivered using a complementary currency, similar to Alberta's old Prosperity Certificates, it would be more clear that the funds represent a kind of birthright. If the funds were electronic, it would be simple to apply a small negative interest rate to discourage hoarding and cover administration costs (no stamps required). In practice this charge would be equivalent to a normal account fee, with the difference that the charge scales with the amount held. The currency could also borrow ideas from corporate currencies to help achieve agreed goals such as carbon reduction or debt cancellation.[41]

Local currencies or mutual credit schemes—which can exist independent of either the state or private banks—do not threaten to replace national currencies but can play an important complementary role. As we've seen, their use can be encouraged simply by the local government accepting them as payment for taxes. In some respects the situation today resembles the Middle Ages, with multiple overlapping currency zones. That period saw the advent of virtual instruments such as bills of exchange, which ultimately reshaped the world financial order. In the next chapter, we consider an alternative, deliberately scarce virtual currency that is truly international (or postnational)—and which its advocates believe will provide the gold standard for the global village.

9

Changing the Dominant Monetary Regime, Bit by Bitcoin

I think that the Internet is going to be one of the major forces for reducing the role of government. And the one thing that's missing, but that will soon be developed, is a reliable e-cash, a method whereby on the Internet you can transfer funds from A to B, without A knowing B or B knowing A, the way in which I can take a 20 dollar bill and hand it over to you and there's no record of where it came from. . . . Of course, it has its negative side. It means the gangsters, the people who are engaged in illegal transactions, will also have an easier way to carry on their business.

MILTON FRIEDMAN, "FULL INTERVIEW ON ANTI-TRUST AND TECH"

The root problem with conventional currency is all the trust that's required to make it work. The central bank must be trusted not to debase the currency, but the history of fiat currencies is full of breaches of that trust. Banks must be trusted to hold our money and transfer it electronically, but they lend it out in waves of credit bubbles with barely a fraction in reserve. We have to trust them with our privacy, trust them not to let identity thieves drain our accounts. . . . With e-currency based on cryptographic proof, without the need to trust a third party middleman, money can be secure and transactions effortless.

SATOSHI NAKAMOTO, "BITCOIN OPEN SOURCE
IMPLEMENTATION OF P2P CURRENCY"

The state/bank's shared monopoly over money has suddenly been challenged by what first appeared to be a mere toy of geeks and cyberanarchists in 2008. At second glance, Bitcoin, and more generally cybercurrencies, seemed to be a perfect answer to much of the malaise of the current economic regime that people started to recognize and criticize as a result of the crisis. And thus, like lightning out of a blue sky, these moneys started to be seriously discussed by mainstream media and Wall Streeters alike. Some predicted an ephemeral life for them, while others praised their revolutionary potential—or warned against it. Several years down the road, Bitcoin, *the* symbol of cybercurrencies, is still largely perceived as a means to get guns and drugs from the darkest corners of the Net. At the same time, however, the biggest corporates—including banks like JP Morgan— are getting their hands dirty, either accepting it or exploring its logic.

The Great Financial Crisis of 2007/2008 put a lot of people off the world's financial system, and even the concept of money itself. But one person or group (for grammatical convenience we'll assume it's a guy), operating under the male Japanese pseudonym Satoshi Nakamoto, decided to take matters into his own hands by designing a completely new currency that would be minted neither by central banks, nor by private banks, but by the people. Or to be more accurate, by the people's computers.

The electronic currency known as Bitcoin was first proposed in a paper posted online by the elusive Nakamoto in November 2008, and open-source software to run it became available at the start of the new year.[1] On January 3, to time-stamp the code creating the first coins (the so-called Genesis block), he included a headline from the *Times* that captured the spirit of the age: "Chancellor on Brink of Second Bailout for Banks."

Other cybercurrencies had been proposed in the past, and many of Bitcoin's design elements grew out of the anarchist/cryptographic Cypherpunk movement in the 1990s, which also spawned Julian Assange's WikiLeaks. But Nakamoto was the first to make it work. His invention also came at exactly the right time. Just when trust in the finance system was at its lowest ebb, here was a currency that only required trust in an algorithm. As he put it in an introductory post, "With e-currency based on cryptographic proof, without the need to trust a third party middleman, money can be secure and transactions effortless."

Bitcoin didn't take off straight away. That January, Nakamoto ran his own program and produced or "mined" himself about 43,000 bitcoins. As will be discussed, the point of the mining algorithm is to maintain the payment system, and the bitcoins are a reward. Of course they had no value, because there was nothing to spend them on, so he gave ten of them to a coder called Hal Finney who he'd met on a discussion forum. Finney tried out the mining algorithm, helped debug it, let it run for about a week, and produced about 1,000 coins—then stopped when the intensive number crunching appeared to be wearing out the fan on his computer.[2]

By then, a community of users was developing. (Finney died in 2014 from the degenerative disease ALS; his Bitcoin hoard was used to keep his body cryogenically frozen, in the hope that a cure is found and he can be revived.) Each time a computer was added to the network, the mining task became incrementally more difficult, requiring a little more computer power and electricity to produce the same number of coins. In October, users set up a website quoting a price that corresponded to the cost of electricity required to mint a coin. This worked out at the time to about $0.0008 per bitcoin, so 1,000 coins was worth about $0.80. With Bitcoin, a labor theory of value is appropriate—if you count the labor of computers.

Once a price was available, people began to trade. The price became extremely volatile, but it was still just a game. At least until May 22 , 2010, when a software engineer in Florida called Laszlo Hanyecz managed to buy two pizzas for 10,000 bitcoins, by posting a request on the Bitcoin forum. Someone in Britain accepted the bitcoins and ordered the pizzas from a restaurant in Jacksonville using a credit card.

Bitcoins were taking their first tentative steps out of the virtual world, into the real world—they were becoming *things*. And they never looked back. At the time of this writing, the price paid for one of those pizzas works out to more than $1 million.

Bitcons

Hanyecz had plenty of bitcoins, because he had worked out how to speed up the mining process by programming his computer's graphic card to handle the computations. This was the digital equivalent of inventing a new prospecting technique and sparked a competitive race among miners that became increasingly intense as the price started to climb. And climb. However, the killer app for Bitcoin, which brought it into widespread use, turned out to be not pizza delivery but drugs (and a few killers).

As Milton Friedman had predicted, foremost among the early adopters were "the gangsters, the people who are engaged in illegal transactions."

The most notorious example was the Bitcoin-driven website known as Silk Road, which specialized in narcotics. Set up in March 2011, it soon became very popular, with about 1 million accounts, and did a roaring trade right up until October 2013 when the FBI acted to close down the site. Its founder, Ross Ulbricht, was charged with money laundering, conspiracy to traffic narcotics, and trying to arrange no fewer than six hits. No evidence that the murders were actually carried out was provided—although the very next month a new site called Kuwabatake Sanjuro was set up to cater to that need.

One of the clearer expositions of how Bitcoin works was provided in the FBI's testimony to a district court in New York. As the FBI explained to the judge and jury, who probably thought they were learning about some new hallucinogenic substance, Bitcoin is a "decentralized form of electronic currency, existing entirely on the Internet and not in any physical form. The currency is not issued by any government, bank, or company, but rather is generated and controlled automatically through computer software operating on a 'peer-to-peer' network."[3] Thus, instead of swapping songs, as in the defunct Napster, people swap virtual money, which can be used to buy real things, such as pizza or drugs. To acquire bitcoins (the technology has a capital B; the currency unit, a lower-case b), a user typically must purchase them from a Bitcoin 'exchanger.' In return for a commission, Bitcoin exchangers accept payments of currency in some conventional form (cash, wire transfer, etc.) and exchange the money for a corresponding number of bitcoins, based on a fluctuating exchange rate. Exchangers also accept payments of bitcoins and exchange the bitcoins back for conventional currency, again charging a commission for the service." The bitcoins are stored in a Bitcoin wallet, which is a kind of secure account accessed by a private key contained in a text file.

To make a payment, the user's computer releases the transaction details to the peer-to-peer network. The information is bundled together with an electronic signature that identifies the issuer's account but not his or her personal identity. Bitcoin is sometimes known as a "cryptocurrency," because it uses cryptographic techniques to ensure security and anonymity: "Only if one knows the identities associated with each Bitcoin address involved in a set of transactions is it possible to meaningfully trace funds through the system." However, exchanges often require personal information to open an account. Other computers in the network, the miners, check the payment details and incorporate them into a public ledger known as the "blockchain," which serves as a record of all Bitcoin transactions that have occurred in the system's history. It is a database that keeps track of changes, not by erasing or modifying entries, but by growing larger. Its memory goes all the way back to the Genesis block, so it never forgets where the coins are or where they came from. The blockchain was the key innovation that made Bitcoin possible, because by tracking every coin in existence, as the FBI noted, it protects against fraud and "serves to prevent a user from spending the same bitcoins more than once." About every ten minutes, a block of transactions is confirmed, time-stamped, and added to the blockchain. As of early-2016, the size of the blockchain is over 50 gigabytes and counting.[4] Bitcoin is therefore both public and private—the ledger is public, but the addresses it contains are anonymous and private.

The task of adding a new block is made artificially difficult by requiring miners to perform a so-called proof-of-work, which is comparable to tossing a coin millions of times (electronically, of course) until they get a certain number of heads in a row. The computing power required to do this puts a price on the blockchain and makes it economically unattractive to try and trick the system by producing a fraudulent version. As a reward for successful completion of this work, miners also receive a certain number of freshly created bitcoins. This represents a seigniorage fee, and because the addition of new coins dilutes the worth of existing ones, the expense is shared over the network. The difficulty of the task is progressively ramped up so that the blockchain is updated at the same rate of one block every ten minutes no matter how fast computers get.

Mining is expensive because to do it efficiently now requires dedicated facilities—heavily air-conditioned warehouses stacked with racks of computers—along with large amounts of electricity.[5] Environmentally friendly, it is not. Popular locations include Iceland (cheap geothermal energy) and Washington State (cheap hydropower). This expense can be seen as the cost of maintaining trust in the network, measured in computers and gigawatts, but it may also prove to be a competitive disadvantage for Bitcoin, as discussed later.

The issuance of new bitcoins, like the discovery of gold, therefore has a random component but favors large miners. The money supply is thus diversified to a degree and allowed to gradually expand. However, the system is designed so that the maximum number of bitcoins in existence does not exceed the apparently arbitrary limit of 21 million. We are currently about two-thirds of the way there, and the limit is expected to be reached around 2140, after which miners will receive only transaction fees, which are currently small or even zero. As this limit approaches, fees will therefore have to increase, though by how much is a subject of debate.[6] In principle, users could collectively decide to change the rules and introduce more coins, but only if 51 percent of the computing power in the network agreed (a potential vulnerability, should the system be taken over by a consortium).

The system has therefore been cunningly designed to enable cheap, secure transactions in a completely decentralized way. Napster could be shut down because it ran off a centralized server, but Bitcoin lives on the Internet. From the point of view of a judge, listening to FBI testimony, it probably resembled some kind of sinister conspiracy, which is ironic given that many of its proponents feel the same way about the conventional banking system. The "stamp" on a bitcoin is provided not by a government or central bank but by the network-confirmed and time-stamped blockchain. A bitcoin by itself has no inherent worth; like a fiat currency such as the dollar it attains value through the markets it has itself created. Unlike a traditional currency, it is not (yet) issued by the state or accepted as payment for taxes. Because its code is open source, anyone can download it and play around with it, and as discussed later, Bitcoin has already spawned a number of copycats and variants, known as "altcoins," but Bitcoin is currently far larger than any of its competitors and is holding onto its first-mover advantage.

The addresses of the first coins, from the Genesis block on, are written there in the blockchain, and it is relatively easy to figure out which anonymous figures they belong to and to see whether they have moved. Satoshi Nakamoto no longer stays in touch with the Bitcoin community—his last known e-mail was in April 2011—but he is believed to be a Bitcoin millionaire, which at the currency's peak was a dollar billionaire. (Nakamoto can mean "central" and Satoshi "intelligence" in Japanese, so it all points to the CIA.) Whether his creation will pass the test of time remains to be seen, but cybercurrencies as a whole seem unlikely to go away soon—and not just as a means to buy contraband or avoid taxes.

Wild West

One group that Bitcoin appeals to is the masses of migrant workers (see box 8.2), whose remittances totaled $530 billion in 2012 and who—if they were a single economy—would place twenty-second, ahead of Iran or Argentina. As Bitcoin's founder pointed out, the main disadvantage of the conventional banking system is the massive overhead costs, which appear as transaction fees. These are particularly high for cross-border exchange.

Specialized firms such as Western Union and banks alike charge around 10 percent, and as high as 20 percent in some instances, to send these funds home. Add exchange rate costs, and the total cut can reach 30 percent. The process also takes a few days. With Bitcoin, in contrast, users swap the original currency for bitcoins for a fee of typically 1 percent, transfer it to the intended destination, and swap it again for the local tender—all in a matter of minutes.[7]

Another group that naturally gravitates toward cybercurrencies are citizens of nondemocratic or outright authoritarian countries. In Venezuela, for example, Bitcoin is gaining a foothold for a number of reasons. One is rebellion against the system, against the order of things where access to consumer goods and hard currency is limited to the affluent. Another is that, with hyperinflation of over 50 percent, bitcoins do not seem so risky.[8] It also helps that Bitcoin miners have access to cheap, subsidized electricity.

Finally, there are also the 2.5 billion adults who are collectively referred to as the "unbanked" (which sounds like the financial version of unwashed). Given that this group amounts to over half the adult population, it is an attractive target for cybercurrencies. Even in the United States, 12 percent don't have bank accounts, which makes it hard to either save or borrow.[9] Of course, it might seem that the unbanked will also be unreceptive to new technologies—but as discussed in chapter 8, this is far from the case, which is why countries in Africa have spearheaded mobile banking. They can skip over the legacy banking system in the same way they skipped over landlines and went straight to mobile. One reason Bitcoin has captured the imagination of so many people is that it holds the promise to democratize finance and change lives for the better. There is a kind of utopian fervor around Bitcoin meet-ups that is in marked contrast to the jaded careerism that characterizes most of the financial sector.

Given the novelty of the whole concept, most countries do not know what to do with it, while seeing it both as a potential and a threat. Some countries, such as Switzerland, Germany, and Cyprus, have been supportive. A group of forty-five Swiss members of Parliament called for the evaluation of the opportunities that Bitcoin yields for the country's banking system in 2013. Germany labeled it private money and treats it as such. The Cypriot University of Nicosia, one of the largest accredited English-language universities in the Euro-Mediterranean region, became the first university to accept tuition in bitcoins (the Cyprus banking crisis, which led to confiscation of savings accounts in 2013, may have been a motivating factor). In the United States, the Treasury Department released a statement recognizing "the innovation virtual currencies provide, and the benefits they offer society," which was enough to boost the price to a record of $1,242 in November 2013—thus briefly surpassing by 2 cents the price of an ounce of gold.

The Chinese had a different view, and soon spoiled the party when they barred financial companies (though not the public) from making Bitcoin transactions. Bitcoin, like other cryptocurrencies, ignores physical boundaries and restrictions that come with them, such as limits to capital flows. Once Beijing realized that Bitcoin created a backdoor through which money was being siphoned out of the country, it opted for an abrupt stop, since the Chinese economy needs to keep money in the domestic banks that fuel its rapid expansion with their credits. The attempt to rein in Bitcoin has not scared off the general public in China; at the time of this writing, nearly 80 percent of transactions are yuan–bitcoin, most of them speculative (one reason for the large number of trades is that Chinese exchanges often don't charge trading fees).[10] However, it triggered a fall in the virtual currency's price of about one-third from its peak.

Things got even worse after the collapse of the Mt. Gox Bitcoin exchange. Mt. Gox originally began as a platform for a card-trading game (the name does not refer to a mystical mountain, but comes from Magic: The Gathering Online Exchange). When Bitcoin began to take off, Magic's founder, Jed McCaleb, switched to trading bitcoins. The site moved to Japan and became the leading Bitcoin exchange, at its peak handling over 75 percent of trades, until early 2014, when it turned out someone had magicked away about 850,000 bitcoins, which by then was worth around $500 million. The security flaw apparently lay with the exchange, rather than the design of Bitcoin, but again it sent the price plunging.

To chronic naysayers, this was a clear sign that Bitcoin was done, or nearing its end as a subject of any notable interest beyond the geek community that gave birth to it in the first place. However, every idea has to suffer through its childhood illnesses. And for most of its end users, such as those sending remittances abroad, such price perambulations are a secondary concern, since they only hold the currency for a matter of minutes.

Under the Table

In his "Crypto Anarchist Manifesto," published well before Friedman's 1999 interview on the topic, Tim May wrote with some prescience about the social and economic impact of cryptographic methods: "The State will of course try to slow or halt the spread of this technology, citing national security concerns, use of the technology by drug dealers and tax evaders, and fears of societal disintegration."[11] Indeed, much of the public discourse around Bitcoin, fueled regularly by some central bankers and government officials, seems to stress the connection between cybercurrencies and illegal activities such as drug dealing, tax evasion, funding for terrorism, and organized crime. This is why it is so important to understand what Bitcoin is and what it is not.

One thing that Bitcoin is not, is cash. "King" cash offers the certainty one can rely on even during the financial earthquake, as the market proverb goes. It seems solid, understandable, accountable, which is why many economies, including the most advanced ones, such as Germany, still largely rely on it; in the current period of rapid time and space compression, wherein more and more familiar things are turning into series of zeros and ones, banknotes and coins simply evoke a cozy feeling that resembles fond memories, like grandma's apple pie. Cash is a money object that you can hold in your hand and feel in your pocket.

However, many of the attractive properties that cash is supposed to have are largely an illusion. Given the inflationary character of fiat currencies, meaning the ingrained principle that a certain level of inflation is good and is thus targeted by central banks, to hold onto cash is like holding a candy cane in the rain; no matter how well you protect it, it will disappear, so enjoy it while it lasts, and enjoy it fast, the environment tells you. At least with Bitcoin, the biggest meddler of all, the central bank, is out of the picture. As Nakamoto put it in a 2009 post that echoed Nicolas Oresme in the Middle Ages: "Escape the arbitrary inflation risk of centrally managed currencies!"[12]

While Bitcoin has a reputation as being used by criminals, cash remains the medium of choice for most underground dealings, and its use has shown no sign of being supplanted by cybercurrencies. In the United States, for instance, cash use increased by 20 percent from 2011 to 2014, which means that there is around $1.2 trillion in cash outside American banks and the average American has about $4,000 stacked under the mattress. It has been estimated that the American economy loses more than $100 billion due to the evasion of taxes on unacknowledged incomes.[13] In Britain, some 70 percent of banknotes in circulation are said to be used for tax evasion, drug deals, bribery, and so on.[14] The study showing that 99 percent of banknotes in circulation in London are tainted with cocaine can only be considered a punch line in this context.[15]

Cash use for small general transactions, meanwhile, is being gradually supplanted by electronic payment systems. In 1776, Adam Smith announced that paper money outnumbered the coins in circulation; according to the UK Payments Council, 2015 would be the first year in which more is spent electronically than with both coins and notes.[16] Moreover, there are economies in which cash is on the very fringe of the monetary spectrum. In Sweden, transactions involving notes and coins equal a mere 3 percent of the national economy, and the country is expected to go completely cashless by 2030.[17] Some have argued that we should do away with coin and paper money altogether, though it isn't just criminals who would miss the liberating anonymity of cash.[18]

Banknotes (and coins), as well as gold and diamonds, thus enable organized crime as much as cybercurrencies do. Bitcoin, no doubt, attracts especially those who browse the dark Web to score or sell illegal matter or engage in illicit deeds. Its lack of complete anonymity explains why there is demand for an alternative in the dark pockets of the World Wide Web that is being met with altcoins such as Darkcoin and Zerocoin. These are based on the same protocols as Bitcoin, but are designed to compromise attempts at blockchain tracing via, for instance, encrypted swaps of coins among two or more users. It appears that at least some of the potential clients are paying attention. At the end of 2014, one could thus pay for LSD, cocaine, or counterfeit euros in Darkcoin on sites like Nucleus and Diabolus.[19]

Digital Gold

Another common criticism of Bitcoin is that it has no "intrinsic value" and is a poor store of wealth.[20] This is justified both by its currently volatile exchange rate and the fact that the entire system, which after all is based only on information encoded in the blockchain, could suddenly disappear into the ether, like a group illusion that suddenly shatters. But even gold, as discussed earlier, is ultimately considered valuable on the basis that it has been considered valuable for thousands of years (unlike other metals, such as copper, gold's industrial applications are limited). This is obviously a good reason for keeping the stuff, but essentially it is still a statement about fashion—just one that happens to have lasted with its ups and downs over a remarkably long time. Cybercurrencies will be worthless if the global Internet crashes and never recovers, but in that event gold might be rather useless as well: it is too soft and thus could not be used to forge simple instruments should some apocalyptic prophecy materialize and we all go back to being self-sufficient and relying on simple techniques of tool-making. (What *will* be useful? Social skills, probably.)

Bitcoin seems to be distinct from something like gold because it has no physical counterpart that you can hold in your hands (although you can buy "coins" with the Bitcoin data embedded in them). Indeed, the appeal of gold probably has as much to do with its reassuring heft as with its beauty: with a density nineteen times greater than that of water, a standard gold bar has a length of only seven inches but weighs 27.5 pounds. Bitcoins weigh nothing in themselves, but they still have a physical presence. This was demonstrated when someone mistakenly threw out a computer hard drive containing 7,500 bitcoins, purchased in 2009 when they were almost free. Somewhere in a Welsh landfill, if the story is right, lies a few million dollars, worth of digital gold.[21] The distinction between physical matter and digital information is blurry, since both ultimately consist of atomic configurations: what counts is possession. And while the apparent immateriality of a bitcoin may to many be its greatest disadvantage, it is at the same time its greatest strength.

Moving or making payments with gold is difficult, not just because it is heavy, but also because of the security risks. Someone has to keep an eye on the stuff as it goes from point A to point B. The same holds true for any kind of monetary transaction, which adds significant costs. For example, while credit card purchases can be made electronically over the Internet, credit cards were never designed with that in mind. The process is clunky and involves a number of middlemen who charge transaction fees that amount to between 2 and 3 percent. Their involvement is necessary to make sure the money has left your account and is deposited in the seller's account. Middlemen also provide both credit and a degree of consumer protection, so goods can sometimes be returned and transactions reversed. However, the purchaser needs to supply information such as address, credit card number, and the CVV number on the back of the card, and the process is not completely secure. Underwriting fraud is one reason credit card fees are expensive. The other is that the process is dominated by the Visa/MasterCard duopoly, together with their associated banks, so until recently there has been little competition.

Bitcoin transactions, in contrast, are tracked in the blockchain and do not require additional information to be submitted, making fraud more difficult, though certainly not impossible. For example, bitcoins can be stolen by hackers or malware that searches computers for the text file containing the private key to a wallet (a number of companies supply secure wallets and authentication schemes that give an added layer of protection). As discussed earlier, gold has historically been used as money not just for its beauty and scarcity but also because its properties—stability, fungibility, and divisibility—make it rather like number. But in a number-based society, why not just use code?

If anything, Bitcoin's biggest problem may be that it is *too much* like gold. As with ounces of gold, the total number of bitcoins is capped (subject again to a quorum of the mining community not agreeing to change the cap), so the system is not designed to adapt to the supply of goods and services. In fact, the number of bitcoins would actually shrink over time as some are permanently lost, in Welsh landfills or elsewhere. A Bitcoin economy, if it grows, will therefore tend to be deflationary, which will encourage hoarding, since the currency should—speculative swings aside—become progressively more valuable with time. Under the gold standard, banks gained extra flexibility through fractional-reserve banking, that is, lending more money than they had on their books; however, with Bitcoin there is less incentive for people to store their money with banks that will lend it to someone else. Over time, control of the currency could therefore accumulate in the hands of a small elite. One imagines a future version of William Jennings Bryan refusing to "crucify mankind upon a cross of digital cybercurrency."

Bitcoin's artificially high mining costs, which serve as a security feature to deter tampering with the blockchain, were perhaps also intended to emulate gold. As discussed in chapter 6, Adam Smith equated the cost of gold with the labor required to procure it, so gold money is in a sense backed by mining labor. With Bitcoin's proof-of-work protocol, human labor is replaced with the labor of computers and the electricity needed to power them. Bitcoin price and mining costs are coupled. If the price spikes too high above costs, then miners will mine more coins, which will increase supply and drive down the price; and as mining technology improves, costs go down, but the system makes fewer coins available to mine, which drives up the price. (When the number of bitcoins reaches its cap, mining of new coins will come to an end, so the existing coins will be backed, we suppose, by *historic* computer labor.) One of the criticisms of gold is the environmental damage and waste caused by mining, and the same can be said of Bitcoin; proponents will argue this is the cost of maintaining a secure network.

Bitcoin's exchange rate is volatile in part because much of the trading is speculative and does not involve the purchase of actual goods and services.[22] This volatility is not of direct concern to people who use bitcoins only as an intermediary for money transfers; however, it is certainly a headache for people like merchants. Volatility should reduce with time as the currency becomes more widely accepted, and this appears to be happening at a fairly quick pace—so much so, that even some of the people involved with the development of Bitcoin were surprised (see the section "Bitcoin: An Insider's Audit"). As one of the authors of this book, Chlupatý, found out, in Berlin, dubbed the world's Bitcoin capital, one could even live entirely on this currency in 2014, from renting a place, through getting a meal or a cup of coffee, to buying collectibles. Berlin business owners from Kreuzberg, the very heart of it all, say they mostly save the bitcoins they earn today, liking Bitcoin's philosophy, its rebellious antiestablishment feel, and its potential to disrupt the status quo, and hoping for the best to happen tomorrow. They both fear the currency's gradual shift toward the mainstream and, on a certain level, wish for it.

Money 5.n

While Bitcoin is by far the leading cybercurrency, it may not represent the last word on cybercurrency design. Competitors include so-called proof-of-stake altcoins such as the Paris-based NeuCoin, launched in July 2015, which rewards miners based on holdings rather than proof-of-work. As NeuCoin's founders point out in a white paper, Bitcoin miners currently earn in aggregate about $1 million a day, which works out to about $10 per transaction.[23] Users don't notice this, because transaction fees average only 5 cents. The remaining $9.95 comes from the new coins awarded to miners, and most of this is swapped out of Bitcoin to pay for expenses such as electricity. Mining rewards are set to decline as fewer new coins become available in the future, so total transaction fees will have to go up to compensate. The idea is that the sum value of transactions should increase enough to keep fees low.

NeuCoin, which is focusing initially on microtransactions such as tipping for online services, gets around this potential problem in another way, by simplifying the mining process and rewarding miners with new coins based on the number they hold (effectively an interest payment). Miners are motivated to secure the system because they will be substantial holders of the currency. Some coins are also granted to new or existing users or companies that adopt the currency. The process is overseen by three nonprofit foundations located in the Isle of Man, which are ultimately controlled by NeuCoin users on the basis of one vote per coin. The idea is to distribute coins strategically to encourage widespread adoption—while the Greeks and Romans used the army, NeuCoin is going for gaming, music, and video sites, with ads such as: "Go ad-free today for 10 NeuCoins. Click here to get 20 free." The money supply will therefore expand, rapidly at first and then more slowly, with a long-term target of 3 percent per year. Whether NeuCoin will succeed remains to be seen, but it and other competitors may well give the champ a run for its money.

Bitcoin's key technology, the blockchain, can also be used for purposes other than tracking coins. The company Ethereum, for example, has developed a software platform that uses the blockchain to certify digital contracts, powered by its own Bitcoin-like currency called ether (symbol Ξ, as in Ξther).[24] When we asked a representative from the firm at a Bitcoin conference to show a useful application, he pointed at his T-shirt, which displayed a few lines of code describing a decentralized drop box for large files. The file to be saved is broken up and distributed to multiple computers owned by different users. The owner can then redownload the file by making a micropayment in ethers. It doesn't sound that exciting, until you think of the massive quantities of underutilized but potentially valuable storage space that could be tapped, instead of building more data centers in Iceland or wherever.

In principle, anything that can be represented mathematically can be implemented using the language, from voting systems to derivatives contracts to stock markets to ownership of physical assets such as cars, houses, and gold. Trading expensive items usually involves middlemen such as real estate agents or brokers to verify the identity of each party and make sure the transaction takes place properly. But if the ownership of the goods is tied to a digital token and verified through the blockchain, then the assets can be tracked and traded in the same way as bitcoins.

The blockchain has, for example, been proposed for the music industry as a way to keep track of artists' royalties, which are currently handled through a notoriously labyrinthine procedure involving layers of middlemen.[25] In other areas, the problem is not so much middlemen but the lack of a functioning system at all. As the Peruvian economist Hernando de Soto points out, billions of people around the world are excluded from the formal economy because there is no "public memory" of who owns what—which means among other things that they have no collateral for loans.[26] One answer—currently being tested in Honduras, one of the poorest countries in Latin America—is to build a secure land registry based on an enlarged version of the blockchain.[27] The trust that the blockchain gives Bitcoin can be generalized to any type of contract or document that would usually require a third party such as a lawyer. The distinction between money, things, and information becomes increasingly blurred.

In fact, with the much-vaunted Internet of Things, things could start to pay one another. An appropriately configured washing machine could order laundry detergent, negotiate the price, monitor the shipment, and alert the owner by phone, tracking everything on the blockchain as it went.[28] A self-driving car could set itself up as a taxi service.[29] Toasters and dishwashers will presumably be owning their own bank accounts and doing some speculation in derivatives on the side. And so on.

The endless possibilities are being explored in fintech hubs around the world, from Sydney to Tel Aviv, from London's Silicon Roundabout (situated around the Old Street Roundabout) to Zug's Crypto-Valley (described as a Swiss mecca for fintech because of its open legal environment).[30] A number of start-ups are being supported by investors such as BitAngels, whose cofounder Michael Terpin believes at least 10 percent of the world's e-commerce could be done over the blockchain, and the $4 billion venture capital firm Andreessen Horowitz, whose Marc Andreessen coinvented the first widely used Internet browser, Mosaic.[31] And in a replay of the "coder versus suits" dynamic that fueled the PC revolution in the 1970s, the equally revolutionary appeal of Bitcoin has not been lost on large financial companies such as JP Morgan and technology firms such as (yesterday's upstart) Apple. Even Goldman Sachs described Bitcoin as part of a "megatrend" that will shape the future of finance and backed it up by making a major investment in the Bitcoin company Circle.[32] In 2015 it also filed a patent application for its own cybercurrency, dubbed SETLcoin, which uses the blockchain to execute transactions involving financial assets such as stocks and bonds.

What will emerge from these financial laboratories remains to be seen, but the world of money is experiencing a greater wave of innovation than at any time since someone first transcribed an IOU onto a clay tablet.

Bitcoin: An Insider's Audit

Marek Palatinus, a freelance programmer, is well known in the Bitcoin community. He is creator of the Bitcoin mining pool concept and a core programmer of TREZOR, the world's first hardware bitcoin valet. He was also one of the victims of a publicized cyberattack in 2012 during which hackers stole bitcoins worth roughly $228,000. Despite—or perhaps because of—this, Palatinus remains loyal to the development of this cryptocurrency.[33]

AUTHORS: In less than two and a half years, Bitcoin's value spiked from approximately $100 to $1,000, dropped back toward $200 and then grew to the current $400 level. How do you view speculations with this currency?

PALATINUS: Bitcoin as a technology is simply a tool that can be used in a number of ways. One is as money, another is for speculation. For me personally Bitcoin is not about speculation but I do not think it will harm it. It helps stabilize it and determine its market value. Bitcoin is a relatively new tool, and people are still looking for a stable price level at which it could find itself with respect to regular currencies such as the dollar.

AUTHORS: But could significant volatility not harm its exchange rate?

PALATINUS: People certainly look at this a lot; it is in a way a reflection of confidence in the system. If they do not understand a technology, then they observe how much faith others put in it. Bitcoin has as a result died a hundred times already, which is why every time it fell markedly articles started to appear about its failure. Nevertheless its volatility is slowly declining, which confirms that the more people speculating or trading, the smaller the fluctuations.

AUTHORS: Bitcoin's exchange rate fell five percent after bitcoin community legend Mike Hearn, a former senior software engineer at Google who left the company in 2014 to focus on bitcoin development stated at the start of 2016 that "bitcoin has failed," pointing out that the cryptocurrency faces technological collapse. What is your view?

PALATINUS: There are two factions in the Bitcoin community and each has its own view of what bitcoin is. It is a tool that works according to some principles but how it is used is really up to people. According to Mike, Bitcoin should be a transaction method for regular spending. The second faction claims that it should be a rare digital commodity that either quotes a value or around which other tools are created. I believe that in the long run the second option is more advantageous than a hugely inflated blockchain.

AUTHORS: Going back to the idea of bitcoin's technical failure: Do you think it is possible that it will encounter an irresolvable technological problem?

PALATINUS: Of course this can happen. On the other hand, with each new day, it is less and less probable for a truly major mistake to appear in the technological arena. But Bitcoin can fail in the sense that it will not fulfill the expectations of the general public.

AUTHORS: Another crucial issue raised lately has been the concentration of power. Mining is supposedly currently dominated by several Chinese entities, two of which control more than 50 percent of the hash power. What is your take on this?

PALATINUS: Centralization is in this sense under way. I consider this a problem but not a fatal one. China is today a technological superpower and mineries there are more accessible and cost at least 20 percent less. Intended decentralization is thus interrupted by physical borders, which has nothing to do with bitcoin as such. The market is simply skewed due to the fact that there are few producers, that they do not compete with each other and that they are connected to large Chinese farms. But in principle nothing prevents natural competition from fixing this as time passes.

AUTHORS: What if an entity without economic interests (in profits) but one interested in controlling bitcoin tries to enter the game? There are, for example, speculations about secret services, scared of cryptocurrencies, of their disruptive potential. What happens then?

PALATINUS: Of course, with an essentially unlimited budget, one can gain a monopoly or control. In the end this is about the degree of likelihood. I think it is possible but I am not sure it is probable.

AUTHORS: In the past two years signals indicating that bitcoin and the technology it depends on have attracted mainstream attention have been multiplying. Large banks such as Goldman Sachs are buying up startups that use the blockchain principle to develop various products and services. Is this shift towards the mainstream—or its interest—positive or negative for Bitcoin?

PALATINUS: It is without a doubt excellent PR for Bitcoin, it legitimizes the technology. This is because many people want to know if politicians, well-known companies, and the like approve of something. But I must add that in my opinion corporate blockchain use is nonsense. This is just buzz, an effort to show that they are keeping an eye on things and going with the times. As far as I know, no bank has introduced so much as an app or even functional concept indicating what blockchain should be used for.

AUTHORS: And what is your opinion about the fact that the Chinese central bank is mulling launching its own cryptocurrency while certainly having a different motivation than global commercial entities?

PALATINUS: Issuing a decentralized currency with controlled circulation seems strange to me. I do not believe that China would let people mine their own currency, that it would not want control. In such a case, it makes no sense. Blockchain has huge overhead, which ensures decentralization. If someone issues a cryptocurrency that they want to control, all they have is an expensive technology.

AUTHORS: Predicting further development is of course very difficult in the case of young and organically growing projects such as bitcoin. But let's try anyway: Where do you see Bitcoin in five years, technologically and, shall we say, ideologically?

PALATINUS: In terms of technology the protocol is in place and current discussions indicate that it will not change easily. But I think that various startups and services able to use the technology will emerge around the existing model. This means various sidechain technologies, that is, opportunities to create your own blockchains, currencies, which enjoy the same security as the main bitcoin blockchain. In terms of ideology, I think Bitcoin will be demystified within a few years in part thanks to how often we now talk about blockchain. People will simply get used to the fact that it is here and that there is no need to fear it.

Veni-check, Vidi-check, Vici-pending

So how does the future look for Bitcoin in particular? As Palatinus hints, the result will depend not just on technology but also on the interplay of social, political, and economic forces. There are myriad possibilities, but as we peer into the virtual tea leaves, three of the more extreme scenarios are as follows.

Napstercoin

Bitcoin becomes yet another short-lived star that turns into a black hole; some of its principle shall be carried on by other tools and projects, but this currency per se will run its course. In this Napster-like scenario, Bitcoin would cause a massive industry shake-up, of the sort that led to Apple's iTunes, and then fulfill the adage that "the revolution devours its children."

The main attraction of Napster was not just the fact that it was free but that users could access a huge and decentralized catalogue of digital music. Apple iTunes offered a similar catalogue, but now it was centralized. It also had a simple and elegant interface, which users were willing to pay to use. Some of the moves done by big players, including Apple, indicate that they might be thinking the same approach can work again. Apple Pay basically turns a phone into a standard credit card. While its technology relies on credit card infrastructure and is creaky compared to Bitcoin, to the consumer it might make little difference. And given Apple's design brilliance and its ability to partner with Visa, Whole Foods, or Disney, the advantage seems to be clearly on its side. Apple will take a hefty cut of the payment charges and enjoy access to consumer data previously monopolized by banks.

However, one must not forget that "the Apple ecosystem is a closed system that does a tremendous job at retaining customers but leaves it vulnerable to the innovation of open source projects. This is a flaw that Google's Android has exploited brilliantly and profitably," as the investor and author Brian Kelly argues.[34] Perhaps this time around the mainstream will enable the revolutionary feature to establish itself—in early 2015, Google announced that it was testing a new system known as Plaso that allows Bitcoin payments. Which leads us to the next scenario.

Supercoin

Bitcoin (or an improved version thereof) becomes an established parallel currency that functions alongside fiat moneys and other legal tenders including a handful of cybercurrencies. Enjoying its momentum, it grows in size until it becomes a challenge to the status quo just by the virtue of its sheer existence. If it succeeds in this way, Bitcoin could prove disruptive for not only authoritarian regimes such as China but also standard liberal democracies. "The politicians are still not fully aware of the destructive potential the Bitcoin has vis-à-vis their power," says Jaroslav Brychta, chief economist at brokerage X-Trade Brokers and a staunch supporter of the Austrian school of economics.[35] The banks' focal role in the economy is given by their monopoly over the system of payments, but if Bitcoin goes mainstream anyone could make payments and handle other financial operations without a bank account. "At that point, bank deposits would be meaningless. And once you take away deposits from the banks, if they cannot take deposits and multiply them, it is game over," concludes Brychta.

To achieve this level of dominance, Bitcoin would probably need some major support, from either a powerful corporation or even a government—for example it could be chosen as the basis for a national or regional currency.[36] Another route, in a country such as Venezuela, would be for the rest of the financial system to collapse—note that Bitcoin was born in a financial crisis and might hold its value quite well in the next one.

Selloutcoin

Bitcoin's blockchain technology is taken over by financial firms to serve as the back end for lucrative money-transfer services, in either bitcoins or some other currency (such as dollars).[37] Independent fintech services manage to cream off some of the banks' profit streams, but the power structure remains in place. It will be ironic if Bitcoin, which grew out of the same utopian, antigovernment, anticorporation ethos that gave us WikiLeaks, ends up being co-opted by the very institutions it sought to protect us from. When Cypherpunks claimed that cryptographic methods would "fundamentally alter the nature of corporations and of government interference in economic transactions," they didn't mean strengthen them.[38]

An additional possibility, of course, is that Bitcoin could implode in such a spectacular manner that it scares everyone off the idea of cybercurrencies for a long time, just as John Law put the French off banks, or at least the word *banque*. At this moment, though, Bitcoin seems to be enjoying decent momentum. The idea behind it has succeeded in a rational test—which is why big money got involved—and also appeals to the emotions of many, since it works with concepts such as freedom and collective will.

Of course, some fear even the idea of a financial system that lacks central control. To them, the interventions of central banks and the creative policies of commercial banks are largely a force for good, and inflation, banking fees, and occasional bailouts are externalities worth their cost. Bitcoin should only be accepted if it can reinforce the existing (power) structure; otherwise anarchy would arise. The campaigner and former derivatives broker Brett Scott revived a famous discussion between two Enlightenment political philosophers: Thomas Hobbes argued that people are inherently in conflict and thus, to escape "a war of all against all," they need to delegate some of their freedom to a sovereign who mediates. Jean-Jacques Rousseau countered with the idea that it does not have to be a sovereign but could be collective or general will. "So it goes with Bitcoin," says Scott. "In place of a centralised, hierarchical group of banks keeping score of the money, a decentralised network of individuals records every transaction on a virtual ledger."[39] Perhaps the most likely outcome will involve some blend of the two—a kind of compromise between hierarchy (state or corporate) and decentralization (Bitcoin or other) that echoes the accommodation between sovereign power and financial innovation that led to the foundation of the Bank of England.

Emerging Currency

One of the reasons cybercurrencies, and alternative currencies in general, have met with resistance is that they don't conform to traditional ideas about money. A price in bitcoins does not measure labor (at least the human sort) or utility (it's not a hedonometer), and the cybercurrency's emergence into the world relied neither on commodity value or the sanction of the state. Georg Friedrich Knapp wrote in 1905 that "the metallists fail to explain currency systems that have no metal. The chartalist has no trouble in explaining them; they are the touchstone of his theory."[40] But both these schools, along with many economists in general, struggle with something like Bitcoin. As Alan Greenspan said: "I do not understand where the backing of Bitcoin is coming from. There is no fundamental issue of capabilities of repaying it in anything which is universally acceptable, which is either intrinsic value of the currency or the credit or trust of the individual who is issuing the money, whether it's a government or an individual."[41] According to Eugene Fama, Bitcoin is "not a store of value. Unless it has some other value, the core value has to come from something."[42]

Nonetheless, cybercurrencies have proved their "metal"—you can buy things with them. So maybe the problem is not with cybercurrencies, but with our theories of money (box 9.1).[43] Implicit to all these theories is the idea that money has to be backed by something. It therefore inherits its value from some preexisting outside source, be it physical (metal), virtual (the law of the state), or some combination (labor or utility). But when we treat money as a fundamental rather than a derived quantity and acknowledge that money objects have contradictory but also mutually reinforcing aspects, it is possible to see how a currency can boot itself up out of the ether, based on nothing more than some code and an Internet connection. Money objects are desirable in themselves, so the more something looks like money, the more valuable its numbers become. And just as market prices emerge from the use of money objects, so the power of the money system expands with its markets.

A decentralized cybercurrency is supported not by metal or the state but by something much more distributed and amorphous—its network of users. A property of networks is that their power expands rapidly with size (sometimes called the fax effect, since fax machines were of little use until enough people had them). The value of a cybercurrency—and the trust it embodies—grows in the same way with the size of the network, so it can

Box 9.1

Seeing the Light

The debate over whether money is made of solid metal (as bullionists believe) or is a virtual system (chartalists) mirrors the much older debate over the nature of light. Democritus, in the fourth century B.C.E., believed that light was a form of physical matter that consisted, like everything else, of *atomos*, or atoms. Aristotle argued instead that light was a kind of wave in the ether. In the seventeenth century, Isaac Newton proposed a corpuscular theory in which light was a stream of particles, just as money was a stream of golden coins.

In 1801, Thomas Young tested this hypothesis in his famous double-slit experiment, in which light was shone from a point source through two small slits and projected onto a screen. The surprising result was an undulating pattern of bright and dark bands, which was similar to the interference patterns produced when two waves come together, with points where the crests reinforced one another and others where they canceled out.

The balance of evidence therefore seemed to favor the wave hypothesis—but then the advent of quantum physics at the start of the twentieth century showed that light was actually made of individual photons. In 1909 Geoffrey Taylor repeated the double-slit experiment, this time with an extremely weak light source, and showed that even when individual photons passed through the slit, the interference pattern was still reproduced. The crests corresponded to places with a high probability of seeing a photon, while the troughs were places with a low probability. Even though individual photons were passing through only one of the slits, they somehow reacted to the presence of the other slit. According to Niels Bohr, the only way to make sense of this was to see the wave–particle properties as complementary aspects of a unified whole.

The debate over money has followed a similar trajectory. Prior to the early twentieth century, most experts (including Newton) believed that money was precious metal—something physical you can touch and weigh. The chartalist movement then countered with the idea that money is actually a virtual system—an information wave in the ether. As we have argued, though, money is best understood as having dual, complementary, real/virtual properties—in which case economics really is like physics, just a century behind. Viewed in this light, far from being an aberration or a curiosity of the digital age, cybercurrencies are a natural step in the evolution of money; the latest manifestation of its quantum nature.

initially be near zero. Note that the two sides of money, which represent positive credit and negative debt, remain in oppositional balance, so a kind of conservation principle is observed, as when matter–antimatter particles are created from the quantum void. It is therefore not necessary to begin with an external debt or a source of value, because the two can expand together.

In many respects, buying a stake in a new cybercurrency is the same as funding a business—you are betting that it will take off and your investment will be worth something. In 2014 Ethereum crowdfunded its development through an online sale of ethers, which raised over $18 million, a record at the time. The business exchange network Ripple Labs was similarly funded by issuing its own blockchain-based altcoin known as XRP and keeping 20 billion of the maximum 100 billion that can be issued.[44] NeuCoin granted its nonprofit foundations an initial endowment of NeuCoins. If these currencies gain value, so do the holdings of their founders, investors, and organizations. They are making money by coining (in the sense of inventing) a new form of the stuff—just as Nakamoto did in 2009.

The traditional notion that a currency must be explicitly backed by something of value may in fact have affected the design of Bitcoin: as discussed earlier, the capped limit and the energy-intensive mining seem clearly to be attempts to emulate the properties of gold. Adam Smith, who equated value with labor, might have approved—assuming that the labor of computers counts.[45] If instead money is seen as a fundamental quantity, and market value as an emergent property of the money system, these restrictions begin to seem less relevant or desirable. Money doesn't so much need to be backed as it needs to be used. This raises the question of whether an algorithm that simplifies the mining process, such as proof-of-stake or another, may turn out to be a superior approach. It will be ironic if the world's leading cybercurrency founders because it is too much like metal.

Since the 1970s, we have moved from having one gold-linked global reference currency, to enjoying a wide menu of choices. The dollar, the euro, and the yuan, along with smaller national currencies, are complemented by both local currencies and global currencies such as Bitcoin. As fintech firms around the world compete to find new ways to mesh computer technology with finance, the results promise to revolutionize not just money but everything around it from wealth management to funding business loans to trading options. Such tools, notes author Nathan Schneider, are "a testing ground for whatever virtual utopias people are able to translate into code, and the tests will have nonvirtual effects. . . . As for any utopia, though, the power struggles of the real world are sure to find their way in as well."[46] Whatever form that money takes—from clay tablets to gold coins to banknotes to computer bits—it still retains the same quantum, dualistic nature that binds virtual number to real value; and the struggle between these two sides is far from over. In the final chapter, we take an envious look at different visions of utopia and ask whether the design of money can hold practical solutions to some of our most pressing problems.

10

Utopia

Money is a new form of slavery, and distinguishable from the old simply by the fact that it is impersonal—that there is no human relation between master and slave.

LEO TOLSTOY, "WHAT SHALL WE DO THEN?"

Money often costs too much.

RALPH WALDO EMERSON

As seen in previous chapters, modern fiat currencies are based on the public–private partnership between the state and private banks that was developed during the years of the gold standard. Today, though, many alternative forms of money exist, from local time-share schemes to modern cybercurrencies, that fundamentally renegotiate the relationship between number and value at the core of money. But is money, which always points toward number and profit, ultimately incompatible with values such as ethics and with long-term projects such as preventing environmental degradation? What will be the future monetary order?

Of all human inventions, money must be the most deceptively powerful. It helped spark the development of writing and the organization of the first city-states. Its use contributed to a great flowering of thought in the Axial Age. It has been the cause of epic bloodlust and the focus of scientific geniuses. It arouses overpowering emotions but also a kind of detachment. It has the nuclear power to make or destroy nations. We revere it but also see it as corrupting—even evil. And yet our economic theories treat it as a mere tool for exchange and accounting, nothing special in itself.

Neoclassical economics, for example, began as a kind of utopian vision for society—aiming to achieve what Francis Edgeworth called "the maximum energy of pleasure, the Divine love of the universe."[1] One property of such visions is that money never plays much of a role. The original Utopia, after all, was that of Thomas More, who in his book of the same name wrote in 1516: "Men's fears, solicitudes, cares, labours, and watchings would all perish in the same moment with the value of money; even poverty itself, for the relief of which money seems most necessary, would fall."[2]

The word was a pun on the Greek words *ou topia* (no place) and *eu topia* (good place), and meant a good place that doesn't exist—and another property of utopias is that attempts to build them on earth routinely fail, whether they are led by religious cranks or staid academics. The neoclassical version certainly didn't work out quite as its inventors planned. While the economy has grown enormously, and many people around the world have escaped poverty, not everyone has achieved "the maximum energy of pleasure," and we are now faced with a number of interlinked problems that are in a way related to that success. Two of the most prominent and frequently discussed are environmental limits to growth and economic inequality. Like a projection of money's two sides, each is associated with a different kind of debt—the physical with the planet and the numerical between groups. There is a symmetry between the slow but inexorable rise in global debt and the rise in global carbon emissions. Techno-utopians will argue that the answer to either problem is more economic growth, based on the idea that we can buy our way out of trouble, but so far the evidence seems to point the other way. It's not that technology has disappointed—we are all impressed with the Internet and smartphones—but that the impact of the most important technology—money—doesn't usually get taken into account.[3]

Perhaps the defining issue of our age is that the human economy has grown to a scale where it affects the environment at every level: on land, in the oceans, and in the air. As Kenneth Boulding put it, we are transitioning from a cowboy economy, where the world is an open frontier, to a spaceman economy, where we are restrained by natural limits. This transition, ecologist Eugene Odum argued, resembles that followed by ecosystems as they become established.[4] At the early stages of an ecosystem's development, available energy (whose ultimate source is the sun) is rapidly exploited by a few species in a sudden bloom of growth. As the ecosystem matures, the food chain switches from a linear chain—carnivores eating herbivores eating plants—to a more web-like, decentralized structure in which multiple species interact in increasingly complex ways. The waste of one organism is recycled as food for another, and resources such as nutrients and minerals are conserved. An example of a mature ecosystem is a tropical rain forest, where most of the nutrients are not in the ground but in the trees and the species that live in them. The land itself has little agricultural productivity, as farmers discover if they cut down the trees and try to grow soy or provide pasture for cattle.

Economies also develop in a similar manner. In a society of pioneers, wrote Odum, "high birth rates, rapid growth, high economic profits, and exploitation of accessible and unused resources are advantageous."[5] As the economy matures, the emphasis switches to "considerations of symbiosis (i.e., civil rights, law and order, education, and culture)" and the recycling of resources. However this transition is a work in progress: "Until recently mankind has more or less taken for granted the gas-exchange, water-purification, nutrient-cycling, and other protective functions of self-maintaining ecosystems, chiefly because neither his number nor his environmental manipulations have been great enough to affect regional and global balances. Now, of course, it is painfully evident that such balances are being affected, often detrimentally."[6] And matters have not improved in the ensuing half-century, as carbon dioxide emissions have climbed and the life-support abilities of the planet have continued to degrade. We have grown richer in monetary terms but the hidden charges are mounting up.

In her book *This Changes Everything* (whose uncompromising stance has led to critics calling it a "utopian call to arms" in the climate battle),[7] the author and activist Naomi Klein asks, "What is wrong with us? I think the answer is far more simple than many have led us to believe: we have not done the things that are necessary to lower emissions because those things fundamentally conflict with deregulated capitalism, the reigning ideology for the entire period we have been struggling to find a way out of this crisis."[8] Indeed, as we argued in chapter 6, mainstream economics is an ideology that has shaped our attitudes toward both the economy and the natural world. But while this ideology has certainly been influential, it has never been left alone behind the wheel. Neoclassical theory was started with the best of intentions but was co-opted or exploited by market fundamentalists to justify the existing power structure. Economics, along with its bank-sponsored Nobel Prizes, was bought, the same way anything else can be bought in a market economy. Its argument that "money is a distraction" just distracts from that fact.

So perhaps the answer, at least in a technical sense, is even simpler: the design of money. After all, it is our monetary system as much as any particular ideology that dictates how we move energy and resources around the economy, and the technology was never intended to be environmentally friendly. Money is created primarily by private banks and lent out at interest. The interest can be repaid only if the economy and money supply constantly inflate. Prices emerge from the use of money in markets to trade goods between people and firms, but the process does not work at the edges of the system—that is, with the input of natural resources or the output of pollution. Much economic growth comes from transforming preexisting natural systems and services—land, oil, gold, trees, fish, water—into money. But the earth does not trade or haggle over price; it just passively supplies, up to a point. If money, as Tolstoy said, is a new form of slavery, then the planet is the biggest slave of all.

Some economists argue that we can create an artificial market for the planet's services and harness Adam Smith's invisible hand to the task of environmental protection.[9] But if the connection between price and value is tenuous for goods traded on human markets, it becomes looser still when you try to attach numbers to nonhuman systems. What is the price of a species if it is not an obvious service-provider? Or the price of fresh water that we don't plan to drink? And if modelers can't accurately calculate financial risk, such as the chance of a company going bankrupt, how can we price the risk of, say, a fishery's collapse? By translating environmental problems into monetary terms, we can justify anything, because the numbers are easily rigged by whoever holds power and stands to profit—a fact excluded from economic models that focus on abstract calculations of utility.[10]

Environmental conflict is therefore hardwired into the design of our monetary system—built for funding wars with kings and empires and now, as Klein documents, with the planet (one that, if it continues, the planet will win—it's bigger). Dazzling us with number, it distracts us from the costs. This, rather than ideology, is why the GDP produced in a city like Beijing is booming, but people are leaving because they can't breathe the air (and why, a little late, the National Congress of the Communist Party wrote the goal of an "ecological civilization" into its constitution in 2012). Like a toxic algal bloom on a lake, the economy is doing fine, but it is asphyxiating everything around it.

Of course, money works only if we believe in it, and economic ideas are part of maintaining and feeding that belief. How can we redesign money—and our mind-set—for a mature economy or an ecological civilization?

Bread Spread

The continuous growth required by our monetary system for its survival also dominates the structure of our working lives. In his essay "Economic Possibilities for Our Grandchildren" (1930), John Maynard Keynes predicted that economic and technological growth would mean that people in rich countries could support themselves on a fifteen-hour work week. In 1967, the *New York Times*, with a slightly more restrained degree of optimism, reported that "by the year 2000, people will work no more than four days a week and less than eight hours a day. With legal holidays and long vacations, this could result in an annual working period of 147 days worked and 218 days off."[11] Today many are working longer hours than ever, so what happened?

Part of the reason is a shift in the composition of jobs. According to a 2006 report on the American job market, "professional, managerial, clerical, sales, and service workers (except private household service workers) grew from one-quarter to three-quarters of total employment between 1910 and 2000."[12] Technology has indeed meant that we can produce more with less, as the utopians promised, but somehow we have conspired to maintain our workload, by managing one another.[13] Another reason, already discussed in chapter 7, is that as we get richer, we increase our expectations and bid up the prices of things like real estate. But this still doesn't completely explain why we collectively feel compelled to work so hard in what should be an age of plenty. And again the answer is related to the design of our monetary system, which to an excessive degree fosters competition and inequality.

Keynes wrote in his thesis that "we shall endeavour to spread the bread thin on the butter—to make what work there is still to be done to be as widely shared as possible."[14] But money has a different idea. While we certainly seem to be trying to spread the *work* around, the actual *reward*—that is, the bread—has tended to be more concentrated, with most going to the very top tier of earners. The picture is complex, and growth in China and India has helped to reduce global measures of inequality, but within many countries wealth distribution has become increasingly skewed toward the rich. According to Thomas Piketty, this is because the rate of return on capital has long tended to exceed the rate of economic growth, with the result that money builds on itself as it is passed on within families through inheritance.

Piketty's proposed solution of a global tax on capital is, he admits, politically infeasible—a "utopian idea."[15] And again, the main problem is with money itself. Money begets money, in a positive-feedback loop, through interest but also through its association with power and status. Instead of spreading evenly, it clumps and clusters. As capital accumulates with the wealthy, so its opposite—debt—accumulates with everyone else. Gains in productivity due to technology are captured by the elite class of CEOs and investors. In the United States, the pay ratio of CEOs to unskilled workers is 354:1 (a survey showed that most people thought the real ratio was 30:1 and the ideal ratio 7:1).[16] Wages for the middle classes stagnate, while those people further down the income scale are essentially wage slaves—rather than enjoying the much-anticipated age of leisure, they are working to break even or get out of debt. The tension, inherent in money, between positive wealth and negative debt has grown to a point where it threatens social stability.

In the Organisation for Economic Co-operation and Development countries, for example, the average income of the richest 10 percent is about nine times higher than that of the 10 percent at the bottom, and the gap is widening even in traditionally more egalitarian places such as Germany and Scandinavia.[17] And things only became worse in the aftermath of the GFC and the rescue operations that flooded the system with liquidity via quantitative easing, profiting the disproportionately affluent who are active market players. As the Bank of England reported in 2012, its monetary rescue mission had boosted the price of domestic stocks and bonds by 26 percent—and about 40 percent of resulting gains went to the richest 5 percent of British households. Quantitative easing was thus "exacerbating already extreme income inequality and the consequent social tensions that arise from it," according to Dhaval Joshi of BCA Research. In the United States, the top 5 percent own 60 percent of individually held financial assets, so QE represented a regressive redistribution program.[18]

Upward social mobility, or a chance that "one will have enough to be able to stop elbowing the others," has thus been severely limited in the course of the past three decades or so. In some Western countries like Great Britain, the generation of recent graduates is the first in a long time that does not have a better prospect of social advancement than their parents, an Oxford University study shows.[19] And the same goes for the United States, where people believed in the American Dream the least in nearly two decades in 2014 (when only 64 percent of those polled said hard work could result in riches, down from 74 percent in the midst of the GFC in 2009).[20]

According to mainstream economics, prices correspond to utility, so things like pay inequality just reflect economic reality. As Eugene Fama of CEO compensation said in a 2007 interview: "You're just looking at market wages. They may be big numbers; that's not saying they're too high."[21] But as discussed in chapter 7, prices are influenced by power relationships. The financial system, for example, is dominated by a relatively small number of highly connected firms. Profits flow to these companies and their employees largely because they occupy a privileged position in the network. Of course, they must compete to retain that position—they are all working very hard, managing away like crazy—but that competition appears to provide no real constraint on wages.

Economic inequality is a matter not just of fairness—or the perception of it, which is crucial for social cohesion and thus stability—but also of economic health.[22] In other words, the rising inequality orchestrated by "the relentless apostles of efficiency" hurts what they cherish the most—efficiency. This full circle seems to suggest that we have reached the natural limits of the current system, the monetary empire is overstretched, and a way forward cannot be powered by business as usual. As former governor of the Federal Reserve Henry Wallich said: "Growth is a substitute for equality of income. So long as there is growth there is hope, and that makes large income differentials tolerable."[23] But when growth slows, inequality becomes very obvious.

Also, while predictions for an age of leisure (or unemployment) have consistently been proven wrong, the revolution in areas such as robotics and artificial intelligence has barely begun; and as discussed in chapter 7, this will affect everything from factory work to legal work. The labor market will certainly adapt, and new occupations will appear, but if the whole point of robots is to replace people, then at some level they will probably succeed. This should be a good thing, but again, benefits will primarily flow to investors and managers. Which would you rather do, compete with a robot or own the robot?

From the viewpoint of neoclassical economics, people are rather like robots anyway, since we are driven by similarly mechanical impulses (as one student from the University of Glasgow put it, "Whenever I sit an economics exam, I have to turn myself into a robot").[24] The only difference is that robots are programmed by us, while we are programmed by our desire to "optimize utility"; and we want to be happy, while robots (like slaves) just need to be maintained. However, extreme social inequality combined with environmental collapse does not seem the ideal circumstance to achieve Bentham's "greatest happiness principle." How can we redesign our monetary system to "spread the bread" and produce a fair society in which the benefits and the hazards of economic prosperity are more equally shared—even when growth is constrained to an extent by environmental factors?

Wrong Number

Mainstream economics has long argued that the market economy, at least in its idealized form, is a rational, efficient process that optimizes utility. At its heart is the idea that price equals value. But when we see price as an emergent phenomenon that depends on the complex properties of money objects and their use in society, that raises some questions. Money is a way of stamping numbers onto the world, but what do we do when the numbers look wrong? When the incentives they produce no longer make sense? When they are leading us on a dangerous course? Money may have been described as a form of memory, but what if its use is actually erasing local memories and creating a kind of cultural amnesia—a massive blind spot in the way we see the world?

As the Harvard political philosopher Michael J. Sandel explains, "We have drifted from *having* market economies to *becoming* market societies. The difference is this: A market economy is a tool—a valuable and effective tool—for organizing productive activity. A market society, by contrast, is a place where almost everything is up for sale." In this case: "What role should money and markets play in a good society?"[25]

One option, as in More's utopia, would be to move away from the idea of money altogether. Such an approach was favored by Athens's great rival in ancient Greece, the city-state of Sparta, whose highly militaristic society had no need for money, which it saw as corrupt. Post-revolutionary Russia made a game attempt to eliminate money and create a Communist version of utopia in 1920. Today we have people such as the Irish activist Mark Boyle, known as the Moneyless Man because of his unorthodox career choice to live without money.[26] However, apart from a few such holdouts, money has been in continuous use since the time it was invented and seems unlikely to go away any time soon. That leaves us with a few other options. One is to exploit its positive qualities while trying to contain its worst excesses through regulations, another is to redesign its basic features, and a third is to actively cultivate arenas that magnetically shield us from some of its effects.

The first option is the default one, and there has been some progress on improving the financial regulatory framework since the crisis, for example, by increasing reserve requirements for banks and strengthening oversight of things like complex derivatives. However, it is generally agreed that these changes have been largely cosmetic and have done little to address the underlying problem, which is that the financial sector is far too large and unstable.[27] Of course, we should continue to press for change in areas such as regulation of derivatives trading, the bonus culture, and so on, but if even a crisis of that magnitude did not result in truly transformatory change, it only shows how entrenched and resistant to change the monetary system has become.

The second option—redesigning money—was discussed in chapters 8 and 9. Complementary currencies tend to become popular during times of crisis and less popular when the crisis is over (and before the next one arrives). However, there are a number of reasons why the current enthusiasm for new solutions may not be a temporary phenomenon. One is that the existing monetary structure, with its gold standard institutions, is based on a pretense that is becoming harder to maintain, as alternative currencies highlight its inconsistencies and threaten its monopoly. At the same time, technological advances such as the blockchain mean that alternative currencies can spread quickly and become global phenomena. And an unconditional basic income, which could be paid in a complementary currency, might seem particularly applicable if robots end up doing all the grunt work. Currencies bearing negative interest would have seemed a stretch a decade ago, but in the anemic recovery from the GFC many central banks, including the European Central Bank, have successfully experimented with bonds that do exactly that, effectively charging to store money in a safe place. (Though when debt levels are a problem, negative interest seems like throwing fuel on a fire.)

Of course, one should again not underestimate the inertia of our financial system, the power of entrenched interests, and the great advantage enjoyed by official currencies, which is that they have a large captive market—taxpayers. The reason money caught on in ancient Greece was not just because the coins were handy and looked great but also because they were demanded back as taxes, thus closing the loop and guaranteeing their acceptance. Note that in principle there is nothing to stop a government from one day adopting an altcoin as an official currency. In 2014, before his spell as the Greek finance minister, Yanis Varoufakis proposed a blockchain-based currency denominated in euros and backed by future taxes—buy the altcoins now and use them to get a discount on taxes in two years. As mentioned in chapter 9, China is also said to be contemplating its own digital currency.[28]

Giving

In addition to these, there is the third option, which is to explore and develop the space around money and create a kind of oasis from it. Money hasn't always been as important as it is today. We might not be able to live without the stuff, but—armed with a knowledge of its true nature—we can learn to better control, moderate, and direct its lines of force. Doing so will require finding ways to renegotiate the relationship—at the core of money—between number and value.

As the behavioral psychologist Dan Ariely observes, "We live in two worlds: one characterized by social exchanges and the other characterized by market exchanges."[29] The former include offers of help, exchange of gifts, neighborly collaborations, and volunteer work; immediate reciprocity is not expected, demanded, or even wanted. Market exchanges, in contrast, are "sharp-edged" and based on left-brained, numerical calculations of wages and prices. The difference between the two spheres therefore comes down to the use of number. Confusing them can result in problems. "Imagine that you help me move and I give you twenty-two euros and seventy-five cents at the end of the day. You would be offended," notes economist and philosopher Tomáš Sedláček, adding that once it is a nice meal and a glass of wine of the same price everybody suddenly feels happy.[30]

One of the powers of money, because of the way it points toward number, is that its mere presence is enough to make us shift from social norms to market norms. This has been demonstrated by a number of experiments in which subjects are primed to think about money before carrying out some tasks, for example, by seating them in view of a pile of Monopoly cash. The effect of the exposure to money was to make them less likely to ask for help, offer help, or collaborate in any way. They even preferred to sit farther apart from each other.[31] (Unsurprisingly, given its mantras of scarcity, competition, self-optimizing behavior, rational economic man, etc., the study of economics appears to make people more self-centered.)[32] A study at the University of California, Los Angeles, found that over the past 200 years there has been an increase in use of words such as "get," "unique," "individual," and "self," but a decrease in words such as "give" and "obliged."[33] The researchers put this down to English-speaking countries moving from "a predominantly rural, low-tech society to a predominantly urban, hi-tech society" but another reason could be the growing importance of money. An oft-stated advantage of money is that it removes the need for personal relationships to conduct business, but a side effect is that personal relationships get replaced by money.

However, while the pull of money sometimes seems an unstoppable force, it can be countered with some effort and organization. The Global Freecycle Network, for instance, is made up of more than 5,000 communities totaling 9.3 million members worldwide. It is one of many grassroots, nonprofit groups built upon the premise that not everything should be viewed through the prism of a price tag. Be it Haizhu, China; Hermosillo, Mexico; or any other participating city in one of the 110 countries on all inhabited continents, they are ready to give and get stuff for free, working with the principle that it is better to share than hoard and to reuse than fill landfills with usable things.

How much stuff (and money, by extension) could be saved this way? Numbers delivered by Freecycle alone are impressive: we are talking about 32,000 items that change hands a day or more than 100 million tons of potential landfill content a year. The gift economy is an alternative to the exactness of the market economy, on the one hand, and the impracticality of barter, on the other. It seems to offer a place where "there is enough for everyone's need, but not for everyone's greed" as a banner reads in a Give-away shop in Utrecht, the Netherlands.

This type of economic interaction could historically be found everywhere—and seems to be in direct contravention to the market econ-omy and the assumptions of mainstream economics (what would rational economic man think?).[34] Furthermore, there are spaces of overlap that were long considered a realm of the work-for-pay economy only to be invaded by people expecting other than a monetary reward. The online world, in particular, seems to encourage this type of interaction. Famous examples include Wikipedia, where people write and edit articles for no compensa-tion; designs for 3D printing and the "maker" community; and open-source software that is used by organizations from NASA to Google to Bitcoin. The Internet itself runs largely on open-source code, as do components of smartphones. Those who pitch in cite "learning, working with interest-ing people, or satisfying an itch" and other nonmonetary rewards such as peer recognition as their primary motivations.[35] The work might be unpaid, but its economic impact is significant. In Europe alone, programmer Carlo Daffara argues, open-source software lowers costs and increases efficiency by €116 billion a year.[36]

Open-source code is often issued under a general public license (GPL), which was invented in 1980s by the hacker-activist Richard Stallman. He called the GPL a copyleft law, because in many respects it is the opposite of copyright: instead of asserting the right to exclusive use, it asserts that the resource must remain in the digital commons, freely available to all under certain conditions (e.g., any program that incorporates the code must also be GPL). People can therefore contribute to the community without wor-rying that their ideas are going to be appropriated by a corporation. The legal framework was later emulated by Creative Commons licenses, which are used by artists, writers, and other creative types to similarly protect (or keep unprotected) their output, and in academia by open-access online journals that subvert the expensive publication model favored by established academic publishers (which is fitting since universities were created in the Middle Ages as a way to keep knowledge a common shared resource). As the author and commons activist David Bollier notes, "Among the 'born digital' generation, many conventional ideas about private property rights—the exclusivity of control, commercial motives and indifference to the common good over the long term—seem decidedly old-fashioned, if not antisocial."[37] If the Romans (with later input from John Locke) gave us our customs of property laws and ownership, then the open-source community is showing us how to give stuff away. (Though open-source code is not really a human invention—the ultimate example is DNA, which has evolved precisely because it has been shared and tinkered with by countless organisms. About 8 percent of the human genome consists of recycled viral genes.)[38]

A research group set up by the government of Ecuador, for example, recently created a transition plan, known as FLOK (Free-Libre, Open Knowledge), which proposes to reinvent everything from agriculture to design to government along "principles that are the basic foundations of the internet: peer-to-peer collaboration and shared knowledge."[39] The aim is not to optimize GDP, but instead something closer to the indigenous people's fuzzy concept of *buen vivir* (good living). Perhaps uncoincidentally, the same country was the first to produce its own purely digital currency. It is based on the U.S. dollar, which is the country's present currency, but some see it as presenting a possible route out of dollarization.[40]

The gift economy, together with shared stewardship of common areas such as the Internet, can therefore produce something that yields monetary value or, better yet, something that has a real value for the economy and by extension society. The reason why it is not expressed in those terms very often is that doing so would involve a switch from social norms to market norms, which is what is being avoided. Monetizing something means putting a number on it, a process actively resisted by many of the most important things in life (such as life itself, the ultimate gift). And when something is a gift, the usual principles of economics and commerce simply don't apply. In the past, economic growth has come in part from bringing into the money economy resources previously shared for free or services such as housework or caring for the young or the old. Growing the gift economy means putting this process into reverse—the numbers look bad, but the end result might be a happier or at least more connected and resilient society.

Sharing

The growth in giving has been equaled by the growth in sharing. Be it schemes focused on transportation (Uber), accommodation (Airbnb), or finance (Kickstarter), they all have two things in common: first, the premise that the person next door can be as good a driver/host/banker as a professional with an official stamp; and second, the premise that technologies, rather than top-down regulation, can guarantee that those who do not deliver shall be quickly identified by the constant flow of consumer reviews and shortly thereafter excluded by the resulting lack of demand for their services.

The primary motivation for using or providing such services still appears to be about saving or making money, with the biggest profits made by the companies running them.[41] On Facebook, for example, you share the details of your life with friends, but also with Facebook, Inc., whose lead underwriters for its 2012 initial public offering were those seasoned power brokers Morgan Stanley, JP Morgan, and Goldman Sachs. At the time of this writing, similar IPOs are anticipated for Uber and Airbnb. However, other models are also possible.

Tool libraries, for example, have been around in the United States since 1970s, but the idea took off after the success of the West Seattle Tool Library (founded in 2009) gained media attention. Now more than seventy cities in North America and others around the world, have similar libraries. The emphasis is on borrowing things such as power tools but some also offer workspaces fitted out with equipment such as laser cutters and 3D printers. The Toronto Tool Library, for example, offers access to more than 3,000 tools for $50 per year. Or in exchange for three shifts per week, workers gain 24/7 access to the facilities. According to its founders, Ryan Dyment and Lawrence Alvarez, the aim of the project is not just about tools but about engineering a change in "cultural consciousness"—a kind of mental retooling that will change our perception of ownership, remove barriers to access, and get us out of our single-use mentality, which is "disrespectful to the resources."[42] The boxer Floyd Mayweather Jr. is said to wear his shoes only once, and we often treat tools the same way (also books, which is why we have book libraries). Scarcity is often self-imposed or artificially created by corporations and can be circumvented with different organizational structures, which by making better use of resources reduce the burden on the environment. Whether the structure is peer-to-peer or centralized, or how fees are handled, is in a sense secondary to this end result.

It is no coincidence that most of these companies and organizations started in the years following the financial crisis (Airbnb was founded in 2008, Uber and Kickstarter in 2009) and were embraced by a generation whose neo-thrifty attitudes—especially an interest in using rather than owning—were shaped by that crisis; and whose environmental concerns were shaped by worries over climate change. Again, of course, according to conventional metrics, all of this sharing is bad for the economy, because it will reduce jobs in areas such as tool manufacturing. And if users don't need to buy and own tools, they might work less hard themselves. But this just highlights the inappropriateness of our current economic model. It makes as much sense as saying that the creatures in the rain forest should stop sharing the trees because it is making things too easy.

The sharing economy and the cybercurrency movement are based on a shared ethos: there is a synergy between the idea of sharing tools and Ethereum's idea of sharing computer storage space. And they point toward a system in which money plays a smaller role, with the Internet taking over the task of matching users—thus solving the problem of William Stanley Jevons's "double coincidence of wants"—and online reputation emerging as a new kind of social currency. Of course, gift and sharing economies have their shadow side—they're not utopian—especially when they grow up in the cracks of a failing, distorted economy. In Venezuela, for example, there is a thriving "gift" economy. Price controls mean that many critical goods, from foods to drugs, are set at artificially low prices by the state. Instead of selling items at these prices, shopkeepers prefer to keep the goods for certain clients who will in turn reward them with favors. The system resembles the graft networks, known as *blat*, in the former Soviet Union. The need for money is therefore replaced by the need for connections, which in many respects seems even less fair.[43]

Even in rich countries where corruption might be low, unpaid interns and many authors and artists contribute their work in the hope that it will give them experience or exposure, though they would probably prefer a paycheck. Academics rightly celebrate their own gift economy of sharing research, but only because their universities reward them with salary, merit points, and tenure. Robert Reich, meanwhile, argues that work-on-demand services such as Uber and Airbnb are "hurtling us backwards" to the nineteenth century: a world without basic protections for laborers, where many tasks are automated and "human beings do the work that's unpredictable—odd jobs, on-call projects, fetching and fixing, driving and delivering, tiny tasks needed at any and all hours—and patch together barely enough to live on."[44] It is often said that "markets loathe uncertainty," as if they are delicate flowers that must be left undisturbed so they can get on with their important job of optimizing utility, but they seem to have a knack for *producing* uncertainty. Gift and sharing economies will work only if they are honored rather than exploited—if our sense of community is itself treated as a commons rather than yet another area to be colonized by number.

Going Medieval

Perhaps the best way forward, in monetary terms rather than social organization, is in fact to reach backward—not to the nineteenth century, but even further, a thousand years back. Few people today would want to give up the incredible developments in technology and living standards of the past few centuries. But in a search for new monetary ideas, much can be learned from the last era when virtual currencies were in the ascendant phase, the High Middle Ages of the eleventh to thirteenth centuries, before finance was Medicified.

While neoclassical economics was developed by idealists who had a vision of a good society, one of the more notable features of both modern capitalism and economic theory to have made itself evident by its absence during the GFC was any sense of right and wrong, of good and evil.[45] Economic theory teaches that market price measures intrinsic value, which itself is a measure of utility. As economists M. Neil Browne and J. Kevin Quinn note, "Economists distinctly do not question the moral worth of market prices and wages."[46] According to Sedláček, mainstream economics has neglected ethics to the point where "it is almost heretical to even talk about it."[47] Instead, this subject was outsourced to the invisible hand of the markets.

As we have seen, though, while money is a tool for setting numerical prices in the market, the relationship it produces between exact price and fuzzy value is uncertain, unstable, and often misleading. The idea that the market knows best, or that maximizing profit is the same as doing "God's work" in Lloyd Blankfein's phrase, is very far from the view that prevailed in the Middle Ages, with its concept of the just price. The idea that the state—and everyone else—must borrow its own money at interest stands in marked contrast to medieval ideas about usury. The idea that the economy has to continuously grow would have been equally foreign.

Our aim is certainly not to romanticize the High Middle Ages or sell it as a utopian vision—and few would want to see an economy based on undernourished and disease-prone serfs doing digital piecework, where what counts is social standing and control of land (though that sometimes seems to be the way we are heading). But the comparison does point the way to a monetary system that would address issues such as limits to growth, economic inequality, and societal happiness and resilience.

By harnessing the powers of virtual currencies and the extraordinary wave of invention overtaking finance, we can realign the basic incentives of our monetary system away from an exclusive focus on short-term profit. Seignorage earned on national and regional currencies can be recycled back to the state rather than being sequestered by private banks (the Medicis of our day). Alternative currencies will play an important complementary role, and local currencies can help align money with the needs of a community. Currencies with negative interest rates, appropriately used, will both discourage hoarding, and—by not discounting the future—encourage long-term thinking. We also need imaginative strategies—such as basic income–style cash handouts or restrictions on lending—to tackle the mounting debt whose charge hangs over every region of the world economy, holding us in awe and fear of its next unpredictable lightning strike (given the mathematical tendency of unpaid debts to climb toward infinity, one suspects that debt write-offs will also be involved at some stage). A first step is to come out of denial about the true nature of our current virtual money system, with its easy money creation and gold standard debt collection.

At the same time, we can reinvigorate the idea of a commons and fight back against the modern enclosure of land, water, and even our thought processes by corporate interests (then the commons were reserved for grazing animals, now we need some unbranded space for our minds to wander). We can reduce the size of the financial sector, so that it no longer dominates the flow of money in the economy. Perhaps a modern version of *caritas* will even emerge as a nonmonetary measure of personal and societal worth. In this context, a shrinking GDP would by no means be a disaster if it represents a kind of reclaiming of space from the money economy.

Money Is the Message

Faced with worries over resource shortages, environmental disaster, extreme wealth inequality, out-of-control debt, mass unemployment, and so on, it is easy to be pessimistic about the future—especially since we have borrowed so much from it already in both financial and environmental terms. However, these problems are in many respects the product of our old money system, and its associated ideology, which say that numbers accurately reflect value, that debt is just a neutral transfer from one group of people to another, and that money is inert. We live in a time of change when, having been trained to equate value with scarcity, we perceive everything as being scarce, except for information—and information is the most precious commodity of all. If we are worried that computers and robots are going to remove the need for work, it only shows how perverse economic incentives have become—and how urgently we need to embrace the new paradigm that is emerging in piecemeal fashion from the tremors of the Nixon shock and the later financial crises. Some of the most interesting developments will take place in the areas that are least well-served by our conventional money system, where the gap between number and value is the greatest.

While it is impossible to predict how currencies and the economy itself will evolve, here are some thoughts based on general trends that we expect to continue:

• We will have a range of overlapping currencies, on a local, national, regional, and global scale. Some moneys will be state managed, others corporate or open source. Some will be open, so switching in or out will be fluid and easy; others will try to insulate themselves. Some, like Bitcoin, will be mostly pseudonymous; others, such as corporate currencies, will track information about users.

• The main spawning ground and incubator for alternative currencies and ideas about money will be the online, virtual economy. One outcome will be a "just price" for digital content, though it may not be measured in dollars.

• Online and mobile purchases will automatically incorporate a variety of reward schemes. Some of these will become so popular that they will serve as forms of money.

• Alternative currencies will eventually become a part of everyday life for most people, just as precious metal coins once were, with the difference that they will be held in a digital wallet rather than a leather purse.

• Money of any type will play a smaller role as the Internet allows for a broader range of transactions, including sharing, gifting, and direct barter.

• An already nascent gift economy will emerge, where it is online reputation that opens doors and creates opportunities, rather than net worth.

• Monetary developments will be further accelerated by debt crises that force people, or countries, to adopt alternatives.

- The age of robotics, along with a basic income, will allow people more time to pursue nonmonetary goals.
- According to conventional measures, the economy's metabolism—deprived of its heady levels of debt oxygen—will slow, but it will be more resilient.
- The emerging economy will be better placed to address issues such as climate change, inequality, and societal happiness than our current model.
- New theories of economics will develop that will put the dualistic, dynamic, and creative properties of money at their heart.
- Money will continue to be a source of human drama and tension, no matter what form it takes.

Although some aspects of this picture may sound radical, its components have been works in progress for decades. It is just that they have captured little attention, exactly because they don't register as part of the normal economy. Creating a new cybercurrency or writing some open-source code does not boost GDP—it might even subtract from it by destroying someone's business model. If Wikipedia were a company, it has been estimated that its market capitalization would be in the tens of billions of dollars—but it is not a company; instead it is something that prevents companies from making money by doing the same thing.[48] Such projects represent a new type of organization in which money plays no role; another way to coordinate people and get them on the same page.

Our view of money has been shaped by a mainstream economic theory that—with its emphasis on principles such as stability, linearity, symmetry, unity, and rationality—conforms to an idea about what is good and beautiful that dates back to the Pythagoreans. It came into its own during the growth phase of the Industrial Age, but is now running out of room. The resulting breakdown in this mental monoculture, documented in chapter 7, is mirrored by a breakdown in the monoculture of mainstream currencies. Perhaps the greatest contribution of inventions such as Bitcoin is to present a new aesthetic, based (like a mature ecosystem) on decentralized networks rather than on linear hierarchy; a picture that makes our fool's gold traditional currencies look corny and antiquated in comparison and opens our minds to unforeseen possibilities. Artists and writers may turn out to be as important as economists or scientists in reshaping our view of money.[49]

Money has played a determining role in history from ancient Mesopotamia to the present day, and this latest transition will have lasting consequences. The High Middle Ages saw the building of cathedrals that still provide both spiritual inspiration and tourist dollars to their regions. So what will be our comparable long-term civilization-building projects—our gifts to future generations? Can we at least buy some time? And if money is a medium of communication like writing, what story will we leave? As Marshall McLuhan famously said, "the medium is the message," and the answers to these questions will depend on the money systems that evolve.

NOTES

Introduction

1. Catherine Eagleton and Jonathan Williams, *Money: A History* (Richmond Hill, Ont.: Firefly, 2007), 256.

2. Lydia Saad, "Americans' Money Worries Unchanged from 2014," Gallup, April 20, 2015, www.gallup.com/poll/182768/americans-money-worries-unchanged-2014.aspx.

3. Tim Adams, "Anxious, Atomised . . . and Not in It Together: The State of Britain in 2015," *Observer*, April 19, 2015.

4. Elizabeth W. Dunn, Lara B. Aknin, and Michael I. Norton, "Spending Money on Others Promotes Happiness," *Science* 319, no. 5870 (2008): 1687–1688.

5. As author George Cooper told World Finance: "We've got a very interesting debate going on that's just started a few weeks ago with the Bank of England publishing a new paper saying that the old model of how money is made in the economy is wrong. . . . Now they've published this paper, and a lot of people are getting very excited about it. And really it should be radically changing monetary policy. But it's actually having no impact at all" (interview in *World Finance: The Voice of the Market*, April 4, 2014, www.worldfinance.com/banking/economics-is-a-broken-science-dr-george-cooper-on-his-new-book-money-blood-and-revolution-video).

1. Origins

1. Philip Brickman, Dan Coates, and Ronnie Janoff-Bulman, "Lottery Winners and Accident Victims: Is Happiness Relative?" *Journal of Personality and Social Psychology* 36, no. 8 (1978): 917–927.

2. Tim Kreider, "Slaves of the Internet, Unite!" *New York Times*, October 27, 2013.

3. F. A. Harper, *Why Wages Rise* (Irvington, N.Y.: Foundation for Economic Education, 1957). David Hume earlier wrote that money "is none of the wheels of trade: It is the oil which renders the motion of the wheels more smooth and easy" (*Essays, Moral, Political, and Literary*, ed. Eugene F. Miller [Indianapolis: Liberty Fund, 1987], www.econlib.org/library/LFBooks/Hume/hmMPL26.html).

4. Aristotle, *Politics* (Mineola, N.Y.: Dover, 2000), 42.

5. Adi Setia, "Ja'far Ibn 'Ali al-Dimashqi on Community, Money, and Prudent Management in Trading and Spending: Four Excerpts from His *Kitab Al-Isharat Ila Mahasin Al-Tijarat*," *Islam & Science* 9, no. 1 (2011): 11–32.

6. Adam Smith, *An Inquiry into the Nature and Causes of the Wealth of Nations* (London: Strahan & Cadell, 1776), I.4.2.

7. William Stanley Jevons, *Money and the Mechanism of Exchange* (New York: Appleton, 1875), I.4.

8. Karl Menger, "On the Origins of Money," *Economic Journal* 2, no. 3 (1892): 239–255.

9. Geoffrey Crowther, *An Outline of Money* (London: Nelson, 1941), 15.

10. Paul A. Samuelson, *Economics*, 9th ed. (New York: McGraw-Hill, 1973), 274–276.

11. John Smithin, "What Is Money? Introduction," in *What Is Money?* ed. John Smithin (New York: Routledge, 2000), 4.

12. Christopher T. S. Ragan and Richard G. Lipsey, *Economics*, 13th ed. (Toronto: Pearson Education Canada, 2011), 672–673.

13. "Origin and Evolution of Money," Banco Central do Brasil, www.bcb.gov .br/?ORIGINMONEY.

14. Alfred Mitchell-Innes, "What Is Money?" *Banking Law Journal*, May 1913, 377–408. Another author to raise the question was Effingham Wilson, *What Is Money?* (London: Wilson, 1872).

15. L. Randall Wray, ed., *Credit and State Theories of Money: The Contributions of A. Mitchell-Innes* (Cheltenham: Elgar, 2004).

16. Quoted in David Graeber, *Debt: The First 5000 Years* (Brooklyn, N.Y.: Melville House, 2011), 29.

17. Maria Eugenia Aubet, *Commerce and Colonization in the Ancient Near East* (Cambridge: Cambridge University Press, 2013), 147.

18. James B. Pritchard, ed., *The Ancient Near East: An Anthology of Texts and Pictures* (Princeton, N.J.: Princeton University Press, 2010).

19. Indeed, prices fluctuated significantly during this period. See: Howard Farber, "A Price and Wage Study for Northern Babylonia During the Old Babylonian Period," *Journal of the Economic and Social History of the Orient* 21, no. 1 (1978): 1–51.

20. Éric Tymoigne and L. Randall Wray, "Money: An Alternative Story," in *A Handbook of Alternative Monetary Economics*, ed. Philip Arestis and Malcolm C. Sawyer (Northampton, Mass.: Elgar, 2007), 1–16.

21. Together the Federal Reserve and the Bank of England vaults contain about one-third of the gold supply.

22. Federal Reserve Bank of New York, "Gold Vault," www.newyorkfed.org/about-thefed/goldvault.html.

23. Not everyone is convinced. See Vernon Silver, "Where Is Germany's Gold?" February 5, 2015, Bloomberg Business, www.bloomberg.com/news/features/2015-02-05/germany-s-gold-repatriation-activist-peter-boehringer-gets-results.

24. According to Morris Silver, "That in the earlier second millennium Mesopotamia knew negotiable loans of a two-party promissory-note type is suggested by numbers of surviving loan documents specifying repayment not to the lender but to the '*bearer* of this tablet'" ("Karl Polanyi and Markets in the Ancient Near East: The Challenge of the Evidence," *Journal of Economic History* 43, no. 4 [1983]: 804).

25. This interest rate was mentioned in both the Eshnunna code and the Hammurabi code from about two centuries later. See Catherine Eagleton and Jonathan Williams, *Money: A History.* (Richmond Hill, Ont.: Firefly Books, 2007), 18. See also Michael Hudson, "How Interest Rates Were Set, 2500 BC–1000 AD," *Journal of the Economic and Social History of the Orient* 43, no. 2 (2000): 132–161.

26. As cited in the book of Leviticus, 25:8. See Michael Hudson, *The Lost Tradition of Biblical Debt Cancellations* (New York: Schalkenbach, 1993).

27. Glyn Davies, *A History of Money: From Ancient Times to the Present Day*, 3rd ed. (Cardiff: University of Wales Press, 2002), 52.

28. According to Jack Weatherford, "The Egyptians buried more gold and other precious commodities in the earth than any other known civilization in history" (*The History of Money* [New York: Three Rivers, 1997], 10).

29. François de Callatay, "White Gold: An Enigmatic Start to Greek Coinage," *American Numismatic Society Magazine* 12, no. 2 (2013): 6–17.

30. Weatherford, *History of Money*, 32.

31. Michael H. Crawford, "Money and Exchange in the Roman World," *Journal of Roman Studies* 60 (1970): 40–48.

32. David Schaps, "The Invention of Coinage in Lydia, in India, and in China" (paper presented at the XIV International Economic History Congress, August 21–25, 2006, Helsinki).

33. Manuela Saragosa, "Libyan Gold Valued at $6.5bn," March 23, 2011, BBC, www.bbc.com/news/business-12833866.

34. Karl Jaspers, *The Way to Wisdom: An Introduction to Philosophy* (New Haven, Conn.: Yale University Press, 2003), 98.

35. According to Alan Pense, "If you consider the whole army of legionnaires and auxiliaries at the time of Augustus, 250,000 men, the total annual requirement of the army for silver denarii (or equivalent copper coins) was at least 75,000,000 per year!" ("The Decline and Fall of the Roman Denarius," *Materials Characterization* 29, no. 2 [1992]: 213–222).

36. Ibid.

37. Marcus Tullius Cicero, *On Duties*, trans. Walter Miller (Cambridge, Mass.: Harvard University Press, 1913).

38. Pliny the Younger, *The Letters of the Younger Pliny: With an Introductory Essay*, trans. John B. Firth (London: Scott, 1909), 3.19.

39. Eagleton and Williams, *Money*, 49.

40. Ovid, *Ovid's Art of Love (in Three Books), the Remedy of Love, the Art of Beauty, the Court of Love, the History of Love, and Amours*, ed. Anne Mahoney (New York: Blanchard, 1855), book I.

41. Eagleton and Williams, *Money*, 51.

42. Weatherford, *History of Money*, 52. For comparison, the modern Italian army employs about 180,000.

43. W. V. Harris, *The Monetary Systems of the Greeks and Romans* (Oxford: Oxford University Press, 2008), 205.

44. According to Matthew 20:2, the wages for a day's labor were one denarius. Wages for a Roman legionary soldier went from 225 denarii under Caesar (ca. 46 B.C.E.) to 1,800 denarii under Maximinus (235–238 C.E.). See Eagleton and Williams, *Money*, 54.

45. Pense, "Decline and Fall of the Roman Denarius."

46. Things got worse from there, as a pound of gold was worth 2.12 billion denarii in the middle of the fourth century in Egypt. See Davies, *History of Money*, 108.

47. Before Diocletian, who was Roman emperor from 284 to 305 and who drew up the first budget. See Davies, *History of Money*, 103.

48. Orlando Patterson, *Slavery and Social Death: A Comparative Study* (Cambridge, Mass.: Harvard University Press, 1982), 31.

49. Jerry Toner, *The Roman Guide to Slave Management: A Treatise by Nobleman Marcus Sidonius Falx* (New York: Overlook, 2014), quoted in Manuela Hoelterhoff, "'The Roman Guide to Slave Management' Is Brilliant," Bloomberg Business, October 15, 2014, http://www.bloomberg.com/news/articles/2014-10-15/-the-roman-guide-to-slave -management-is-brilliant-hoelterhoff.

50. David Noble, "11% of UK Businesses Say Slavery in Their Supply Chains Is 'Likely,'" *Guardian*, August 18, 2014. For more information, see https://agenda.weforum. org/2015/12/are-you-benefitting-from-slave-labour.

51. C. F. Kolbert, *The Digest of Roman Law: Theft, Rapine, Damage, and Insult* (New York: Penguin, 1979), 7.

52. Edward Gibbon, *The History of the Decline and Fall of the Roman Empire* (New York: Harper, 1845), Volume 3, 176.

53. Edward Castronova stresses that anything can be used as money: "In the end, 'money' is an abstract quality that can be applied to almost anything" (*Wildcat Currency: How the Virtual Money Revolution Is Transforming the Economy* [New Haven, Conn.: Yale University Press, 2014], 44). But in the games he cites, the money is usually designed by programmers.

54. As Graeber puts it: "[F]or there even to be a discipline called 'economics,' a discipline that concerns itself first and foremost with how individuals seek the most advantageous arrangement for the exchange of shoes for potatoes, or clothes for spears,

it must assume that the exchange of such goods need have nothing to do with war, passion, adventure, mystery, sex, or death" (*Debt*, 32–33).

55. Geoffrey Ingham, "'Babylonian Madness': On the Historical and Sociological Origins of Money," in *What Is Money?* ed. John Smithin (New York: Routledge, 2000), 17.

56. Todd Hirsch, "The Future of Money," TED^xEdmonton, 2013, YouTube, www .youtube.com/watch?v=Kon3BGId9nU.

57. Narayana R. Kocherlakota, "Money Is Memory," Staff Report 218 (Federal Reserve Bank of Minneapolis, 1996).

58. Stephanie Kelton, "Money Is No Object: Accounting for Deficits, Taxes, and Trust in the 21st Century" (presentation at the Financial Planning Association Annual Retreat Conference, May 5–8, 2012).

59. Felix Martin, *Money: The Unauthorized Biography* (New York: Knopf, 2013), 224.

2. The Money Magnet

1. Aristotle, *Nicomachean Ethics, Book V*, trans. W. D. Ross (Kitchener, Ont.: Batoche, 1999), 80.

2. Felix Martin, *Money: The Unauthorized Biography* (New York: Knopf, 2013), 79.

3. Russell, Bertrand. *A History of Western Philosophy, and Its Connection with Political and Social Circumstances from the Earliest Times to the Present Day* (New York: Simon and Schuster, 1945), 3.

4. Iamblichus, *The Life of Pythagoras*, trans. T. Taylor (Kila, Mont.: Kessinger, 1918).

5. W. K. C. Guthrie, *A History of Greek Philosophy*, vol. 1, *The Earlier Presocratics and the Pythagoreans* (Cambridge: Cambridge University Press, 1962), 221–22.

6. Benoit Mandelbrot, *The Fractal Geometry of Nature* (New York: Freeman, 1982), 1.

7. Aristotle, *Generation of Animals*, trans. A. L. Peck (Cambridge, Mass.: Harvard University Press, 1943), 184.

8. This compares with K. Hart, who wrote: "One side [heads] reminds us that states underwrite currencies and the money is originally a relation between persons in society, a token perhaps. The other [tails] reveals the coin as a thing, capable of entering into definite relations with other things." ("Heads or Tails: Two Sides of the Coin," *Man* 21, no. 3 [1986]: 638). Rather than persons versus things, our version is numbers versus value. The key difference is again our emphasis on the importance of number.

9. "U.S. Nickel Melt Value Calculator," CoinApps.com, http://coinapps.com/nickel /us/calculator.

10. In 2014, the Financial Conduct Authority fined Barclays £26 million for charges including manipulation of the gold price on June 28, 2012. See Financial Conduct Authority, "Barclays Fined £26m for Failings Surrounding the London Gold Fixing and Former Barclays Trader Banned and Fined for Inappropriate Conduct," press release, May 23, 2014.

11. Edward Castronova, *Wildcat Currency: How the Virtual Money Revolution Is Transforming the Economy* (New Haven, Conn.: Yale University Press, 2014), 6.

12. William Thomson, *Popular Lectures and Addresses* (London: Macmillan, 1889), 73.

13. Alfred Marshall, *Principles of Economics* (New York: Cosimo, 2006), 14.

14. An "emergent definition of value" is provided by K. R. Srinivasiengar, who wrote that "value may be defined as the variable status of an object emerging out of contemplation of it by a subject attached to a given universe of desire realizable by that object" ("Outline of an Emergent Theory of Value," *International Journal of Ethics* 45, no. 4 [1935]: 416). The theory we provide here is better described as an "emergent theory of price."

15. Roger Wolcott Sperry, "Left-Brain, Right-Brain," *Saturday Review*, August 9, 1975, 30–33.

16. Iain McGilchrist, *The Master and His Emissary: The Divided Brain and the Making of the Western World* (New Haven, Conn.: Yale University Press, 2009), 209.

17. Ibid., 279.

18. Quoted in Adam Levy, "Mapping the Trader's Brain," *Bloomberg Markets*, February 1, 2006, 34–45.

19. Christopher T. S. Ragan and Richard G. Lipsey, *Economics*, 13th ed. (Toronto: Pearson Education Canada, 2011), 609.

20. Paul A. Samuelson and William D. Nordhaus, *Economics*, 17th ed. (Boston: McGraw-Hill, 2001), 511.

21. Effingham Wilson, *What Is Money?* (London: Wilson, 1872).

22. The following discussion of the quantum properties of money is based on David Orrell, "A Quantum Theory of Money and Value," June 28, 2015, Social Science Research Network, http://ssrn.com/abstract=2624371. It is also partly based on Orrell's 2015 Marshall McLuhan Lecture "Money Is the Message," hosted by Transmediale and the Canadian Embassy in Berlin (www.youtube.com/playlist?list=PL9olnMFdRIwshkq 3nfaF2nBzbFAQRvLmy).

23. Georg Friedrich Knapp, *The State Theory of Money*, 4th ed. (London: Macmillan, 1924), 32.

24. Ibid., 38–39.

25. Alfred Mitchell-Innes, "The Credit Theory of Money," *Banking Law Journal*, December–January 1914, 151–168.

26. Martin, *Money*, 29.

27. According to David Graeber, "What we call 'money' isn't a 'thing' at all, it's a way of comparing things mathematically, as proportions: of saying one of X is equivalent to six of Y. As such it is probably as old as human thought" (*Debt: The First 5000 Years* [Brooklyn, N.Y.: Melville House, 2011], 52).

28. Bernard Lietaer, *The Future of Money: Creating New Wealth, Work and a Wiser World* (London: Century, 2001), 39.

29. According to Knapp, "The metallist defines the unit of value as a given quantity of metal. . . . The chartalist defines the unit of value historically. It therefore becomes a notion which derives its meaning from a particular pay-community in which it finds itself" (*State Theory of Money*, 302).

30. Marshall McLuhan and W. Terrence Gordon, *Understanding Media: The Extensions of Man*, critical ed. (Corte Madera, Calif.: Gingko, 2003), 179–195.

31. This special property of money objects is illustrated graphically for gold in figure 7.1.

32. Glyn Davies, *A History of Money: From Ancient Times to the Present Day*, 3d ed. (Cardiff: University of Wales Press, 2002), 44.

33. Part of the problem is the "shut up and calculate" Copenhagen interpretation of quantum physics, which, like money, attempts to reduce the quantum world to hard number. See David Orrell, *Truth or Beauty: Science and the Quest for Order* (New Haven, Conn.: Yale University Press, 2012), 109–111.

34. "Hold Funds Policy," TD Canada Trust, www.tdcanadatrust.com/document /PDF/520866.pdf.

35. Lietaer, *Future of Money*, 34.

36. Herodotus, *The Landmark Herodotus: The Histories*, ed. Robert B. Strassler, trans. Andrea L. Purvis (New York: Anchor, 2009), 55.

37. Including in the area of finance, as we found after doing a search. As far as we are aware, the theory we develop here is a novel one, but we are certainly not the first to make comparisons between money and quantum physics. The book that seemed to come closest to our approach is Charles Eisenstein, *Sacred Economics: Money, Gift, and Society in the Age of Transition* (Berkeley, Calif.: Evolver Editions, 2011). In an appendix called "Quantum Money and the Reserve Question," Eisenstein notes "the similarity between fractional-reserve money and the superposition of states of a quantum particle," in the sense that money can seem to exist in more than one place at the same time (454–455). He uses this as an argument in favor of fractional-reserve banking. He does not explicitly link this to the dualistic nature of money (e.g., as debt and credit) but notes that money eludes simple definitions and calls for a "multi-jective" approach to understanding it.

38. Graeber, *Debt*, 214; Graeber states that money is "just an 'IOU'" (46). See also David Graeber, "The Truth Is Out: Money Is Just an IOU, and the Banks Are Rolling in It," *Guardian*, March 18, 2014. However, he also acknowledges the commodity aspect of money, even if the commodity is sometimes psychological: "Credit money is based on trust, and in competitive markets, trust itself becomes a scarce commodity" (*Debt*, 73). We would argue that money has many special properties and is not just an IOU (which can represent any form of debt, such as the need to return a favor).

3. Virtual Money

1. Christopher Hibbert, *Rome: The Biography of a City* (New York: Norton, 1985), 79.

2. David Graeber, *Debt: The First 5000 Years* (Brooklyn, N.Y.: Melville House), 252–270.

3. The first two numbers of the Fibonacci sequence are 0 and 1, and the others are defined as the sum of the two preceding numbers, so it reads 0, 1, 1, 2, 3, 5, 8, 13, 21, and so on.

4. Laurence E. Sigler, *Fibonacci's Liber Abaci: A Translation into Modern English of Leonardo Pisano's Book of Calculation* (New York: Springer, 2002).

5. Glyn Davies, *A History of Money: From Ancient Times to the Present Day*, 3d ed. (Cardiff: University of Wales Press, 2002), 235.

6. The French historian Marc Bloch described feudal society in the following terms: "A subject peasantry; widespread use of the service tenement (i.e. the fief) instead of a salary, which was out of the question; the supremacy of a class of specialized warriors; ties of obedience and protection which bind man to man and, within the warrior class, assume the distinctive form called vassalage; fragmentation of authority—leading inevitably to disorder; and, in the midst of all this, the survival of other forms of association, family and State" (*Feudal Society*, trans. L. A. Manyon [Chicago: University of Chicago Press, 1965], 446).

7. As Laurent Feller notes, "Buying and selling were not prompted by trading considerations alone but also obeyed social logics, themselves determined by kinship, friendship and neighbourhood as well as by adherence to a particular group of equivalent status" (quoted in Jacques Le Goff, *Money and the Middle Ages* [Oxford: Polity, 2012], 115).

8. *The Dialogue Concerning the Exchequer*, circa 1180, The Avalon Project, Yale Law School, http://avalon.law.yale.edu/medieval/excheq.asp.

9. M. T. Clanchy, *From Memory to Written Record: England, 1066–1307* (Cambridge, Mass.: Harvard University Press, 1979), 96.

10. Graeber, *Debt*, 268.

11. Davies, *History of Money*, 253.

12. Jack Weatherford, *The History of Money* (New York: Three Rivers, 1997), 67.

13. Le Goff, *Money and the Middle Ages*, 62–64.

14. Aristotle wrote that "money has become by convention a sort of representative of demand; and this is why it has the name 'money' (*nomisma*)—because it exists not by nature but by law (*nomos*) and it is in our power to change it and make it useless" (*Nicomachean Ethics*. http://classics.mit.edu/Aristotle/nicomachaen.5.v.html).

15. Aristotle, *Politics*, http://classics.mit.edu/Aristotle/politics.1.one.html.

16. Thomas Aquinas, *Sententia Ethica*, lib. 5, l. 9, n. 12.

17. Le Goff, *Money and the Middle Ages*, 42.

18. Ibid., 70.

19. Ibid., 72.

20. An example of such an insurance contract was the following from Francesco di Prato and Co., of Venice, on August 3, 1384: "We insure Baldo Ridolfo and Co. for 100 gold florins of wool, loaded onto the boat of Bartolomeo Vitale in transit from Penisola to Porto Pisano. Of these 100 florins which we insure against all risk, we will receive four gold florins in cash." Below the text is a note that "the said boat arrived safely 4 August 1384" (quoted in ibid., 97).

21. Marco Polo, *The Book of Ser Marco Polo, the Venetian, Concerning the Kingdoms and Marvels of the East*, trans. and ed. Henry Yule (London: Murray, 1903).

22. Charles Poor Kindleberger, *A Financial History of Western Europe* (London: Allen & Unwin, 1984), 22.

23. Fairs were highly organized and followed fixed schedules over the course of a few weeks with days for settlement at the end. See ibid., 36.

24. Because this did not include an exchange rate, it was usurious. See ibid., 40.

25. This example is from Weatherford, *History of Money*, 76.

26. Diego Laynez, *Disputationes Tridentinae*, trans. Hartmann Grisar (Oeniponti: Rauch, 1886), 2:228.

27. Felix Martin, *Money: The Unauthorized Biography* (New York: Knopf, 2013), 69.

28. David Bollier, *Think Like a Commoner: A Short Introduction to the Life of the Commons* (Gabriola Island, B.C.: New Society, 2014).

29. Paris demographics from "Historical Population of Paris (59 B.C.E.–1789)," http://en.wikipedia.org/wiki/Demographics_of_Paris#mediaviewer/File:Paris_historical_population_1.png.

30. Karl Marx, *Economic and Philosophic Manuscripts of 1844*, trans. Martin Mulligan (Moscow: Progress, 1959), 60.

31. Bernard Lietaer, "The Mystery of Money" (unpublished manuscript, 2002), 156, http://www.scribd.com/doc/294011240/Bernard-Lietaer-The-Mystery-of-Money-287pp-full-pdf-download.

32. Jackson Spielvogel, *Western Civilization: A Brief History*, vol. 2, *Since 1500* (Belmont, Calif.: Wadsworth, 2008), 281.

33. Vanessa Thorpe, "Black Death Was Not Spread by Rat Fleas, Say Researchers," *Guardian*, March 29, 2014.

34. In upper Normandy, for example, skilled wages went from 2 sous tournois per day in 1320–1340, to 4 in 1340–1405, and 5 in 1405–1520. See Le Goff, *Money and the Middle Ages*, 116.

35. Ibid., 98.

36. Ibid., 145; Anita Guerreau-Jalabert, "Caritas y don en la sociedad medieval occidental," *Hispania: Revista española de historia* 60, no. 204 (2000): 27–62.

37. Quoted in Le Goff, *Money and the Middle Ages*, 128.

38. Ibid., 145.

39. Francis of Assisi, *The Writings of St. Francis of Assisi*, trans. Paschal Robinson (Philadelphia: Dolphin, 1906).

40. Lietaer, "Mystery of Money," 156.

41. "The more severe inequality becomes, the more entitled people may feel and less likely to share resources they become. The wealthier [that] segments of society become then, the more vulnerable communities may be to selfish tendencies and the less charity the least among us can expect" (Lisa Miller, "The Money-Empathy Gap," *New York*, July 1, 2012).

42. Quoted in Michael Lewis, "Extreme Wealth Is Bad for Everyone—Especially the Wealthy," *New Republic*, November 12, 2014.

43. Maryam Kouchaki, Kristin Smith-Crowe, Arthur P. Brief, and Carlos Sousa, "Seeing Green: Mere Exposure to Money Triggers a Business Decision Frame and Unethical Outcomes," *Organizational Behavior and Human Decision Processes* 121, no. 1 (2013): 53–61.

4. New World

1. The fact that Columbus's diary mentions gold sixty-five times over the course of a voyage that lasted less than 100 days, suggests that the search for it was one of

his main motivations. See Charles Poor Kindleberger, *A Financial History of Western Europe* (London: Allen & Unwin, 1984), 25.

2. Michael E. Smith, *The Aztecs*, 3d ed. (Malden, Mass.: Wiley-Blackwell, 2012), 119; Jack Weatherford, *The History of Money* (New York: Three Rivers, 1997), 15.

3. Quoted in Mark Cocker, *Rivers of Blood, Rivers of Gold: Europe's Conquest of Indigenous Peoples* (New York: Grove, 1998), 88.

4. Dale M. Brown, *Aztecs: Reign of Blood & Splendor* (Alexandria, Va.: Time-Life, 1992), 30.

5. Simon L. Lewis and Mark A. Maslin, "Defining the Anthropocene," *Nature* 519 (2015): 171–180.

6. Cocker, *Rivers of Blood*, xiii.

7. Weatherford, *History of Money*, 99.

8. Juan Forero, "Bolivia's Cerro Rico: The Mountain That Eats Men," NPR, September 25, 2012, www.npr.org/2012/09/25/161752820/bolivias-cerro-rico-the-mountain-that-eats-men.

9. Glyn Davies, *A History of Money: From Ancient Times to the Present Day*, 3d ed. (Cardiff: University of Wales Press, 2002), 222.

10. Lewis S. Feuer, *The Scientific Intellectual: The Psychological & Sociological Origins of Modern Science* (New York: Basic, 1963), 120.

11. Henry William Spiegel, *The Growth of Economic Thought*, 3d ed. (Durham, N.C.: Duke University Press, 1991), 88–89.

12. Quoted in Weatherford, *History of Money*, 103.

13. Peter L. Bernstein, *The Power of Gold: The History of an Obsession* (New York: Wiley, 2000), 139.

14. Richard Cantillon, *Essay on the Nature of Trade in General*, trans. Henry Higgs (London: Cass, 1959), 68–69.

15. Quoted in Catherine Eagleton and Jonathan Williams, *Money: A History* (Richmond Hill, Ont.: Firefly, 2007), 162.

16. Such inflation occurred, for example, in 1160. See Davies, *History of Money*, 182.

17. Ibid., 190.

18. Weatherford, *History of Money*, 107.

19. Davies, *History of Money*, 549.

20. Eagleton and Williams, *Money*, 108.

21. Quoted in Murray N. Rothbard, *An Austrian Perspective on the History of Economic Thought* (Auburn, Ala.: Ludwig von Mises Institute, 2006), 1:291.

22. Kindleberger, *Financial History of Western Europe*, 51.

23. According to Davies, "This position was reached by the 1660s" (*History of Money*, 252).

24. Quoted in Kindleberger, *Financial History of Western Europe*, 51.

25. The Amsterdam Exchange accounts were supposed to be backed by metal reserves, although some suspected a cheat—Sir Edward Forde wrote in his 1666 "Experimented Proposals how the King may have money" that "no considerate man can believe that they have so much Money in their Banks as they give out bills for." In 1760 the

metallic stock was 16.3 million florins, compared with total liabilities of 18.7 million florins. See ibid., 49.

26. Kindleberger notes "the private purpose of making a profit through lending newly issued bank notes" as a motivation (ibid., 53). The public-private nature of the bank's partnership is described in Martin, *Money*, 117.

27. Until 1759, no notes were issued for amounts smaller than £20, which was about the average annual wage, so these large notes were primarily used as a substitute for gold in large transactions, and most people never came near them. However, their usage steadily increased as smaller denominations became available, and they officially became legal tender in 1833. See Kindleberger, *Financial History of Western Europe*, 77.

28. Often attributed to former Bank of England director Josiah Stamp, but the source appears to be a British investment adviser, according to Lawrence Angas, *Slump Ahead in Bonds* (New York: Somerset, 1937).

29. Geoffrey Madan, *Geoffrey Madan's Notebooks*, ed. J. A. Gere and John Sparrow (Oxford: Oxford University Press, 1981). The Banking Department had reserves in the range of 42 to 52 percent in the period 1845 to 1900, according to figures in R. H. Inglis Palgrave, *Bank Rate and the Money Market in England, France, Germany, Holland, and Belgium 1844–1900* (London: Murray, 1903), 86.

30. John Locke, *The Second Treatise on Civil Government* (Amherst, N.Y.: Prometheus Books, 1986), chap. 5, sec. 28, 21.

31. It was named after the English financier Sir Thomas Gresham.

32. An example was the new U.S. silver dollar, which was preferred to its Spanish counterpart. See Davies, *History of Money*, 470.

33. Bernstein, *Power of Gold*,196.

34. Demonetization of silver did not occur until 1774. See Kindleberger, *Financial History of Western Europe*, 59.

35. Davies, *History of Money*, 469.

36. Adam Smith, *An Inquiry into the Nature and Causes of the Wealth of Nations* (London: Strahan & Cadell, 1776), II.2.85.

37. Quoted in Martin, *Money*, 203–204.

38. France switched to gold in 1878. The United States was effectively on the gold standard by 1873, officially by 1900.

39. John Kenneth Galbraith, *Money: Whence It Came, Where It Went* (New York: Houghton Mifflin, 1995), 30. The strength of its reputation, of course, allowed it to operate on relatively small reserves. In the period 1850 to 1890, reserves were no more than 4 percent of the bank's domestic deposit liabilities. See Davies, *History of Money*, 359.

40. Weatherford, *History of Money*, 155.

41. Quoted in Bernstein, *Power of Gold*, 240.

42. Weatherford, *History of Money*, 161.

43. Kindleberger, *Financial History of Western Europe*, 87.

44. Davies, *History of Money*, 184.

45. Stefan Zweig, *The World of Yesterday* (London: Cassell, 1943), 13.

46. The effect is also reflected in the stance of central European central bankers, whose belief that "inflation is the predominant threat to macroeconomic stability . . . reflects the hyperinflation of the 1920s. In contrast, for those in English speaking countries, unemployment is seen as the biggest threat. This reflects their experience of the Great Depression" (William R. White, "Is Monetary Policy a Science? The Interaction of Theory and Practice over the Last 50 Years," in *50 Years of Money and Finance: Lessons and Challenges*, ed. Morten Balling and Ernest Gnan [Vienna: SUERF, 2013], 90).

5. A Wonderful Machine

1. James Buchan, *Frozen Desire: The Meaning of Money* (New York: Farrar, Straus and Giroux, 1997), 144.

2. An exception was the Bank of France, founded in 1800. See Charles Poor Kindleberger, *A Financial History of Western Europe* (London: Allen & Unwin, 1984), 98.

3. Glyn Davies, *A History of Money: From Ancient Times to the Present Day*, 3d ed. (Cardiff: University of Wales Press, 2002), 459.

4. Farley Grubb, *Benjamin Franklin and the Birth of a Paper Money Economy* (Philadelphia: Federal Reserve Bank of Philadelphia, 2006).

5. J. A. Leo Lemay, *The Life of Benjamin Franklin*, vol. 1, *Journalist, 1706–1730* (Philadelphia: University of Pennsylvania Press, 2006), 399.

6. The French stayed away from paper currencies until the time of the French Revolution, when the new Republican leaders issued a note known as the *assignat*. It was intended initially as a bond with an interest rate of 5 percent and was supposed to be backed by land confiscated from the Church. See Catherine Eagleton and Jonathan Williams, *Money: A History* (Richmond Hill, Ont.: Firefly, 2007), 228. This was not a huge hit, either—mismanagement of the money supply again led to massive inflation— and in 1796 the printing machines and plates were destroyed in public (but were quickly replaced by a new paper currency with a different name, the *mandat*). The Russian Revolution saw a similar use (and abuse) of paper money.

7. As John Kenneth Galbraith notes, "The United States came into existence on a full tide not of inflation but of hyperinflation" (*Money: Whence It Came, Where It Went* [New York: Houghton Mifflin, 1995], 60). The notes were eventually redeemed at the relatively generous rate of 40 paper dollars to one silver dollar. See Eagleton and Williams, *Money*, 228.

8. Its notes formed about one-fifth of the total currency supply and were allowed to circulate freely alongside other notes issued by state banks.

9. This bank held only a 20 percent coin reserve. See Eagleton and Williams, *Money*, 225.

10. Davies, *History of Money*, 483.

11. Ibid., 502.

12. Andrew Jackson, "Veto of the Bank of the United States," in *A Compilation of the Messages and Papers of the Presidents, 1787–1897*, ed. James D. Richardson (Washington, D.C.: Government Printing Office, 1896), 576–591.

13. Abraham Lincoln, "Senate document 23," 1865, 91.

14. Benjamin Butler, Speech in the House of Representatives, *Congressional Globe,* 40th Cong., 3d sess., January 12, 1869, 303.

15. Eagleton and Williams, *Money,* 227.

16. William Jennings Bryan, "Cross of Gold" speech, in *Official Proceedings of the Democratic National Convention Held in Chicago, Illinois, July 7, 8, 9, 10, and 11, 1896* (Logansport, Ind.: 1896), 226–234, in *The Annals of America,* vol. 12, *1895–1904: Populism, Imperialism, and Reform* (Chicago: Encyclopaedia Britannica, 1968), 100–105.

17. The Reconstruction Finance Corporation was created in 1932 to better fulfill the role of lender of last resort. It later became part of the Federal Deposit Insurance Corporation. See Galbraith, *Money,* 196–200.

18. Simon van Zuylen-Wood, "Feces and the Gold Standard: A Psychological Explanation of Goldbuggery," *New Republic,* August 28, 2012, www.newrepublic.com/article /106601/feces-and-gold-standard-psychological-explanation-goldbuggery.

19. According to the Fed's own website, it is not "owned" by anyone. The Fed charges interest on the money it provides to the government, but most of that is returned to the Treasury. See "Who Owns the Federal Reserve?," Board of Governors of the Federal Reserve System, last updated August 2, 2013, www.federalreserve.gov/faqs/about_14986.htm.

20. Quoted in Satyajit Das, "Trapped Central Banks and the Semiotics of Monetary Policy," *Independent,* July 12, 2013.

21. The price equated to $4.87 per ounce. Galbraith called the 1925 return to the gold standard "perhaps the most decisively damaging action involving money in modern times" (*Money,* 170).

22. Stephen Daggett, "Costs of Major U.S. Wars" (Congressional Research Service, Washington, D.C., 2010).

23. John Noble Wilford, *We Reach the Moon: The New York Times Story of Man's Greatest Adventure* (New York: Bantam, 1969), 67.

24. Milton Friedman, "A Proposal for Resolving the U.S. Balance of Payments Problem: Confidential Memorandum to President-elect Richard Nixon," in *The Merits of Flexible Exchange Rates: An Anthology,* ed. Leo Melamed (Fairfax, Va.: George Mason University Press, 1988), 429–438.

25. Richard Nixon, "Address to the Nation Outlining a New Economic Policy: 'The Challenge of Peace,'" August 15, 1971, The American Presidency Project, www .presidency.ucsb.edu/ws/?pid=3115.

26. Galbraith, *Money,* 301.

27. Quoted in James Rickards, *The Death of Money: The Coming Collapse of the International Monetary System* (New York: Portfolio/Penguin, 2014), 213.

28. Jill Treanor and Dominic Rushe, "Banks Hit by Record Fine for Rigging Forex Markets," *Guardian,* May 20, 2015.

29. Peter Cohan, "Big Risk: $1.2 Quadrillion Derivatives Market Dwarfs World GDP," DailyFinance, June 9, 2010, http://www.dailyfinance.com/2010/06/09/risk-quadrillion -derivatives-market-gdp/.

30. The money supply is "ultimately determined" by the central bank, with banks functioning only as "cooperating partners in this process" (Paul A. Samuelson and William D. Nordhaus, *Economics,* 17th ed. [Boston: McGraw-Hill, 2001], 551).

31. Michael McLeay, Amar Radia, and Ryland Thomas, "Money Creation in the Modern Economy," *Quarterly Bulletin* [Bank of England], no. 1, March 14, 2014, 1.

32. Adair Turner, "Printing Money to Fund Deficit Is the Fastest Way to Raise Rates," *Financial Times*, November 10, 2014.

33. McLeay, Radia, and Thomas, "Money Creation in the Modern Economy," 1–14.

34. Margrit Kennedy, *Interest and Inflation Free Money, Creating an Exchange Medium That Works for Everybody and Protects the Earth* (Philadelphia: New Society, 1987).

35. L. Randall Wray, *Understanding Modern Money: The Key to Full Employment and Price Stability* (Cheltenham: Elgar, 1998), 77–80.

36. To maintain this balance, we should have $R + I + B > D$, where R is the growth rate of GDP, I is the inflation rate, B is borrowing costs as percentage of GDP, and D is the primary deficit—that is, the difference between spending and taxes, again expressed as percentage of GDP. See Rickards, *Death of Money*, 178.

37. Quoted in G. Edward Griffin, *The Creature from Jekyll Island: A Second Look at the Federal Reserve*, 4th ed. (Westlake Village, Calif.: American Media, 2002), 187–188.

38. "Debt to GDP Ratio Historical Chart," Macrotrends, www.macrotrends.net/1381/debt-to-gdp-ratio-historical-chart.

39. Ben Bernanke, interview by Scott Pelley, "Ben Bernanke's Greatest Challenge," *60 Minutes*, CBS, March 12, 2009.

40. David Orrell, "Making Sausages," *World Finance*, March 4, 2013.

41. Jack Weatherford, *The History of Money* (New York: Three Rivers, 1997), 48.

42. Ralph Abraham, *Chaos, Gaia, Eros: A Chaos Pioneer Uncovers the Three Great Streams of History* (New York: HarperCollins, 1994), 92.

43. Along with a major shift in science toward areas such as complexity. See David Orrell, *The Other Side of the Coin: The Emerging Vision of Economics and Our Place in the World* (Toronto: Key Porter, 2008), 150.

44. Bernard Lietaer, "The Mystery of Money" (unpublished manuscript, 2002), http://www.scribd.com/doc/294011240/Bernard-Lietaer-The-Mystery-of-Money-287pp-full-pdf-download.

45. Lietaer, for example, describes gold as a yang currency in "Mystery of Money." Peter L. Bernstein wrote that since the fall of the gold standard, "gold has been emasculated. . . . We have relegated gold to its traditional role in jewelry and adornment" (*The Power of Gold: The History of an Obsession* [New York: Wiley, 2000], 368).

46. James Dawson, "When It Comes to Coins, Isis Is Clearly Not as Good as Gold," *New Statesman*, November 19, 2014.

47. Alison Smale and Melissa Eddy, "Greek Debt Crisis Pits Greeks Against Germans," *New York Times*, July 11, 2015.

6. The Money Power

1. Frederick Soddy, *Wealth, Virtual Wealth and Debt: The Solution of the Economic Paradox* (New York: Dutton, 1926), 69.

2. Richard Dobbs, Susan Lund, Jonathan Woetzel, and Mina Mutafchieva, "Debt and (Not Much) Deleveraging" (McKinsey Global Institute, 2015), www.mckinsey.com /insights/economic_studies/debt_and_not_much_deleveraging; Ami Sedghi, "Global Debt Has Grown by $57 Trillion in Seven Years Following the Financial Crisis," *Guardian*, February 5, 2015.

3. Bill Gross, "Barron's 2015 Roundtable Highlight," *Barron's*, January 17, 2015, http://online.barrons.com/articles/bill-gross-1421929674.

4. International Monetary Fund, "Global Financial Stability Report: Risk Taking, Liquidity, and Shadow Banking: Curbing Excess While Promoting Growth," October 2014, www.imf.org/external/pubs/ft/gfsr/2014/02/index.htm.

5. Norbert Häring and Niall Douglas, *Economists and the Powerful: Convenient Theories, Distorted Facts, Ample Rewards* (London: Anthem, 2012), x.

6. M. Neil Browne, and J. Kevin Quinn, "The Lamentable Absence of Power in Mainstream Economics," in *Future Directions for Heterodox Economics*, ed. John T. Harvey and Robert F. Garnett (Ann Arbor: University of Michigan Press, 2008), 240–261.

7. Frederick Soddy, *The Role of Money: What it Should Be, Contrasted with What it Has Become*, 1934. Reprint, London: Routledge, 2003, ix–x.

8. Murray N. Rothbard, *Wall Street, Banks, and American Foreign Policy* (Burlingame, Calif.: Center for Libertarian Studies, 1996).

9. Howard Zinn, *A People's History of the United States* (New York: Harper Perennial, 2003).

10. Ibid., 242.

11. Ibid., 255.

12. Quoted in Stephen Gandel, "By Every Measure, the Big Banks Are Bigger," *Fortune*, September 13, 2013.

13. Quoted in Marcus Baram, "Government Sachs: Goldman's Close Ties to Washington Arouse Envy, Raise Questions," *Huffington Post*, July 3, 2009, www.huffingtonpost.com/2009/06/02/government-sachs-goldmans_n_210561.html.

14. Joris Luyendijk (journalist and author), private conversation with Roman Chlupatý, April 2013.

15. Nick Mathiason and Melanie Newman, "Finance Industry's Multimillion-Pound Lobbying Budget Revealed," *Guardian*, July 9, 2012.

16. Essential Information, Consumer Education Foundation, "Sold Out: How Wall Street and Washington Betrayed America", March 2009, www.wallstreetwatch.org/reports/sold_out.pdf.

17. Ian Bremmer and Cliff Kupchan, "Top Risks 2015: Weaponization of Finance," January 5, 2015, www.eurasiagroup.net/pages/top-risks-2015#4.

18. Quoted in Roman Chlupatý, "(Ne)konečná krize: 4 expertní názory na současné i budoucí turbulence" [(Never)ending crisis: 4 expert takes on current and future turbulences], InvestičníWeb.cz, http://www.investicniweb.cz/2014/6/11/nekonecna-krize-4-expertni-nazory-na-soucasne-i-budouci-turbulence.

19. "Reserve Currency," Wikipedia, http://en.wikipedia.org/wiki/Reserve_currency.

20. Jeffrey Gundlach, "Americký dolar zpívá labutí píseň," Investicniweb, June 16, 2014, www.investicniweb.cz/2014/6/17/jeffrey-gundlach-americky-dolar-zpiva-labuti-pisen.

21. Joseph R. Peden, "Mises Daily: Inflation and the Fall of the Roman Empire," Mises Institute, September 7, 2009, http://mises.org/library/inflation-and-fall-roman-empire.

22. Susan Strange, *Authority and Markets: Susan Strange's Writings on International Political Economy*, ed. Roger Tooze and Christopher May (New York: Palgrave Macmillan, 2002), 138.

23. "Handle with Care," *Economist*, March 26, 2009.

24. Shannon Tiezzi, "China to Be World's Largest Economy in 2014?" *Diplomat*, May 1, 2014.

25. An imploding Chinese real estate market could threaten global financial stability, as the Bank of England implicitly admitted in 2015 by stress testing the ability of British banks to withstand such an event.

26. Mark Leonard, *What Does China Think?* (New York: PublicAffairs, 2008), 84–86.

27. Sebastian Mallaby and Olin Wethington, "The Future of the Yuan: China's Struggle to Internationalize Its Currency," *Foreign Affairs* 91, no. 1 (2012): 135–146.

28. Quoted in ibid.

29. Ansuya Harjani, "Yuan Trade Settlement to Grow by 50% in 2014: Deutsche Bank," CNBC, December 11, 2013, www.cnbc.com/id/101263663.

30. V. N. Sreeja, "Yuan Overtakes Euro as Second-Most Used Currency in International Trade Settlement: SWIFT," *International Business Times*, December 3, 2013, www.ibtimes.com/yuan-overtakes-euro-second-most-used-currency-international-trade-settlement-swift-1492476.

31. Mallaby and Wethington, "Future of the Yuan," 135–146.

32. Parag Khanna, *How to Run the World: Charting a Course to the Next Renaissance* (New York: Random House, 2011), 58.

33. Greg Palast, "Robert Mundell, Evil Genius of the Euro," *Guardian*, June 26, 2012.

34. Quoted in David Marsh, *The Euro: The Politics of the New Global Currency* (New Haven, Conn.: Yale University Press, 2009), 106.

35. John G. Ruggie, "Territoriality and Beyond: Problematizing Modernity in International Relations," *International Organization* 47, no. 1 (1993): 139–174.

36. Marwan Kraidy, *Hybridity: The Cultural Logic of Globalization* (Philadelphia: Temple University Press, 2005).

37. L. Randall Wray, *Understanding Modern Money: The Key to Full Employment and Price Stability* (Cheltenham: Elgar, 1998).

38. Harris Dellas and George S. Tavlas, "The Gold Standard, the Euro, and the Origins of the Greek Sovereign Debt Crisis," *Cato Journal* 33, no. 3 (2013): 491–520.

39. Martin Feldstein, "The Failure of the Euro," *Foreign Affairs* 91, no. 1 (2012): 105–116.

40. Michael Hudson, "The Financial Attack on Greece: Where Do We Go From Here?" CounterPunch, July 8, 2015. www.counterpunch.org/2015/07/08/71809.

41. A "former Mexican diplomat," quoted in Khanna, *How to Run the World*, 52.

42. Benedict Anderson, *Imagined Communities: Reflections on the Origin and Spread of Nationalism* (London: Verso, 1991).

43. Quoted in Dean Carroll, "Latvia's Membership Shows Euro Is 'Major Achievement'—claims EU," PubAffairs: Public Affairs Networking, December 2013, www.policyreview.eu/latvias-membership-shows-euro-is-major-achievement-claims-eu.

44. "Russian Ruble Becomes Only Valid Currency in Crimea," RT, June 2, 2014, http://rt.com/business/162992-crimea-adopts-ruble-currency.

45. Jeffrey Cavanaugh, "FOREX Africa: The CFA Franc aka the African Euro," AKF Insider, February 12, 2014, http://afkinsider.com/41946/forex-africa-african-euro.

46. Henry Kyambalesa and Mathurin C. Houngnikpo, *Economic Integration and Development in Africa* (Aldershot: Ashgate, 2006), 88.

47. Mervyn King, *The Political Economy of European Monetary Union* (Florence: European University Institute, 1998).

48. Martin Dokoupil, "Gulf Arabs Shouldn't Delay Single Currency—Qatar Central Bank Official," Reuters, July 26, 2012.

49. Steve H. Hanke, "Why the World Should Be Rallying for the 'Yuan-ization' of North Korea," *Business Insider*, June 22, 2013.

50. Pew Charitable Trusts, "The Complex Story of American Debt," July 29, 2015. www.pewtrusts.org/en/research-and-analysis/reports/2015/07/the-complex-story-of-american-debt.

7. Solid Gold Economics

1. Thomas Pownall, *A Letter from Governor Pownall to Adam Smith, Being an Examination of Several Points of Doctrine* (London: Printed for J. Almon, 1776).

2. The principle of an "invisible hand" that guides market forces is an ancient idea that was developed long before Smith, as noted by Tomáš Sedláček, *Economics of Good and Evil: The Quest for Economic Meaning from Gilgamesh to Wall Street* (New York: Oxford University Press, 2011), 10.

3. William Stanley Jevons, *The Theory of Political Economy*, 5th ed. (New York: Kelley and Millman, 1957), p. 1.

4. Jevons writes, for example: "Suppose that a person possesses one single kind of commodity, which we may consider to be money, or income" (ibid., 138).

5. John Stuart Mill, *Principles of Political Economy* (London: Parker, 1848).

6. Gilles Dostaler and Bernard Maris, "Dr. Freud and Mr. Keynes on Money and Capitalism," in *What Is Money?*, ed. John Smithin (New York: Routledge, 2000), 235–256.

7. Irving Fisher, *The Purchasing Power of Money*, 2d ed. (New York: Macmillan, 1922).

8. Federal Reserve Bank of St. Louis, "Velocity of M2 Money Stock," 2014, http://research.stlouisfed.org/fred2/series/M2V.

9. David Hume, *Essays, Moral, Political, and Literary*, ed. Eugene F. Miller (Indianapolis: Liberty Fund, 1987), www.econlib.org/library/LFBooks/Hume/hmMPL26.html.

10. Irving Fisher, *Mastering the Crisis* (London: Allen & Unwin, 1934).

11. Milton Friedman, *The Counter-revolution in Monetary Theory* (London: Institute of Economic Affairs, 1970), 24.

12. Milton Friedman, interview by Russell Roberts, "An Interview with Milton Friedman," September 4, 2006, http://www.econlib.org/library/Columns/y2006/Friedmantranscript.html.

13. The media also play a role. As Marshall McLuhan wrote in 1974, "Whereas all current inflation theories tend toward Newtonian rationality and balance, there is a huge disequilibrium factor of irrationality that results from information movement" ("A Media Approach to Inflation," *New York Times*, September 21, 1974).

14. Quoted in Felix Martin, *Money: The Unauthorized Biography* (New York: Knopf, 2013), 170.

15. Quoted in Todd G. Buchholz, *New Ideas from Dead Economists: An Introduction to Modern Economic Thought* (London: Penguin, 2008), 237.

16. John Maynard Keynes, "Economic Possibilities for Our Grandchildren," in *Essays in Persuasion* (New York: Norton, 1963), 369.

17. Glyn Davies, *A History of Money: From Ancient Times to the Present Day*, 3d ed. (Cardiff: University of Wales Press, 2002), 410.

18. Friedrich A. Hayek, *Denationalisation of Money: The Argument Refined* (1978; repr., London: Institute of Economic Affairs, 1990). 23–24.

19. Paul A. Samuelson, *Economics*, 9th ed. (New York: McGraw-Hill, 1973), 55.

20. Paul A. Samuelson, "An Exact Consumption-Loan Model of Interest with or Without the Social Contrivance of Money," *Journal of Political Economy* 66, no. 6 (1958): 467–482. Our answer to the question of how money attains value, as discussed in chapter 2, is that it is assigned value.

21. John Maynard Keynes once wrote: "If we speak frankly, we have to admit that our basis of knowledge for estimating the yield ten years hence of a railway, a copper mine, a textile factory, the goodwill of a patent medicine, an Atlantic liner, a building in the City of London amounts to little and sometimes to nothing" (*The General Theory of Employment, Interest and Money* [New York: Harcourt, Brace, 1936]).

22. Steve Keen, "Will We Crash Again? FT/Alphaville Talk," YouTube, 2015, www.youtube.com/watch?t=130&v=JKy6_yy3C3U.

23. Kenneth J. Arrow and Gérard Debreu, "Existence of a Competitive Equilibrium for a Competitive Economy," *Econometrica* 22 (1954): 65–90.

24. Yanis Varoufakis, Joseph Halevi, and Nicholas Theocarakis discuss the "propaganda value" of the Arrow–Debreu model, while emphasizing that this use was not the intention of the modelers, in *Modern Political Economics: Making Sense of the Post-2008 World* (New York: Routledge, 2011), 253–254.

25. Johanna Bockman, *Markets in the Name of Socialism: The Left-Wing Origins of Neoliberalism* (Stanford, Calif.: Stanford University Press, 2011), 47.

26. So presumably this book qualifies!

27. The usual technique was to offer a country loans and investment in return for it opening its economy; engineering a crisis; and offering debt relief in exchange for a fire sale of state assets. See Naomi Klein, *The Shock Doctrine: The Rise of Disaster Capitalism* (Toronto: Knopf Canada, 2007).

28. Frederick Soddy, *The Role of Money: What It Should Be, Contrasted with What It Has Become* (1934; repr., London: Routledge, 2003).

29. Gary S. Becker, *The Economic Approach to Human Behavior* (Chicago: University of Chicago Press, 1976).

30. Andrew Haldane, "The Revolution in Economics," in *Economics, Education and Unlearning: Economics Education at the University of Manchester* (Manchester: Post-Crash Economics Society, 2014), 3–6. For a discussion of the role of aesthetics in economics, see David Orrell, *Truth or Beauty: Science and the Quest for Order* (New Haven, Conn.: Yale University Press, 2012).

31. William R. White, "Is Monetary Policy a Science? The Interaction of Theory and Practice over the Last 50 Years," in *50 Years of Money and Finance: Lessons and Challenges*, ed. Morten Balling and Ernest Gnan (Vienna: SUERF, 2013), 84. An exception is that used in Jaromir Benes and Michael Kumhof, "The Chicago Plan Revisited" (working paper, International Monetary Fund, 2013), which Steve Keen described as "the first theoretical neoclassical paper to acknowledge the actual nature of banking, and to try to take this into account in a mathematical model" ("The IMF Gets Radical?," November 5, 2012, www.businessspectator.com.au/article/2012/11/5/business-spectator/imf-gets-radical).

32. White, "Is Monetary Policy a Science?," 85

33. David Orrell, *Economyths: How the Science of Complex Systems Is Transforming Economic Thought* (London: Icon, 2010), 32.

34. Quoted in Eric D. Beinhocker, *Origin of Wealth: Evolution, Complexity, and the Radical Remaking of Economics* (Boston: Harvard Business School Press, 2006), 59.

35. Eugene F. Fama, "Random Walks in Stock-Market Prices", Selected Papers, no. 16 (Graduate School of Business, University of Chicago, 1965).

36. John Cassidy, "Interview with Eugene Fama," *New Yorker*, January 13, 2010.

37. J. Doyne Farmer and John Geanakoplos, "The Virtues and Vices of Equilibrium and the Future of Financial Economics," *Complexity* 14, no. 3 (2009): 25.

38. R. Shiller, "Stock Prices and Social Dynamics," *Brookings Papers on Economic Activity* 2 (1984): 457–510.

39. Gillian Tett and Anuj Gangahar, "Limitations of Computer Models," *Financial Times*, August 14, 2007.

40. Adair Turner, "Printing Money to Fund Deficit Is the Fastest Way to Raise Rates," *Financial Times*, November 10, 2014.

41. Hites Ahir and Prakash Loungani, "Can Economists Forecast Recessions? Some Evidence from the Great Recession," *Oracle*, March 2014, forecasters.org/wp/wp-content/uploads/PLoungani_OracleMar2014.pdf.

42. Quoted in John Cassidy, "Letter from Chicago: After the Blowup," *New Yorker*, January 11, 2010.

43. According to White, despite the work of Minsky and others on the nature of financial crises, "All of this publically available literature was essentially ignored by major central banks. So too were any warnings implicit in the papers prepared for the private meetings of central bankers at the BIS itself. Thus, when the crisis broke in 2007, it came as a complete shock to many central bankers" ("Is Monetary Policy a Science?", 97).

44. Alan Greenspan, *The Map and the Territory: Risk, Human Nature, and the Future of Forecasting* (New York: Penguin, 2013), 7.

45. Thomas Sargent, interview by Art Rolnick, "Interview with Thomas Sargent" (Federal Reserve Bank of Minneapolis, September 2010).

46. Robert Lucas, "In Defence of the Dismal Science," *Economist*, August 6, 2009.

47. Cassidy, "Interview with Eugene Fama."

48. Ha-Joon Chang and Jonathan Aldred. "After the Crash, We Need a Revolution in the Way We Teach Economics," *Observer*, May 11, 2014.

49. Thomas Piketty, *Capital in the Twenty-First Century*, trans. Arthur Goldhammer (Cambridge, Mass.: Belknap Press of Harvard Unversity Press, 2014), 32.

50. Quoted in Claire Jones, " 'Dismal Science' Seeks Fresh Thinking After Failure in Crisis," *Financial Times*, November 11, 2013.

51. Alfred Marshall, *Principles of Economics*, 8th ed. (New York: Cosimo, 2006), xx.

52. Peter L. Bernstein, *The Power of Gold: The History of an Obsession* (New York: Wiley, 2000), 357–358.

53. Former Bank of England governor Gordon Richardson wrote, "I regret to say that I have little direct experience with economic equilibrium—indeed, so far as I am aware, none at all. I sometimes see suggestions that we shall be moving towards equilibrium next year or perhaps the year after: but somehow this equilibrium remains firmly in the offing" ("The Pursuit of Equilibrium," *Euromoney*, October 1979, 28–37).

54. Quoted in Alex Hern, "Bitcoin Hype Worse Than 'Tulip Mania,' Says Dutch Central Banker," *Guardian*, December 4, 2013.

55. Hyman Minsky, "Financial Instability Revisited: The Economics of Disaster," in *Reappraisal of the Federal Reserve Discount Mechanism* (Washington, D.C.: Board of Governors of the Federal Reserve System, 1972), 95–136.

56. Quoted in Stephen Mihm, "Why Capitalism Fails," *Boston Globe*, September 13, 2009.

57. Ibid.

58. Ben Bernanke, "The Macroeconomics of the Great Depression: A Comparative Approach," *Journal of Money, Credit, and Banking* 27, no. 1 (1995): 1–28.

59. Paul Krugman, *End This Depression Now!* (New York: Norton, 2012), 112.

60. The resulting dynamics can be simulated and visualized using the nonlinear dynamics program Minsky, which was originated by Steve Keen. The program is available at "Minsky: System Dynamics Program with Additional Features for Economics," SourceForge, http://sourceforge.net/projects/minsky/files.

61. Keen, "Will We Crash Again?"

62. Wolfgang Munchau, "Macroeconomists Need New Tools to Challenge Consensus," *Financial Times*, April 12, 2015.

63. Jeffrey Dew, Sonya Britt, and Sandra Huston, "Examining the Relationship Between Financial Issues and Divorce," *Family Relations* 61, no. 4 (2012): 615–628.

64. Daniel Kahneman and Amos Tversky, "Prospect Theory: An Analysis of Decision Under Risk," *Econometrica* 47 (1979): 263–291.

65. According to one study, we will pay on average 50 percent more for a dessert at a restaurant when we see it on a dessert cart than when we choose it from a

menu. See B. Bushong et al., "Pavlovian Processes in Consumer Choice: The Physical Presence of a Good Increases Willingness-to-Pay," *American Economic Review* 100 (2010): 1–18.

66. A. R. Hirsch, "Effects of Ambient Odors on Slot-Machine Usage in a Las Vegas Casino," *Psychology & Marketing* 12, no. 7 (1995): 585–594.

67. Francis Ysidro Edgeworth, *Mathematical Psychics: An Essay on the Application of Mathematics to the Moral Sciences* (London: Paul, 1881).

68. Pew Research Center, "The Happiness Trend Line: Barely a Ripple," 2010, www .pewsocialtrends.org/2006/02/13/are-we-happy-yet/37-3.

69. John Stuart Mill, "Posthumous Essay on Social Freedom," *Oxford and Cambridge Review*, January 1907.

70. L. Rainwater, "Poverty and Equivalence as Social Constructions," Luxembourg Income Study Working Paper, no. 91 (Center for Policy Research, Maxwell School, Syracuse, N.Y., 1990).

71. Graeme Wood, "Secret Fears of the Super-Rich," *Atlantic*, February 24, 2011.

72. Peter Singer, "Happiness, Money, and Giving It Away," *Project Syndicate*, July 12, 2006, http://www.project-syndicate.org/commentary/happiness--money--and-giving-it-away.

73. Quoted in Daniel Vasella and Clifton Leaf, "Temptation Is All Around us," *Fortune*, November 18, 2002, 109. See also Sanford E. DeVoe, Jeffrey Pfeffer, and Byron Y. Lee, "When Does Money Make Money More Important? Survey and Experimental Evidence," *ILRREVIEW* 66, no. 5 (2013): 1076–1094; and Eilene Zimmerman, "Research: All Money Is Not Created Equal" (Insights by Stanford Business, Stanford Graduate School of Business, January 6, 2014), www.gsb.stanford.edu/insights/ research-all-money-not-created-equal.

74. Singer, "Happiness, Money, and Giving It Away."

75. Brad Tuttle, "Got Stuff? Typical American Home Is Cluttered with Possessions—and Stressing Us Out," *Time*, July 19, 2012.

76. Donald Nordberg (Bournemouth University, U.K.), private conversation with Roman Chlupatý, April 2012.

77. Ida Kubiszewski et al., "Beyond GDP: Measuring and Achieving Global Genuine Progress," *Ecological Economics* 93 (2013): 57–68.

78. K. E. Boulding, "The Economics of the Coming Spaceship Earth," in *Environmental Quality in a Growing Economy*, ed. H. Jarrett (Baltimore: Johns Hopkins University Press, 1966), 3–14.

79. According to Laura Gottesdiener, "Workers here overwhelming call this place 'the Wild West'" ("What My Time in America's New Oil Boomtown Taught Me About Our Climate Madness," Alternet, October 12, 2014, www.alternet.org/environment /what-my-time-americas-new-oil-boomtown-taught-me-about-our-climate-madness).

80. As Bank of Sweden Prize–winner Robert Solow once said, "If it is very easy to substitute other factors for natural resources, then there is in principle 'no problem.' The world can, in effect, get along without natural resources" ("The Economics of Resources or the Resources of Economics," *American Economic Review* 64, no. 2 [1974]: 11).

81. Samuel Smiles, *Lives of Boulton and Watt: Principally from the Original Soho Mss.* (London: Murray, 1865).

82. Quoted in Sarah van Gelder, "Beyond Greed and Scarcity," *Yes!*, June 30, 1997.

83. For example, in Great Britain in the 1970s, people in the financial sector used to earn less than most other professionals, but now "the average London financial services salary is about £102,000 including bonuses while academics are paid about £48,000, natural scientists average about £42,000 and mechanical engineers £46,000" (Sarah Neville and Keith Fray, "The Fractured Middle: UK Salary Split Sees Übers Pull Ahead," *Financial Times*, February 14, 2014).

84. Stewart Brand, *The Media Lab: Inventing the Future at MIT* (New York: Viking, 1987), 202.

85. Boston Consulting Group, "Takeoff in Robotics Will Power the Next Productivity Surge in Manufacturing," press release, February 10, 2015.

86. Cahal Milmo, "Robot Revolution Gathers Pace—But at What Cost to Jobs?," *Independent*, February 10, 2015.

87. Simon Kennedy, "Half of Europe's Jobs Threatened by Machines in U.S. Echo," Bloomberg News, www.bloomberg.com/news/articles/2014–07–22/half-of-europe-s-jobs -threatened-by-machines-in-u-s-risk-echo.

88. Orrell, *Truth or Beauty*.

89. White, "Is Monetary Policy a Science?," 73–115.

90. "International Student Initiative for Pluralism in Economics," www.isipe.net /supportus.

91. "Pour un enseignement pluraliste de l'économie au Québec," May 13, 2014, Economie Autrement, http://economieautrement.org/pour-un-enseignement-pluraliste-de -leconomie-au-quebec.

92. James Trimarco, "Students for Economic Pluralism, Unite!," *Yes!*, February 20, 2015, www.yesmagazine.org/new-economy/students-for-economic-pluralism-unite -keith-harrington. See also Tomáš Sedláček, David Orrell, and Roman Chlupatý, *Soumrak Homo Economicus* (Prague: 65.pole, 2012); the title of the German version translates to *Humility: For a New Economy*.

93. Orrell, *Economyths*.

94. According to White,

> Perhaps the best candidate to replace extant theories would be models that recognize the importance of fiat credit in influencing economic decisions (to both spend and to produce), the importance of stocks (in particular stocks of debt) and the endogeneity of risk in the financial system. These models can produce highly non-linear results similar to those observed in real life crises. This approach has similarities with some pre-War business cycle models. As well, insights can also be gained from the new, and rapidly developing, study of complexity economics. This approach is at the other end of the stability spectrum from DSGE models in that complexity economics assumes many agents (no representative agent), each acting according to local rules (no concept of rational expectations), and it eschews all concepts of equilibrium. There are many parallels in this regard with evolutionary biology. ("Is Monetary Policy a Science?," 86)

95. Commonly attributed quotes are that quantum mechanics is "fundamentally incomprehensible" (Niels Bohr); "If you think you understand quantum mechanics,

you don't understand quantum mechanics" (Richard Feynman); "You don't understand quantum mechanics, you just get used to it" (John von Neumann).

96. Abbot Gilles li Muisis of Tournai, quoted in Bernstein, *Power of Gold*, 103.

97. For a discussion of economic decision making, see Daniel Kahneman, *Thinking, Fast and Slow* (New York: Farrar, Straus and Giroux, 2011).

98. Quoted in Mark Buchanan, "Quantum Minds: Why We Think Like Quarks," *New Scientist*, September 5, 2011.

99. Stephen Cecchetti, M. S. Mohanty, and Fabrizio Zampolli, "The Real Effects of Debt," Working Paper No. 352 (Bank for International Settlements, Basel, 2011).

100. For our own experience of this, see David Orrell, "Book Burning Economists," *World Finance*, July 1, 2015.

8. New Money

1. Ed Conway, "Basle's Secretive Bankers Have All the Power," *Times* (London), January 20, 2015.

2. Michael Romancov, "Dolar není mrtev, přežil i své kritiky. Jaké jsou vyhlídky americké měny?" [Dollar is not dead, it outlived even its critics. What are the prospects of the American currency?], *Ekonom*, November 9, 2014. This is an interview with Jan Jedlička, Erste Group's EU office manager.

3. Derek Hum and Wayne Simpson, "A Guaranteed Annual Income? From Mincome to the Millennium," *Policy Options*, January–February 2001, 78–82.

4. Paul Slade, "Money: Are You Ready to Rock 'n' Dole?" *Independent*, June 23, 1998.

5. Geoff Dyer, "Gissa Job! Writers on the Dole," *Guardian*, August 1, 2015.

6. For basic income in Utrecht, see Louis Doré, "Dutch City of Utrecht to Experiment with a Universal, Unconditional 'Basic Income,'" *Independent*, June 26, 2015. For Alberta, see Joseph Brean, "Old Anti-poverty Idea—Guaranteed Minimum Income—Getting New Life in Alberta," *National Post*, June 8, 2015.

7. Clifford Hugh Douglas, "Address at the Melbourne Town Hall, Australia," January 22, 1934.

8. Marshall McLuhan, Quentin Fiore, and Jerome Agel, *The Medium Is the Massage: An Inventory of Effects* (Corte Madera, Calif: Gingko, 2001), 9.

9. Adair Turner, "Printing Money to Fund Deficit Is the Fastest Way to Raise Rates," *Financial Times*, November 10, 2014.

10. In 1998, Hans Tietmeyer, then governor of the Deutsche Bundesbank, praised national governments for preferring "the permanent plebiscite of global markets" to the "plebiscite of the ballot box" (quoted in Slavoj Žižek, "How Capital Captured Politics," *Guardian*, July 13, 2014).

11. "The preferences of the average American appear to have only a miniscule, near-zero, statistically non-significant impact upon public policy" (Martin Gilens and Benjamin I. Page, "Testing Theories of American Politics: Elites, Interest Groups, and Average Citizens," *Perspectives on Politics* 12, no. 3 [2014]: 575).

12. Frank Knight, "Money," *Saturday Review of Literature*, April 16, 1927, 732.

13. Irving Fisher, *100% Money* (New York: Adelphi, 1936). For a more recent analysis, see Jaromir Benes and Michael Kumhof, "The Chicago Plan Revisited," Working Paper (International Monetary Fund, 2013).

14. Martin Wolf, "Strip Private Banks of Their Power to Create Money," *Financial Times*, April 24, 2014.

15. Frosti Sigurjónsson, "Monetary Reform—A Better Monetary System for Iceland" (Reykjavik, 2015).

16. Bernard Lietaer, Robert E. Ulanowicz, Sally J. Goerner, and Nadia McLaren, "Is Our Monetary Structure a Systemic Cause for Financial Instability? Evidence and Remedies from Nature," *Journal of Futures Studies*, April 2010, 1–21.

17. For a discussion from a biology perspective, see Marie E. Csete, and John C. Doyle, "Reverse Engineering of Biological Complexity," *Science* 295 (2002): 1664–1669.

18. Parag Khanna (global strategist, author), private conversation with Roman Chlupatý, April 2010.

19. Wojtek Kalinowski, "Currency Pluralism and Economic Stability: The Swiss Experience" (Veblen Institute for Economic Reforms, Paris), October 2011, www.veblen-institute.org/IMG/pdf/currency_pluralism_and_economic_stability_eng_oct_2011_.pdf.

20. James Stodder, "Complementary Credit Networks and Macroeconomic Stability: Switzerland's Wirtschaftsring," *Journal of Economic Behavior & Organization* 72, no. 1 (2009): 79–95.

21. Irving Fisher, Hans R. L. Cohrssen, and Herbert W. Fisher, *Stamp Scrip* (New York: Adelphi, 1933).

22. Bernard Lietaer, *The Future of Money: Creating New Wealth, Work and a Wiser World* (London: Century, 2001), 151–155.

23. Helena Smith, "Euros Discarded as Impoverished Greeks Resort to Bartering," *Guardian*, January 2, 2013.

24. Alternatives Credit Union, "Ithaca Hours," www.alternatives.org/ithacahours.html.

25. Jana Fortier, "Underthrowing the System: How Low Finance Undermines Corporate Culture," *Journal of Ecology and Healthy Living* 9, no. 5 (1996): 61–63.

26. Such "fiscal localism," according to the *San Francisco Chronicle*, is the answer to "big-box stores, online shopping, and globalization" (Carolyn Said, Communities Issue Currency, Promote Local Spending," *San Francisco Chronicle*, July 6, 2011, www.sfgate.com/bayarea/article/Communities-issue-currency-promote-local-spending-2355723.php).

27. Quoted in John Murray Brown, "Bristol Pound Counts in Local Economy," *Financial Times*, July 27, 2015. See also Judith Evans, "British City Goes Rogue with Own Currency," *AFP*, August 16, 2012.

28. Hélène Joachain and Frédéric Klopfert, "Emerging Trend of Complementary Currencies Systems as Policy Instruments for Environmental Purposes: Changes Ahead?" *International Journal of Community Currency Research* 16, no. D (2012): 156–168.

29. Blake Ellis, "Funny Money? 11 Local Currencies," CNN, January 27, 2012, http://money.cnn.com/galleries/2012/pf/1201/gallery.community-currencies/index.html.

30. Rui Izumi, "The Wat System, an Exchange Based on Mutual Appreciation" (Gesell Research Society, Japan, 2001), www.watsystems.net/watsystems-translation /english.html.

31. Gerald Wheatley, "Complementary Currency and Quality of Life: Social and Economic Capital Effects on Subjective Well-Being" (Ph.D. diss., University of Calgary, 2006).

32. Tyler Durden, "The Most Rapidly Depreciating Currency in the World," Zero Hedge, November 27, 2013, www.zerohedge.com/news/2013–11–27/most-rapidly -depreciating-currency-world.

33. Jay Sorensen and Eric Lucas. "Loyalty by the Billions" (Loyalty Marketing Report Series for 2011, IdeaWorks, Shorewood, Wis., 2011).

34. Wheatley, "Complementary Currency and Quality of Life"; Canadian Tire, "Canadian Tire 'Money,'" 2007, www2.canadiantire.ca/CTenglish/ctmoney.html.

35. Unnamed source, private conversation with Roman Chlupatý, November 2014.

36. Marcus Wohlsen, "The Next Big Thing You Missed: How Starbucks Could Replace Your Bank," Wired, March 4, 2014.

37. Wayne Busch and Juan Pedro Moreno, "Banks' New Competitors: Starbucks, Google, and Alibaba," Harvard Business Review, February 20, 2014.

38. Jack C. Liu, "Bitcoin Backed Corporate Currencies Are Coming," November 9, 2014, http://jackcliu.com/post/102166140017/bitcoin-backed-corporate-currencies-are-coming.

39. Nathan Lewis, "Bitcoin Ignites Ron Paul's Parallel Currency Revolution," Forbes, January 1, 2014.

40. Bernard Lietaer, "Why This Crisis? And What to Do About It?" TED×Berlin, November 30, 2009, YouTube, www.youtube.com/watch?v=nORI8r3JIyw.

41. Steve Keen has suggested a "modern Jubilee," with money earmarked for paying off existing debts, though this would be a one-off payment rather than a basic income, in "The Debtwatch Manifesto," January 1, 2012, http://keenomics.s3.amazonaws. com/debtdeflation_media/2012/01/TheDebtwatchManifesto.pdf.

9. Changing the Dominant Monetary Regime, Bit by Bitcoin

1. Satosh Nakamoto, "Bitcoin: A Peer-to-Peer Electronic Cash System," November 1, 2008, https://bitcoin.org/bitcoin.pdf.

2. Paul Vigna and Michael J. Casey, The Age of Cryptocurrency: How Bitcoin and Digital Money Are Challenging the Global Economic Order (New York: St. Martin's Press, 2015), 44–49.

3. United States District Court, Southern District of New York, Sealed Complaint in the Case of USA v. Ross Ulbricht, 2013, www.cs.columbia.edu/~smb/UlbrichtCrimi-nalComplaint.pdf.

4. "Blockchain Size," https://blockchain.info/charts/blocks-size.

5. Total consumption so far has been more than 150,000 mWh; for compari-son, an average American uses about 10 mWh per year. See Jason Clenfield and

Pavel Alpeyev, "The Other Bitcoin Power Struggle," Bloomberg Business, April 24, 2014, www.bloomberg.com/bw/articles/2014-04-24/bitcoin-miners-seek-cheap-electricity -to-eke-out-a-profit..

6. Kerem Kaskaloglu, "Near Zero Bitcoin Transaction Fees Cannot Last Forever," in *The International Conference on Digital Security and Forensics (DigitalSec2014)* (Ostrava, Czech Republic, 2014), 91–99.

7. Michael Hiltzik, "Bye-Bye, Bitcoin? The Crypto-Currency's Price Agonies Intensify," *Los Angeles Times*, October 6, 2014.

8. Girish Gupta, "Venezuelans Turn to Bitcoins to Bypass Socialist Currency Controls," Reuters, October 8, 2014, www.reuters.com/article/2014/10/08/us-venezuela -bitcoin-idUSKCN0HX11O20141008.

9. Vigna and Casey, *Age of Cryptocurrency*, 190.

10. Joon Ian Wong, "Goldman Sachs Report Says Bitcoin Could Shape 'Future of Finance,'" CoinDesk, March 11, 2015, http://www.coindesk.com/goldman-sachs -report-says-bitcoin-could-shape-future-of-finance.

11. Timothy C. May, "The Crypto Anarchist Manifesto," November 22, 1992, www. activism.net/cypherpunk/crypto-anarchy.html.

12. Quoted in Vigna and Casey, *Age of Cryptocurrency*, 63.

13. Ben Steverman, "Why Bitcoins and Apple Pay Can't Kill Off Cash," Bloomberg Business, September 12, 2014, www.bloomberg.com/news/articles/2014-09-12 /why-bitcoins-and-apple-pay-can-t-kill-off-walter-white-s-stash.

14. David Birch, "The Future of Money," YouTube, January 19, 2012, www.youtube .com/watch?v=RTWpbAyqXfs.

15. "UK Banknotes 'Tainted with Cocaine,'" BBC, October 4, 1999. http://news .bbc.co.uk/2/hi/uk_news/464200.stm.

16. Tracy McVeigh, "Buses, Canteens, Parking—Is Cash on the Way Out?" *Observer*, March 8, 2015.

17. "Top 5 Cashless Countries," TotalPayments, 2013, www.totalpayments.org/2013 /07/08/top-5-cashless-countries.

18. Kenneth Rogoff, "Costs and Benefits to Phasing Out Paper Currency," in *NBER Macroeconomics Annual 2014*, ed. Jonathan Parker and Michael Woodford (Chicago: University of Chicago Press, 2015), 29:445–456.

19. Andy Greenberg, "Online Drug Dealers Are Now Accepting Darkcoin, Bitcoin's Stealthier Cousin," *Wired*, November 4, 2014, www.wired.com/2014/11 /darkcoin-and-online-drug-dealers.

20. Investment manager Josh Stein, quoted in Vigna and Casey, *Age of Cryptocurrency*, 183.

21. Alex Hern, "Missing: Hard Drive Containing Bitcoins Worth £4m in Newport Landfill Site," *Guardian*, November 27, 2013.

22. This is a problem with conventional currencies as well. See Izabella Kaminska, "Democratising Finance: Vision for Bitcoin Is Beginning to Fade," *Financial Times*, February 3, 2015.

23. Kourosh Davarpanah, Dan Kaufman, and Ophelie Pubellier, "NeuCoin: The First Secure, Cost-Efficient and Decentralized Cryptocurrency," version 1.0, March 25, 2015, www.neucoin.org/en/whitepaper/download.

24. "Ethereum Frontier Release," www.ethereum.org.

25. D. A. Wallach, "Bitcoin for Rockstars," Backchannel, December 10, 2014, https://medium.com/backchannel/bitcoin-for-rockstars-ca8366802f9.

26. Hernando de Soto, "The Destruction of Economic Facts," Bloomberg Business, April 28, 2011, http://www.bloomberg.com/news/articles/2011-04-28/the-destruction-of-economic-facts.

27. Gertrude Chavez-Dreyfuss, "Honduras to Build Land Title Registry Using Bitcoin Technology," Reuters, May 15, 2015, http://in.reuters.com/article/2015/05/15/usa-honduras-technology-idINKBN0O01V720150515.

28. Stan Higgins, "IBM Reveals Proof of Concept for Blockchain-powered Internet of Things," CoinDesk, January 17, 2015, www.coindesk.com/ibm-reveals-proof-concept-blockchain-powered-internet-things.

29. Leo Kelion, "Could Driverless Cars Own Themselves?" BBC News, February 16, 2015, www.bbc.com/news/technology-30998361.

30. Michael J. Casey and Paul Vigna, "Crypto Innovators Find Fertile Ground in Soft-Touch Switzerland," Wall Street Journal, August 4, 2014.

31. Olga Kharif, "Bitcoin 2.0 Shows Technology Evolving Beyond Use as Money," Bloomberg Business, March 28, 2014, www.bloomberg.com/news/2014-03-28/bitcoin-2-0-shows-technology-evolving-beyond-use-as-money.html.

32. Wong, "Goldman Sachs Report Says Bitcoin Could Shape 'Future of Finance' "; Rob Cox, "Bitcoin Comes out of the Shadows and into Wall Street's Sights," New York Times, May 1, 2015.

33. Marek Palatinus, private conversation with Roman Chlupatý, January 2016.

34. Brian Kelly, "Is Apple Pay a Bitcoin Killer?" CNBC, September 10, 2014, www.cnbc.com/id/101988826.

35. Jaroslav Brychta, private conversation with Roman Chlupatý, December 2013.

36. Mexico, for example, has looked into the idea of using a blockchain-based currency. See Tanaya Macheel, "The Case for Merging Mexico's Peso with Block Chain Technology," CoinDesk, July 26, 2014, www.coindesk.com/case-merging-mexicos-peso-block-chain-technology.

37. At the time of this writing, IBM is considering a blockchain-based cash and payment system for conventional currencies. See Gertrude Chavez-Dreyfuss, "IBM Looking at Adopting Bitcoin Technology for Major Currencies," Reuters, March 12, 2015, www.reuters.com/article/2015/03/12/us-bitcoin-ibm-idUSKBN0M82KB20150312.

38. May, "Crypto Anarchist Manifesto."

39. Brett Scott, "Riches Beyond Belief," Aeon, August 28, 2013, https://aeon.co/essays/so-you-want-to-invent-your-own-currency.

40. Georg Friedrich Knapp, The State Theory of Money, 4th ed. (London: Macmillan, 1924), 303.

41. Quoted in Jeff Kearns, "Greenspan Says Bitcoin a Bubble Without Intrinsic Currency Value," Bloomberg Business, December 4, 2013, http://www.bloomberg.com/news/articles/2013-12-04/greenspan-says-bitcoin-a-bubble-without-intrinsic-currency-value.

42. Omar Bessa, "Nobel Prize Winner Eugene Fama on Bitcoin," CoinTelegraph, November 8, 2015, http://cointelegraph.com/news/115593/nobel-prize-winner-eugene-fama-on-bitcoin.

43. This section is based on David Orrell, "A Quantum Theory of Money and Value," *Social Science Research Network*, June 28, 2015, http://ssrn.com/abstract=2624371.

44. Tom Simonite, "Ripple Labs," *MIT Technology Review*, February 18, 2014.

45. Paul Krugman wrote that "Adam Smith hates Bitcoin" on the basis that Smith pointed out the wastefulness of using gold as a currency, but that is not the same thing as hating it ("Adam Smith Hates Bitcoin," *The Conscience of a Liberal* [blog], *New York Times*, April 12, 2013, http://krugman.blogs.nytimes.com/2013/04/12/adam-smith-hates-bitcoin).

46. Nathan Schneider, "A New 'Lego of Cryptofinance' Enables Users to Design Social Contracts," *Al Jazeera*, April 7, 2014.

10. Utopia

1. Francis Ysidro Edgeworth, *Mathematical Psychics: An Essay on the Application of Mathematics to the Moral Sciences* (London: Paul, 1881), 12.

2. Thomas More, *Utopia*, www.gutenberg.org/files/2130/2130-h/2130-h.htm.

3. The success of mobile phones has been used to justify everything from mainstream economics ("The Invisible Hand Gives You the iPhone") to multiverse theory. See Peter Foster, "Biting the Invisible Hand," *National Post*, September 14, 2012; and Matthew Kleban, "Re: 'An Imperfect Truth,' by David Orrell," Related Letters, *Literary Review of Canada*, April 2015, http://reviewcanada.ca/magazine/2015/04/letters.

4. K. E. Boulding, "The Economics of the Coming Spaceship Earth," in *Environmental Quality in a Growing Economy*, ed. Henry Jarrett (Baltimore: Johns Hopkins University Press, 1966), 3–14; Eugene P. Odum, "The Strategy of Ecosystem Development," *Science* 164 (1969): 262–270.

5. Odum, "Strategy of Ecosystem Development", 269.

6. Ibid., 266–267.

7. Steven Poole, "Could Climate Change Action Rejuvenate Worldwide Democracy?" *New Statesman*, September 18, 2014.

8. Naomi Klein, *This Changes Everything: Capitalism vs. the Climate* (New York: Simon & Schuster, 2014), 33.

9. Environmental economics is based on an underlying faith in the ability of "Adam Smith's invisible hand to achieve what is best for society as a collective," as one textbook on environmental economics puts it, so long as market principles can be adequately applied. See Nick Hanley, Jason E. Shogren, and Ben White, *Environmental Economics in Theory and Practice* (New York: Oxford University Press, 1997), 358.

10. As one forester puts it:

> Perhaps the hard truth is that there may be areas of human activity that are so important for reasons other than financial gains, that the narrow criterion of individual economic gain cannot be the basis of decisions. In other words, the decision rules of neo-classical utility theory may be operative mainly in a narrow range of choices at the margin, between a few units of resources or commodities this way or that, but this cannot be extrapolated in a grand way to the

society-wide policy choices in a manner that may spell doom in the long run. (Dilip Kumar, "Applying Economics to Sustained Yield Forestry: Why Foresters Don't Listen to Social Scientists," *Forest Matters* [blog], February 26, 2015, http://forestmatters.blogspot.ca/2015/02/13-applying-economic-analysis-to.html)

11. Interview with Herman Kahn, *New York Times*, October 19, 1967.

12. Ian D. Wyatt and Daniel E. Hecker, "Occupational Changes During the 20th Century," *Monthly Labor Review*, March 2006: 35–57.

13. David Graeber, "On the Phenomenon of Bullshit Jobs," *Strike!*, August 17, 2013, http://strikemag.org/bullshit-jobs.

14. John Maynard Keynes, "Economic Possibilities for Our Grandchildren," in *Essays in Persuasion* (New York: Norton, 1963), 369.

15. Thomas Piketty, *Capital in the Twenty-First Century*, trans. Arthur Goldhammer (Cambridge, Mass.: Belknap Press of Harvard Unversity Press, 2014), 515.

16. Kiatpongsan Sorapop and Michael I. Norton, "How Much (More) Should CEOs Make? A Universal Desire for More Equal Pay," *Perspectives on Psychological Science* 9, no. 6 (2014): 587–593.

17. See, for instance, OECD, "Crisis Squeezes Income and Puts Pressure on Inequality and Poverty," 2013, www.oecd.org/els/soc/OECD2013-Inequality-and-Poverty-8p.pdf.

18. Robert Frank, "Why the Rich Recovered and the Rest Didn't," CNBC, June 13, 2012. www.cnbc.com/id/47802283.

19. Patrick Butler, "Decline in Professional Jobs Fuels Increase in Downward Mobility," *Guardian*, November 6, 2014.

20. Andrew Ross Sorkin and Megan Thee-Brenan, "Many Feel the American Dream Is out of Reach, Poll Shows," *New York Times*, December 10, 2014, http://dealbook.nytimes.com/2014/12/10/many-feel-the-american-dream-is-out-of-reach-poll-shows.

21. Douglas Clement, "Interview with Eugene Fama," *Region*, December 2007.

22. Richard Wilkinson and Kate Pickett, *The Spirit Level: Why Greater Equality Makes Societies Stronger* (London: Bloomsbury, 2009).

23. Quoted in ibid., 221.

24. Aditya Chakrabortty, "University Economics Teaching Isn't an Education: It's a £9,000 Lobotomy," *Guardian*, May 9, 2014.

25. Michael J. Sandel, "The Moral Limits of Markets," *Project Syndicate*, December 31, 2012.

26. "We have no longer any real appreciation for the embodied energy, destruction, and suffering that goes into every stage of the supply chain," notes Mark Boyle, "The Moneyless Man," TED*ˣ*O'Porto, July 11, 2011, YouTube, www.youtube.com/watch?v=-PuyYVVVkIM. Because money always points toward number (a left-brain specialty), it deprives us of any sense of context (which is typically handled by the right brain).

27. The OECD noted that "there can be too much finance. When the financial sector is well developed, as has been the case in OECD economies for some time, further increases in its size usually slow longterm growth" (Boris Cournède, Oliver Denk, and

Peter Hoeller, "Finance and Inclusive Growth," OECD Economic Policy Paper [Paris: OECD, 2015], 7).

28. Yanis Varoufakis, "Bitcoin: A Flawed Currency Blueprint with a Potentially Useful Application for the Eurozone," February 15, 2014, http://yanisvaroufakis.eu/2014/02/15/bitcoin-a-flawed-currency-blueprint-with-a-potentially-useful-application-for-the-eurozone; Lulu Yilun Chen and Justina Lee, "China Mulls Answer to Bitcoin with Digital Currency Study," Bloomberg Business, January 21, 2016, http://www.bloomberg.com/news/articles/2016-01-21/chinese-central-bank-studies-prospect-of-own-digital-currency.

29. Dan Ariely, *Predictably Irrational: The Hidden Forces That Shape Our Decisions* (London: HarperCollins, 2009), 68, 76.

30. Tomáš Sedláček, David Graeber, and Roman Chlupatý, *(R)evoluční Ekonomie O Systéma a Lidech* (Prague: 65.pole, 2013).

31. Kathleen D. Vohs, Nicole L. Mead, and Miranda R. Goode, "The Psychological Consequences of Money," *Science* 314, no. 5802 (2006): 1154–1156.

32. Robert H. Frank, Thomas Gilovich, and Dennis T. Regan, "Does Studying Economics Inhibit Cooperation?" *Journal of Economic Perspectives* 7, no. 2 (1993): 159–171.

33. Owen Hatherley, "Be a User, Not a Consumer: How Capitalism Has Changed Our Language," *Guardian*, August 11, 2013.

34. David J. Cheal, *The Gift Economy* (New York: Routledge, 1988). See also Charles Eisenstein, *Sacred Economics: Money, Gift, and Society in the Age of Transition* (Berkeley, Calif.: Evolver Editions, 2011).

35. Ruth Suehle, "An Anthropologist's View of an Open Source Community," January 31, 2011, http://opensource.com/life/11/1/anthropologists-view-open-source-community.

36. Carlo Daffara, "The Economic Value of Open Source Software." July 23, 2012, http://carlodaffara.conecta.it/the-economic-value-of-open-source-software/.

37. David Bollier, *Think Like a Commoner: A Short Introduction to the Life of the Commons* (Gabriola Island, B.C.: New Society, 2014), 126.

38. Cédric Feschotte, "Virology: Bornavirus Enters the Genome," *Nature* 463, no. 7277 (2010): 39.

39. Bethany Horne, quoted in Jonathan Dawson, "A Wave of Disruption Is Sweeping in to Challenge Neoliberalism," *Guardian*, March 12, 2015.

40. Everett Rosenfeld, "Ecuador Becomes the First Country to Roll Out Its Own Digital Cash," CNBC, February 9, 2015, www.cnbc.com/id/102397137.

41. F. Bardhi and G. M. Eckhardt, "Access-based Consumption: The Case of Car Sharing," *Journal of Consumer Research* 39, no. 4 (2012): 881–898.

42. Sheetal Lodhia and Paul Kennedy, "Why Money Isn't Everything," CBC, May 12, 2015, www.cbc.ca/radio/ideas/why-money-isn-t-everything-1.3069430.

43. Anatoly Kurmanaev, "Venezuela Squanders Its Oil Wealth," Bloomberg Business, February 18, 2015, www.bloomberg.com/news/articles/2015-02-18/venezuela-goes-from-bling-to-blat-as-oil-wealth-squandered.

44. Robert Reich, "The Share-the-Scraps Economy," February 2, 2015, http://robertreich.org/post/109894095095.

45. William Stanley Jevons, for example, wrote in a letter to his sisters that he wanted to be "powerfully good, that is to be good, not towards one, or a dozen, or a hundred, but towards a nation or the world" (*Letters and Journal of W. Stanley Jevons*, ed. Harriet A. Jevons [London: Macmillan, 1886], 96).

46. M. N. Browne and J. K. Quinn, "The Lamentable Absence of Power in Mainstream Economics," in *Future Directions for Heterodox Economics*, ed. John T. Harvey and Robert F. Garnett (Ann Arbor: University of Michigan Press, 2008) 240–261.

47. Tomáš Sedláček, *Economics of Good and Evil: The Quest for Economic Meaning from Gilgamesh to Wall Street* (New York: Oxford University Press, 2011), 10.

48. Jonathan Band and Jonathan Gerafi, "Wikipedia's Economic Value," infojustice. org, 2013, http://infojustice.org/wp-content/uploads/2013/10/band-gerafi10032013.pdf.

49. Tomáš Sedláček, Gloria Benedikt, Merlijn Twaalfhoven, and Roman Chlupatý, "Bridging the Divide: Arts, Economics and the Irrational—A Debate in 3 Acts" (presentation at the Museum of Modern Art, Vienna, November 29, 2014).

BIBLIOGRAPHY

Abraham, Ralph. *Chaos, Gaia, Eros: A Chaos Pioneer Uncovers the Three Great Streams of History*. New York: HarperCollins, 1994.

Adams, Tim. "Anxious, Atomised . . . and Not in It Together: The State of Britain in 2015." *Observer*, April 19, 2015.

Ahir, Hites, and Prakash Loungani. "Can Economists Forecast Recessions? Some Evidence from the Great Recession." *Oracle*, March 2014. forecasters.org/wp/wp-content/uploads/PLoungani_OracleMar2014.pdf.

Alternatives Credit Union. Ithaca Hours. www.alternatives.org/ithacahours.html.

Anderson, Benedict. *Imagined Communities: Reflections on the Origin and Spread of Nationalism*. London: Verso, 1991.

Angas, Lawrence. *Slump Ahead in Bonds*. New York: Somerset, 1937.

——. *New York Times*, October 19, 1967.

Aquinas, Thomas. *Summa Theologica*. Translated by Fathers of the English Dominican Province. London: Washburne, 1918.

Ariely, Dan. *Predictably Irrational: The Hidden Forces That Shape Our Decisions*. London: HarperCollins, 2009.

Aristotle. *Generation of Animals*. Translated by A. L. Peck. Cambridge, Mass.: Harvard University Press, 1943.

Aristotle. *The Metaphysics*. Translated by John H. McMahon. Mineola, N.Y.: Dover, 2007.

Aristotle. *Nicomachean Ethics, Book V*. Translated by W. D. Ross. Kitchener, Ont.: Batoche Books, 1999.

Aristotle. *Politics*. Translated by Benjamin Jowett. Mineola, N.Y.: Dover, 2000.

Arrow, Kenneth J., and Gérard Debreu. "Existence of a Competitive Equilibrium for a Competitive Economy." *Econometrica* 22 (1954): 65–90.

Aubet, Maria Eugenia. *Commerce and Colonization in the Ancient Near East*. Cambridge: Cambridge University Press, 2013.

Band, Jonathan, and Jonathan Gerafi. "Wikipedia's Economic Value." infojustice.org. 2013. http://infojustice.org/wp-content/uploads/2013/10/band-gerafi10032013.pdf.

Baram, Marcus. "Government Sachs: Goldman's Close Ties to Washington Arouse Envy, Raise Questions." *Huffington Post*, July 3, 2009. www.huffingtonpost.com/2009/06/02/government-sachs-goldmans_n_210561.html.

Bardhi, F., and G. M. Eckhardt. "Access-based Consumption: The Case of Car Sharing." *Journal of Consumer Research* 39, no. 4 (2012): 881–898.

Becker, Gary S. *The Economic Approach to Human Behavior*. Chicago: University of Chicago Press, 1976.

Beinhocker, Eric D. *Origin of Wealth: Evolution, Complexity, and the Radical Remaking of Economics*. Boston: Harvard Business School Press, 2006.

Benes, Jaromir, and Michael Kumhof. "The Chicago Plan Revisited." Working Paper. International Monetary Fund, 2013.

Bernanke, Ben, interview by Scott Pelley. "Ben Bernanke's Greatest Challenge." *60 Minutes*. CBS. March 12, 2009.

——. "The Macroeconomics of the Great Depression: A Comparative Approach." *Journal of Money, Credit, and Banking* 27, no. 1 (1995): 1–28.

Bernstein, Peter L. *The Power of Gold: The History of an Obsession*. New York: Wiley, 2000.

Bessa, Omar. "Nobel Prize Winner Eugene Fama on Bitcoin." CoinTelegraph, November 8, 2015, http://cointelegraph.com/news/115593/nobel-prize-winner-eugene-fama-on-bitcoin.

Birch, David. "The Future of Money." YouTube. January 19, 2012. www.youtube.com/watch?v=RTWpbAyqXfs.

Bloch, Marc. *Feudal Society*. Translated by L. A. Manyon. Chicago: University of Chicago Press, 1965.

Bockman, Johanna. *Markets in the Name of Socialism: The Left-Wing Origins of Neoliberalism*. Stanford, Calif.: Stanford University Press, 2011.

Bollier, David. *Think Like a Commoner: A Short Introduction to the Life of the Commons*. Gabriola Island, B.C.: New Society, 2014.

Boston Consulting Group. "Takeoff in Robotics Will Power the Next Productivity Surge in Manufacturing." Press release, February 10, 2015.

Boulding, K. E. "The Economics of the Coming Spaceship Earth." In *Environmental Quality in a Growing Economy*, edited by Henry Jarrett, 3–14. Baltimore: Johns Hopkins University Press, 1966.

Boyle, Mark. "The Moneyless Man." TED×O'Porto, July 11, 2011. YouTube. www.youtube.com/watch?v=-PuyYVVVkIM.

Brahmagupta. *Brahmasphutasiddhanta* (The Opening of the Universe), 628. https://archive.org/details/Brahmasphutasiddhanta_Vol_1.

Brand, Stewart. *The Media Lab: Inventing the Future at MIT.* New York: Viking, 1987.

Brean, Joseph. "Old Anti-Poverty Idea—Guaranteed Minimum Income—Getting New Life in Alberta." *National Post,* June 8, 2015.

Bremmer, Ian, and Cliff Kupchan. "Top Risks 2015: Weaponization of Finance." Eurasia Group. January 5, 2015. www.eurasiagroup.net/pages/top-risks-2015#4.

Brickman, P., D. Coates, and R. Janoff-Bulman. "Lottery Winners and Accident Victims: Is Happiness Relative?" *Journal of Personality and Social Psychology* 36, no. 8 (1978): 917–927.

Brown, Dale M. *Aztecs: Reign of Blood and Splendor.* Alexandria, Va.: Time-Life, 1992.

Brown, John Murray. "Bristol Pound Counts in Local Economy." *Financial Times,* July 27, 2015.

Browne, M. Neil, and J. Kevin Quinn. "The Lamentable Absence of Power in Mainstream Economics." In *Future Directions for Heterodox Economics,* edited by John T. Harvey and Robert F. Garnett, 240–261. Ann Arbor: University of Michigan Press, 2008.

Bryan, William Jennings. "Cross of Gold" Speech. In *Official Proceedings of the Democratic National Convention Held in Chicago, Illinois, July 7, 8, 9, 10, and 11, 1896* (Logansport, Ind., 1896), 226–234. In *The Annals of America.* Vol. 12, *1895–1904: Populism, Imperialism, and Reform,* 100–105. Chicago: Encyclopaedia Britannica, 1968.

Buchan, James. *Frozen Desire: The Meaning of Money.* New York: Farrar, Straus and Giroux, 1997.

Buchanan, Mark. "Quantum Minds: Why We Think Like Quarks." *New Scientist,* September 5, 2011.

Buchholz, Todd G. *New Ideas from Dead Economists: An Introduction to Modern Economic Thought.* London: Penguin, 2008.

Busch, Wayne, and Juan Pedro Moreno. "Banks' New Competitors: Starbucks, Google, and Alibaba." *Harvard Business Review,* February 20, 2014.

Bushong, B., L. M. King, C. F. Camerer, and A. Rangel. "Pavlovian Processes in Consumer Choice: The Physical Presence of a Good Increases Willingness-to-Pay." *American Economic Review* 100 (2010): 1–18.

Butler, Benjamin. Speech in the House of Representatives, *Congressional Globe,* 40th Cong., 3rd sess., January 12, 1869, 303.

Butler, Patrick. "Decline in Professional Jobs Fuels Increase in Downward Mobility." *Guardian,* November 6, 2014.

Callatay, François de. "White Gold: An Enigmatic Start to Greek Coinage." *American Numismatic Society Magazine* 12, no. 2 (2013): 6–17.

Campbell, Joseph, and Bill Moyers. *The Power of Myth.* New York: Doubleday, 1988.

Canadian Tire. "Canadian Tire 'Money.'" 2007. www2.canadiantire.ca/CTenglish /ctmoney.html.

Cantillon, Richard. *Essay on the Nature of Trade in General.* Translated by Henry Higgs. London: Cass, 1959.

Carroll, Dean. "Latvia's Membership Shows Euro Is 'Major Achievement'—Claims EU." PubAffairs: Public Affairs Networking. December 2013. www.policyreview.eu /latvias-membership-shows-euro-is-major-achievement-claims-eu.

Casey, Michael J., and Paul Vigna. "Crypto Innovators Find Fertile Ground in Soft-Touch Switzerland." *Wall Street Journal*, August 4, 2014.

Cassidy, John. "Interview with Eugene Fama." *New Yorker*, January 13, 2010.

——. "Letter from Chicago: After the Blowup." *New Yorker*, January 11, 2010.

Castronova, Edward. *Wildcat Currency: How the Virtual Money Revolution Is Transforming the Economy*. New Haven, Conn.: Yale University Press, 2014.

Cavanaugh, Jeffrey. "FOREX Africa: The CFA Franc aka the African Euro." AKF Insider. February 12, 2014. http://afkinsider.com/41946/forex-africa-african-euro.

Cecchetti, Stephen, M. S. Mohanty, and Fabrizio Zampolli. "The Real Effects of Debt." Working Paper, no. 352. Bank for International Settlements, Basel, 2011.

Chakrabortty, Aditya. "University Economics Teaching Isn't an Education: It's a £9,000 Lobotomy." *Guardian*, May 9, 2014.

Chang, Ha-Joon, and Jonathan Aldred. "After the Crash, We Need a Revolution in the Way We Teach Economics." *Observer*, May 11, 2014.

Chavez-Dreyfuss, Gertrude. "Honduras to Build Land Title Registry Using Bitcoin Technology." Reuters, May 15, 2015. http://in.reuters.com/article/2015/05/15/usa -honduras-technology-idINKBN0O01V720150515.

——. "IBM Looking at Adopting Bitcoin Technology for Major Currencies." Reuters, March 12, 2015. www.reuters.com/article/2015/03/12/us-bitcoin-ibm -idUSKBN0M82KB20150312.

Cheal, David J. *The Gift Economy*. New York: Routledge, 1988.

Chen, Lulu Yilun, and Justina Lee. "China Mulls Answer to Bitcoin with Digital Currency Study." Bloomberg Business, January 21, 2016. http://www.bloomberg.com/news /articles/2016-01-21/chinese-central-bank-studies-prospect-of-own-digital-currency.

Chlupatý, Roman. "John Hardy: Konec QE? Konec virtuální reality" [John Hardy: The end of the QE? The end of virtual reality!]. *Investiční magazín*, December 2013.

——. "(Ne)konečná krize: 4 expertní názory na současné i budoucí turbulence" [(Never)ending crisis: 4 expert takes on current and future turbulences]. InvestičníWeb.cz. http://www.investiciniweb.cz/2014/6/11/nekonecna-krize-4-expertni -nazory-na-soucasne-i-budouci-turbulence.

Cicero, Marcus Tullius. *On Duties*. Translated by Walter Miller. Cambridge, Mass.: Harvard University Press, 1913.

Clanchy, M. T. *From Memory to Written Record: England, 1066–1307*. Cambridge, Mass.: Harvard University Press, 1979.

Clement, Douglas. "Interview with Eugene Fama." *Region*, December 2007.

Clenfield, Jason, and Pavel Alpeyev. "The Other Bitcoin Power Struggle." Bloomberg Business, April 24, 2014. www.bloomberg.com/bw/articles/2014–04–24/bitcoin -miners-seek-cheap-electricity-to-eke-out-a-profit.

Cocker, Mark. *Rivers of Blood, Rivers of Gold: Europe's Conquest of Indigenous Peoples*. New York: Grove, 1998.

Cohan, Peter. "Big Risk: $1.2 Quadrillion Derivatives Market Dwarfs World GDP." DailyFinance, June 9, 2010.

Conway, Ed. "Basle's Secretive Bankers Have All the Power." *Times* (London), January 20, 2015.

Cook, Tom. "What Is a Good Approximation of How Much Money Skyler Had in the Storage Unit When She Showed Walt How She Stopped Counting It?" *Slate*, September 6, 2012. www.slate.com/blogs/quora/2012/09/06/what_is_a_good_approximation _of_how_much_money_skyler_had_in_the_storage_unit_when_she_showed _walt_how_she_stopped_counting_it_.html.

Cooper, George. Interview. *World Finance: The Voice of the Market*, April 4, 2014. www .worldfinance.com/banking/economics-is-a-broken-science-dr-george-cooper -on-his-new-book-money-blood-and-revolution-video.

Cournède, Boris, Oliver Denk, and Peter Hoeller. *Finance and Inclusive Growth*. OECD Economic Policy Paper. Paris: OECD, 2015.

Cox, Rob. "Bitcoin Comes out of the Shadows and into Wall Street's Sights." *New York Times*, May 1, 2015.

Crawford, Michael H. "Money and Exchange in the Roman World." *Journal of Roman Studies* 60 (1970): 40–48.

Crowther, Geoffrey. *An Outline of Money*. London: Nelson, 1941.

Csete, Marie E., and John C. Doyle. "Reverse Engineering of Biological Complexity." *Science* 295 (2002): 1664–69.

Daffara, Carlo. "The Economic Value of Open Source Software." July 23, 2012. http: //carlodaffara.conecta.it/the-economic-value-of-open-source-software.

Daggett, Stephen. "Costs of Major U.S. Wars." Congressional Research Service, Washington, D.C., 2010.

Das, Satyajit. "Trapped Central Banks and the Semiotics of Monetary Policy." *Independent*, July 12, 2013.

Davarpanah, Kourosh, Dan Kaufman, and Ophelie Pubellier. "NeuCoin: The First Secure, Cost-Efficient and Decentralized Cryptocurrency." Version 1.0. March 25, 2015. www.neucoin.org/en/whitepaper/download.

Davies, Glyn. *A History of Money: From Ancient Times to the Present Day*. 3d ed. Cardiff: University of Wales Press, 2002.

Dawson, James. "When It Comes to Coins, Isis Is Clearly Not as Good as Gold." *New Statesman*, November 19, 2014.

Dawson, Jonathan. "A Wave of Disruption Is Sweeping in to Challenge Neoliberalism." *Guardian*, March 12, 2015.

De Soto, Hernando. "The Destruction of Economic Facts." Bloomberg Business, April 28, 2011. http://www.bloomberg.com/news/articles/2011-04-28/the-destruction-of -economic-facts.

"Debt to GDP Ratio Historical Chart." Macrotrends. www.macrotrends.net/1381 /debt-to-gdp-ratio-historical-chart.

Dellas, Harris, and George S. Tavlas. "The Gold Standard, the Euro, and the Origins of the Greek Sovereign Debt Crisis." *Cato Journal* 33, no. 3 (2013): 491–520.

DeVoe, Sanford E., Jeffrey Pfeffer, and Byron Y. Lee. "When Does Money Make Money More Important? Survey and Experimental Evidence." *ILRREVIEW* 66, no. 5 (2013): 1076-1094.

Dew, Jeffrey, Sonya Britt, and Sandra Huston. "Examining the Relationship Between Financial Issues and Divorce." *Family Relations* 61, no. 4 (2012): 615–628.

The Dialogue Concerning the Exchequer, circa 1180, The Avalon Project, Yale Law School, http://avalon.law.yale.edu/medieval/excheq.asp.

Dilip Kumar, P. J. "Applying Economics to Sustained Yield Forestry: Why Foresters Don't Listen to Social Scientists." *Forest Matters* (blog), February 26, 2015. http://forestmatters.blogspot.ca/2015/02/13-applying-economic-analysis-to.html.

Dobbs, Richard, Susan Lund, Jonathan Woetzel, and Mina Mutafchieva, "Debt and (Not Much) Deleveraging." McKinsey Global Institute. 2015. www.mckinsey.com/insights/economic_studies/debt_and_not_much_deleveraging.

Dokoupil, Martin. "Gulf Arabs Shouldn't Delay Single Currency—Qatar Central Bank Official." Reuters, July 26, 2012.

Dolan, Ed. "Whatever Became of the Money Multiplier?" *EconBlog*, September 23, 2013. www.economonitor.com/dolanecon/2013/09/23/whatever-became-of-the-money-multiplier.

Doré, Louis. "Dutch City of Utrecht to Experiment with a Universal, Unconditional 'Basic Income.'" *Independent*, June 26, 2015.

Dostaler, Gilles, and Bernard Maris. "Dr. Freud and Mr. Keynes on Money and Capitalism." In *What Is Money?*, edited by John Smithin, 235–256. New York: Routledge, 2000.

Douglas, Clifford Hugh. "Address at the Melbourne Town Hall, Australia." January 22, 1934.

Dunn, E. W., L. B. Aknin, and M. I. Norton. "Spending Money on Others Promotes Happiness." *Science* 319, no. 5870 (2008): 1687–1688.

Durden, Tyler. "The Most Rapidly Depreciating Currency in the World." Zero Hedge. November 27, 2013. www.zerohedge.com/news/2013-11-27/most-rapidly-depreciating-currency-world.

Dyer, Geoff. "Gissa Job! Writers on the Dole: Geoff Dyer." *Guardian*, August 1, 2015.

Eagleton, Catherine, and Jonathan Williams. *Money: A History*. Richmond Hill, Ont.: Firefly, 2007.

Edgeworth, Francis Ysidro. *Mathematical Psychics: An Essay on the Application of Mathematics to the Moral Sciences*. London: Paul, 1881.

Eisenstein, Charles. *Sacred Economics: Money, Gift, and Society in the Age of Transition*. Berkeley, Calif.: Evolver, 2011.

Ellis, Blake. "Funny Money? 11 Local Currencies." CNN. January 27, 2012. http://money.cnn.com/galleries/2012/pf/1201/gallery.community-currencies/index.html.

Essential Information, Consumer Education Foundation. "Sold Out: How Wall Street and Washington Betrayed America." March 2009. www.wallstreetwatch.org/reports/sold_out.pdf.

Evans, Judith. "British City Goes Rogue with Own Currency." *AFP*, August 16, 2012.

Fama, Eugene F. "Random Walks in Stock-Market Prices." Selected Papers, no. 16. Graduate School of Business, University of Chicago, 1965.

Farber, Howard. "A Price and Wage Study for Northern Babylonia During the Old Baby-lonian Period." *Journal of the Economic and Social History of the Orient* 21, no. 1 (1978): 1-51.

Farmer, J. Doyne, and John Geanakoplos. "The Virtues and Vices of Equilibrium and the Future of Financial Economics." *Complexity* 14, no. 3 (2009): 11-38.

Federal Reserve Bank of St. Louis. "Velocity of M2 Money Stock." 2014. http://research .stlouisfed.org/fred2/series/M2V.

Feldstein, Martin. "The Failure of the Euro." *Foreign Affairs* 91, no. 1 (2012): 105-116.

Feschotte, Cédric. "Virology: Bornavirus Enters the Genome." *Nature* 463, no. 7277 (2010): 39.

Feuer, Lewis S. *The Scientific Intellectual: The Psychological and Sociological Origins of Modern Science.* New York: Basic, 1963.

Financial Conduct Authority. "Barclays Fined £26m for Failings Surrounding the London Gold Fixing and Former Barclays Trader Banned and Fined for Inappropriate Con-duct." Press release, May 23, 2014.

Fisher, Irving. *Mastering the Crisis.* London: Allen & Unwin, 1934.

——. *100% Money.* New York: Adelphi, 1936.

——. *The Purchasing Power of Money.* 2d ed. New York: Macmillan, 1922.

Fisher, Irving, Hans R. L. Cohrssen, and Herbert W. Fisher. *Stamp Scrip.* New York: Adelphi, 1933.

Forero, Juan. "Bolivia's Cerro Rico: The Mountain That Eats Men." NPR, September 25, 2012. www.npr.org/2012/09/25/161752820/bolivias-cerro-rico-the-mountain-that -eats-men.

Fortier, Jana. "Underthrowing the System: How Low Finance Undermines Corporate Culture." *Journal of Ecology and Healthy Living*, 9, no. 5 (1996): 61-63.

Foster, Peter. "Biting the Invisible Hand." *National Post*, September 14, 2012.

Francis of Assisi. *The Writings of St. Francis of Assisi.* Translated by Paschal Robinson. Philadelphia: Dolphin, 1906.

Frank, Robert. "Why the Rich Recovered and the Rest Didn't." CNBC. June 13, 2012. www.cnbc.com/id/47802283.

Frank, Robert H., Thomas Gilovich, and Dennis T. Regan. "Does Studying Economics Inhibit Cooperation?" *Journal of Economic Perspectives* 7, no. 2 (1993): 159-171.

Friedman, Milton. "Full Interview on Anti-trust and Tech." National Taxpayers Union, 1999, https://www.youtube.com/watch?v=mlwxdyLnMXM.

——. Interview by Russell Roberts. "An Interview with Milton Friedman." September 4, 2006, http://www.econlib.org/library/Columns/y2006/Friedmantranscript.html.

——. *The Counter-revolution in Monetary Theory.* London: Institute of Economic Affairs, 1970.

——. "A Proposal for Resolving the U.S. Balance of Payments Problem: Confidential Memorandum to President-Elect Richard Nixon." In *The Merits of Flexible Exchange Rates: An Anthology*, edited by Leo Melamed, 429-438. Fairfax, Va.: George Mason University Press, 1988.

Galbraith, John Kenneth. *Money: Whence It Came, Where It Went.* New York: Houghton Mifflin, 1995.

Gandel, Stephen. "By Every Measure, the Big Banks Are Bigger." *Fortune*, September 13, 2013.

Garrett, Reginald H., and Charles M. Grisham. *Biochemistry*. Fort Worth, Tex.: Saunders, 1995.

Gelder, Sarah van. "Beyond Greed and Scarcity." *Yes!*, June 30, 1997.

Gesell, Silvio. *The Natural Economic Order*. Translated by Philip Pye. London: Peter Owen, 1958.

Gibbon, Edward. *The History of the Decline and Fall of the Roman Empire*. New York: Harper, 1845.

Gilens, Martin, and Benjamin I. Page. "Testing Theories of American Politics: Elites, Interest Groups, and Average Citizens." *Perspectives on Politics* 12, no. 3 (2014): 564–581.

Gottesdiener, Laura. "What My Time in America's New Oil Boomtown Taught Me About Our Climate Madness." Alternet. October 12, 2014. www.alternet.org /environment/what-my-time-americas-new-oil-boomtown-taught-me-about-our -climate-madness.

Graeber, David. *Debt: The First 5000 Years*. Brooklyn, N.Y.: Melville House, 2011.

——. "On the Phenomenon of Bullshit Jobs." *Strike!*, August 17, 2013. http://strikemag. org/bullshit-jobs.

——. "The Truth Is Out: Money Is Just an IOU, and the Banks Are Rolling In It." *Guardian*, March 18, 2014.

Greenberg, Andy. "Online Drug Dealers Are Now Accepting Darkcoin, Bitcoin's Stealthier Cousin." *Wired*, November 4, 2014. www.wired.com/2014/11/darkcoin -and-online-drug-dealers.

Greenspan, Alan. *The Map and the Territory: Risk, Human Nature, and the Future of Forecasting*. New York: Penguin, 2013.

Griffin, G. Edward. *The Creature from Jekyll Island: A Second Look at the Federal Reserve*. 4th ed. Westlake Village, Calif.: American Media, 2002.

Gross, Bill. "Barron's 2015 Roundtable Highlight." *Barron's*, January 17, 2015. http://online .barrons.com/articles/bill-gross-1421929674.

Grubb, Farley. *Benjamin Franklin and the Birth of a Paper Money Economy*. Philadelphia: Federal Reserve Bank of Philadelphia, 2006.

Guerreau-Jalabert, Anita. "Caritas y don en la sociedad medieval occidental." *Hispania: Revista española de historia* 60, no. 204 (2000): 27–62.

Gundlach, Jeffrey. "Americký dolar zpívá labutí píseň." Investicniweb, June 16, 2014. www .investicniweb.cz/2014/6/17/jeffrey-gundlach-americky-dolar-zpiva-labuti-pisen.

Gupta, Girish. "Venezuelans Turn to Bitcoins to Bypass Socialist Currency Controls." Reuters, October 8, 2014. www.reuters.com/article/2014/10/08/us-venezuela-bitcoin -idUSKCN0HX11O20141008.

Guthrie, William Keith Chambers. *A History of Greek Philosophy*. Vol. 1, *The Earlier Presocratics and the Pythagoreans*. Cambridge: Cambridge University Press, 1962.

Haldane, Andrew. "The Revolution in Economics." In *Economics, Education and Unlearning: Economics Education at the University of Manchester*, 3–6. Manchester: Post-Crash Economics Society, 2014.

"Handle with Care." *Economist*, March 26, 2009.

Hanke, Steve H. "Why the World Should Be Rallying for the 'Yuan-ization' of North Korea." *Business Insider*, June 22, 2013.

Hanley, Nick, Jason E. Shogren, and Ben White. *Environmental Economics in Theory and Practice*. New York: Oxford University Press, 1997.

Häring, Norbert, and Niall Douglas. *Economists and the Powerful: Convenient Theories, Distorted Facts, Ample Rewards*. London: Anthem, 2012.

Harjani, Ansuya. "Yuan Trade Settlement to Grow by 50% in 2014: Deutsche Bank." CNBC, December 11, 2013. www.cnbc.com/id/101263663.

Harper, F. A. *Why Wages Rise*. Irvington, N.Y.: Foundation for Economic Education, 1957.

Harris, W. V. *The Monetary Systems of the Greeks and Romans*. Oxford: Oxford University Press, 2008.

Hart, K. "Heads or Tails: Two Sides of the Coin." *Man* 21, no. 3 (1986): 637–656.

Hatherley, Owen. "Be a User, Not a Consumer: How Capitalism Has Changed Our Language." *Guardian*, August 11, 2013.

Hayek, Friedrich A. *Denationalisation of Money: The Argument Refined*. 1978. London: Institute of Economic Affairs, 1990.

Hern, Alex. "Bitcoin Hype Worse Than 'Tulip Mania,' Says Dutch Central Banker." *Guardian*, December 4, 2013.

——. "Missing: Hard Drive Containing Bitcoins Worth £4m in Newport Landfill Site." *Guardian*, November 27, 2013.

Herodotus. *The Landmark Herodotus: The Histories*. Edited by Robert B. Strassler. Translated by Andrea L. Purvis. New York: Anchor, 2009.

Hibbert, Christopher. *Rome: The Biography of a City*. New York: Norton, 1985.

Higgins, Stan. "IBM Reveals Proof of Concept for Blockchain-powered Internet of Things." CoinDesk. January 17, 2015. www.coindesk.com/ibm-reveals-proof-concept -blockchain-powered-internet-things.

Hiltzik, Michael. "Bye-Bye, Bitcoin? The Crypto-Currency's Price Agonies Intensify." *Los Angeles Times*, October 6, 2014.

Hirsch, A. R. "Effects of Ambient Odors on Slot-Machine Usage in a Las Vegas Casino." *Psychology & Marketing* 12, no. 7 (1995): 585–594.

Hirsch, Todd. "The Future of Money." TED^XEdmonton, 2013. YouTube. www.youtube .com/watch?v=Kon3BGId9nU.

Hoelterhoff, Manuela. "'The Roman Guide to Slave Management' Is Brilliant." Bloomberg Business, October 15, 2014. http://www.bloomberg.com/news/articles/2014-10 -15/-the-roman-guide-to-slave-management-is-brilliant-hoelterhoff.

Hudson, Michael. "The Financial Attack on Greece: Where Do We Go from Here?" CounterPunch, July 8, 2015. www.counterpunch.org/2015/07/08/71809.

——. "How Interest Rates Were Set, 2500 BC–1000 AD." *Journal of the Economic and Social History of the Orient* 43, no. 2 (2000): 132–161.

——. *The Lost Tradition of Biblical Debt Cancellations*. New York: Schalkenbach, 1993.

Hum, Derek, and Wayne Simpson. "A Guaranteed Annual Income? From Mincome to the Millennium." *Policy Options*, January–February 2001: 78–82.

Hume, David. *Essays, Moral, Political, and Literary*. Edited by Eugene F. Miller. Indianapolis: Liberty Fund, 1987. www.econlib.org/library/LFBooks/Hume/hmMPL26.html.

Iamblichus. *The Life of Pythagoras*. Translated by T. Taylor. Kila, Mont.: Kessinger, 1918.

Ingham, Geoffrey. "'Babylonian Madness': On the Historical and Sociological Origins of Money." In *What Is Money?* edited by John Smithin, 16–41. New York: Routledge, 2000.

International Monetary Fund. "Global Financial Stability Report: Risk Taking, Liquidity, and Shadow Banking: Curbing Excess While Promoting Growth." October 2014. www.imf.org/external/pubs/ft/gfsr/2014/02/index.htm.

Izumi, Rui. "The Wat System, An Exchange Based on Mutual Appreciation." Gesell Research Society, Japan. 2001. www.watsystems.net/watsystems-translation/english.html.

Jackson, Andrew. "Veto of the Bank of the United States." In *A Compilation of the Messages and Papers of the Presidents, 1787–1897*, edited by James D. Richardson, 576–591. Washington, D.C.: Government Printing Office, 1896.

Jaspers, Karl. *The Way to Wisdom: An Introduction to Philosophy*. New Haven, Conn.: Yale University Press, 2003.

Jenkins, Patrick, and Tom Braithwaite. "New Platforms Vie to Take Finance to the Masses." *Financial Times*, January 29, 2015.

Jevons, William Stanley. *Letters and Journal of W. Stanley Jevons*. Edited by Harriet A. Jevons. London: Macmillan, 1886.

——. *Money and the Mechanism of Exchange*. New York: Appleton, 1875.

——. *The Theory of Political Economy*. 5th ed. New York: Kelley and Millman, 1957.

Joachain, Hélène, and Frédéric Klopfert. "Emerging Trend of Complementary Currencies Systems as Policy Instruments for Environmental Purposes: Changes Ahead?" *International Journal of Community Currency Research* 16, no. D (2012): 156–168.

Jones, Claire. "'Dismal Science' Seeks Fresh Thinking After Failure in Crisis." *Financial Times*, November 11, 2013.

Kahneman, Daniel. *Thinking, Fast and Slow*. New York: Farrar, Straus and Giroux, 2011.

Kahneman, Daniel, and Amos Tversky. "Prospect Theory: An Analysis of Decision Under Risk." *Econometrica* 47 (1979): 263–291.

Kalinowski, Wojtek. *Currency Pluralism and Economic Stability: The Swiss Experience*. Veblen Institute for Economic Reforms, Paris. October 2011. www.veblen-institute.org/IMG/pdf/currency_pluralism_and_economic_stability_eng_oct_2011_.pdf.

Kaminska, Izabella. "Democratising Finance: Vision for Bitcoin Is Beginning to Fade." *Financial Times*, February 3, 2015.

Kaskaloglu, Kerem. "Near Zero Bitcoin Transaction Fees Cannot Last Forever." In *The International Conference on Digital Security and Forensics (DigitalSec2014)*, 91–99. Ostrava, Czech Republic, 2014.

Kearns, Jeff. "Greenspan Says Bitcoin a Bubble Without Intrinsic Currency Value." Bloomberg Business, December 4, 2013. http://www.bloomberg.com/news/articles/2013-12-04/greenspan-says-bitcoin-a-bubble-without-intrinsic-currency-value.

Keen, Steve. "The Debtwatch Manifesto." January 1, 2012. http://keenomics.s3.amazonaws.com/debtdeflation_media/2012/01/TheDebtwatchManifesto.pdf.

——. "The IMF Gets Radical?" November 5, 2012. www.businessspectator.com.au/article/2012/11/5/business-spectator/imf-gets-radical.

——. "Will We Crash Again? FT/Alphaville Talk." YouTube. 2015. www.youtube.com /watch?t=130&v=JKy6_yy3C3U.

Kelion, Leo. "Could Driverless Cars Own Themselves?" BBC News, February 16, 2015. www.bbc.com/news/technology-30998361.

Kelly, Brian. "Is Apple Pay a Bitcoin Killer?" CNBC. September 10, 2014. www.cnbc.com /id/101988826.

Kelton, Stephanie. "Money Is No Object: Accounting for Deficits, Taxes, and Trust in the 21st Century." Presentation at the Financial Planning Association Annual Retreat Conference, May 5–8, 2012.

Kennedy, Margrit. *Interest and Inflation Free Money: Creating an Exchange Medium That Works for Everybody and Protects the Earth.* Philadelphia: New Society, 1987.

Keynes, John Maynard. "Economic Possibilities for Our Grandchildren." In *Essays in Persuasion,* 358–373. New York: Norton, 1963.

——. *The General Theory of Employment, Interest and Money.* New York: Harcourt, Brace, 1936.

Khanna, Parag. *How to Run the World: Charting a Course to the Next Renaissance.* New York: Random House, 2011.

Kharif, Olga. "Bitcoin 2.0 Shows Technology Evolving Beyond Use as Money." Bloomberg Business, March 28, 2014. www.bloomberg.com/news/2014-03-28/bitcoin -2-0-shows-technology-evolving-beyond-use-as-money.html.

Kiatpongsan, Sorapop, and Michael I. Norton. "How Much (More) Should CEOs Make? A Universal Desire for More Equal Pay." *Perspectives on Psychological Science* 9, no. 6 (2014): 587–593.

Kindleberger, Charles Poor. *A Financial History of Western Europe.* London: Allen & Unwin, 1984.

King, Mervyn. *The Political Economy of European Monetary Union.* Florence: European University Institute, 1998.

Kleban, Matthew. "Re: 'An Imperfect Truth,' by David Orrell." Related Letters. *Literary Review of Canada,* April 2015. http://reviewcanada.ca/magazine/2015/04/letters.

Klein, Naomi. *The Shock Doctrine: The Rise of Disaster Capitalism.* Toronto: Knopf Canada, 2007.

——. *This Changes Everything: Capitalism vs. the Climate.* New York: Simon & Schuster, 2014.

Knapp, Georg Friedrich. *The State Theory of Money.* 4th ed. London: Macmillan, 1924.

Knight, Frank. "Money." *Saturday Review of Literature,* April 16, 1927, 732.

Kocherlakota, Narayana R. "Money Is Memory." Staff Report 218. Federal Reserve Bank of Minneapolis, 1996.

Kolbert, C. F. *The Digest of Roman Law: Theft, Rapine, Damage, and Insult.* New York: Penguin, 1979.

Kouchaki, Maryam, Kristin Smith-Crowe, Arthur P. Brief, and Carlos Sousa. "Seeing Green: Mere Exposure to Money Triggers a Business Decision Frame and Unethical Outcomes." *Organizational Behavior and Human Decision Processes* 121, no. 1 (2013): 53–61.

Kraidy, Marwan. *Hybridity: The Cultural Logic of Globalization*. Philadelphia: Temple University Press, 2005.

Kreider, Tim. "Slaves of the Internet, Unite!" *New York Times*, October 27, 2013.

Krugman, Paul. "Adam Smith Hates Bitcoin." *The Conscience of a Liberal* (blog). *New York Times*, April 12, 2013. http://krugman.blogs.nytimes.com/2013/04/12 /adam-smith-hates-bitcoin.

——. *End This Depression Now!* New York: Norton, 2012.

Kubiszewski, Ida, Robert Costanza, Carol Franco, Philip Lawn, John Talberth, Tim Jackson, and Camille Aylmer. "Beyond GDP: Measuring and Achieving Global Genuine Progress." *Ecological Economics* 93 (2013): 57–68.

Kupka, Martin. "Bitcoin čeká ještě mnoho bublin, věří programátor Marek Palatinus" [Bitcoin is still bound to experience many bubbles, says programmer Marek Palatinus]. *Ekonom*, January 18, 2014.

Kurmanaev, Anatoly. "Venezuela Squanders Its Oil Wealth." Bloomberg Business, February 18, 2015. www.bloomberg.com/news/articles/2015-02-18/venezuela-goes-from -bling-to-blat-as-oil-wealth-squandered.

Kyambalesa, Henry, and Mathurin C. Houngnikpo. *Economic Integration and Development in Africa*. Aldershot: Ashgate, 2006.

Laynez, Diego. *Disputationes Tridentinae*. Vol. 2. Translated by Hartmann Grisar. Oeniponti: Rauch, 1886.

Le Goff, Jacques. *Money and the Middle Ages*. Oxford: Polity, 2012.

Ledgard, Jonathan, and John Clippinger. "How a Digital Currency Could Transform Africa." *Financial Times*, October 29, 2013.

Lemay, J. A. Leo. *The Life of Benjamin Franklin*. Vol. 1, *Journalist, 1706–1730*. Philadelphia: University of Pennsylvania Press, 2006.

Leonard, Mark. *What Does China Think?* New York: PublicAffairs, 2008.

Levy, Adam. "Mapping the Trader's Brain." *Bloomberg Markets*, February 1, 2006, 34–45.

Lewis, Michael. "Extreme Wealth Is Bad for Everyone—Especially the Wealthy." *New Republic*, November 12, 2014.

Lewis, Nathan. "Bitcoin Ignites Ron Paul's Parallel Currency Revolution." *Forbes*, January 1, 2014.

Lewis, Simon L., and Mark A. Maslin. "Defining the Anthropocene." *Nature* 519 (2015): 171–180.

Lietaer, Bernard. *The Future of Money: Creating New Wealth, Work and a Wiser World*. London: Century, 2001.

——. "The Mystery of Money." Manuscript, 2002. http://www.scribd.com/doc/294011240/ Bernard-Lietaer-The-Mystery-of-Money-287pp-full-pdf-download.

——. "Why This Crisis? And What to Do About It?" TEDˣBerlin, November 30, 2009. YouTube. www.youtube.com/watch?v=nORI8r3JIyw.

Lietaer, Bernard, Robert E. Ulanowicz, Sally J. Goerner, and Nadia McLaren. "Is Our Monetary Structure a Systemic Cause for Financial Instability? Evidence and Remedies from Nature." *Journal of Futures Studies*, April 2010, 1–21.

Lincoln, Abraham. "Senate document 23." 1865.

Liu, Jack C. "Bitcoin Backed Corporate Currencies Are Coming." November 9, 2014. http://jackcliu.com/post/102166140017/bitcoin-backed-corporate-currencies-are-coming.

John Locke, *The Second Treatise on Civil Government*, Amherst, N.Y.: Prometheus Books, 1986.

Lodhia, Sheetal, and Paul Kennedy. *Why Money Isn't Everything.* CBC. May 12, 2015. www.cbc.ca/radio/ideas/why-money-isn-t-everything-1.3069430.

Lucas, Robert. "In Defence of the Dismal Science." *Economist*, August 6, 2009.

MacBeth, Hilliard. *When the Bubble Bursts: Surviving the Canadian Real Estate Crash.* Toronto: Dundurn, 2015.

Macheel, Tanaya. "The Case for Merging Mexico's Peso with Block Chain Technology." CoinDesk. July 26, 2014. www.coindesk.com/case-merging-mexicos-peso-block-chain-technology.

Madan, Geoffrey. *Geoffrey Madan's Notebooks.* Edited by J. A. Gere and John Sparrow. Oxford: Oxford University Press, 1981.

Mallaby, Sebastian, and Olin Wethington. "The Future of the Yuan: China's Struggle to Internationalize Its Currency." *Foreign Affairs* 91, no. 1 (2012): 135–146.

Mandelbrot, Benoit B. *The Fractal Geometry of Nature.* New York: Freeman, 1982.

Marsh, David. *The Euro: The Politics of the New Global Currency.* New Haven, Conn.: Yale University Press, 2009.

Marshall, Alfred. *Principles of Economics.* 8th ed. New York: Cosimo, 2006.

Martin, Felix. *Money: The Unauthorized Biography.* New York: Knopf, 2013.

Marx, Karl. *Economic and Philosophic Manuscripts of 1844.* Translated by Martin Mulligan. Moscow: Progress, 1959.

Mathiason, Nick, and Melanie Newman. "Finance Industry's Multimillion-Pound Lobbying Budget Revealed." *Guardian*, July 9, 2012.

Mathiason, Nick, Melanie Newman, and Maeve McClenaghan. "Revealed: The £93m Lobby Machine." July 9, 2012. Bureau of Investigative Journalism. www.thebureauinvestigates.com/2012/07/09/revealed-the-93m-city-lobby-machine / (accessed November 18, 2015).

May, Timothy C. "The Crypto Anarchist Manifesto." November 22, 1992. www.activism.net/cypherpunk/crypto-anarchy.html.

McGilchrist, Iain. *The Master and His Emissary: The Divided Brain and the Making of the Western World.* New Haven, Conn.: Yale University Press, 2009.

McLeay, Michael, Amar Radia, and Ryland Thomas. "Money Creation in the Modern Economy." *Quarterly Bulletin* [Bank of England], no. 1, March 14, 2014, 1–14.

McLuhan, Marshall. "A Media Approach to Inflation." *New York Times*, September 21, 1974.

McLuhan, Marshall, Quentin Fiore, and Jerome Agel. *The Medium Is the Massage: An Inventory of Effects.* Corte Madera, Calif: Gingko, 2001.

McLuhan, Marshall, and W. Terrence Gordon. *Understanding Media: The Extensions of Man.* Critical ed. Corte Madera, Calif.: Gingko, 2003.

McVeigh, Tracy. "Buses, Canteens, Parking—Is Cash on the Way Out?" *Observer*, March 8, 2015.

Menger, Karl. "On the Origins of Money." *Economic Journal* 2, no. 3 (1892): 239–255.

Mihm, Stephen. "Why Capitalism Fails." *Boston Globe*, September 13, 2009.

Mill, John Stuart. "Posthumous Essay on Social Freedom." *Oxford and Cambridge Review*, January 1907.

———. *Principles of Political Economy*. London: Parker, 1848.

Miller, Lisa. "The Money-Empathy Gap." *New York*, July 1, 2012.

Milmo, Cahal. "Robot Revolution Gathers Pace—But at What Cost to Jobs?" *Independent*, February 10, 2015.

Minsky, Hyman P. "Financial Instability Revisited: The Economics of Disaster." In *Reappraisal of the Federal Reserve Discount Mechanism*, 95–136. Washington, D.C.: Board of Governors of the Federal Reserve System, 1972.

Mitchell-Innes, Alfred. "The Credit Theory of Money." *Banking Law Journal*, December–January 1914, 151–168.

———. "What Is Money?" *Banking Law Journal* May 1913, 377–408.

Mokyr, Joel. *The Oxford Encyclopedia of Economic History*. Vol. 2. Oxford: Oxford University Press, 2003.

More, Thomas. *Utopia*. www.gutenberg.org/files/2130/2130-h/2130-h.htm.

Munchau, Wolfgang. "Macroeconomists Need New Tools to Challenge Consensus." *Financial Times*, April 12, 2015.

Nakamoto, Satosh. "Bitcoin: A Peer-to-Peer Electronic Cash System." November 1, 2008. https://bitcoin.org/bitcoin.pdf.

———. "Bitcoin Open Source Implementation of P2P Currency." P2P Foundation: The Foundation for Peer to Peer Alternatives. February 11, 2009. http://p2pfoundation. ning.com/forum/topics/bitcoin-open-source.

Neville, Sarah, and Keith Fray. "The Fractured Middle: UK Salary Split Sees Übers Pull Ahead." *Financial Times*, February 14, 2014.

Nixon, Richard. "Address to the Nation Outlining a New Economic Policy: 'The Challenge of Peace.'" August 15, 1971. The American Presidency Project. www.presidency .ucsb.edu/ws/?pid=3115.

Noble, David. "11% of UK Businesses Say Slavery in Their Supply Chains Is 'Likely.'" *Guardian*, August 18, 2014.

Odum, Eugene P. "The Strategy of Ecosystem Development." *Science* 164 (1969): 262–270.

Oresme, Nicole. *The De Moneta of Nicholas Oresme, and English Mint Documents*. Translated by Charles Johnson. London: Nelson, 1956.

Organisation for Economic Co-operation and Development. "Crisis Squeezes Income and Puts Pressure on Inequality and Poverty." 2013. www.oecd.org/els/soc /OECD2013-Inequality-and-Poverty-8p.pdf.

Orrell, David. "Book Burning Economists." *World Finance*, July 1, 2015.

———. *Economyths: How the Science of Complex Systems Is Transforming Economic Thought*. London: Icon, 2010.

———. "Making Sausages." *World Finance*, March 4, 2013.

———. "Money Is the Message." Marshall McLuhan Lecture. Transmediale, 2015. www .youtube.com/playlist?list=PL9olnMFdRIwshkq3nfaF2nBzbFAQRvLmy.

———. *The Other Side of the Coin: The Emerging Vision of Economics and Our Place in the World*. Toronto: Key Porter, 2008.

——. "The Problem with Predictions." *World Finance*, November 6, 2013.

——. "A Quantum Theory of Money and Value." Social Science Research Network. June 28, 2015. http://ssrn.com/abstract=2624371.

——. *Truth or Beauty: Science and the Quest for Order.* New Haven, Conn.: Yale University Press, 2012.

Ovid. *Ovid's Art of Love (in Three Books), the Remedy of Love, the Art of Beauty, the Court of Love, the History of Love, and Amours.* Edited by Anne Mahoney. New York: Calvin Blanchard, 1855.

Pacioli, Luca. *Summa de Arithmetica, Geometria, Proportioni et Proportionalita.* Venice, 1494.

Palast, Greg. "Robert Mundell, Evil Genius of the Euro." *Guardian*, June 26, 2012.

Palgrave, R. H. Inglis. *Bank Rate and the Money Market in England, France, Germany, Holland, and Belgium, 1844–1900.* London: Murray, 1903.

Patterson, Orlando. *Slavery and Social Death: A Comparative Study.* Cambridge, Mass.: Harvard University Press, 1982.

Peden, Joseph R. "Mises Daily: Inflation and the Fall of the Roman Empire." Mises Institute, September 7, 2009. http://mises.org/library/inflation-and-fall-roman -empire.

Pense, Alan. "The Decline and Fall of the Roman Denarius." *Materials Characterization* 29, no. 2 (1992): 213–22.

Pew Charitable Trusts. "The Complex Story of American Debt." July 29, 2015. www .pewtrusts.org/en/research-and-analysis/reports/2015/07/the-complex-story -of-american-debt.

Pew Research Center. "The Happiness Trend Line: Barely a Ripple." 2010. www.pewso-cialtrends.org/2006/02/13/are-we-happy-yet/37-3.

Piketty, Thomas. *Capital in the Twenty-First Century.* Translated by Arthur Goldhammer. Cambridge, Mass.: Belknap Press of Harvard Unversity Press, 2014.

Pliny the Younger. *The Letters of the Younger Pliny: With an Introductory Essay.* Translated by John B. Firth. London: Scott, 1909.

Polo, Marco. *The Book of Ser Marco Polo, the Venetian, Concerning the Kingdoms and Marvels of the East.* Translated and edited by Henry Yule. London: Murray, 1903.

Poole, Steven. "Could Climate Change Action Rejuvenate Worldwide Democracy?" *New Statesman*, September 18, 2014.

Pownall, Thomas. *A Letter from Governor Pownall to Adam Smith, Being an Examination of Several Points of Doctrine.* London: Printed for J. Almon, 1776.

Pritchard, James B., ed. *The Ancient Near East: An Anthology of Texts and Pictures.* Princeton, N.J.: Princeton University Press, 2010.

Ragan, Christopher T. S., and Richard G. Lipsey. *Economics.* 13th ed. Toronto: Pearson Education Canada, 2011.

Rainwater, L. "Poverty and Equivalence as Social Constructions." Luxembourg Income Study Working Paper, no. 91, Center for Policy Research, Maxwell School, Syracuse, N.Y., 1990.

Reich, Robert. "The Share-the-Scraps Economy." February 2, 2015. http://robertreich .org/post/109894095095.

Richardson, Gordon. "The Pursuit of Equilibrium." *Euromoney*, October 1979: 28–37.

Rickards, James. *The Death of Money: The Coming Collapse of the International Monetary System*. New York: Portfolio/Penguin, 2014.

Rogoff, Kenneth. "Costs and Benefits to Phasing Out Paper Currency." In *NBER Macroeconomics Annual 2014*, edited by Jonathan Parker and Michael Woodford, 29: 445–456 Chicago: University of Chicago Press, 2015.

Romancov, Michael. "Dolar není mrtev, přežil i své kritiky. Jaké jsou vyhlídky americké měny?" [Dollar is not dead, it outlived even its critics. What are the prospects of the American Currency?]. *Ekonom*, November 9, 2014.

Rosenfeld, Everett. "Ecuador Becomes the First Country to Roll Out Its Own Digital Cash." CNBC. February 9, 2015. www.cnbc.com/id/102397137.

Rothbard, Murray N. *An Austrian Perspective on the History of Economic Thought*. 2 vols. Auburn, Ala.: Ludwig von Mises Institute, 2006.

——. *Wall Street, Banks, and American Foreign Policy*. Burlingame, Calif.: Center for Libertarian Studies, 1996.

Ruggie, John G. "Territoriality and Beyond: Problematizing Modernity in International Relations." *International Organization* 47, no. 1 (1993): 139–174.

Russell, Bertrand. *A History of Western Philosophy, and Its Connection with Political and Social Circumstances from the Earliest Times to the Present Day*. New York : Simon and Schuster, 1945.

"Russian Ruble Becomes Only Valid Currency in Crimea." RT. June 2, 2014. http://rt .com/business/162992-crimea-adopts-ruble-currency.

Saad, Lydia. "Americans' Money Worries Unchanged from 2014." Gallup. April 20, 2015. www.gallup.com/poll/182768/americans-money-worries-unchanged-2014.aspx.

Said, Carolyn. "Communities Issue Currency, Promote Local Spending." *San Francisco Chronicle*, July 6, 2011. www.sfgate.com/bayarea/article/Communities-issue-currency -promote-local-spending-2355723.php.

Samuelson, Paul A. *Economics*. 9th ed. New York: McGraw-Hill, 1973.

——. "An Exact Consumption-Loan Model of Interest with or Without the Social Contrivance of Money." *Journal of Political Economy* 66, no. 6 (1958): 467–482.

Samuelson, Paul A., and William D. Nordhaus. *Economics*. 17th ed. Boston: McGraw-Hill, 2001.

Sandel, Michael J. "The Moral Limits of Markets." *Project Syndicate*, December 31, 2012.

Saragosa, Manuela. "Libyan Gold Valued at $6.5bn." March 23, 2011. BBC. www.bbc.com /news/business-12833866.

Sargent, Thomas. Interview by Art Rolnick. "Interview with Thomas Sargent." Federal Reserve Bank of Minneapolis, September 2010.

Schaps, David. "The Invention of Coinage in Lydia, in India, and in China." Paper presented at the XIV International History Congress, August 21–25, 2006, Helsinki.

Schneider, Nathan. "A New 'Lego of Cryptofinance' Enables Users to Design Social Contracts." *Al Jazeera*, April 7, 2014.

Scott, Brett. "Riches Beyond Belief." *Aeon*, August 28, 2013. https://aeon.co/essays/so -you-want-to-invent-your-own-currency.

Sedghi, Ami. "Global Debt Has Grown by $57 Trillion in Seven Years Following the Financial Crisis." *Guardian*, February 5, 2015.

Sedláček, Tomáš. *Economics of Good and Evil: The Quest for Economic Meaning from Gilgamesh to Wall Street.* New York: Oxford University Press, 2011.

Sedláček, Tomáš, Gloria Benedikt, Merlijn Twaalfhoven, and Roman Chlupatý. "Bridging the Divide: Arts, Economics and the Irrational—A Debate in 3 Acts." Presentation at the Museum of Modern Art, Vienna, November 29, 2014.

Sedláček, Tomáš, David Graeber, and Roman Chlupatý. *(R)evoluční Ekonomie O Systému a Lidech.* Prague: 65.pole, 2013.

Sedláček, Tomáš, David Orrell, and Roman Chlupatý. *Soumrak Homo Economicus.* Prague: 65.pole, 2012.

Setia, Adi. "Jaʿfar Ibn ʿAli Al-Dimashqi on Community, Money, and Prudent Management in Trading and Spending: Four Excerpts from His Kitab Al-Isharat Ila Mahasin Al-Tijarat." *Islam & Science* 9, no. 1 (2011): 11–32.

Shiller, R. "Stock Prices and Social Dynamics." *Brookings Papers on Economic Activity* 2 (1984): 457–510.

Sigler, Laurence E. *Fibonacci's Liber Abaci: A Translation into Modern English of Leonardo Pisano's Book of Calculation.* New York: Springer, 2002.

Sigurjónsson, Frosti. "Monetary Reform—A Better Monetary System for Iceland." Reykjavik, 2015.

Silver, Morris. "Karl Polanyi and Markets in the Ancient Near East: The Challenge of the Evidence." *Journal of Economic History* 43, no. 4 (1983): 795–829.

Silver, Vernon. "Where Is Germany's Gold"? Bloomberg Business, February 5, 2015. www.bloomberg.com/news/features/2015-02-05/germany-s-gold-repatriation -activist-peter-boehringer-gets-results.

Simonite, Tom. "Ripple Labs." *MIT Technology Review*, February 18, 2014.

Singer, Peter. "Happiness, Money, and Giving It Away." *Project Syndicate*, July 12, 2006. www.project-syndicate.org/commentary/happiness—money—and-giving-it -away.

Slade, Paul. "Money: Are You Ready to Rock 'n' Dole?" *Independent*, June 23, 1998.

Smale, Alison, and Melissa Eddy. "Greek Debt Crisis Pits Greeks Against Germans." *New York Times*, July 11, 2015.

Smiles, Samuel. *Lives of Boulton and Watt: Principally from the Original Soho Mss.* London: Murray, 1865.

Smith, Adam. *An Inquiry into the Nature and Causes of the Wealth of Nations.* London: Strahan & Cadell, 1776.

Smith, Helena. "Euros Discarded as Impoverished Greeks Resort to Bartering." *Guardian*, January 2, 2013.

Smith, Michael E. *The Aztecs.* 3d ed. Malden, Mass.: Wiley-Blackwell, 2012.

Smithin, John, ed. *What Is Money?* New York: Routledge, 2000.

Soddy, Frederick. *The Role of Money: What It Should Be, Contrasted with What It Has Become.* 1934. Reprint, London: Routledge, 2003.

——. *Wealth, Virtual Wealth and Debt: The Solution of the Economic Paradox.* New York: Dutton, 1926.

Solow, Robert M. "The Economics of Resources or the Resources of Economics." *American Economic Review* 64, no. 2 (1974): 1–14.

Sorensen, Jay, and Eric Lucas. "Loyalty by the Billions." Loyalty Marketing Report Series for 2011. IdeaWorks, Shorewood, Wis., 2011.

Sorkin, Andrew Ross, and Megan Thee-Brenan. "Many Feel the American Dream Is Out of Reach, Poll Shows." *New York Times*, December 10, 2014. http://dealbook.nytimes .com/2014/12/10/many-feel-the-american-dream-is-out-of-reach-poll-shows.

Spencer, Herbert. *Social Statics: or, The Conditions Essential to Human Happiness Specified, and the First of Them Developed*. London: John Chapman, 1851.

Sperry, Roger Wolcott. "Left-Brain, Right-Brain." *Saturday Review*, August 9, 1975, 30-33.

Spiegel, Henry William. *The Growth of Economic Thought*. 3d ed. Durham, N.C.: Duke University Press, 1991.

Spielvogel, Jackson. *Western Civilization: A Brief History*. Vol. 2, *Since 1500*. Belmont, Calif.: Wadsworth, 2008.

Sreeja, V. N. "Yuan Overtakes Euro as Second-Most Used Currency in International Trade Settlement: SWIFT." *International Business Times*, December 3, 2013. www .ibtimes.com/yuan-overtakes-euro-second-most-used-currency-international -trade-settlement-swift-1492476.

Srinivasiengar, K. R. "Outline of an Emergent Theory of Value." *International Journal of Ethics* 45, no. 4 (1935): 413–421.

Stein, Gertrude. *How Writing Is Written*. Edited by Robert Bartlett Haas. Los Angeles: Black Sparrow, 1974.

Steverman, Ben. "Why Bitcoins and Apple Pay Can't Kill Off Cash." Bloomberg Business, September 12, 2014. www.bloomberg.com/news/articles/2014-09-12/why-bitcoins -and-apple-pay-can-t-kill-off-walter-white-s-stash.

Stodder, James. "Complementary Credit Networks and Macroeconomic Stability: Switzerland's Wirtschaftsring." *Journal of Economic Behavior & Organization* 72, no. 1 (2009): 79–95.

Strange, Susan. *Authority and Markets: Susan Strange's Writings on International Political Economy*. Edited by Roger Tooze and Christopher May. New York: Palgrave Macmillan, 2002.

Suehle, Ruth. "An Anthropologist's View of an Open Source Community." January 31, 2011. http://opensource.com/life/11/1/anthropologists-view-open-source-community.

Svensson, Roger. "The Bracteate as Economic Idea and Monetary Instrument." IFN Working Paper No. 973, Research Institute of Industrial Economics, Stockholm, 2013.

TD Canada Trust. "Hold Funds Policy." www.tdcanadatrust.com/document/PDF /520866.pdf.

Tett, Gillian, and Anuj Gangahar. "Limitations of Computer Models." *Financial Times*, August 14, 2007.

Thomson, William. *Popular Lectures and Addresses*. London: Macmillan, 1889.

Thorpe, Vanessa. "Black Death Was Not Spread by Rat Fleas, Say Researchers." *Guardian*, March 29, 2014.

Tiezzi, Shannon. "China to Be World's Largest Economy in 2014?" *Diplomat*, May 1, 2014.

Toner, Jerry. *The Roman Guide to Slave Management: A Treatise by Nobleman Marcus Sidonius Falx*. New York: Overlook, 2014.

"Top 5 Cashless Countries." TotalPayments. 2013. www.totalpayments.org/2013/07/08/top-5-cashless-countries.

Treanor, Jill, and Dominic Rushe. "Banks Hit by Record Fine for Rigging Forex Markets." *Guardian*, May 20, 2015.

Trimarco, James. "Students for Economic Pluralism, Unite!" *Yes!*, February 20, 2015. www.yesmagazine.org/new-economy/students-for-economic-pluralism-unite-keith-harrington.

Turner, Adair. "Printing Money to Fund Deficit Is the Fastest Way to Raise Rates." *Financial Times*, November 10, 2014.

Tuttle, Brad. "Got Stuff? Typical American Home Is Cluttered with Possessions—and Stressing Us Out." *Time*, July 19, 2012.

Tymoigne, Éric, and L. Randall Wray. "Money: An Alternative Story." In *A Handbook of Alternative Monetary Economics*, edited by Philip Arestis and Malcolm C. Sawyer, 1–16. Northampton, Mass.: Elgar, 2007.

"UK Banknotes 'Tainted with Cocaine.'" BBC. October 4, 1999. http://news.bbc.co.uk/2/hi/uk_news/464200.stm.

United States District Court, Southern District of New York. Sealed Complaint in the Case of *USA v. Ross Ulbricht*. 2013. www.cs.columbia.edu/~smb/UlbrichtCriminalComplaint.pdf.

Varoufakis, Yanis. "Bitcoin: A Flawed Currency Blueprint with a Potentially Useful Application for the Eurozone." February 15, 2014. http://yanisvaroufakis.eu/2014/02/15/bitcoin-a-flawed-currency-blueprint-with-a-potentially-useful-application-for-the-eurozone.

Varoufakis, Yanis, Joseph Halevi, and Nicholas Theocarakis. *Modern Political Economics: Making Sense of the Post-2008 World*. New York: Routledge, 2011.

Vigna, Paul, and Michael J. Casey. *The Age of Cryptocurrency: How Bitcoin and Digital Money Are Challenging the Global Economic Order*. New York: St. Martin's Press, 2015.

Vohs, Kathleen D., Nicole L. Mead, and Miranda R. Goode. "The Psychological Consequences of Money." *Science* 314, no. 5802 (2006): 1154–1156.

Wallach, D. A. "Bitcoin for Rockstars." Backchannel. December 10, 2014. https://medium.com/backchannel/bitcoin-for-rockstars-ca8366802f9.

Watson, Andrew. "Back to Gold—and Silver." *Economic History Review*, 2d ser., 20 (1967): 1–34.

Weatherford, Jack. *The History of Money*. New York: Three Rivers, 1997.

Weinstein, Michael M. "Paul A. Samuelson, Economist, Dies at 94." *New York Times*, December 13, 2009.

Wheatley, Gerald. "Complementary Currency and Quality of Life: Social and Economic Capital Effects on Subjective Well-Being." Ph.D. diss., University of Calgary, 2006.

Whipple, John. *The Importance of Stringent Usury Laws: An Answer to Jeremy Bentham*. Boston: Wentworth, 1857.

White, William R. "Is Monetary Policy a Science? The Interaction of Theory and Practice over the Last 50 Years." In *50 Years of Money and Finance: Lessons and Challenges*, edited by Morten Balling and Ernest Gnan, 73–115. Vienna: SUERF, 2013.

"Who Owns the Federal Reserve?" Board of Governors of the Federal Reserve System. Last updated August 2, 2013. www.federalreserve.gov/faqs/about_14986.htm.

Wilford, John Noble. *We Reach the Moon: The* New York Times *Story of Man's Greatest Adventure*. New York: Bantam, 1969.

Wilkinson, Richard, and Kate Pickett. *The Spirit Level: Why Greater Equality Makes Societies Stronger*. London: Bloomsbury, 2009.

Wilson, Effingham. *What Is Money?* London: Wilson, 1872.

Wohlsen, Marcus. "The Next Big Thing You Missed: How Starbucks Could Replace Your Bank." *Wired*, March 4, 2014.

Wolf, Martin. "Hair of the Dog Risks a Bigger Hangover for Britain." *Financial Times*, February 13, 2014.

——. "Strip Private Banks of Their Power to Create Money." *Financial Times*, April 24, 2014.

Woll, Cornelia. "Myths and Realities of the Banking Lobby." *World Politics Review*, July 1, 2014, 1–5.

Wong, Joon Ian. "Goldman Sachs Report Says Bitcoin Could Shape 'Future of Finance.'" CoinDesk. March 11, 2015. http://www.coindesk.com/goldman-sachs-report-says -bitcoin-could-shape-future-of-finance.

Wood, Graeme. "Secret Fears of the Super-Rich." *Atlantic*, February 24, 2011.

Wray, L. Randall, ed. *Credit and State Theories of Money: The Contributions of A. Mitchell Innes*. Cheltenham: Elgar, 2004.

——. *Understanding Modern Money: The Key to Full Employment and Price Stability*. Cheltenham: Elgar, 1998.

Wyatt, Ian D., and Daniel E. Hecker. "Occupational Changes During the 20th Century." *Monthly Labor Review*, March 2006: 35–57.

York, Geoffrey. "How Mobile Phones Are Making Cash Obsolete in Africa." *Globe and Mail*, June 22, 2013.

Zimmerman, Eilene. "Research: All Money Is Not Created Equal." Insights by Stanford Business, Stanford Graduate School of Business, January 6, 2014. www.gsb.stanford .edu/insights/research-all-money-not-created-equal.

Zinn, Howard. *A People's History of the United States*. New York: Harper Perennial, 2003.

Žižek, Slavoj. "How Capital Captured Politics." *Guardian*, July 13, 2014.

Zuylen-Wood, Simon van. "Feces and the Gold Standard: A Psychological Explanation of Goldbuggery," *New Republic*, August 28, 2012. www.newrepublic.com/article /106601/feces-and-gold-standard-psychological-explanation-goldbuggery.

Zweig, Stefan. *The World of Yesterday*. London: Cassell, 1943.

INDEX

GPSR Authorized Representative: Easy Access System Europe, Mustamäe tee
50, 10621 Tallinn, Estonia, gpsr.requests@easproject.com

www.ingramcontent.com/pod-product-compliance
Ingram Content Group UK Ltd.
Pitfield, Milton Keynes, MK11 3LW, UK
UKHW042334300325
456869UK00010B/53/J